# MARVEL
# COOKING WITH
# WOLVERINE

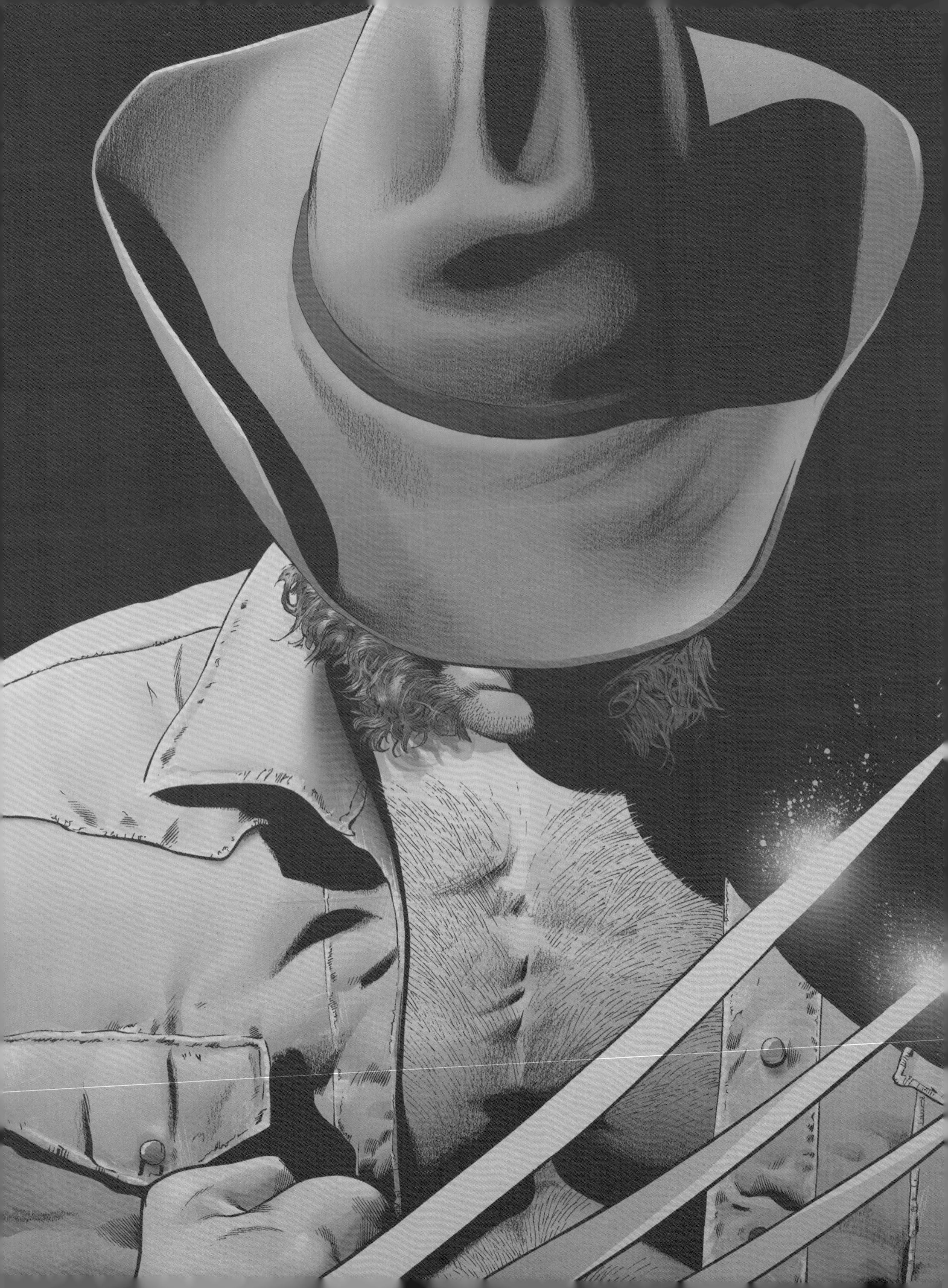

MARVEL

# COOKING WITH WOLVERINE

## RECIPES, TALES, AND TIPS FOR CULINARY SURVIVAL

Recipes and tips by Cassandra Reeder

Guest recipes by Chris Cosentino

Written by James Asmus

INSIGHT EDITIONS

SAN RAFAEL • LOS ANGELES • LONDON

## CONTENTS

Introduction . . . . . . . . . . . . . 8

### 1 KEEP SHARP, BUB: KNIFE SKILLS

The Knives . . . . . . . . . . . . 12
The Grips . . . . . . . . . . . . . 15
The Techniques . . . . . . . . . 16
Blade Maintenance . . . . . . 20
Adamantium . . . . . . . . . . . 21

### 2 ROUGHIN' IT: LIVING OFF THE LAND

How To: Starting a Campfire . . . . . 24
Eggs Howlett . . . . . . . . . . . . . . . . 27
Healing Factor Pemmican . . . . . . . 28
How To: Spice Blends . . . . . . . . . . 30
Moose Jerky . . . . . . . . . . . . . . . . . 31
Salmon Candy . . . . . . . . . . . . . . . 32
How To: Fillet a Fish . . . . . . . . . . . 35
Wojapi . . . . . . . . . . . . . . . . . . . . . 36
Feral Flapjacks . . . . . . . . . . . . . . . 39
Wild Mushroom Rice . . . . . . . . . . 40
Cedar Plank Fish . . . . . . . . . . . . . 43
Ol' Canucklehead's Canard . . . . . . 44
Skunk-Bear Venison Stew . . . . . . . 47
How To: Flavor Bases . . . . . . . . . . 48
Fried Bannock Bread . . . . . . . . . . 49
X-Man's Brewis . . . . . . . . . . . . . . 50
Saskatoon Berry Crumble . . . . . . . 53
Snow Maple Taffy . . . . . . . . . . . . 54
How To: Into the Frying Pan . . . . . 57

### 3 SNIKT!: SKEWERS AND KABOBS

Kuzuri Na Kushikatsu . . . . . . . . . 60
Lowtown Satay . . . . . . . . . . . . . . 62
Tsarina's Shashlik . . . . . . . . . . . . 65
How To: Skewering Like a Pro . . . . 67
Bison Donair Kebabs . . . . . . . . . . 69
How To: Perfectly Cooked Meat . . . 70
Skewered Surf 'n Turf . . . . . . . . . . 73
How To: Steak Cuts . . . . . . . . . . . 74
Stabby Shishliki . . . . . . . . . . . . . . 77
Krakoan Kabobs . . . . . . . . . . . . . 78
Tornado Potato . . . . . . . . . . . . . . 80
Hammer Bay BBQ . . . . . . . . . . . . 83
Yakitori Negima . . . . . . . . . . . . . 84
Mixed Veggie Kushiyaki . . . . . . . . 87
Choco Banana . . . . . . . . . . . . . . . 88

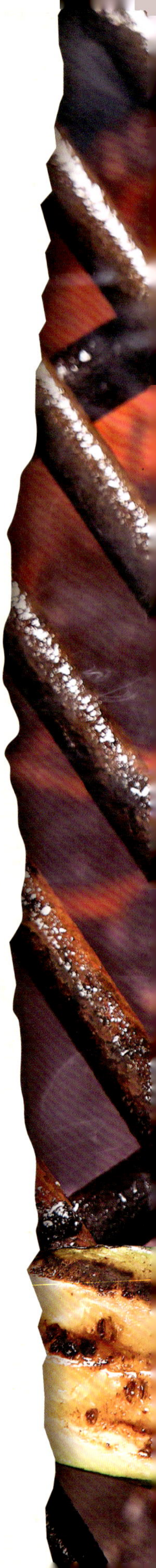

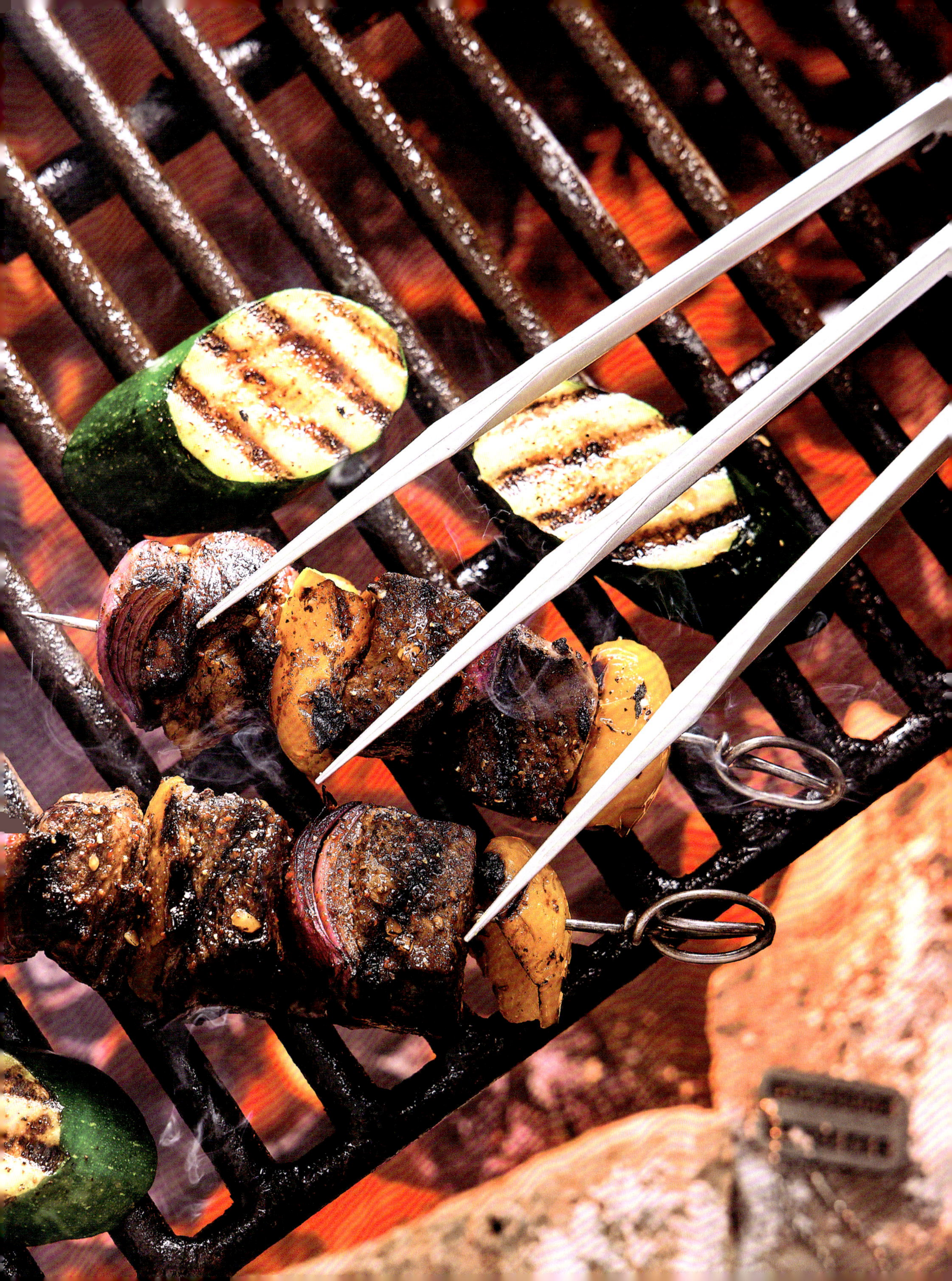

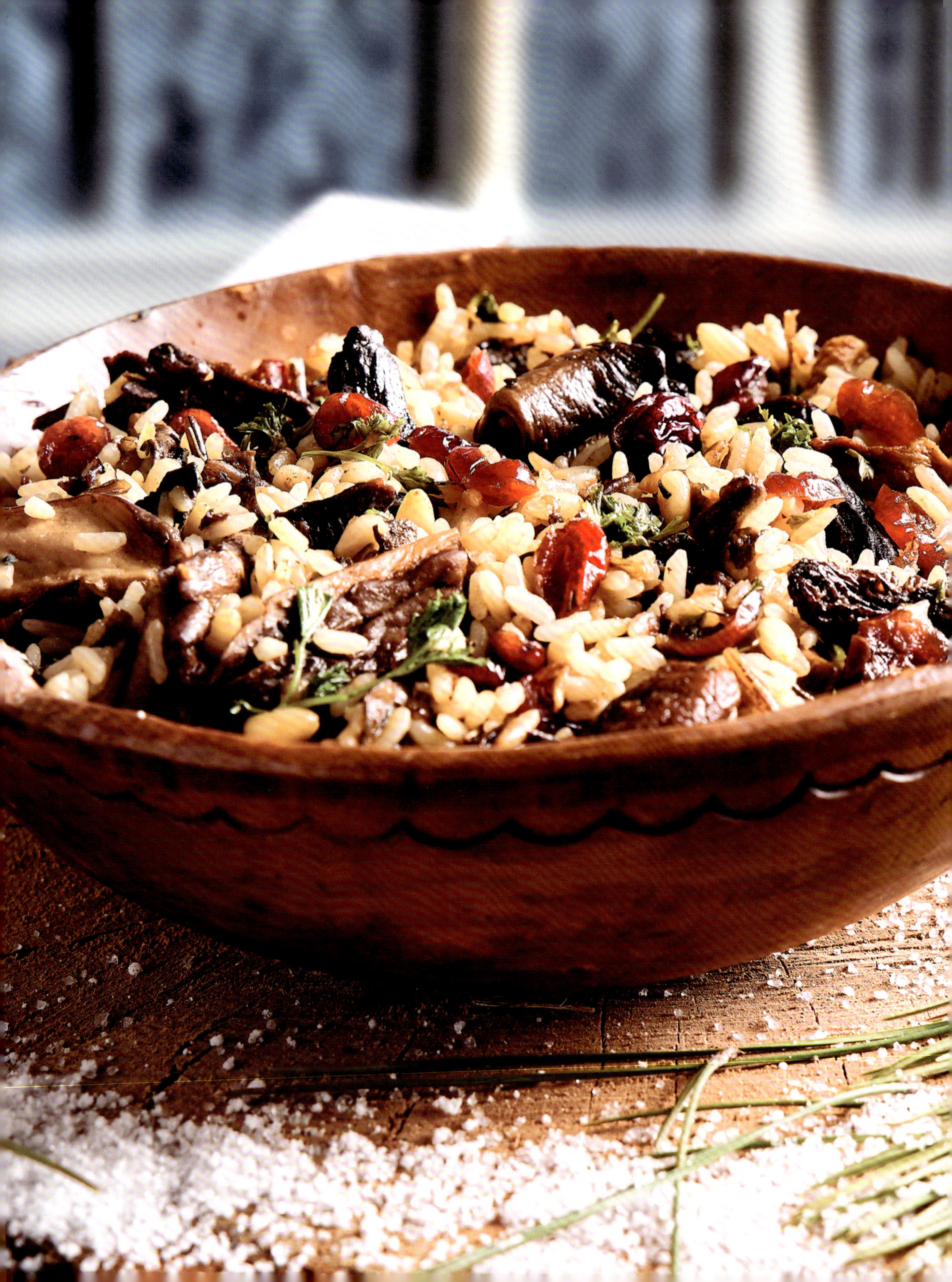

## 4 ON THE ROAD: STREET EATS AND TAVERN BITES

## 5 HOME SWEET HOME: X-MEN FAMILY RECIPES

Canada . . . . . . . . . . . . . . . . . 92
How To: A Poutine Exploration . . . 93
Poutine . . . . . . . . . . . . . . . . . 94
All-Dressed Chips . . . . . . . . . . . 97
Japanese-Style Hot Dog . . . . . . . 98
Ginger Beef . . . . . . . . . . . . . . 101
Nanaimo Bars . . . . . . . . . . . . 102
Japan . . . . . . . . . . . . . . . . . 104
How To : Japanese Convenience Food . . . . . . . . . 105
How To: Holdin' Chopsticks . . . . 105
Tomago Sando . . . . . . . . . . . . 106
Ramen Noodles from Scratch . . . 107
Gaijin's Ramen . . . . . . . . . . . 108
Pickled Daikon . . . . . . . . . . . 111
Salmon Mayo Onigiri . . . . . . . . 112
Korokke . . . . . . . . . . . . . . . 115
Okonomiyaki . . . . . . . . . . . . 116
Madripoor . . . . . . . . . . . . . . 118
How To: Madripoor Dining and Survival Guide . . . . . 119
Ragin' Radishes . . . . . . . . . . . 120
Roti ~~John~~ Steve . . . . . . . . . 123
Mystique's Mei Fun . . . . . . . . . 124
Lowtown Laksa . . . . . . . . . . . 127
Lepat Pisang . . . . . . . . . . . . 128
Jade Giants . . . . . . . . . . . . . 131
Stateside . . . . . . . . . . . . . . . 132
How To: Roadside Diners, Dives, and Other Places Open 24/7 . . . 133
Berserker Burger . . . . . . . . . . 134
Shredded Hero . . . . . . . . . . . 136
Cubano Sandwich . . . . . . . . . 137
Slingin' Chopped Cheese Dogs . . 139
Layered Cake: Assemble! . . . . . .140

The Professor's Cambric Tea . . . . 144
Storm's Bajias . . . . . . . . . . . . 147
Nightcrawler's Bavarian Cheese Dip . 148
Colossus's Buckwheat Blinis . . . . 151
Slim's Cheesesteak Sandwiches . . . 152
Logan's Dry-Smoked Ribs . . . . 153
Jubilee's Food Court Chili Fries . . . 154
How To: Surviving Family Dinners . 155
Logan's "Sophisticated" Grilled Cheese (recipe by way of Chris Cosentino) . . . . . . . . . 156
Jean's Holiday Broccoli Casserole . . 159
Kitty's Kickin' Kugel . . . . . . . . 160
Gambit's "Scoundrel" Beignets . . 163
Iceman's Snowball Special . . . . . 164
Rogue's Boysenberry Pie . . . . . . 167
Reminiscin' Pork Schnitzel (recipe by way of Chris Cosentino) . 168
Student's Danger Room X-Mix . . . 169

Measurement Conversions . . . . . 170
About the Authors . . . . . . . . . 171
Acknowledgments . . . . . . . . . 171

# INTRODUCTION

They say your sense of smell and taste are some of the strongest triggers for old memories. Catch a whiff of something and bang—you're back in an old childhood classroom. Or a certain mix of spices hits your tongue and you get a flash of your Great Aunt Ethel. I can vouch from personal experience—when those senses are heightened, so's the rush down memory lane. And once you've had your head screwed with as much as *I* have, you know how valuable a memory can be. Not knowin' your past, your people, yourself … makes for a cold and lonely road. Sometimes a warm meal is just the cure, and the shortest path to reconnect with the moments and faces you don't wanna forget.

In this crazy world of telepaths, resurrections, shadowy government experiments, and all kinds of other stuff that'll lock up the ol' brain cells, I figured I should scrap together the recipes that do the trick for me. Just in case … These tastes and aromas are tied so strongly to my past—good and bad—that no adamantium claws could cut 'em loose. And if it works for me, I guess it can work for anyone. So next time some wannabe mastermind in the shadows messes with the ol' noggin, you'll be just a home-cooked meal away from feelin' like yourself again.

That's when you remind *them* that you're the best there is at what you do. And what you do isn't very nice.

Logan

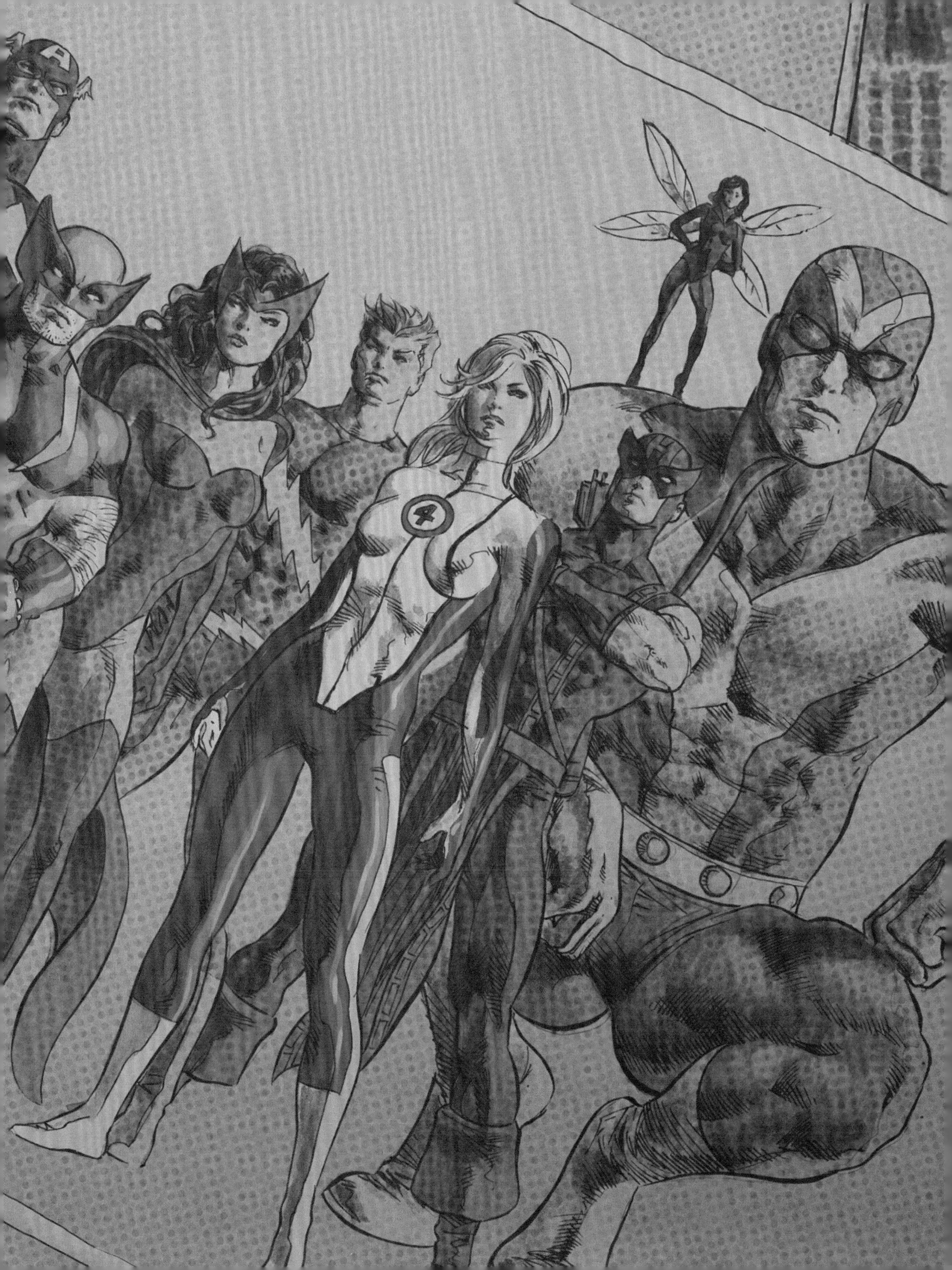

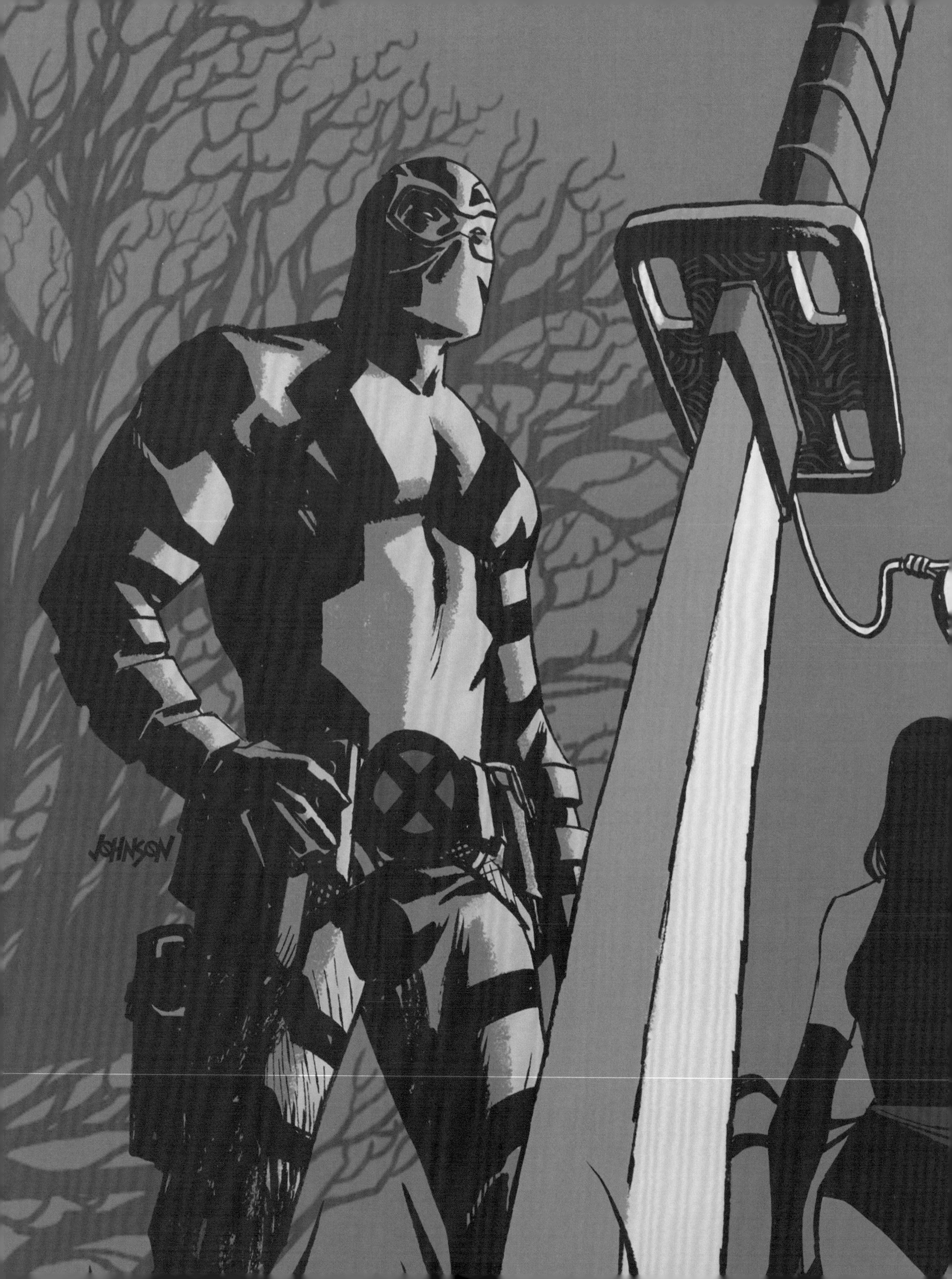
JOHNSON

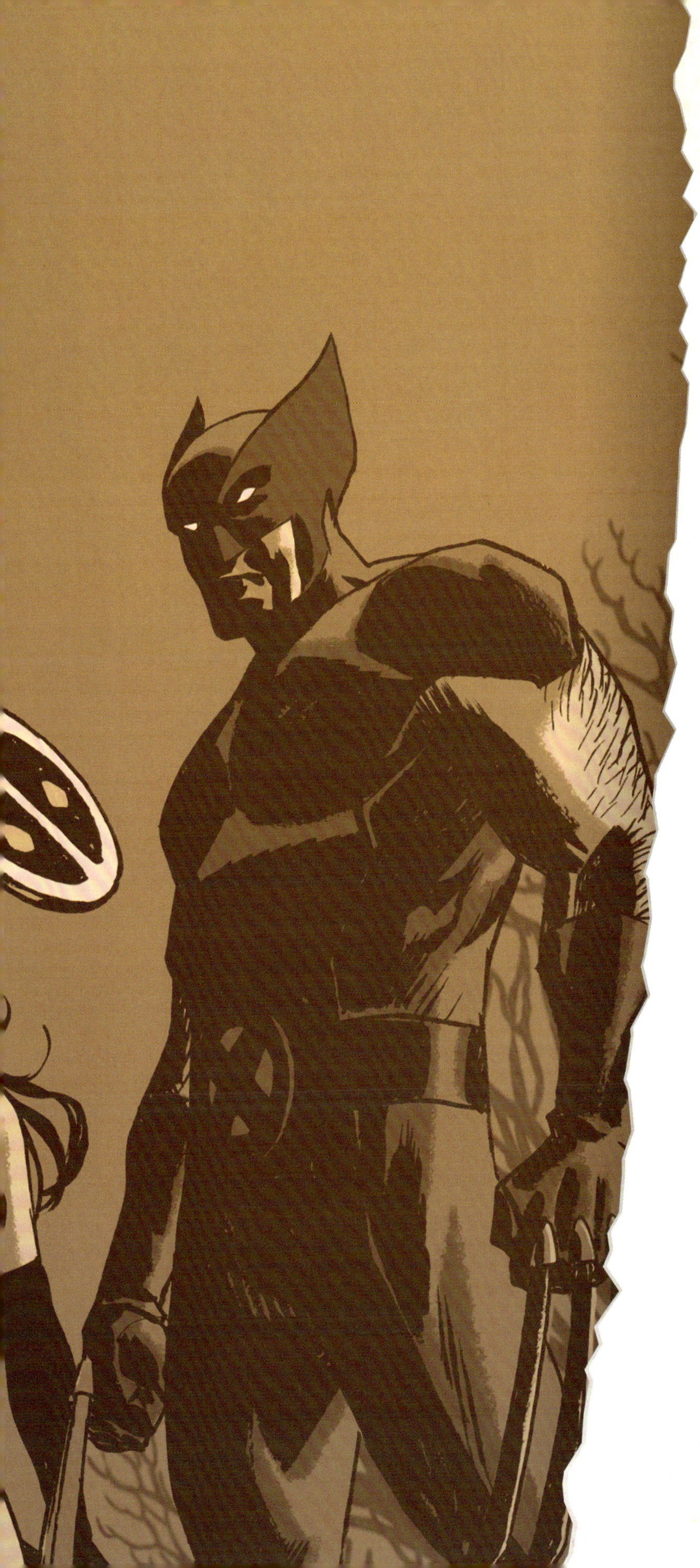

# 1

## KEEP SHARP, BUB: KNIFE SKILLS

I don't step into a kitchen unprepared. And I mean I don't just use these claws for brawlin'. 'Course, I know my way around a knife, too ... I've been inclined to pick 'em up from time to time. No matter if you're using a kitchen knife or your own adamantium claws, these skills are key to any cook's arsenal. Understanding the basics can up your game, so don't rush past 'em. This guide covers some essential Western knife skills, plus a few techniques I picked up in Japan.

# THE KNIVES

## WESTERN KNIVES

### CHEF'S KNIFE (8–10 INCHES) 1
**USE:** All-purpose knife for slicing, dicing, and chopping.
**NOTES:** Versatile and a must-have for any kitchen.

### PARING KNIFE (3–4 INCHES) 2
**USE:** Small, detailed work like peeling, trimming, and slicing fruits.
**NOTES:** Best for precision tasks that need control.

### SERRATED KNIFE (8–10 INCHES) 3
**USE:** Slicing bread, tomatoes, and other soft, delicate foods.
**NOTES:** Ideal for anything with a crust or tough skin but soft inside.

### UTILITY KNIFE (5–7 INCHES) 4
**USE:** Mid-sized knife for slicing and chopping tasks where a chef's knife is too big.
**NOTES:** A good backup when you need something between a paring and chef's knife.

### SLICING KNIFE (8–12 INCHES)
**USE:** Long, narrow blade perfect for slicing cooked meats like roasts, turkey, or ham.
**NOTES:** Its length makes it ideal for smooth, even slices with minimal tearing.

### FILET KNIFE (6–10 INCHES)
**USE:** Long, flexible blade designed for removing bones from fish or poultry, and for fileting delicate proteins.
**NOTES:** The flexibility of the blade allows for precise cuts along the bone and skin, making it perfect for clean, smooth filets.

## JAPANESE KNIVES

### GYUTO (8–10 INCHES, THE JAPANESE EQUIVALENT TO A CHEF'S KNIFE) 5
**USE:** All-around knife for meat, fish, and veggies.
**NOTES:** Slightly more nimble than a Western chef's knife, it's great for precision cuts.

### SANTOKU (5–7 INCHES) 6
**USE:** Multipurpose knife for slicing, dicing, and mincing.
**NOTES:** Shorter and lighter than a Gyuto, great for quick, fine cuts.

### NAKIRI (6–7 INCHES)
**USE:** Specifically designed for cutting vegetables.
**NOTES:** Flat edge makes it perfect for clean, straight cuts on produce.

### DEBA (6–8 INCHES)
**USE:** Heavy-duty knife for breaking down fish and poultry.
**NOTES:** Single-bevel blade, designed for precise, powerful cuts through bones and flesh.

### YANAGIBA (9–12 INCHES) 7
**USE:** Slicing fish for sashimi or sushi.
**NOTES:** Long, slender, and razor-sharp for paper-thin, delicate slices.

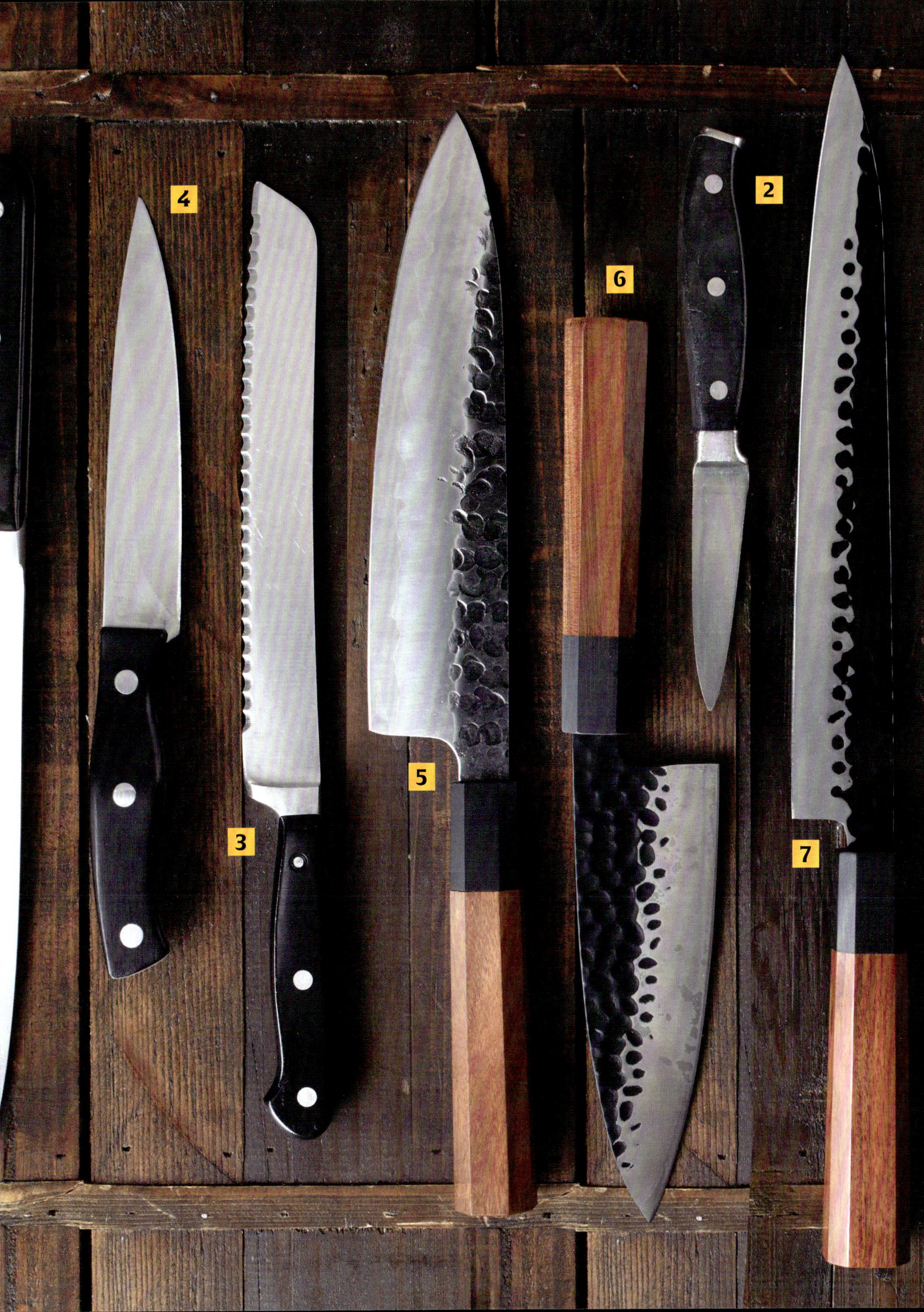

4
2
6
5
3
7

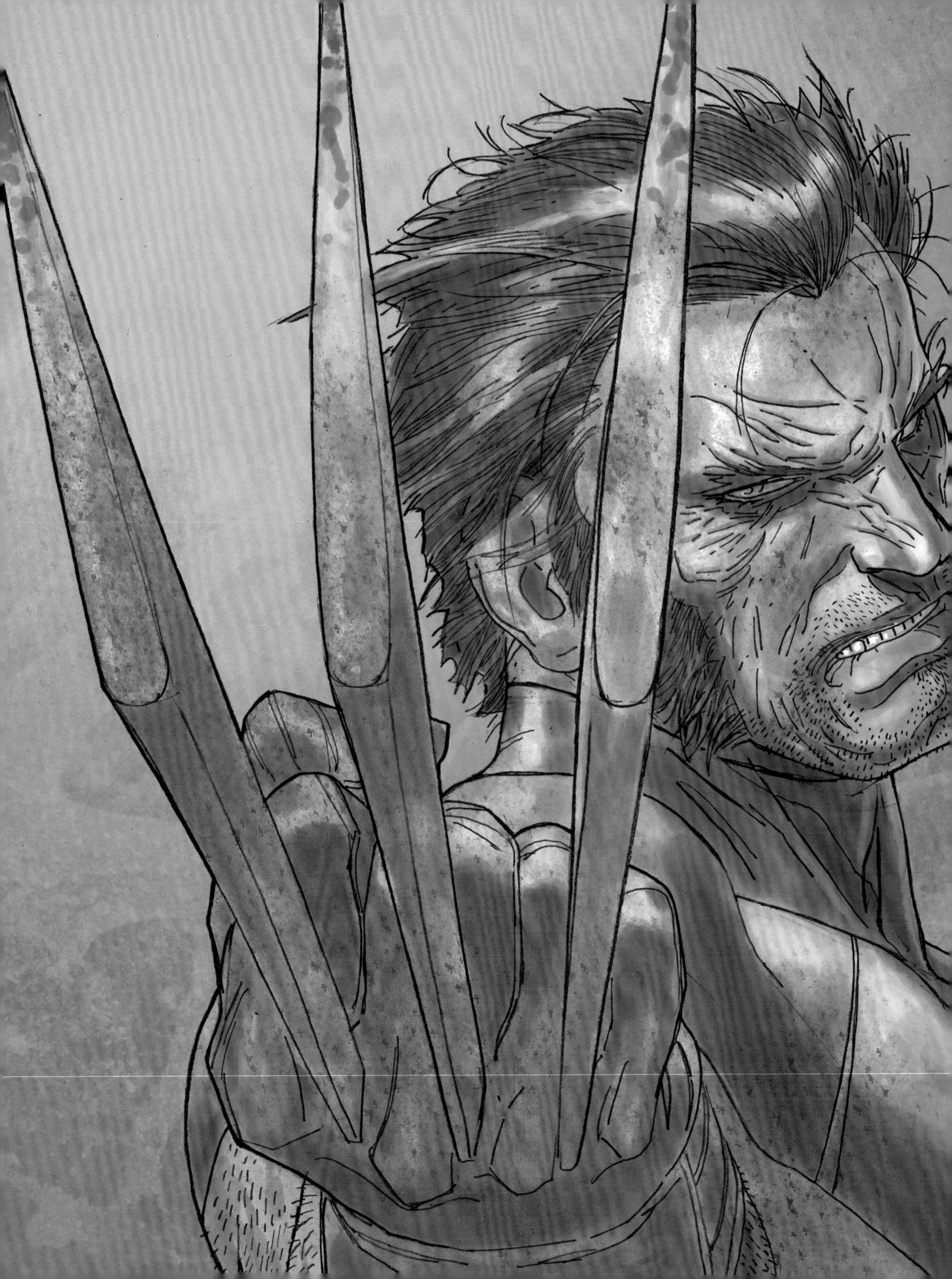

# THE GRIPS

## THE "CLAW"

Before you worry about your knife hand, you'll want to master "The Claw." It keeps the fingers of your non-dominant hand out of harm's way and helps guide your ingredients with precision. Use it whenever you're cutting up food to protect your digits and keep the knife in check.

**HOW TO DO IT:** Curl the fingers of your non-dominant hand inward, tucking your fingertips under and away from the blade. Your knuckles should press against the side of the ingredient, forming a "claw" shape. The claw grip steadies the ingredients, no matter how you handle your knife.

## PINCH OR "BLADE" GRIP

The pinch grip is the professional chef's preferred grip because it gives you both control and stability. Whether you're using a Japanese knife or a Western one, this grip is your ticket to real precision and power.

**HOW TO DO IT:** Firmly pinch the blade or bolster between your thumb and index finger, with your other fingers on the same hand wrapped gently around the handle.

## HANDLE OR "HAMMER" GRIP

I'm told the handle grip is sometimes more comfortable for home cooks. It's good for all kinds of cuttin' tasks but doesn't offer the same control as the pinch grip. It's straightforward, gives a stable hold and comfortable cuts.

**HOW TO DO IT:** Wrap your fingers around the handle tightly, encircling it with the fingers of your dominant hand and resting your thumb on the opposite side of the handle.

## POINT GRIP

The point grip is a go-to for sashimi chefs using a special knife called a *yanagiba*. This grip locks the blade in place, making the knife feel like an extension of your arm, to give you precise control for delicate slicin'.

**HOW TO DO IT:** Rest your forefinger along the top of the blade's spine, with your thumb and other fingers gripping the handle. Make sure the blade is sharp to get the most out of this grip.

# THE TECHNIQUES

## CHOPPING

Chopping's about getting ingredients in chunks quickly. Don't need to be pretty, just fast.

### FINE CHOP

This is for gettin' ingredients to small enough pieces for sauces or for blending into your dish.

**KNIFE:** Chef's Knife or Paring Knife
**HOW TO DO IT:** Use a rocking motion, keeping the tip of the knife on the cutting board, and chop the ingredient into fine pieces about ⅛ inch in size.

### MEDIUM CHOP

Ideal for ingredients you'd like to shape into moderately-sized chunks to make sure they cook even, while keeping some of their texture.

**KNIFE:** Chef's Knife
**HOW TO DO IT:** Use a rocking motion, keeping the tip of the knife on the cutting board, and chop the ingredient into pieces approximately ¼ inch to ½ inch.

### ROUGH CHOP 1

This produces large, uneven pieces, perfect for stews or roasting, or any dish where precision is not the priority.

**KNIFE:** Chef's Knife
**HOW TO DO IT:** Use a rocking motion with the knife's heel, chopping roughly and unevenly to get bigger pieces, usually between ½ inch and 1 full inch, but it can go up to 2 inches.

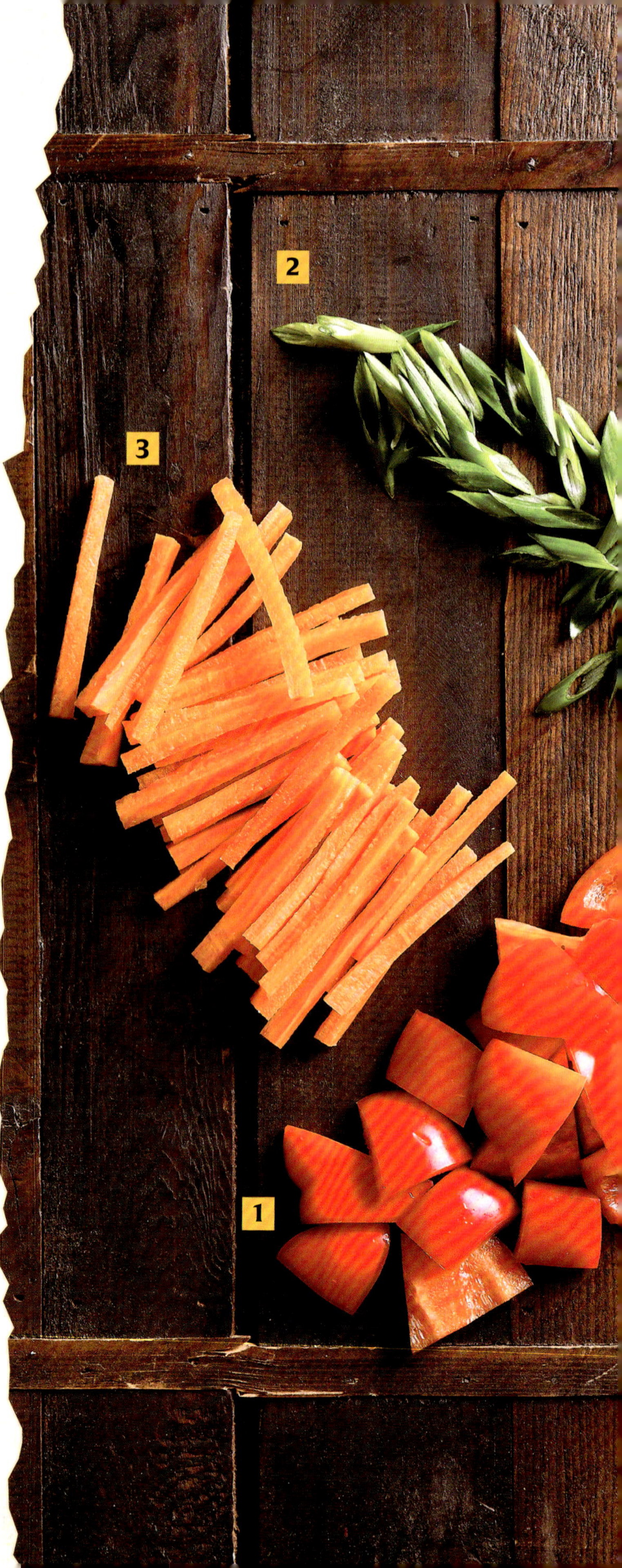
2
3
1

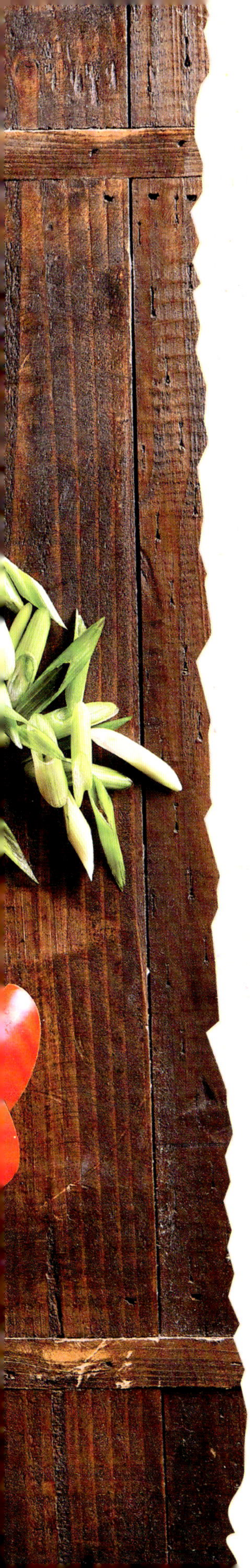

### RANGIRI CUT

A Japanese style that translates to "random shape," it's used for cuttin' vegetables into pieces with a rough appearance, often before they're cooked in soups or stews. It's similar to a rough chop in Western cooking but with a focus on uneven cuts.

**KNIFE:** Gyuto or Santoku
**HOW TO DO IT:** Cut the ingredient into uneven, rustic pieces with a chopping motion, focusing on varying the size and shape for a more natural look. The cuts do not need to be uniform, giving the final dish a hearty texture.

## SLICING

Used for cutting ingredients into thin, uniform pieces, such as slicing meats, vegetables, or fruits.

### STANDARD SLICE

The standard slice is a straightforward cut to shape ingredients into straight, even, well, "slices."

**KNIFE:** Chef's Knife or Slicing Knife
**HOW TO DO IT:** Move the knife in a smooth rocking motion, from tip to heel, to slice clean through the food. Slide your claw hand's fingers back after each cut, keeping the food steady, and let the knife do the work.

### WAGIRI CUT

Wagiri, which translates to "round," involves slicing ingredients into circular pieces, often used for vegetables and fruits where uniformity and presentation are key.

**KNIFE:** Santoku or Nakiri
**HOW TO DO IT:** Slice the ingredient into round pieces with a smooth, controlled motion. Keep the knife perpendicular to the ingredient to ensure even slices.

### BIAS CUT 2

A technique where ingredients are sliced at an angle to increase the surface area for faster cooking and better flavor absorption.

**KNIFE:** Chef's Knife or Paring Knife
**HOW TO DO IT:** Slice diagonally through the ingredient in a smooth, controlled motion, maintaining a consistent angle with each cut.

### NANAMEGIRI CUT

A Japanese slicing technique, very similar to a bias cut. You're slicing ingredients at an angle, not just to get more surface area but also for presentation.

**KNIFE:** Gyuto or Santoku
**HOW TO DO IT:** Like a bias cut but at a slightly steeper angle, often approaching 30 to 45 degrees.

### STRIP STYLES

Strip cuts are used for making long, thin pieces. These cuts are great for when you need quick, even cooking that's also pleasin' to look at.

### JULIENNE 3

Cuttin' vegetables into matchstick-size strips, perfect for garnishes, salads, or stir-fries.

**KNIFE:** Chef's Knife or Utility Knife
**HOW TO DO IT:** Slice the ingredient into thin, even slices. Stack these slices and then cut 'em into thin matchstick-sized strips.

## BATONNET 5

Similar to julienne but creates thicker strips, often used as a precursor to dicing or for dishes where larger pieces are required.

**KNIFE:** Chef's Knife
**HOW TO DO IT:** Slice the ingredient into even, thick planks, then stack the planks and cut them into thick strips, typically about ¼ inch to ½ inch wide.

## KAKUGIRI

Ideal for choppin' your vegetables into precise cubes, particularly in dishes like stir-fries or soups.

**KNIFE:** Santoku or Nakiri
**HOW TO DO IT:** Similar to dicing, but the motion is more of an up-and-down chop, with less rocking. This method allows for precise, even cuts.

# SMALL, FINE CUTS

These techniques are used for cutting ingredients into very fine, delicate pieces for a smooth texture or garnishes.

## MINCING 4

Finely chopping ingredients, often garlic, herbs, or onions, into tiny pieces.

**KNIFE:** Chef's Knife or Paring Knife
**HOW TO DO IT:** Rock the knife back and forth, keeping the tip of the knife on the cutting board, 'til the ingredient is very finely chopped.

## TANZAKU-KIRI CUT

Produces thin, rectangular strips often used for vegetables and garnishes, like a julienne.

**KNIFE:** Gyuto or Nakiri
**HOW TO DO IT:** Cut the ingredient into planks (flat, thick slices). Stack these planks and then cut 'em into long, rectangular strips.

# SQUARE AND CUBE CUTS

## MIREPOIX

Used for makin' a fine dice of onions, carrots, and celery, typically around ¼ inch, to create a flavor base (pg 48) for soups, stews, and sauces.

**KNIFE:** Chef's Knife
**HOW TO DO IT:** Start by doing a julienne cut, then once you have strips, cross-cut them into small, uniform cubes around ¼ inch or less. Aim for consistency so that all the pieces cook at the same rate, releasing their flavors evenly into your dish.

## DICING 6

Creates uniform cubes, commonly used for vegetables like onions, carrots, or potatoes.

**KNIFE:** Chef's Knife
**HOW TO DO IT:** Slice the ingredient into even strips, then cross-cut the strips to create cubes. The size of the dice can be small (¼ inch), medium (½ inch), or large (¾ inch).

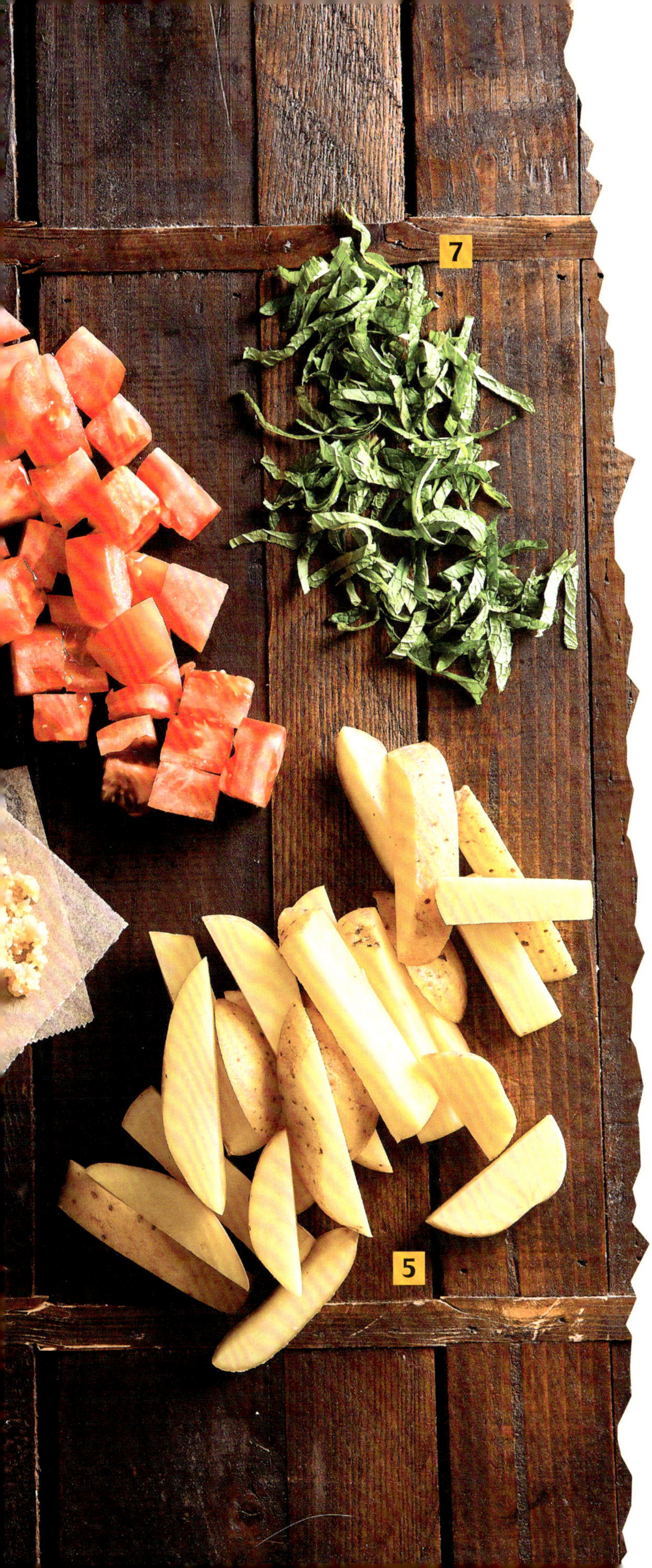
7
5

## MIJINGIRI

Similar to mincing, this is used for cutting ingredients into very small, fine pieces.

**KNIFE:** Santoku or Nakiri
**HOW TO DO IT:** Use a quick, fine chopping motion, often with the entire blade touching the cutting board to create very fine pieces.

## CHIFFONADE 7

Used for cuttin' leafy greens or herbs into thin ribbons, ideal for garnishes or salads.

**KNIFE:** Chef's Knife or Paring Knife
**HOW TO DO IT:** Stack the leaves, roll 'em into a tight bundle, and slice across the bundle to create thin ribbons.

## SENGIRI

Sengiri or "thousand" cut, is a technique for cutting vegetables, especially cabbage, into fine, thin strips.

**KNIFE:** Nakiri or Santoku
**HOW TO DO IT:** Slice the vegetable into very thin, even strips, usually with a straight up-and-down motion. Use this one for Okonomiyaki (pg 116).

# BLADE MAINTENANCE

I don't have to sharpen my claws—one of the perks of the pure adamantium coatin' my bones. But if you're working with regular kitchen knives, you're going to have to put in some work to keep them nice and sharp.

## THE TOOLS

- **WHETSTONE:** Treat this as "Option A." The best tool for sharpening is a whetstone–1000 grit for sharpening, 3000–8000 grit for polishing.
- **ELECTRIC SHARPENER:** My usual "Option B." If I'm short on time, a manual or electric sharpener works well for basic sharpening.
- **HONING ROD:** A honing rod isn't for sharpening, but it's essential for keeping the edges of your knife's blade aligned.

**PREPARING A WHETSTONE:** Soak the whetstone in water for 10–15 minutes 'til no more air bubbles rise. This ensures the stone stays moist during sharpening.

## SHARPENING

- **STEP 1: GET THE ANGLE RIGHT:** Hold the knife at a 15-to-20-degree angle. For Japanese knives, stick to a 15-degree angle.
- **STEP 2: TACKLE THE COARSE SIDE:** Starting with the rougher side of the whetstone or sharpener, and, using gentle pressure, push the knife away from you across the stone, flipping sides after each stroke. Do about 10 to 15 strokes per side.
- **STEP 3: MOVE OVER TO THE FINE SIDE:** Switch to the smoother side of the stone, repeating the same motion with lighter pressure to refine and polish the edge.

**HONING:** After sharpening, or in between sharpening sessions, use a honing rod to align the knife's edge. Hold the rod vertically with the tip on a cutting board, place the knife at a 15-to-20-degree angle against the rod, and swipe the knife down and across, alternating sides for about 6-8 swipes. To test the sharpness, slice through a piece of paper or a tomato—if the knife is sharp, it will cut cleanly without effort.

**TESTING:** Try slicing a tomato or an onion. A properly sharpened knife will cut cleanly and effortlessly, without the tomato gettin' squished or the onion slipping.

**MAINTENANCE:** Hone blades regularly, sharpen them every 2 to 3 months, and store knives properly to maintain their sharpness.

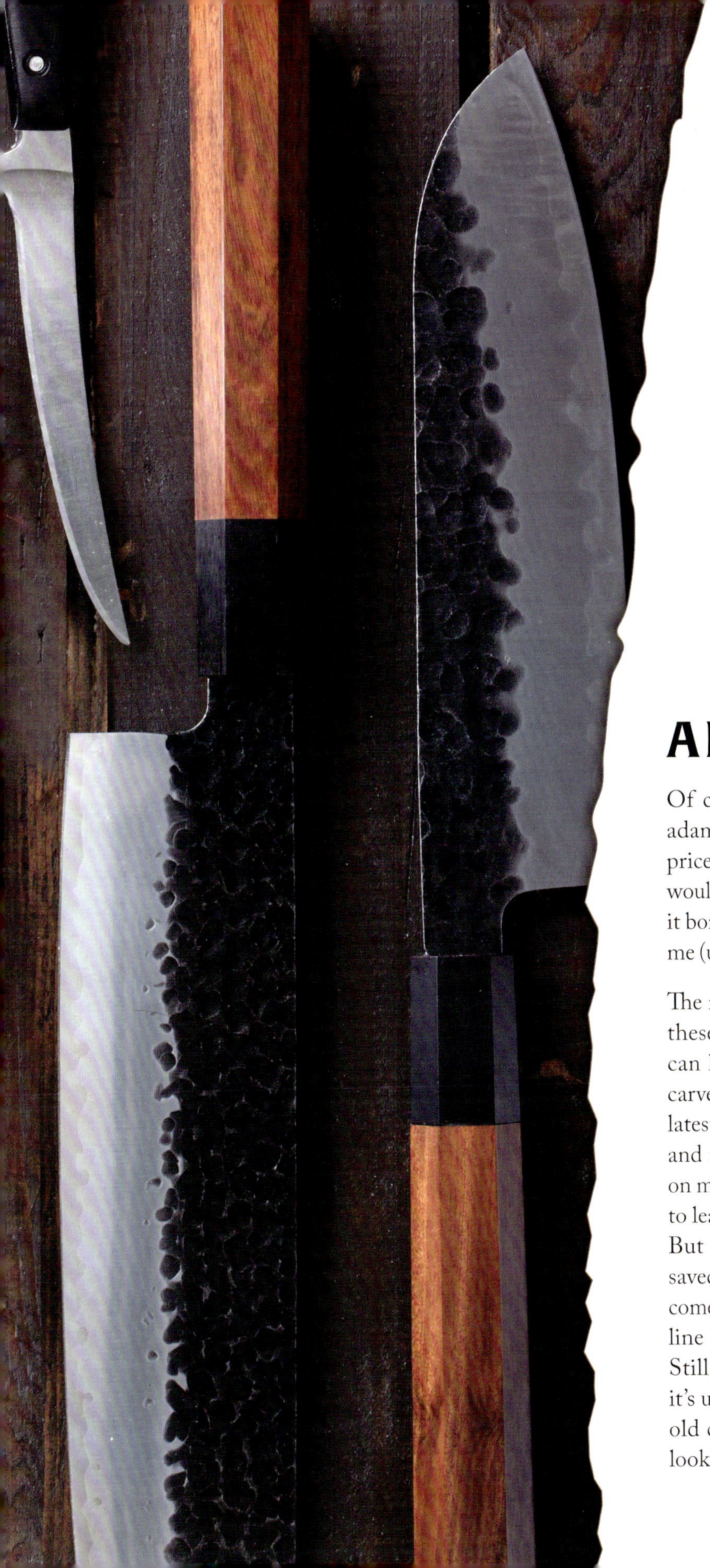

# ADAMANTIUM

Of course, nothing on Earth cuts like adamantium. Extremely rare and near-priceless, but then any unbreakable alloy would be. Not that I recommend folks get it bonded onto their bones like they did to me (unless you got a helluva healing factor).

The razor-sharp finish Weapon X left on these here indestructible claws means I can hack through a concrete wall, fine-carve a hunk of marble, and chop up the latest model of mutant-hunting Sentinels and never dull a blade. It's put a bullseye on my back for all kinds of whackos lookin' to learn the secrets or strip-mine it off me. But I gotta admit that the stuff must've saved my keister ten times as often. Also comes in handy to always have top-of-the-line cutlery whenever the occasion calls. Still, when cooking for polite company, it's usually best to fall back on the regular old chopping set. At least 'til they aren't lookin' ... or they tick me off.

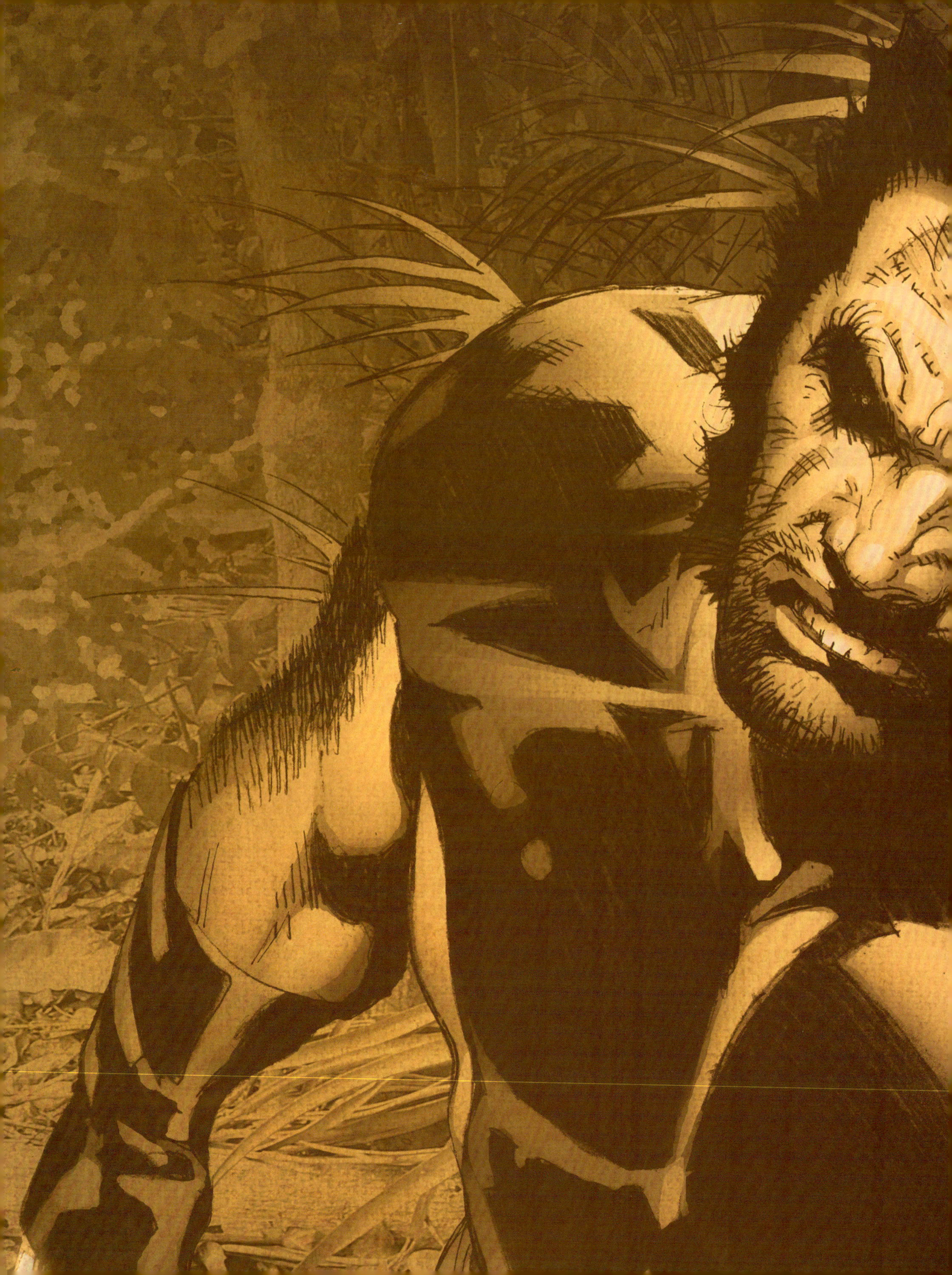

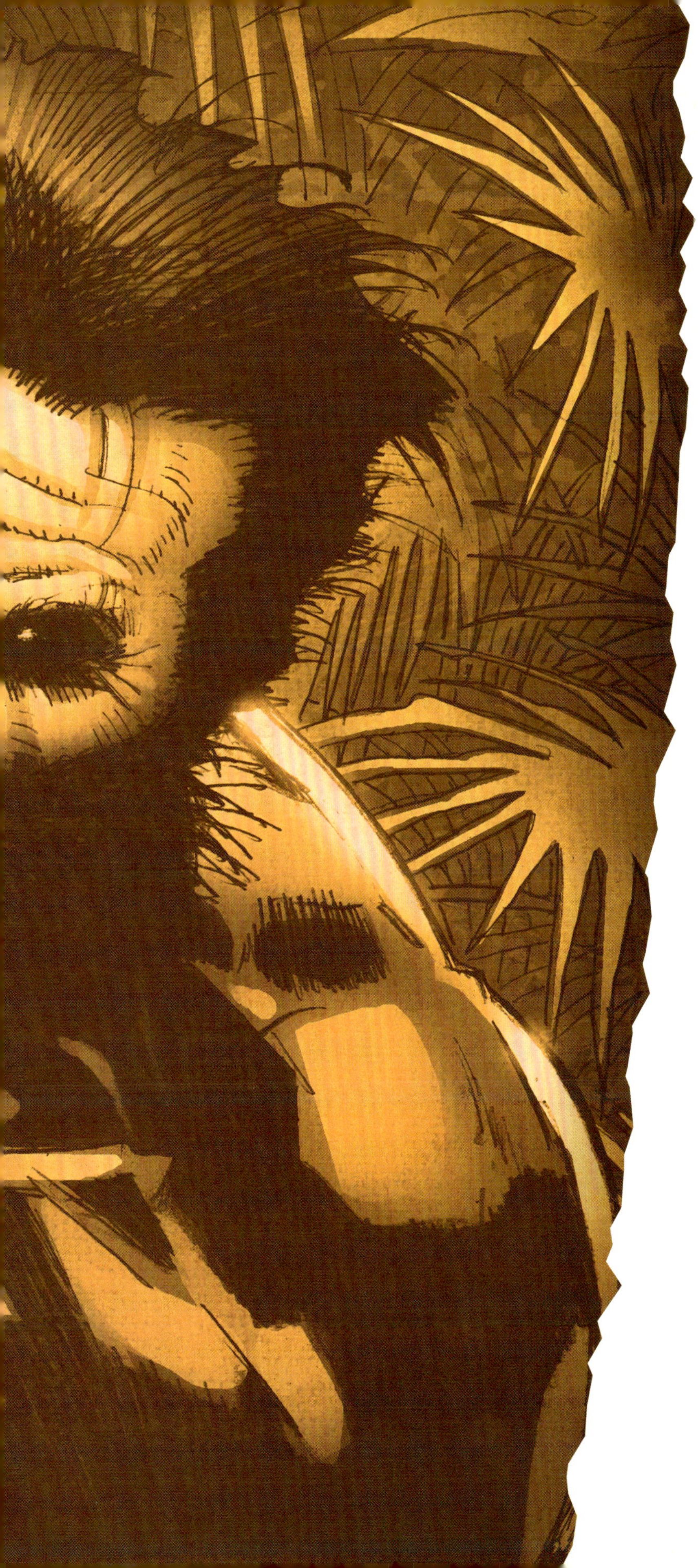

# 2

## ROUGHIN' IT: LIVING OFF THE LAND

A lone animal, stalking through the wilderness, scrappin' to survive. It's how I started life as the Wolverine, and somehow or another—I end up back there time and again. Maybe it's where I belong …

One thing's for sure: fightin' off starvation looks a helluva lot different deep in the wild. Whether laying low in a cabin, holed up in some abandoned remote facility, or half-feral among the wolves in some forest, you might want to know how to forage or hunt. But that don't mean you can't prepare some grub good enough to feel like you got one foot back in civilization.

## HOW TO
# STARTING A CAMPFIRE

Starting a fire ain't just about flicking a match—it's about knowing what you're doing. Out in the wilderness, you either get it right, or you're sittin' out in the cold. Or worse, burning down the whole damn forest. So, let's get down to business.

**WHAT YOU'LL NEED**

- Long matches or a long-necked lighter (see Note)
- Tinder: your dry leaves, small twigs, paper
- Kindling: your small sticks and branches
- Firewood: your larger logs
- Water or an extinguisher

Clear a 10-foot-diameter area around the fire site of any flammable materials like leaves or grass. If there's a fire pit available, use it. Otherwise, dig a small pit and surround it with rocks to contain the fire.

Collect plenty of dry tinder, kindling, and firewood. Make sure everything is dry because wet wood and leaves won't burn.

Place a handful of tinder in the center of your fire pit. Arrange the kindling around the tinder in a teepee shape, leaving a small opening on one side for airflow. Lean larger sticks against the kindling, also in a teepee shape.

Use long matches or a long-necked lighter to ignite the tinder. Light it in several places to ensure it catches.

Once the kindling catches fire, add small pieces of firewood. Gradually add larger logs as the fire grows stronger. Always place wood carefully to maintain airflow.

Keep the fire burning by adding wood as needed. Don't smother it by piling on too much wood at once.

When you're done, pour water on the fire, stir the ashes, and pour more water 'til everything is cool to the touch. Never leave a fire unattended.

**LEAVE NO TRACE:** This bit's a key step. Clean up every bit of trash and food scraps around your fire. Pack it out so the next folks can enjoy the spot and you can enjoy your anonymity.

*Note: If you find yourself without a match or a lighter, locate a piece of flint or a hard rock and strike it against steel or another rock to create sparks and catch the sparks on the tinder. You could also use a shiny object (like a lens or even ice if you can carve it into shape) to focus the sunlight onto the tinder. Or, you know, adamantium might just do the trick ...*

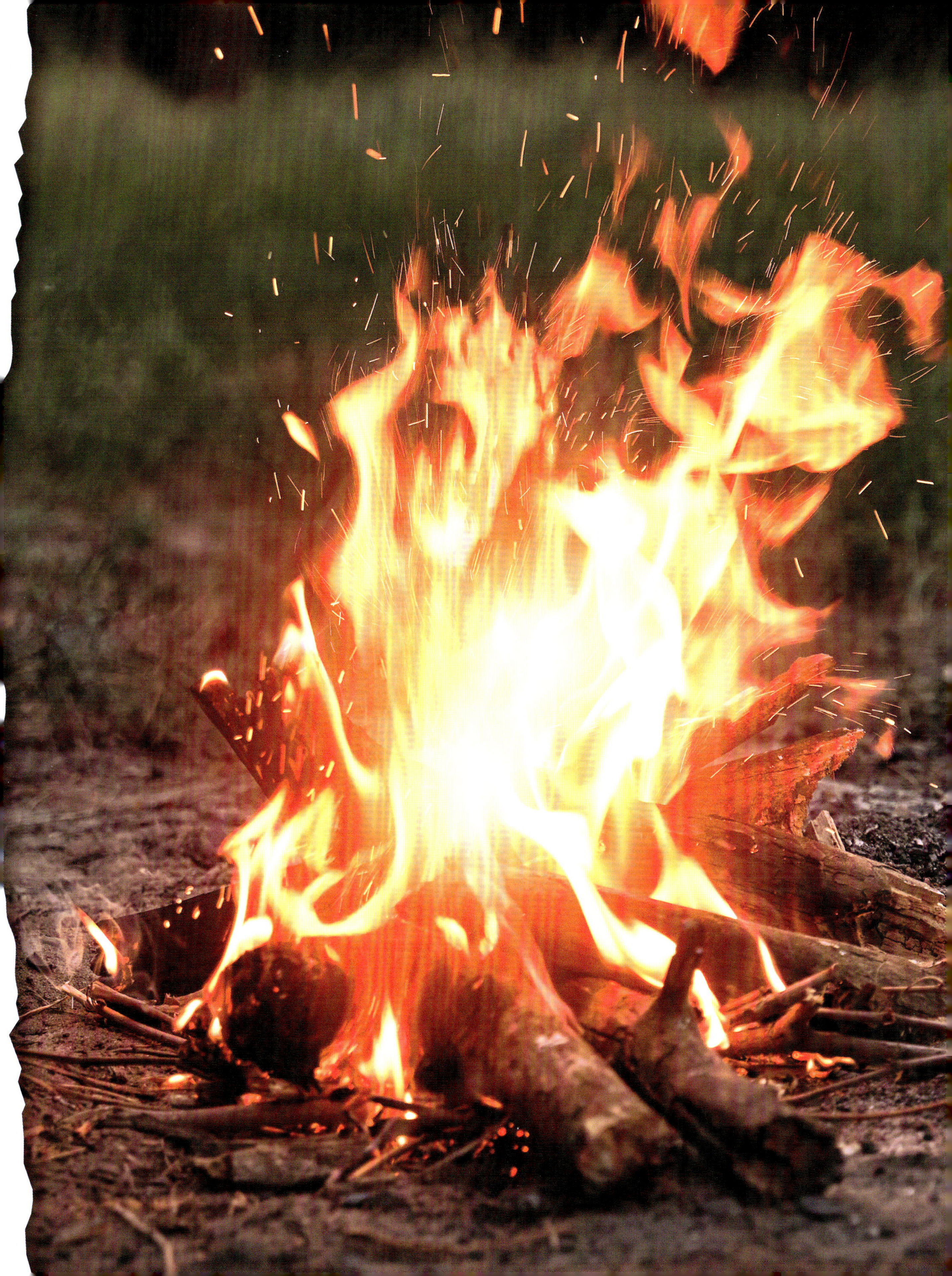

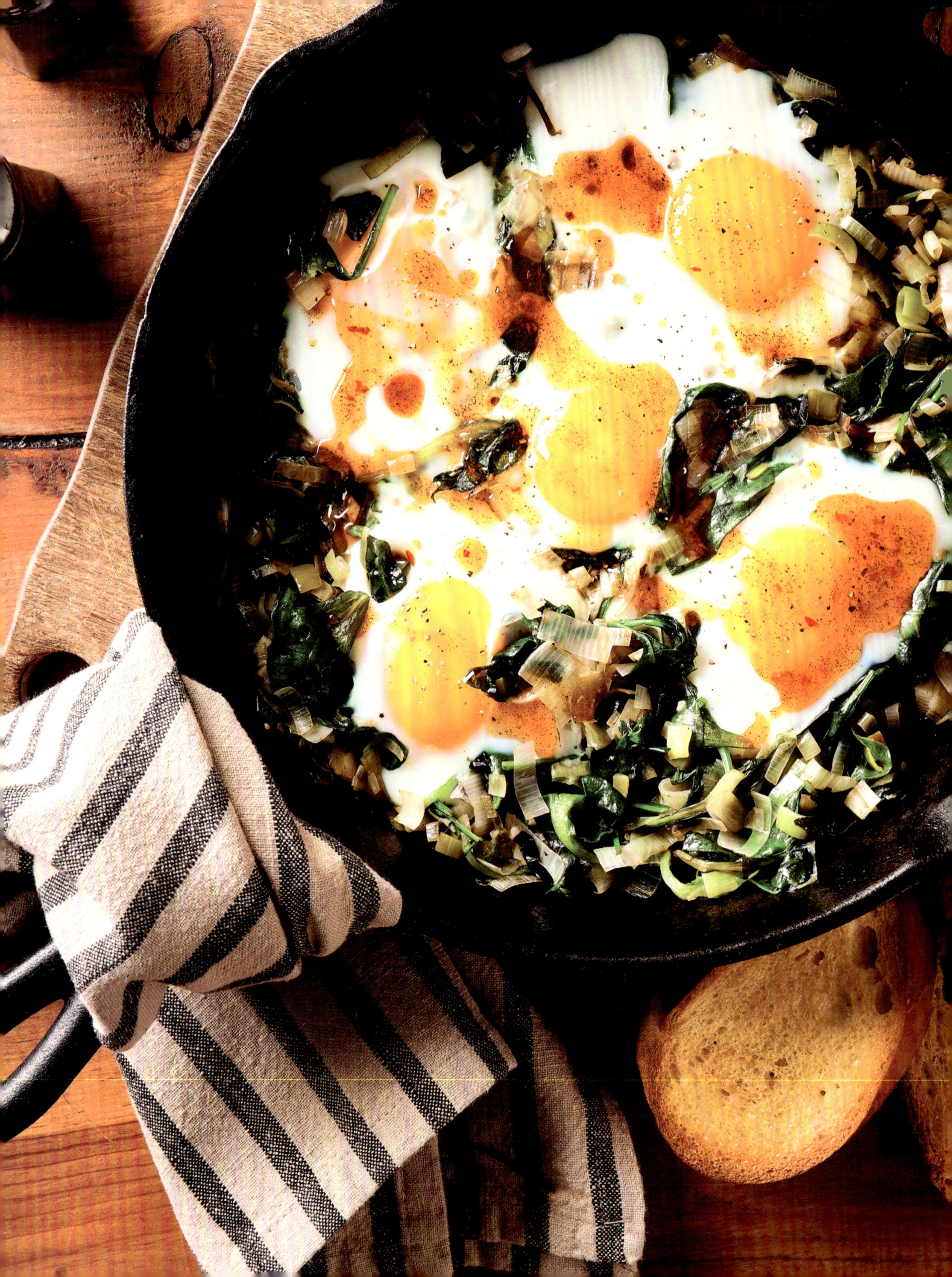

# EGGS HOWLETT

May not look like it now, but the relentless Wolverine started life as scrawny James Howlett, a kid prone to illness. Most days were spent cooped up inside the giant Howlett estate, walled off for fear of allergies and sickness. So, every taste of the outside world had to be savored. When the morning's eggs were cooked with wild greens of the season, I tried to latch onto every scent and let it lead me *away*. Nowadays, cooking this leads me *back*. I didn't get to make enough memories with my family. But this is one of 'em.

**Servings: 2 to 4 • Type: Breakfast • Difficulty: Easy • Prep Time: 15 minutes**
**Cook Time: 20 minutes • Rest Time: None • Dietary Considerations: V\*, GF**
**Pairs well with: Toast or *Fried Bannock Bread* (pg 49)**

2 tablespoons rendered duck fat or butter, adding more as needed

1 leek, washed and chopped

2 cloves garlic, minced

5 cups chopped mixed greens (see Note)

1 tablespoon *Mutant Medley* (pg 30)

¾ teaspoon salt (or to taste)

4 to 5 large chicken eggs

1 tablespoon chile oil or harissa paste, optional

Cracked black pepper (to taste)

Toasted bread or *Fried Bannock Bread* (pg 49), optional, for serving

In a large cast-iron skillet, heat 1 tablespoon of the duck fat or butter over medium-low heat. Add the leeks and cook, covered, 'til softened, about 8 to 10 minutes.

Once the leeks have softened, add the garlic and more fat or butter if needed. Cook for another minute 'til the garlic is fragrant, then add the greens and cook for about 4 to 5 minutes, 'til lightly wilted.

Season the greens with Mutant Medley and salt to taste.

Create 3 to 5 wells in the cooked greens, then drop the eggs into the wells you created. Cover and keep the temperature on medium-low so that the eggs don't burn on the bottom. Do not stir.

Once the egg whites are cooked through, and the yolks done to your preference, add small dollops of chile oil and sprinkle with cracked black pepper, if you like. Serve warm with toast.

*Note: When you're out in the wild, just grab whatever edible greens you can find—wild garlic or spring onions, fiddleheads, watercress, mustard greens, stinging nettle, dandelion greens, or maybe some chopped wild asparagus. But if you're makin' this back in civilization, go ahead and use spinach, arugula, kale, swiss chard, shaved brussels sprouts—fancy stuff like that.*

ROUGHIN' IT: LIVING OFF THE LAND

# HEALING FACTOR PEMMICAN

Bullets, swords, plasma blasts … sure, I can take most any kinda damage you got. But even with a mutant healing factor, stitching myself back together is a *pain*. Especially when I've been cut down to the ol' adamantium bone, it pays to speed up the process. Recipes like this got passed down in Indigenous tribes, including the Cree and Lakota, for packin' plenty of fuel into one dense, chewy package. So next time you're left for dead in the wilderness, scrap these together and get back on your feet and back in the fight.

**Servings: 4 to 6 • Type: Snack • Difficulty: Easy • Prep Time: 15 minutes • Cook Time: None**
**Rest Time: 1 hour • Dietary Considerations: GF, V\*, V+\*(see Notes)**

½ pound (8 ounces) *Moose Jerky* (pg 31), or other jerky or dried meat

4 ounces dried fruit such as blueberries, cherries, cranberries, raisins

4 ounces nuts and seeds such as hazelnuts, walnuts, pumpkin seeds, etc.

4 ounces rendered fat such as duck fat, beef suet, bacon fat, ghee, or coconut oil (see Notes)

1 to 2 tablespoons pure maple syrup, optional or to taste

1 to 2 teaspoons *Danger Room Rub* (pg 30) or other BBQ seasoning, optional or to taste

Pulse the jerky in a food processor 'til you have a coarse powder with no big pieces.

Remove the jerky powder and set it aside. Add the nuts and fruit and pulse so they are also a coarse powder. Set aside.

Heat the fat in a small saucepan over medium-high heat 'til completely liquified. Carefully pour the hot fat through a mesh strainer into a heat-resistant container. Careful not to splatter.

In a large mixing bowl, add the jerky powder, fruit, nuts, maple syrup, and seasonings. Stir to combine.

Add half the liquid fat and stir to combine. Start adding the fat a little bit at a time, adding just enough so the mixture easily holds together when squeezed.

Press the mixture into a pan or mold and allow it to cool and solidify in the refrigerator, about 1 to 2 hours.

Cut the solidified pemmican into 2-inch squares or roll it into small ping-pong-sized balls. Store in the freezer for up to 3 months, in the refrigerator for up to a month, or at room temperature for up to 3 days.

*Notes: Make sure whatever rendered fat you use is one that solidifies at room temperature. Don't use butter because it contains milk solids, which turn bad on ya. Oh and if you're using coconut oil as your rendered fat, you can even make this recipe vegan. Just use jackfruit or mushroom jerky instead of meat and you'll make Bruce Banner and Wanda Maximoff awfully happy.*

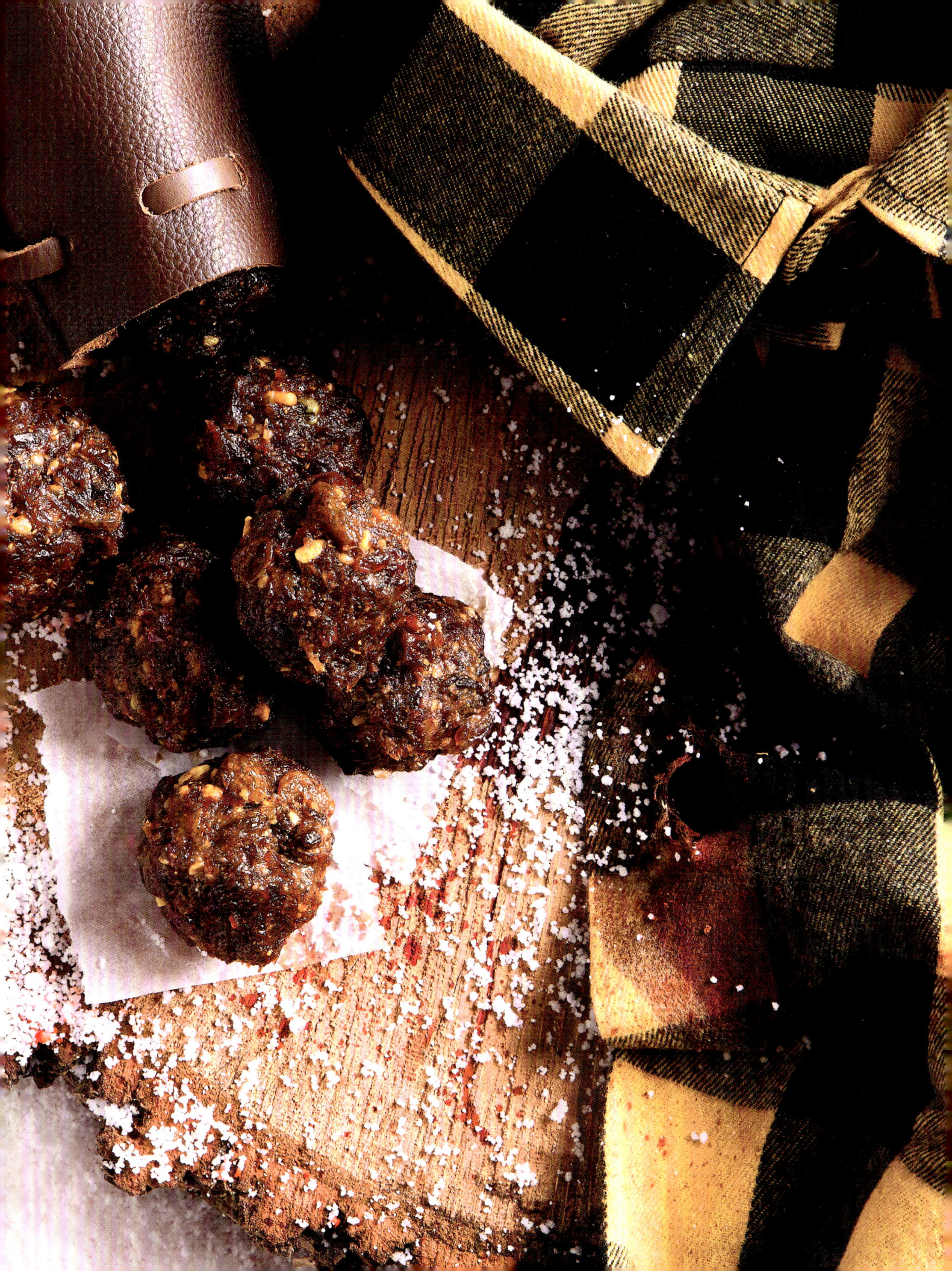

## HOW TO
# SPICE BLENDS

Spice blends come in real handy when you're on the move or just wanna get the job done fast. Nobody wants to be haulin' around a bunch of loose spices while on the go, and you don't have time to be hunting for the oregano while your meal's turning to ash. So just mix 'em up ahead of time. Stir it all up in a bowl, funnel it into a jar, and you're good to go. These are my go-tos. For each, it's as simple as mixing all the ingredients together in a jar or other sealed container and storing, well let's just say I haven't seen any of these go bad and I've been around a while.

**YIELD: ABOUT ½ CUP OR 8 TABLESPOONS EACH**

### MUTANT MEDLEY (ALL-PURPOSE SEASONING)

Used in: Eggs Howlett 27, Moose Jerky 31, Wild Mushroom Rice 40, Skunk-Bear Venison Stew 47, X-Man's Brewis 50, Bison Donair Kebabs 67, Skewered Surf 'n Turf 73, Tornado Potato 80, Hammer Bay BBQ 83, Poutine 94, Gaijin's Ramen 108, Korokke 115, Slingin' Chopped Cheese Dogs 139, Slim's Cheesesteak Sandwiches 152, Jubilee's Food Court Chili Fries 154, Jean's Holiday Broccoli Casserole 159

- 2 tablespoons garlic powder
- 2 tablespoons onion powder
- 1 tablespoon paprika
- 1 tablespoon black pepper
- 1 tablespoon dried parsley flakes

### DANGER ROOM RUB (BBQ SEASONING/RUB)

Used in: Healing Factor Pemmican 28, Tornado Potato 80, Logan's Dry Smoked Ribs 153

- 3 tablespoons brown sugar
- 2 tablespoons smoked paprika
- 2 tablespoons chile powder
- 1 tablespoon dry mustard
- 1 tablespoon cumin
- 1 tablespoon garlic powder
- 1 tablespoon onion powder
- 1 tablespoon black pepper

### DAGGER BAY BLEND (CURRY POWDER)

Used in: Lowtown Satay 62, Hammer Bay BBQ 83, Korokke 115, Roti ~~John~~ Steve 123, Mystique's Mei Fun 124, Storm's Bajias 147

- 3 tablespoons ground turmeric
- 3 tablespoons ground coriander
- 2 tablespoons ground cumin
- 2 teaspoons garlic powder
- 1 teaspoon cinnamon
- 1 teaspoon ground ginger
- ½ teaspoon ground nutmeg

### WEAPON X (STEAK SEASONING)

Used in: Moose Jerky 31, Skewered Surf 'n Turf 73, Slim's Cheesesteak Sandwiches 152

- 2 tablespoons paprika
- 2 tablespoons whole black peppercorns, ground
- 2 tablespoons garlic powder
- 1 tablespoon onion powder
- 1 tablespoon ground coriander
- 1 tablespoon dill seed or dill weed
- 1 tablespoon crushed red pepper flakes

### GAMBIT'S MAGIC (CAJUN SEASONING)

Used in: Ragin' Cajun Poutine 93

- 3 tablespoons paprika
- 1½ tablespoons onion powder
- 1½ tablespoons garlic powder
- 2 teaspoons dried thyme
- 2 teaspoons dried oregano
- 2 teaspoons cayenne pepper
- 1 teaspoon ground black pepper

*Tip: Got a new favorite brand of AP seasoning, curry powder, or BBQ rub? No problem—swap 'em in. Just keep an eye on the salt. Some store-bought seasoning already has salt in it, meaning you'll probably want to reduce the amount of salt added separately to the recipe.*

# MOOSE JERKY

After a hunt—and the feast—a smart survivalist won't let good sustenance go to waste. Moose, venison, beef … most red meat can be preserved as jerky to keep you game without gettin' gamey. And while there are plenty of ways to dry jerky out in the wild, this recipe is how I avoid the risk that the scent'll attract some other animals—from your usual scavengers to a damn blood-thirsty WENDIGO.

**Servings: 6 to 8 • Type: Snack • Difficulty: Average • Prep Time: 30 minutes**
**Cook Time: 4 to 8 hours • Rest Time: 10 minutes • Dietary Considerations: GF**

2 pounds top round (or similar lean cut)
1 cup dark brown sugar
½ cup soy sauce or tamari
½ cup Worcestershire sauce
2 tablespoons *Mutant Medley* (pg 30) or other all-purpose seasoning
1 teaspoon *Weapon X* (pg 30) or other steak seasoning
2 teaspoons black pepper, plus more for later
1 teaspoon meat tenderizer
¼ teaspoon curing salt
1 teaspoon red pepper flakes, optional

**SPECIAL EQUIPMENT:**

Paring knife or kitchen shears, optional
Wooden spoon

*Note: Maybe you're wondering why I'm tellin' ya to use an oven instead of hanging meat out by the fire or stringing it up in the woods. Well, if you got a choice, making jerky is best tackled before you hit the trail. Sure, you could go old school and hang it to dry in the sun, but then you'd be stuck guarding it from critters all day and starin' down squirrels is probably not how you wanna spend your day. Unless you're looking to become a full-time wildlife bouncer, stick with the oven.*

If there's a fat cap on the meat, trim it down with a paring knife or kitchen shears. Slice the meat against the grain into slices about ¼ inch thick. Sometimes it's easier to slice meat when it's been frozen for a while, so put it in the freezer for a couple of hours first. Not 'til it's rock hard, just a bit firmer.

Add the sugar, soy sauce or tamari, Worcestershire sauce, and seasonings to a large zip-sealed bag. Add the meat slices, then shake and massage the meat to coat it evenly in the marinade.

Marinate the meat for 24 to 48 hours, flipping the bag and massaging the meat every 6 to 8 hours to ensure an even soak.

Line a rimmed baking sheet with aluminum foil and set a wire rack on top. After the meat has marinated, take the meat slices out of the bag and shake off any excess marinade. Place the meat slices in a single layer on the wire rack. Make sure the slices aren't overlapping at all. If you want, crack some extra black pepper on one or both sides of the meat strips.

Preheat the oven to 300°F. Place the baking sheet with the meat inside the oven, close the oven door, then immediately reduce the temperature to 275°F. Bake for 10 minutes to bring the internal temperature of the meat to a safe 160°F.

Lower the oven temperature to its lowest setting—around 170°F for most ovens—and prop the oven door open with a wooden spoon to maintain airflow. If your oven has a convection fan, flip it on after about 30 minutes to speed up the drying process. The fan isn't essential, but it helps move things along.

Continue drying the jerky, flipping every hour or so, 'til it passes the bend test—it should bend without breaking and show slight cracks on the surface. Depending on the oven and the thickness of the meat, this process can take anywhere between 4 and 8 hours.

Once the jerky is fully dried, let it cool completely before storing. Place the cooled jerky in an airtight container or resealable bag. If it is fully dried out, it can last up to 2 weeks at room temperature. For longer storage, keep it in the fridge or freeze it for up to 3 months. Make sure to label and date the storage container.

# SALMON CANDY

Even in the harshest winters, the roughest terrain, or our darkest days—there can be some sweetness. And a traditional Indigenous "salmon candy" evokes all three. It was the beautiful Silver Fox who made this smoky and succulent treat all those years ago in our cabin. While memories of that idyllic time together, and her death, are all mixed up with mind-games from our time under Weapon X—one taste of this floods the senses, and the salty-sweet flavors are almost as complicated as the feelings it drags up.

**Servings: 6 • Type: Snack • Difficulty: Average • Prep Time: 30 minutes • Cook Time: 1 hour
Rest Time: 8 hours • Dietary Considerations: GF**

1 pound salmon filets

½ cup dark brown sugar

1 to 2 tablespoons salt

2 teaspoons garlic powder

½ cup maple syrup

1 teaspoon black pepper

1 teaspoon liquid smoke (only if air frying)

2 cups water

Rinse the salmon under cold water and pat it dry with paper towels. If you want, remove the skins. Slice the salmon into 1-inch-wide strips and place in a large sealable bag.

In a medium mixing bowl, whisk together the brown sugar, salt, garlic powder, half the maple syrup, black pepper, and water 'til dissolved. Pour the mixture into the bag with the salmon, seal, and shake and massage gently to coat. Let the salmon marinate for 8 hours in the fridge, flipping the bag once or twice.

Preheat a smoker to 225°F. Remove the salmon from the bag, rinse it under cold water, and pat it dry with paper towels. Carefully place the salmon on a greased wire rack.

Transfer the wire rack with the salmon to the smoker grates. Smoke the salmon for about 1 hour, 'til it reaches an internal temperature of 140°F. Every 15 minutes, brush the salmon with the remaining maple syrup to create a glaze.

Once the salmon is done, brush it one last time with the maple syrup and let it rest. Serve at room temperature or chilled.

**Alternative Method:** If you wanna use an air fryer instead of a smoker, add 1 to 2 teaspoons of liquid smoke to the brine in Step 2. After the fish has brined, preheat the air fryer to 225°F and grease the grates. Remove the salmon from the brine, rinse it under cold water, and pat it dry with paper towels. Place the salmon on the greased grates with enough room in between for air to flow. Cook the salmon for about 1 hour, 'til it reaches an internal temperature of 140°F. Every 15 minutes, brush the salmon with the remaining maple syrup to create a glaze.

ROUGHIN' IT: LIVING OFF THE LAND

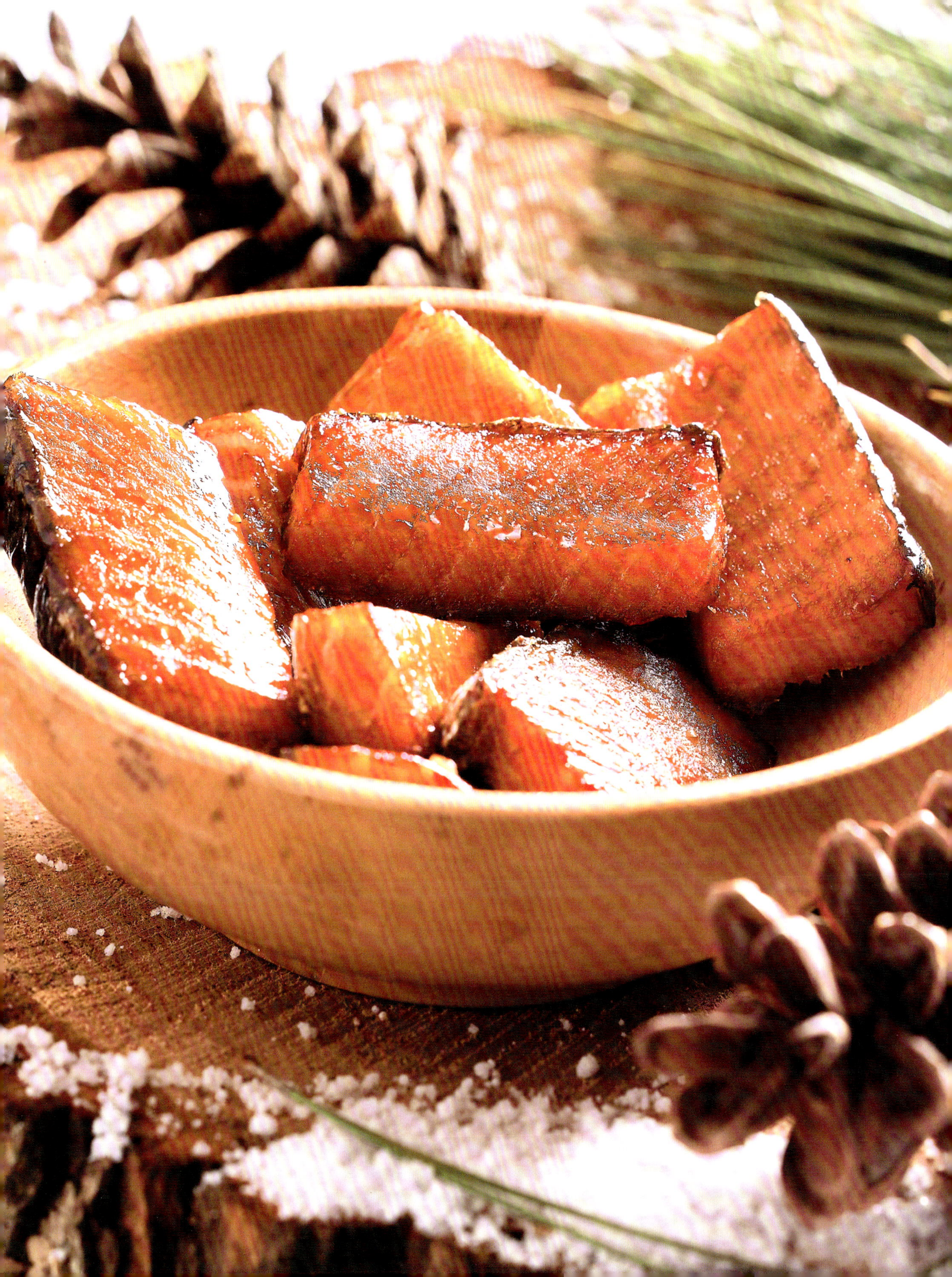

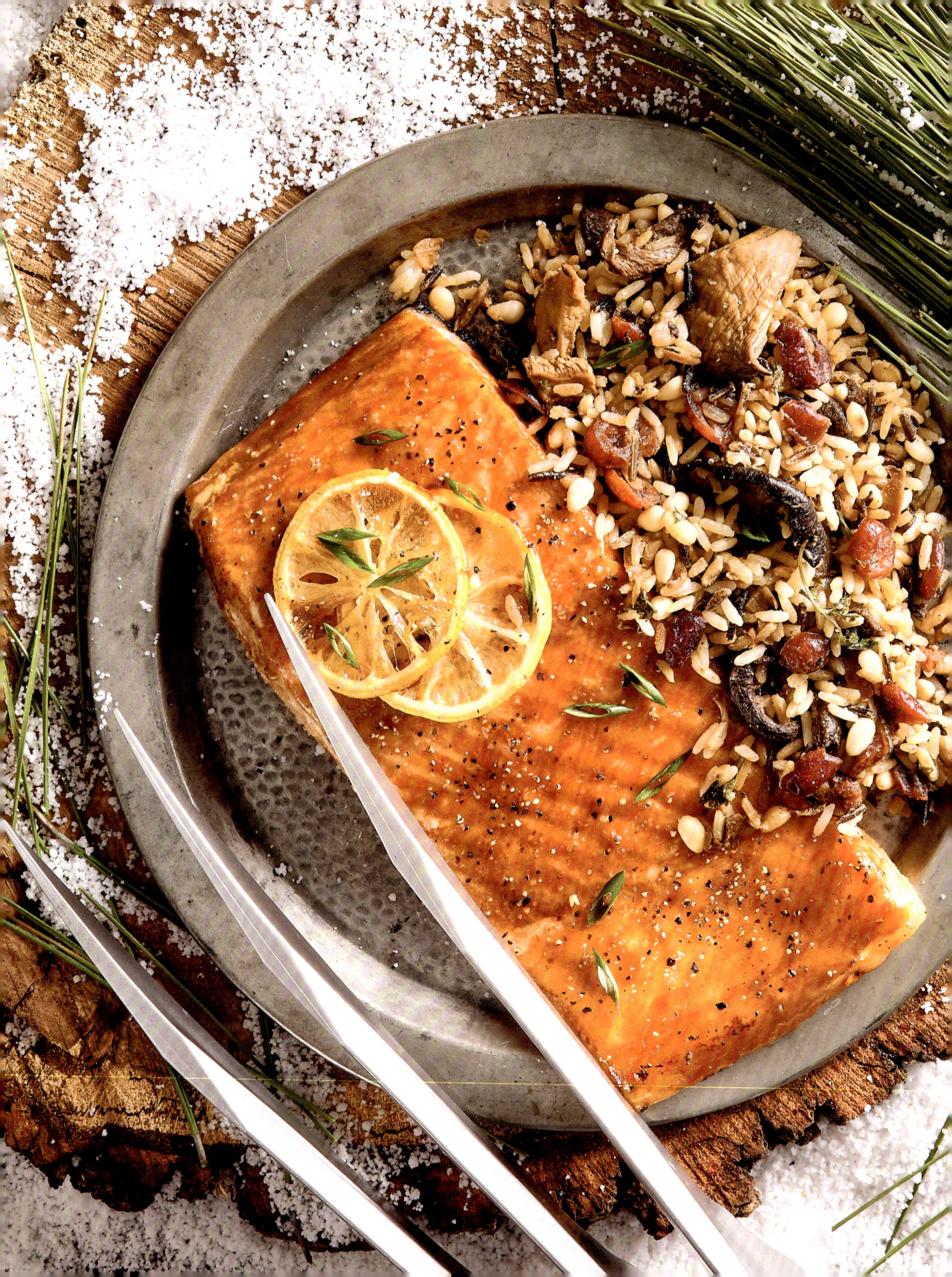

## HOW TO
# FILLET A FISH

It ain't pretty to fillet a fish. Takes a lick of skill and a sharp blade—both of which I got in spades, so stay sharp and you'll fillet like a pro in no time. Whether you're fresh off the water or just grabbed a catch from the market, I'll walk you through the steps to turn that fish into a clean, boneless slab of swim-meat.

**WHAT YOU'LL NEED**
Filet knife
Cutting board
Paper towels
Tweezers (optional)
1 Whole Fish

Rinse the fish under cold water and pat it dry with paper towels. Lay the fish on the cutting board with the belly facing you.

Remove the head if you like, by making a diagonal cut behind the gills, angling toward the head. But leaving it on can help guide your filleting cuts.

Start at the top of the fish near the head (or where the head was). Insert the tip of the knife behind the gills and cut down to the backbone, feeling for the ribs.

Turn the knife flat, with the blade facing the tail, and carefully slide it along the backbone. Keep the knife angled slightly downward to stay close to the bones. Use a gentle sawing motion to separate the flesh from the bones as you work toward the tail. Flip the fish over and repeat the process on the other side to remove the second filet.

Optional: remove the skin. Place the filet skin-side down on the cutting board. Hold the tail end with one hand, and with the knife at a slight angle, carefully slide it between the flesh and the skin, pulling the skin as you go.

Remove any remaining bones with tweezers or your knife. Trim off any unwanted belly fat or dark meat.

ROUGHIN' IT: LIVING OFF THE LAND

35

# WOJAPI

My favorite foraged-berry sauce and one of my least favorite memories all rolled into one. I was barely conscious—lost too much blood, even after the healing kicked in. That vicious bastard Sabretooth had just introduced himself by tearing through Silver Fox, our home, and then me. Left for dead, some kinda survival instinct took over. I guess some deep-down part of me remembered a First Nations recipe Silver Fox would make to put some "pep in our step," called Wojapi. I started makin' my own, grabbing fist-fulls of berries off any branch I passed. The quick hits of natural sugars, tart undertones, and nutrient-rich juices were enough to jolt me back from a black-out and help fuel my recovery.

**Yield: 1 pint • Type: Sauce/Condiment • Difficulty: Easy • Prep Time: <5 minutes**
**Cook Time: 30 minutes • Rest Time: None • Dietary Considerations: V, V+, GF**
**Pairs well with: *Fried Bannock Bread* (pg 49), *Feral Flapjacks* (pg 39), *Ol' Canucklehead's Canard* (pg 44), *Colossus's Buckwheat Blinis* (pg 151), cornbread, yogurt, and cooked meats.**

4 cups mixed berries (see Note)

½ cup water if using fresh berries (or 2 tablespoons if using frozen berries)

1 tablespoon cornstarch or arrowroot powder

Maple syrup or honey, to taste

Add the berries and water to a medium saucepan and bring to a simmer over medium heat.

Once simmering, remove a small amount of the liquid (about 3 or 4 tablespoons) and place it in a cup or small bowl. Whisk in the cornstarch or arrowroot powder to create a slurry, then stir the slurry back into the berries.

Reduce the heat to low and continue to simmer, stirring frequently, 'til the berries have mostly broken down and the mixture has thickened into a sauce. This could take anywhere between 20 and 30 minutes, depending on the type of berries. If the liquid evaporates too much and the berries begin to stick to the bottom of the saucepan, stir in another tablespoon or two of water as needed.

Once the sauce has reached a consistency somewhere between a sauce and a jam, stir in the maple syrup or honey to taste.

Once cool enough to handle, transfer to a mason jar or similar container for storage. Store for up to 2 weeks in the refrigerator.

*Note: Use whatever edible berries you can find. Chokeberries, blueberries, loganberries, huckleberries, strawberries, blackberries, marionberries, everything goes. Aim for a mix of at least three different types of berries. The bigger berries, like strawberries, might need to be halved or quartered 'til the pieces are around the same size as the other berries.*

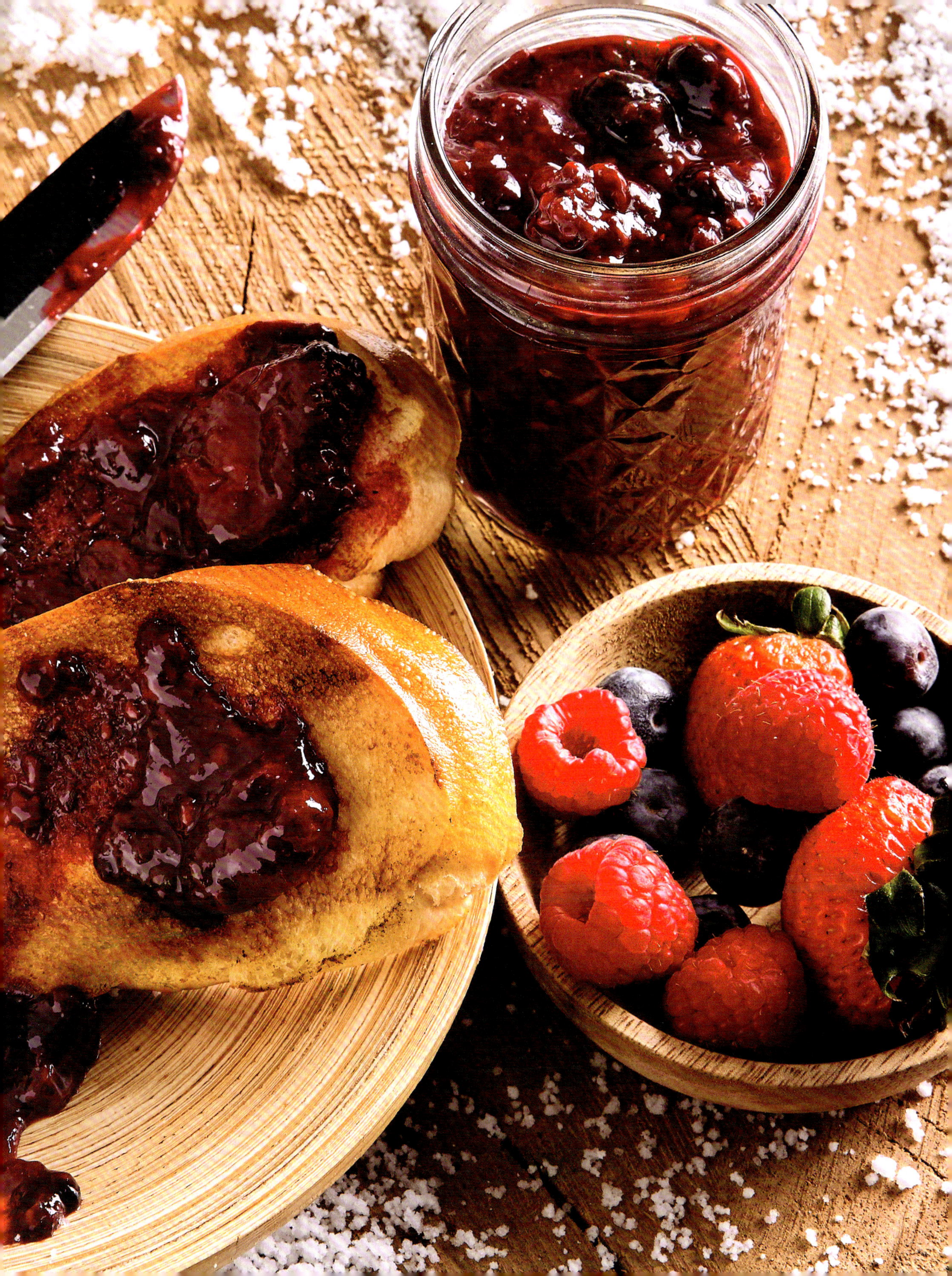

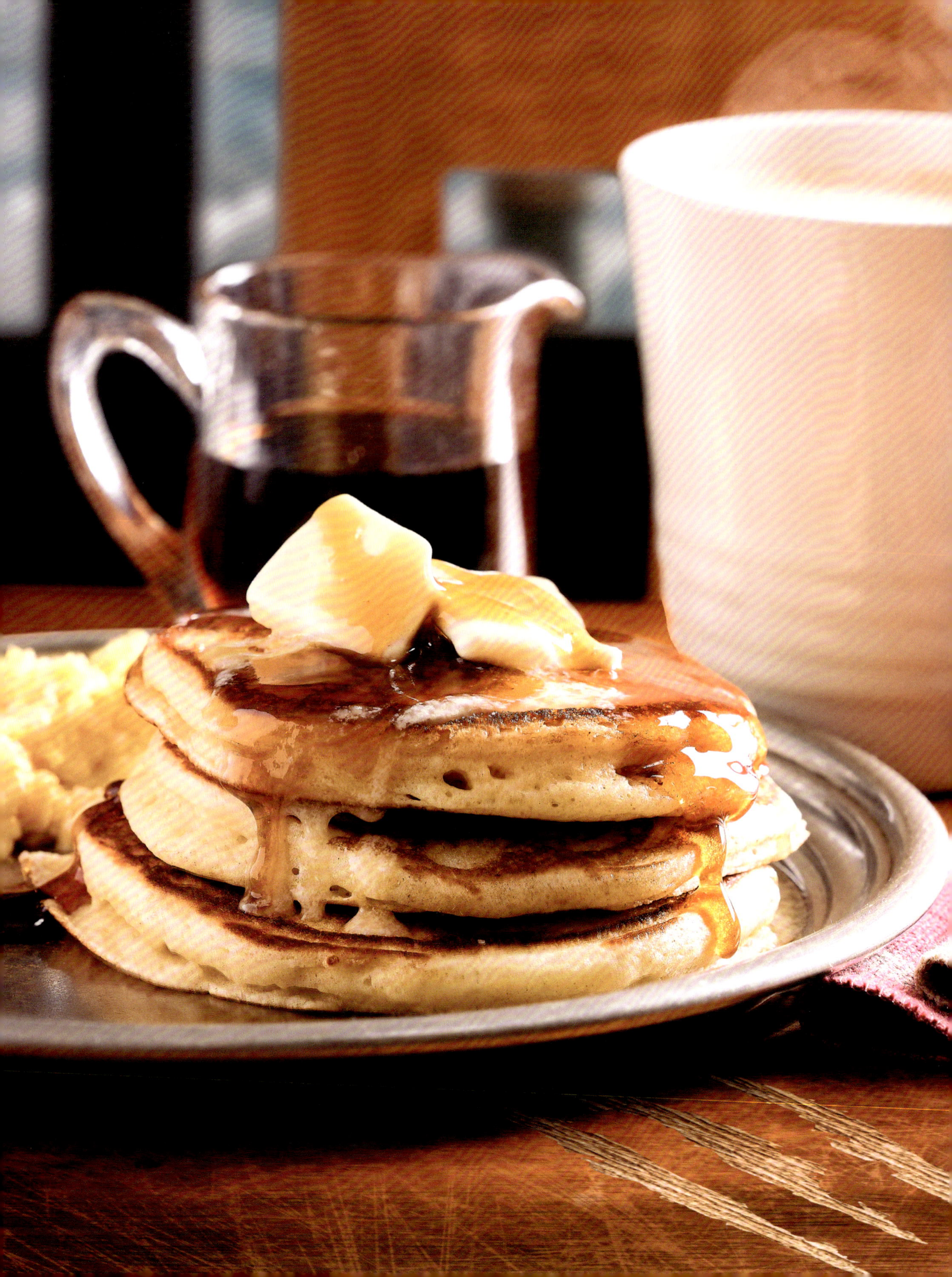

# FERAL FLAPJACKS

What's more Canadian than maple syrup? Dependin' on who you ask: maybe the nation's maple flag waving super team ALPHA FLIGHT. Unfortunately, I first met their star couple James and Heather Hudson (or "Guardian" and "Vindicator" to the spandex set) when I crashed their honeymoon on a feral rampage. This was after escaping from the Weapon X program—with adamantium on my bones and a scrambled brain as parting gifts. Lucky for everyone, they managed to pin me down and bring me back to some kinda sense. In the days it took to bring me around, Heather helped sooth the savage beast with a never-ending stack of sweet and nutty pancakes. She made sure they were drowned in rich, melted butter and freshly tapped maple syrup. Good enough to make a wild dog roll over.

**Yield: 8 to 10 pancakes • Type: Breakfast • Difficulty: Easy • Prep Time: 10 minutes**
**Cook Time: 45 minutes • Rest Time: None • Dietary Considerations: V**
**Pairs well with: Butter and maple syrup or *Wojapi* (pg 36)**

½ cup acorn meal, or use hazelnut, almond, or walnut meal

1½ cup all-purpose flour

1 tablespoon light brown sugar

1 teaspoon baking powder

1 teaspoon baking soda

½ teaspoon salt

2 cups buttermilk

2 large eggs

2 tablespoons unsalted butter, melted (plus more for serving)

Maple syrup or *Wojapi* (pg 36)

Option to start with: toast the acorn or nut meal in a dry skillet over medium heat for 3 to 5 minutes, and stir often, 'til it's golden brown and smells toasty. But stay sharp, it can burn quickly.

In a bowl, whisk together the flour, acorn meal, sugar, baking powder, baking soda, and salt.

In a separate medium mixing bowl, whisk together the buttermilk and the eggs.

Create a well in the flour mixture, then pour the buttermilk-and-eggs mixture in it. Stir 'til you have a thick, wet batter. Let the batter rest for 10 minutes.

Preheat a skillet or griddle to medium-low heat.

Lightly brush some of the butter over the surface of the pan 'til coated. Pour ¼ to ⅓ cup of batter into the hot skillet for each pancake. Depending on the size of your skillet or griddle, cook 1 or 2 pancakes at a time. After 2 to 4 minutes, bubbles will appear on the surface of the pancakes and stay—this is your queue to flip them. Flip the pancakes and cook for an additional 1 to 2 minutes, or 'til the underside is golden brown. Repeat the process with the remaining batter, adding more butter to the skillet as needed.

As each pancake finishes, set it aside on a serving plate and keep them warm (if you're indoors, you can place them in an oven set to low heat) while you finish cooking the rest.

Serve warm with butter and maple syrup or Wojapi.

# WILD MUSHROOM RICE

As plentiful as game is in the woods, there's also plenty o' reasons *not* to pop claws and go hunting every time your guts grumble. So, whether you're layin' low and don't wanna leave a trail or you're just trying to keep your hands clean, you can fill up on hearty, wholesome, and rich flavors gathered from the wild. Full of dynamic flavors—nutty, sweet, earthy—a bowl of this keeps you feeling civilized. (Of course, it can also round out a meaty meal pretty nice, too.)

**Servings: 4 to 6 • Type: Side • Difficulty: Average • Prep Time: 10 minutes**
**Cook Time: 1 hour • Rest Time: None • Dietary Considerations: V, GF, V+***
**Pairs well with:** *Ol' Canucklehead's Canard* (pg 44), *Cedar Plank Fish* (pg 43)

½ cup pine nuts, hazelnuts, and/or walnuts

2 cups water, as needed

8 ounces northern wild rice or other long-grain wild rice

6 to 8 tablespoons unsalted butter

1 large shallot, finely diced

1 pound wild mushrooms (see Note), sliced

1 teaspoon *Mutant Medley* (pg 30)

1 teaspoon mushroom powder or poultry seasoning, optional

1 teaspoon salt, or to taste

½ teaspoon black pepper, or to taste

1 tablespoon apple cider vinegar

¼ cup mushroom or vegetable broth

½ cup dried cranberries, raisins, and/or currants

¼ cup finely chopped parsley, plus more for garnish

Option to start with: toast the nuts in a dry skillet over medium-low heat for 2 to 4 minutes, just 'til lightly toasted. Set aside.

In a medium saucepan over medium-high heat, bring the water to a boil. Stir in the rice, then reduce the heat to low. Cover and cook 'til the rice grains puff and become tender, about 30 minutes. If the rice package has significantly different instructions and water quantity to cook the rice, follow those instead. Drain any extra liquid from the rice and fluff it with a fork. Set the cooked rice aside, covered.

Melt 4 tablespoons of butter in a large skillet over medium-high heat. Add the shallots and cook for 1 to 2 minutes 'til softened, then add the remaining butter and the mushrooms. Cook, stirring occasionally, 'til they have browned and released their juices, about 8 minutes. Season with Mutant Medley, mushroom powder or poultry seasoning, salt, and pepper to taste.

Add the vinegar, broth, and dried fruit and deglaze the pan, scraping up any browned bits on the bottom of the skillet. Cook 'til the excess liquid has evaporated.

Add the cooked rice, nuts, and parsley to the skillet, tossing to mix, and cook for 1 to 2 more minutes so everything melds together. Taste and adjust seasoning.

Garnish with more chopped fresh parsley and serve hot.

*Note: Use whatever 'shrooms you can get your claws on, assuming you know they're safe to eat. If you can't sniff out the difference, just be safe and forage what's available in the local store.*

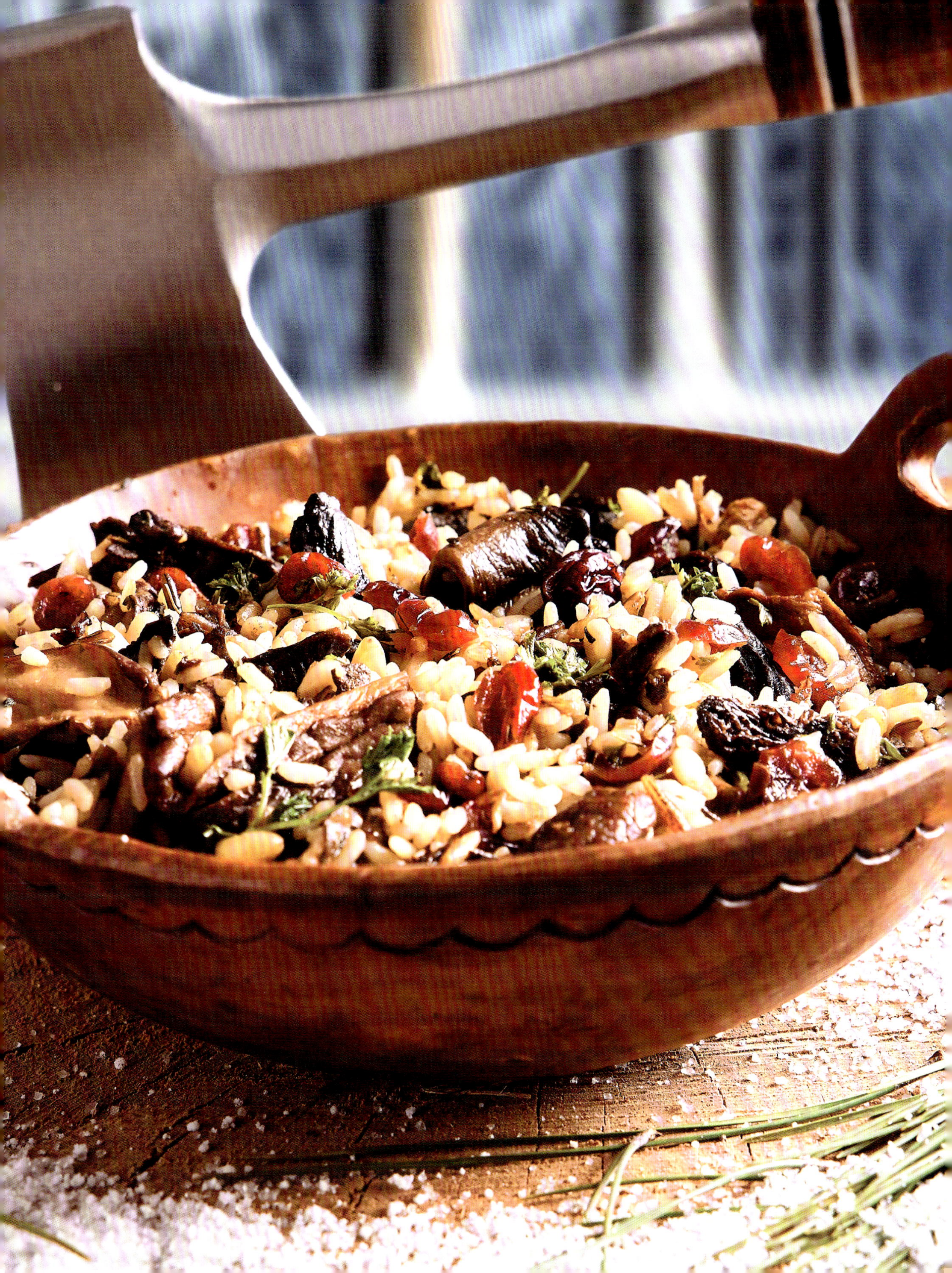

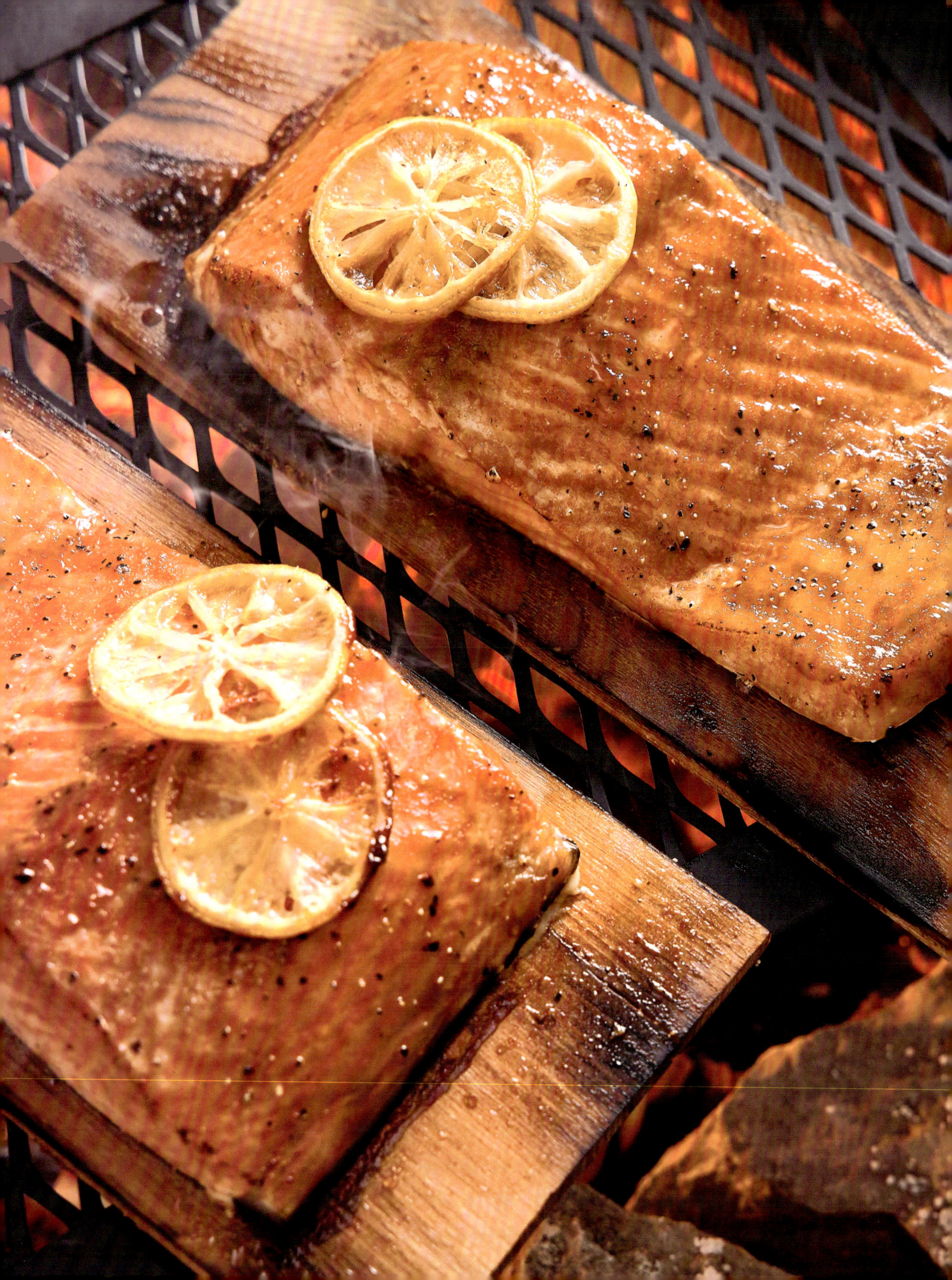

# CEDAR PLANK FISH

While this recipe gets plenty of play with the trappers, loggers, and frontier folks back in Canada, it makes me think of the SAVAGE LAND. After all, you don't visit that hidden tropical world filled with dinosaurs, you get *trapped* there. These days, when it feels like every month I'm jugglin' X-Men, X-Force, some "New" Avengers, plus all the stuff I'd rather work through *solo*, being stranded with Ka-Zar and Shanna in volcano land is about the only chance I get to slow down enough for this kinda meal-prep. The trees down there may not be cedar, but soaked and cooked, they seep just as much smokey flavor into whatever the hell you call those giant, prehistoric fish. The end result is just as crisp, flaky, and buttery too. Just remember to make enough for Zabu, or you'll be wrestlin' a sabretooth tiger for your supper.

**Servings:** 4 • **Type:** Main • **Difficulty:** Easy • **Prep Time:** 15 minutes • **Cook Time:** 25 minutes
**Rest Time:** 2 hours, 15 minutes • **Dietary Considerations:** GF
**Pairs well with:** *Wild Mushroom Rice* (pg 40)

4 filets arctic char, salmon, or trout
1 teaspoon salt, or to taste
Black pepper, to taste
¼ cup dijon mustard
¼ cup pure maple syrup
1 lemon, thinly sliced

**SPECIAL EQUIPMENT:**
1 or 2 cedar planks

Soak the cedar planks in water for at least 2 hours, or up to 24 hours, prior to cooking.

About 30 minutes before cooking, remove the fish filets from the fridge and season them with salt and pepper.

In a small mixing bowl, whisk together the maple syrup and mustard 'til well-combined.

Preheat the grill to medium-high heat, or about 400°F. Once hot, change the setting to indirect heat so the cedar planks don't catch fire. If using a two-burner grill, turn one of the burners off and place cedar planks on the side that's unlit. If using a three- or four-burner grill, turn off the middle burners and place cedar planks in the center of the grill.

Place the soaked cedar planks on the hot grate, over indirect heat, and close the lid. Let the planks heat for about 4 to 5 minutes. Place the filets, skin-side down on top of the planks. Brush about a tablespoon of the mustard mixture on top of each filet. Add 1 to 2 slices of lemon on top of each, if you like.

Close the grill lid and cook the fish on the cedar planks for 15 to 25 minutes or 'til cooked through. This will vary depending on the size of the filets, but you're aiming for about 140°F internal temperature. Careful not to overcook!

Just before the filets are done to your preference (they will continue to cook on the planks), carefully remove the planks from the grill. Cover with aluminum foil and let the fish rest for 10 to 15 minutes before removing them from the planks with a spatula and serve.

**Alternative Method:** To cook cedar plank salmon in the oven instead of the grill, preheat the oven to 375°F. Place the soaked cedar planks in the oven to preheat for about 4 to 5 minutes. Place the fish filets skin-side down on the cedar planks, brush the filets with the maple-mustard glaze and top with the lemon. Bake for 15 to 25 minutes, or 'til the internal temperature reaches 140°F. Remove the planks from the oven, cover with aluminum foil, and let the filets rest for 10 to 15 minutes before serving.

# OL' CANUCKLEHEAD'S CANARD

Sometimes the carnivore instinct takes hold, and you can't be satisfied 'til you're tearing into fresh meat. But you don't gotta sacrifice flavor for fuel. The tricks I picked up from a professional chef buddy in San Francisco work just as good over an open fire in the Canadian wilderness. And sometimes all you need is a bird cooked to perfection. With just a little salt and some know-how on your technique, even traditional game like a duck can become a rich, juicy, succulent feast.

**Servings: 2 • Type: Main • Difficulty: Average • Prep Time: 10 minutes**
**Cook Time: 20 minutes • Rest Time: 15 minutes • Dietary Considerations: GF**
**Pairs well with:** *Wojapi* **(pg 36),** *Wild Mushroom Rice* **(pg 40)**

2 duck breast pieces (breasts of one duck)

1 teaspoon salt, or to taste

½ teaspoon five spice or quatre épices, optional

1 teaspoon rendered duck fat or olive oil

*Wojapi* (pg 36), optional, for serving

Using a very sharp knife, gently score the duck breast skin in a tight crosshatch pattern, with cuts spaced about ⅛ inch apart. Cut into the fat as deep as you can but be careful not to cut into the flesh.

Season duck breasts with salt and spices (if using), more heavily on the skin-side and lightly on the flesh side. Let the breast sit for at least 15 to 20 minutes to give the salt time to absorb and to ensure the breasts are room temperature before going into the pan.

Gently brush a large, cold cast-iron skillet or sauté pan with the fat or oil. Place the duck breasts, skin-side down, into the skillet. Set the skillet over low to medium-low heat. To prevent the edges from curling, press the duck breasts down using a smaller heavy pan or a cooking weight.

After 4 or 5 minutes, the fat should begin to bubble gently. If the fat is silent or spitting, adjust the heat up or down accordingly. Cook 'til the skin is golden brown, much of the fat has rendered, and the internal temperature reaches 125°F, about 12 to 15 minutes. As the breasts cook, pour the excess rendered fat into a sealable glass container. That stuff is liquid gold.

Increase heat to medium and further brown skin for about 1 minute, before flipping and cooking on the flesh side. For medium-rare, cook 'til the breast registers 130°F, about 1 to 2 minutes. Continue cooking 'til the duck registers 140°F (60°C) for medium. Anything above that isn't worth my time, but to each his own.

Remove the duck breasts from the skillet and set them aside to rest for 10 to 15 minutes, before slicing and serving with the Wojapi.

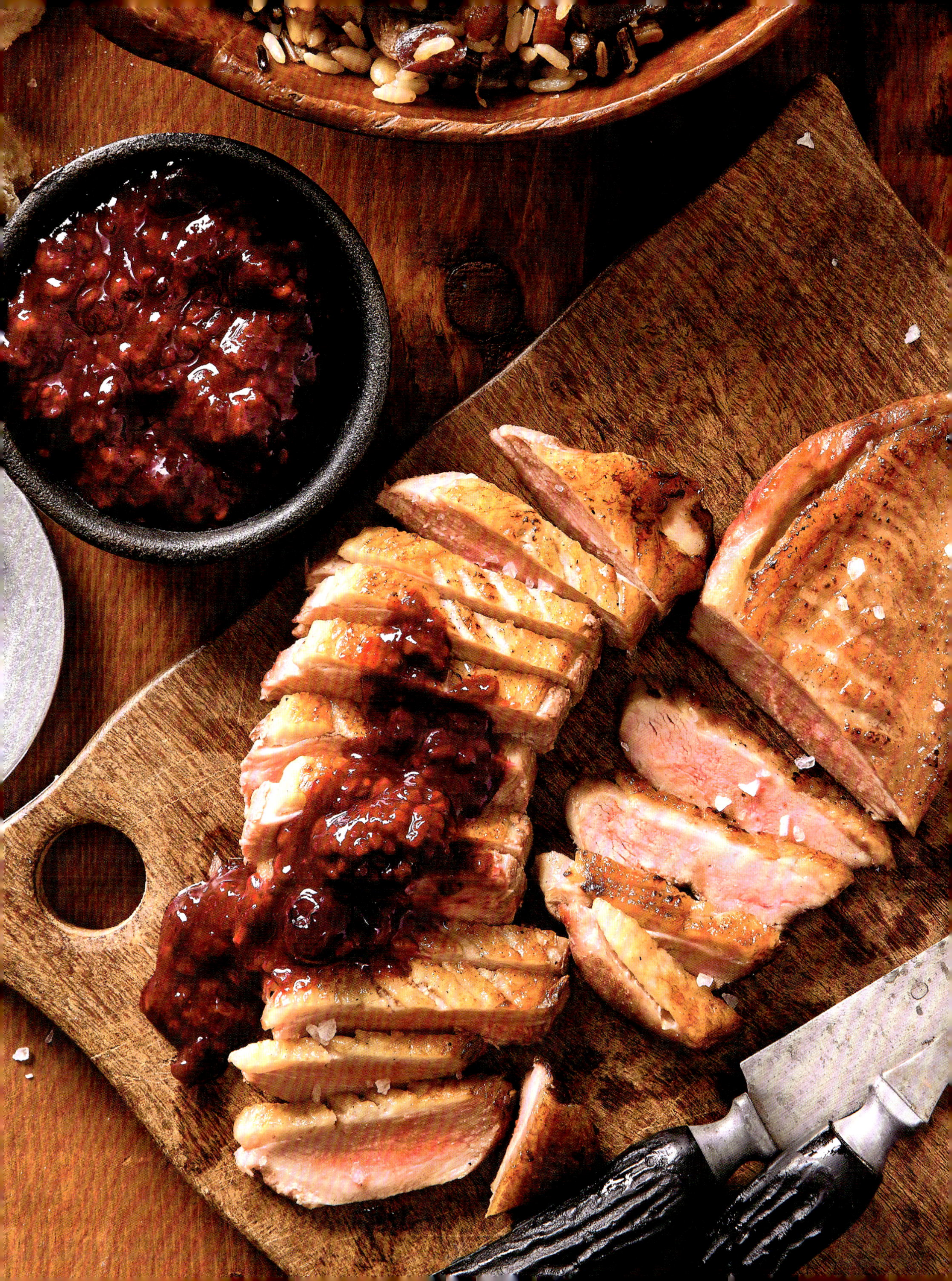

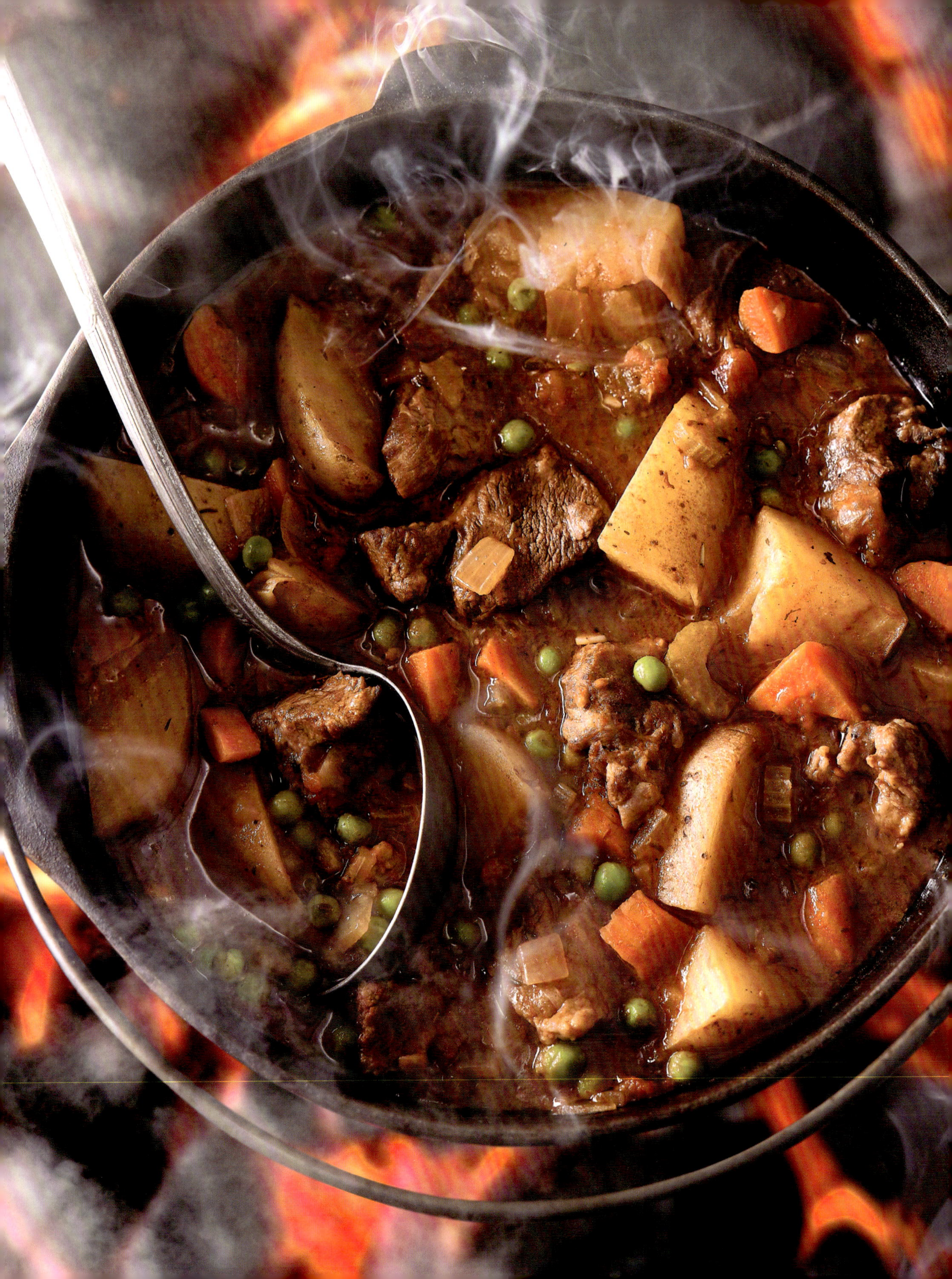

# SKUNK-BEAR VENISON STEW

There was a time when some of the only work a man could find in the Canadian frontier was fur trapping and trading for big companies. Or protecting their business interests ... This meant facin' off against poachers, land disputes, and occasional ancient or demonic creatures. Savin' folks from one particularly nasty something-or-other left me so close to dead that I likely only survived thanks to a few members of the Blackfoot tribe nursing me back to life. We started working together to drive off a few more beasts that'd been causin' havoc and I tried to carry my weight with them every way I could, including at mealtime. They already made a great venison stew, but I liked to throw a few surprises in the mix when it was my turn at the tureen. This recipe in particular turns out thick, meaty, rich, and comforting. And it went over well enough they gave it the same nickname they gave *me*: the "Skunk-Bear"—or as folks may know it, *"The Wolverine."*

**Servings: 6 to 8 • Type: Soup • Difficulty: Average • Prep Time: 45 minutes • Cook Time: 3 hours**
**Rest Time: None • Dietary Considerations: n/a • Pairs well with:** *Wild Mushroom Rice* **(pg 40),**
*Fried Bannock Bread* **(pg 49), or other crusty bread**

2 pounds venison or beef chuck, cut into 1½-inch cubes

2 teaspoons salt, or to taste

1 teaspoon black pepper, or to taste

½ cup all-purpose flour

1 to 2 tablespoons rendered fat or olive oil, or more as needed

1 to 2 tablespoons unsalted butter

1 large onion, medium diced

2 ribs celery, sliced

2 large carrots, roughly chopped

4 garlic cloves, minced

1 tablespoon *Mutant Medley* (pg 30)

2 teaspoons herbes de provence

1 tablespoon tomato paste

2 tablespoons apple cider vinegar

2 to 3 sprigs fresh thyme

1 to 2 sprigs fresh parsley

2 bay leaves

One 15-ounce can diced tomatoes

3 cups venison stock or beef stock

¼ cup Worcestershire sauce

3 large yellow potatoes, cut into 8ths

1 cup frozen peas (optional)

Chopped fresh parsley or chives, optional, for garnish

Pat the meat dry and season with the salt and pepper, then toss the meat in the flour 'til coated.

In a large Dutch oven, heat a tablespoon of the fat or oil over medium-high heat. Brown the meat in batches, being careful to avoid overcrowding the pot, for about 3 to 4 minutes per side. Set the browned pieces aside on a large plate and add more oil as needed.

Melt the butter in the same Dutch oven over medium heat, then add the onions, celery, carrots, and garlic. Cook for 8 minutes 'til slightly softened.

Stir in the seasonings and cook for another 1 to 2 minutes, then add the tomato paste, stirring to coat the veggies and cook for another 2 to 3 minutes. Add the apple cider vinegar and scrape up any browned bits that remain in the pot.

Take a piece of twine and securely tie together the thyme, bay leaves, and parsley. Add this to the Dutch oven, along with the can of diced tomatoes, stock, Worcestershire sauce, and the cooked beef, plus any escaped juices. Turn the heat to low and simmer, covered, for an hour.

Stir in the potatoes and cook, uncovered for 1 hour longer, or 'til the venison, veggies, and potatoes are tender and the sauce has thickened. Remove the herb bundle and stir in the peas, if using, simmering for another 5 minutes. Taste and adjust seasoning.

Divide into serving bowls and garnish with chopped fresh parsley or chives.

ROUGHIN' IT: LIVING OFF THE LAND

# HOW TO
# FLAVOR BASES

Flavor bases are the backbone of a great meal. They're what makes the whole thing come alive. Each one's got its own style, its own punch. You nail that base, and your meal's gonna taste like it was meant to.

### MIREPOIX
- **WHAT'S IN IT:** Onion, Carrot, Celery
- **STANDARD RATIO:** 2-parts onion to 1-part carrot and 1-part celery, but it can vary.
- **USE IT FOR:** Soups, stews, and sauces, particularly those in the French culinary tradition. I use this one in my Venison Stew (pg 47).

### THE HOLY TRINITY
- **WHAT'S IN IT:** Onion, Bell Pepper, Celery
- **USE IT FOR:** Creole and Cajun dishes like gumbo and jambalaya. Basically, anything Gambit rambles on about.

### SOFRITO
- **WHAT'S IN IT:** Onion, Garlic, Bell Peppers, Tomatoes, sometimes herbs like cilantro
- **USE IT FOR:** Spanish, Latin American, and Caribbean dishes.

### BATTUTO
- **WHAT'S IN IT:** Onion, Carrot, Celery, Garlic
- **RATIO:** Typically equal parts onion, carrot, and celery, with garlic added to taste.
- **USE IT FOR:** Italian foods like pasta sauces, soups, and stews.

### GARLIC + GINGER + ONION
- **WHAT'S IN IT:** Garlic, Ginger, Onion (typically green onions or shallots)
- **USE IT FOR:** Stir-fries, curries, and other Asian dishes. You see these popping up in a lot of Madripoorian dishes, like Mei Fun (pg 124) and Laksa (pg 127), and Chinese dishes like Ginger Beef (pg 101).

### TARE
- **WHAT'S IN IT:** Tare is not tied down to just one set of ingredients, it's a flavor powerhouse that flexes with whatever you're cooking. You might find it made from soy sauce ("shoyu"), mirin, dashi, kombu (dried kelp), miso, and sometimes extras like garlic, ginger, yuzu, or sesame.
- **USE IT FOR:** It can be used as a dipping sauce or for marinating or glazing meats. When combined with broth, it's often used as a seasoning base for ramen noodle soup, as in my ramen recipe on pg 108. It's also used in the Yakitori (pg 84) and Kushiyaki (pg 87).

ROUGHIN' IT: LIVING OFF THE LAND

# FRIED BANNOCK BREAD

In almost all my treks through the Great White North—laying low, scraping odd jobs, making barely enough to skip town next time folks caught on I wasn't like them—I could sniff out the buttery, oil-crisped aroma of Bannock. Affectionately referred to as "Fry Bread." It's a staple of Indigenous cooking, as well as a chow-time classic all across Canada. And I must've wolfed down thousands by now. Anytime I get homesick—or got just the bare essentials and a growling gut—I whip up a batch of these. Best when warm, center-soft, and golden, Fry Bread hits home all on its own, or makes a helluva base for all kinds of dishes.

**Yield: 1 dozen • Type: Bread • Difficulty: Easy • Prep Time: 20 minutes • Cook Time: 20 minutes**
**Rest Time: None • Dietary Considerations: V, V+ • Pairs well with: *Wojapi* (pg 36),**
***Venison Stew* (pg 47), maple syrup and powdered sugar, chili, or taco fixings**

3 cups all-purpose flour

2 tablespoons baking powder

1 teaspoon salt

1½ cups warm water, or more as needed

Neutral oil, such as peanut or canola, for frying

In a large mixing bowl, sift half the flour with the baking soda and salt. Add the water and stir 'til the mixture becomes thick and paste-like.

Add more flour, a little at a time, kneading 'til the dough feels soft and pliable.

Add 1 inch of oil to a large skillet or a deep frying pan. Heat over medium-high heat to 375°F, or hot enough that a small piece of dough sizzles immediately upon contact.

Break off palm-sized pieces of the dough and flatten each with your hands to form round patties about ½ inch thick.

Fry the patties for 3 minutes on each side 'til golden brown and puffy. You may have to do this in batches to prevent overcrowding.

Using tongs, transfer the finished bannock on a paper towel–lined plate.

For a sweet breakfast or dessert, serve with Wojapi or maple syrup and powdered sugar. For a savory meal, serve with venison stew, chili, or taco fixings.

# X-MAN'S BREWIS

Let's face it, not all "survival" cooking is created equal. Whether off-grid with the X-Men in the Australian Outback or tryin' to toughen up some X-kids with a few days off from school, most campfire meals these days are more "weekend warrior" than "escape from Weapon X." That's why I like this dish. Don't see much salt cod or salt pork in the States, but you can still get a little taste of the ol' Canadian frontier with this smoky, caramelized take on a Newfoundland classic. And you can make the hardtack on its own for simple, survival rations. As for teaching pampered mutants to appreciate sleeping on forest floors and catching their food …? Still ain't cracked that.

**Servings: 6 to 8 • Type: Main • Difficulty: Average • Prep Time: 20 minutes • Cook Time: 1 hour
Rest Time: 2 hours • Dietary Considerations: n/a**

### FOR THE HARDTACK:

1½ cups all-purpose flour

1 teaspoon salt

½ cup water

### FOR THE BREWIS:

5 or 6 squares Hardtack

4 medium yellow potatoes, peeled and sliced

1 pound thick-cut bacon, sliced or cut with kitchen shears

1 pound boneless, skinless cod filets (or other white fish)

1 to 2 teaspoons salt (or to taste)

1 tablespoon *Mutant Medley* (pg 30) or other AP seasoning

Black pepper (to taste)

2 large yellow onions, sliced

1 lemon, cut into wedges, for serving

Finely chopped parsley or chives, for garnish

### SPECIAL EQUIPMENT:

Kitchen shears, optional

Slotted spoon

Sealable glass jar

Rolling pin

**TO MAKE THE HARDTACK,** preheat the oven to 375°F. Line a baking sheet with parchment paper.

In a medium mixing bowl, combine the flour, salt, and water. Stir to combine. Turn the dough out on a lightly floured surface. Knead 'til the dough becomes elastic, about 5 to 10 minutes. With a floured rolling pin, roll the dough to about ½ inch thick.

Use a sharp knife to cut 2-inch squares. Don't worry too much about the shape of the pieces. Poke holes in the squares using a fork or a chopstick. Place the squares on the lined baking sheet and bake one side for 30 minutes. After 30 minutes turn the hardtack over and cook the other side for another 30 minutes. Set the cookie sheet on a cooling rack after baking 'til cool. After it cools, it's ready to store in airtight containers indefinitely.

**TO MAKE THE BREWIS,** soak the hardtack in water in a glass mixing bowl or other glass storage container for at least 2 hours or overnight, then drain the excess water.

In a large pot bring the potatoes to a simmer and cook for 5 minutes. Add the hardtack to the potato pot to continue to simmer for about 8 to 10 minutes 'til the potatoes are cooked through and there's little resistance when the potatoes are pierced with a fork.

In a large skillet, fry the bacon pieces over medium-high heat 'til they are crisp and golden brown. Use a slotted spoon to set the cooked bacon pieces aside on a paper towel–lined plate. Drain 75 percent of the fat into a sealable jar or similar heat-proof container, reserving it for Steps 8 and 10.

Season the fish liberally with salt and pepper, as well as Mutant Medley, then cook it in the bacon fat in the skillet for 1 to 2 minutes per side 'til browned and cooked through. Remove the fish pieces and set them aside.

Add 1 to 2 tablespoons of bacon fat back into the skillet and sauté the onions 'til they are a deep golden brown, about 15 minutes.

Thoroughly drain the potatoes and hardtack. Transfer them to the skillet with the onions along with the seasonings, fish, and most of the bacon pieces (save some for topping), and stir to combine. Taste and adjust seasonings.

Transfer the whole mixture into an oven safe dish or casserole pan. Top with the remaining bacon drippings (or about 2 more tablespoons) and broil for about 10 to 15 minutes in the oven or 'til a nice golden crust is formed on top.

Garnish with chopped fresh parsley and serve with the lemon wedges on the side.

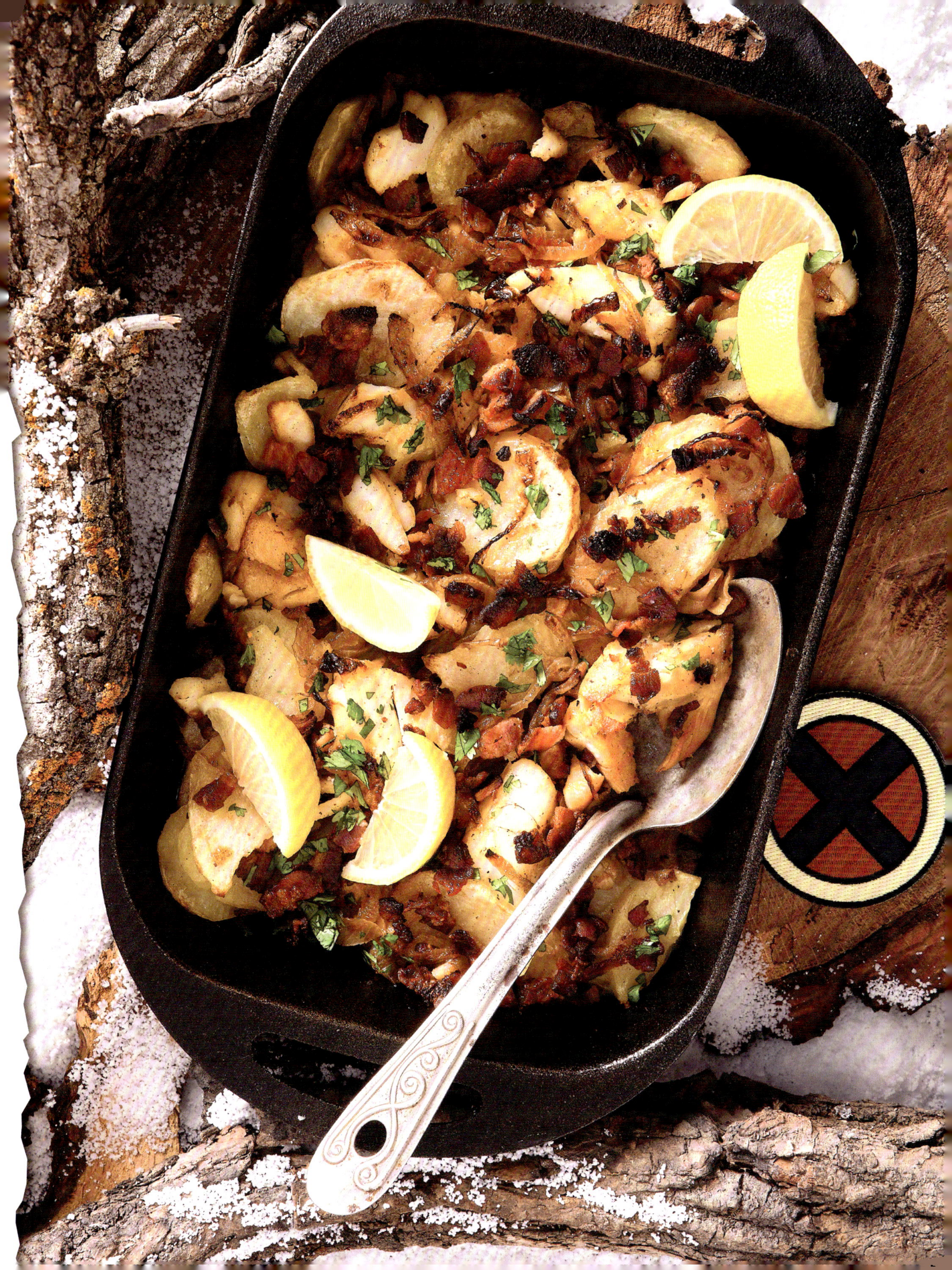

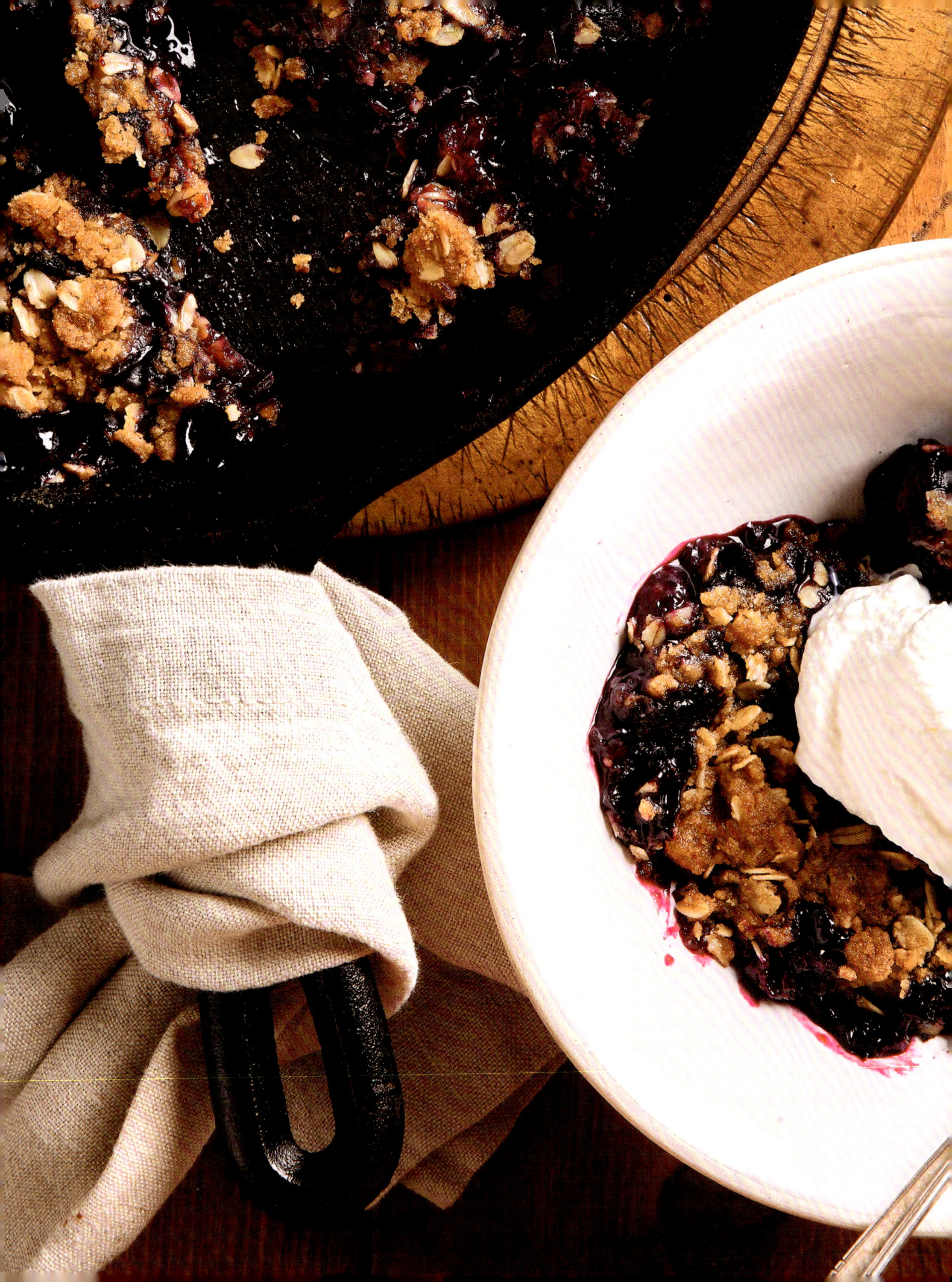

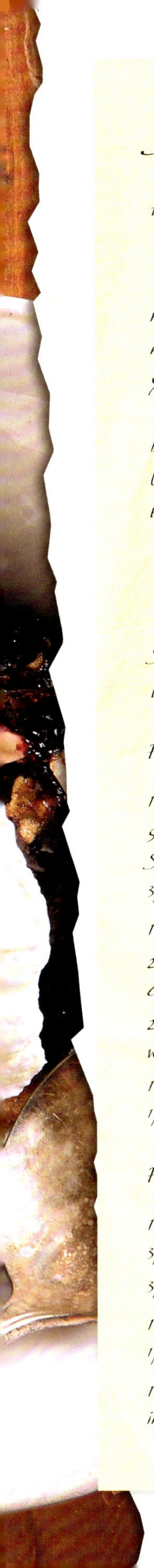

# SASKATOON BERRY CRUMBLE

Hey Logan,

Folks here tell me you're dead, but I'm writing anyways. I mean, they got to be wrong— 'cause I'm you. From the future.

Hell, I guess we both know there's always some "Omega-level" mutant, or a Red Skull screwin' with the timeline or rewriting reality. So maybe you won't end up roamin' the irradiated ruins of a world you didn't save. Maybe we were never the same guy to begin with. But I wish we walked this world together long enough to find out ... and for me to warn you of all the mistakes I made, so you don't have to.

But since there ain't enough time or ink in the world for all that, I leave you this. A recipe. The ingredients should be much easier to come by here in your time. But the taste might take you back. If the crisp and buttery crust or the luscious, sweet, and tangy filling send your mutant senses all the way to special celebrations in Howlett Manor, then we might just be cut from the same cloth after all.

And if that's the case ... I'm sorry.

 "Old Man" Logan

Servings: 8 to 10 • Type: Dessert • Difficulty: Easy • Prep Time: 30 minutes • Cook Time: 1 hour
Rest Time: 10 minutes • Dietary Considerations: V • Pairs well with: Whipped cream, vanilla ice cream, cheddar cheese

## FOR THE FILLING:

- 1 tablespoon unsalted butter
- 5 cups fresh or thawed Saskatoon berries (see Note)
- 3/4 cup granulated sugar
- 1 teaspoon lemon zest
- 2 tablespoons potato starch or cornstarch
- 2 tablespoons grape juice or water, or as needed
- 1 teaspoon vanilla extract
- 1/4 teaspoon salt

## FOR THE TOPPING:

- 1 cup packed dark brown sugar
- 3/4 cup all-purpose flour
- 3/4 cup old-fashioned oats
- 1 teaspoon ground cinnamon
- 1/4 teaspoon salt
- 1 stick cold unsalted butter, cut into small cubes

Grease a 12-inch cast-iron skillet with a tablespoon of butter and set aside. If using an oven, preheat it to 375°F. If using a campfire, make sure it's roarin'.

To make the filling: In a mixing bowl, combine the berries, granulated sugar, and lemon zest. In a separate small bowl, whisk together the cornstarch and juice to make a slurry. If you are using thawed from frozen berries, use the juice from the berries. Stir the slurry into the berries. Pour the mixture into the greased skillet and smooth into an even layer.

To make the topping: In another bowl, add the brown sugar, flour, oats, cinnamon, and salt. Massage or cut in the cold butter into the dry ingredients 'til there's no more dry flour visible and you have a coarse crumb.

Sprinkle the topping evenly over the top of the berries. If using a campfire, cover the skillet with foil and place over the campfire for 45 to 60 minutes. If using the oven, bake, uncovered, 'til the filling is bubbling and the topping is crisp and golden brown, about 30 to 40 minutes.

Remove the skillet from the oven and let sit for at least 10 minutes before serving with vanilla ice cream or whipped cream. Or try it with cheddar cheese.

Note: Saskatoon berries are known as serviceberries in the States. If you can't get 'em where you're at, swap them with blueberries and add 1/2 teaspoon of almond extract to the filling.

ROUGHIN' IT: LIVING OFF THE LAND

# SNOW MAPLE TAFFY

**BEST THERE IS WARNING**

This may read simple, but getting the consistency and balance right can be a tricky one. But then bein' damn near unkillable sounds like it'd make life easy and that's been anything but. You miss the mark on temperatures or don't pack that snow tight enough, these go south real fast. But if your skills are sharp, you'll have a sweet and sticky maple-flavored treat on your claws.

**Yield:** 12 to 16 taffy sticks • **Type:** Dessert • **Difficulty:** Challenging • **Prep Time:** 10 minutes • **Cook Time:** 15 minutes • **Rest Time:** None Dietary Considerations: V, V+, GF

1 gallon clean fresh snow (see Note)

1½ cups pure maple syrup

**SPECIAL EQUIPMENT:**
10 to 15 popsicle sticks

Add clean, fresh snow onto a baking sheet, spreading it out to cover the entire surface. Smooth out the top and pack the ice down as tight as possible. Place it in the freezer to keep it cold.

In a medium to large saucepan, pour in the maple syrup. The syrup should take up less than half of the vessel, this prevents it from overflowing when it heats up. Bring it to a boil over medium-low heat.

Continue cooking 'til the maple syrup is between 240°F to 250°F and has reduced and thickened, or 'til a small drop of syrup, when tested in ice-cold water, forms into a firm ball. This should take about 15 minutes. The syrup will be bubbling up a lot at this stage so make sure it doesn't overflow your vessel or you're in for a sticky mess.

Once the syrup is reduced and thickened, and is in the right temperature range, take the baking sheet of snow out of the freezer and set it on a stable surface.

Using a metal spoon, drizzle thin lines of syrup, about 3 or 4 inches long, onto the snow—or roughly 1 tablespoon of syrup per piece. Let it cool and firm up for about 5 seconds. Once the strips have set slightly, place one end of the popsicle stick at the edge of one of the taffy strips, then roll the taffy onto the stick, lifting it out of the snow as you roll. Repeat 'til you have used all the syrup.

Best to enjoy the taffy while it's still a little warm.

*Note: If you're in a snowless region, or it's just not the right season, blend a bag of ice in batches in the blender 'til you have enough shaved ice to fill a standard baking sheet.*

ROUGHIN' IT: LIVING OFF THE LAND

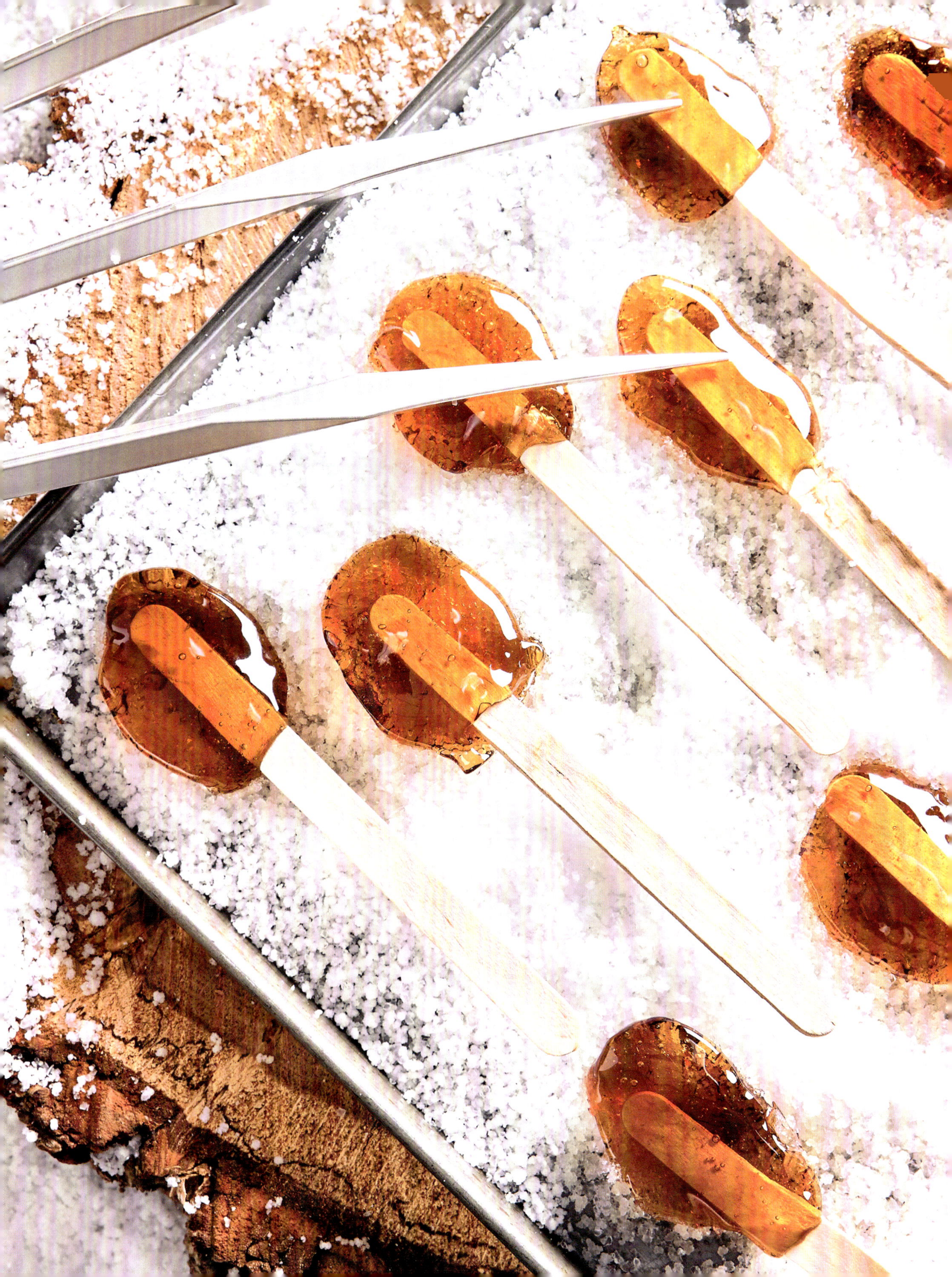

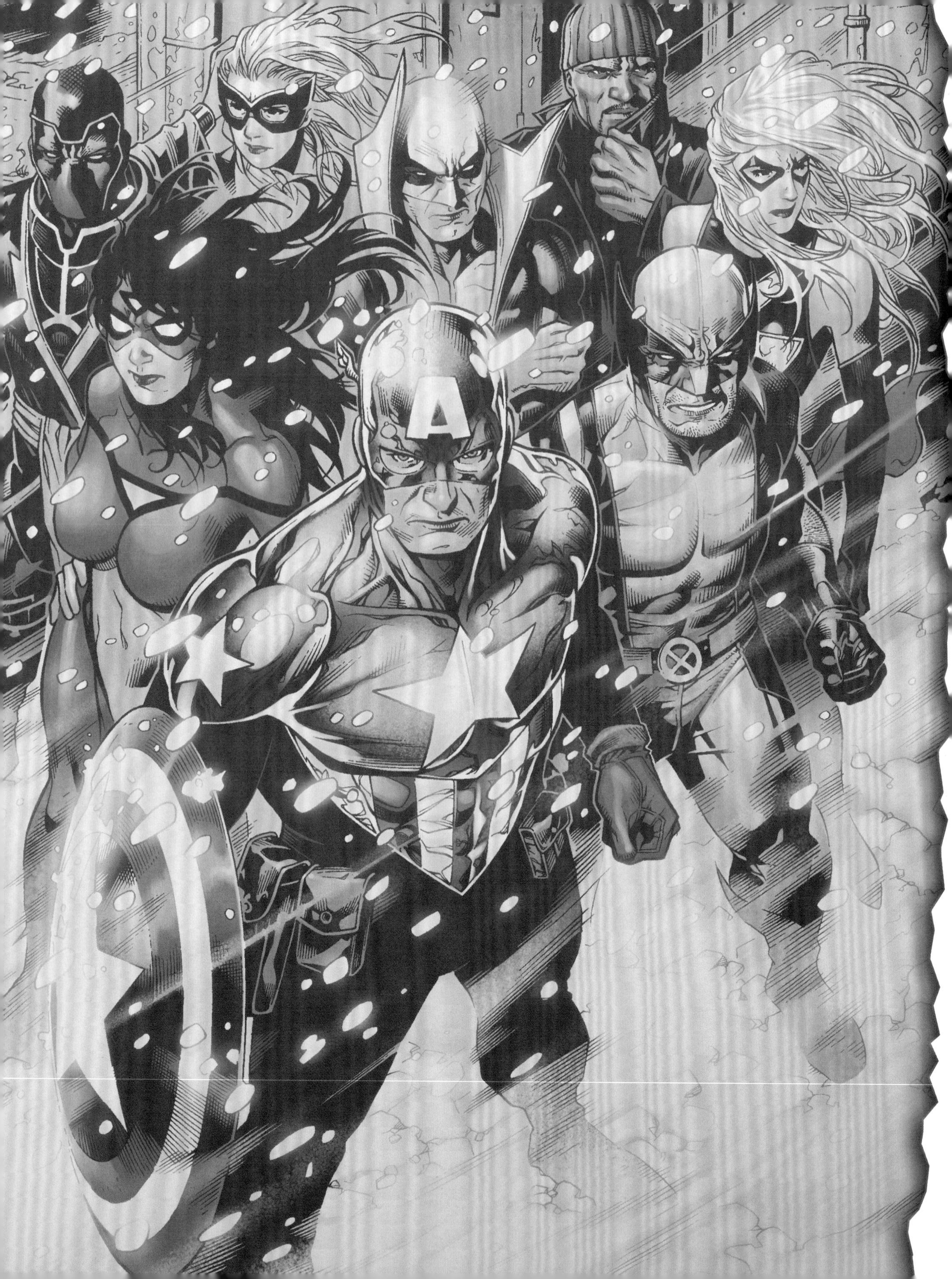

## HOW TO
# INTO THE FRYING PAN

Frying's as sure a way as I know to give your food that crispy, golden crunch. But if you don't know what you're doing, things can go sideways faster than Quicksilver can sprint. Whether you're plunging your food into a hot oil bath or just givin' it a quick sizzle, here's what you need to know:

### CHOOSING THE RIGHT OIL
- **HIGH SMOKE POINT:** Stick with oils that don't start to smoke 'til they reach higher temperatures; like peanut oil, avocado oil, or canola oil. Keeps things from going up in smoke. Literally.
- **NEUTRAL FLAVOR:** Whether deep or shallow frying, you usually want the oil's flavor to stay in the background and let the other ingredients do the talking. Avoid strong-tasting oils like unrefined coconut oil, palm oil, or virgin olive oil.

### NECESSARY EQUIPMENT
- **STURDY COOKING VESSEL:** Nothing flimsy, you need something that can take the heat and won't let you down. A cast-iron skillet's a go-to for shallow frying—tough, reliable, and gets the job done. For deep frying, a heavy-bottomed pot or a proper deep fryer is what you want.
- **THERMOMETER:** Attach a deep-frying or candy thermometer to keep the oil temperature in check. You can eyeball it, but it's best not to guess.
- **TONGS AND/OR SLOTTED SPOON:** You need at least one of these, ideally both. Metal tongs are your best bet for flipping and moving things around. A slotted spoon is better for scooping the food out. Make sure both are metal; plastic's got no place in hot oil.

### HEATING
- **PREHEAT THE OIL:** Get the oil hot before anything touches it. You want that food to start frying the second it hits the oil, not soaking up grease.
- **IDEAL TEMP:** Keep it between 350°F and 375°F. Too hot, and you're burning everything. Too cold, and you're just making greasy sludge.
- **MONITORING:** Keep checking the temperature and adjust the temperature settings when necessary. Don't let it slip out of that sweet spot.

### AVOID OVERCROWDING
- **FRYING IN BATCHES:** You don't need to cook everything all at once. Small batches are often the way to go. Overloading your pot drops the oil's temperature and ruins your fry. Half the oil surface is the max for food at one time.

### EXTRACTION
- **REMOVAL:** Use your metal slotted spoon or tongs to pull the food out of the oil, letting the excess drip back into the pot.
- **DRAINING:** Have a paper towel–lined plate or a wire rack ready to go. This lets the oil drain off and keeps things crispy. You want the oil off and the crunch on.

### CLEAN UP
- **SAFETY EVEN AT THE END:** Don't try to handle hot oil, let it cool down before you deal with it. Even if you've got a healing factor, the burns'll hurt.
- **STORING USED OIL:** If you're the thrifty type and your oil's in decent shape still, strain the oil through a fine-mesh strainer into a clean jar once it's cool. Label it with the date, the type of oil, and what you fried in it. You can reuse it once or twice, but if it starts to smell or look funny, toss it.
- **DISPOSING OF OIL:** Pour the cooled oil into a sealable container, like an old milk jug, before tossing it in the trash. Don't pour it down the drain unless you want clogged pipes.

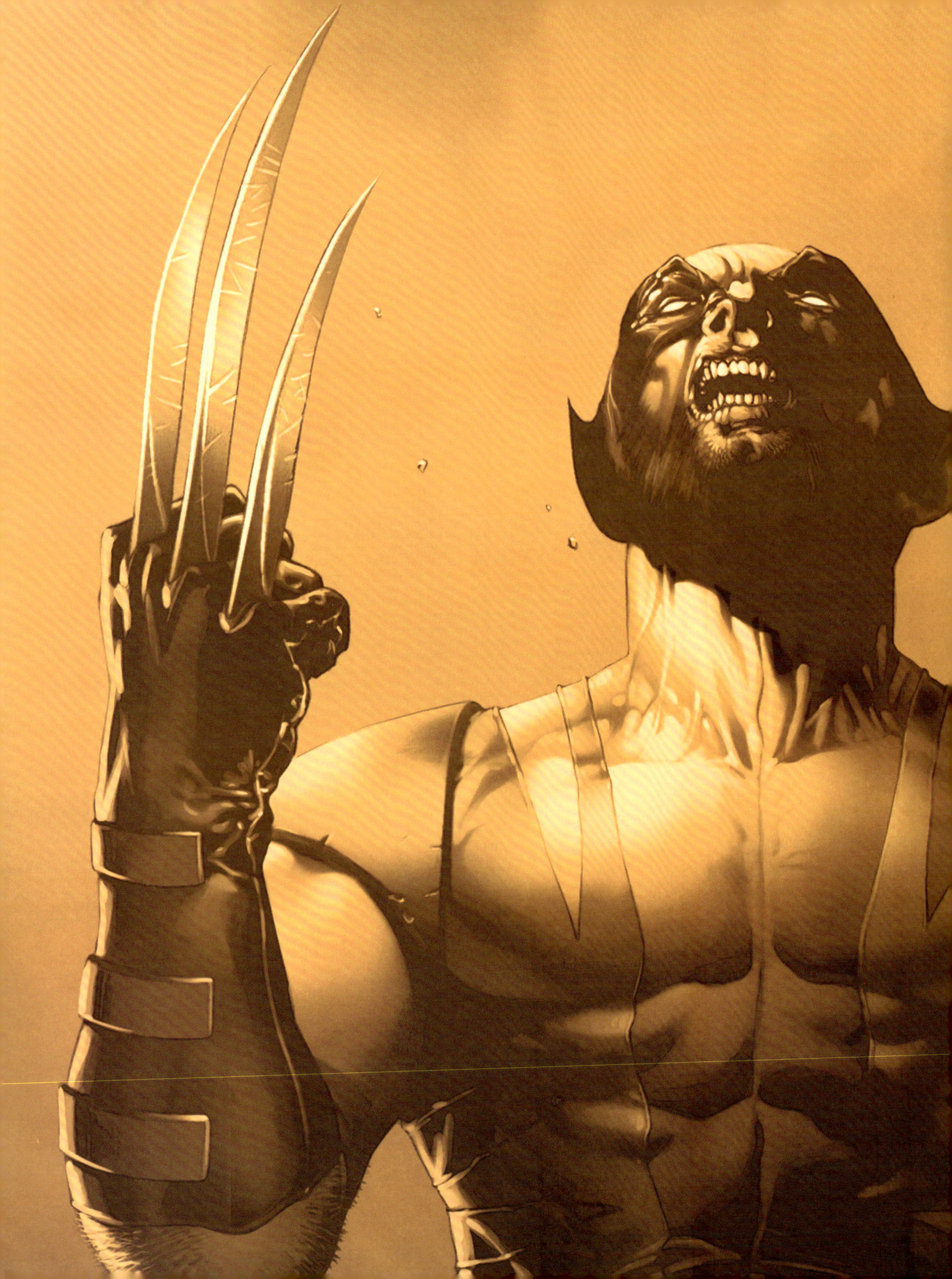

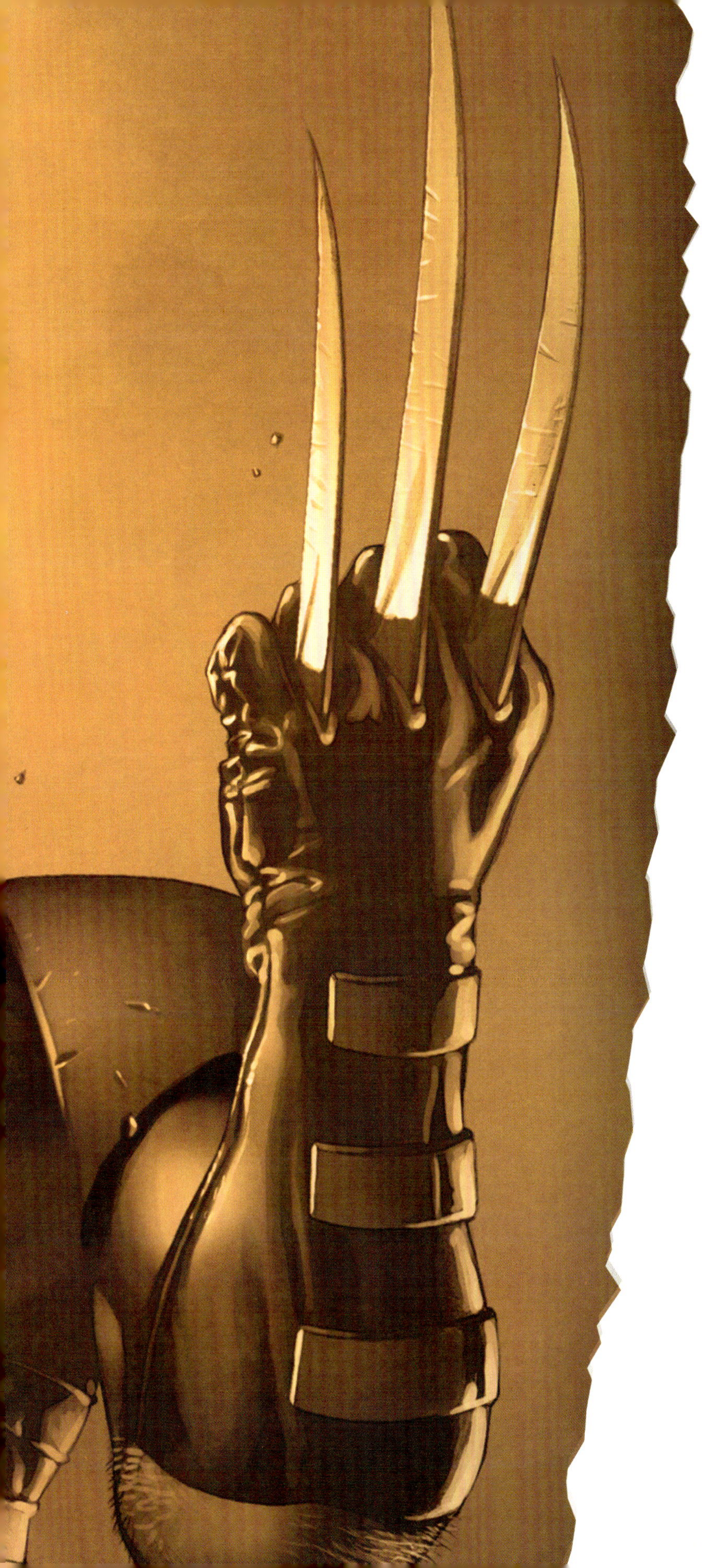

# 3

## SNIKT!: SKEWERS AND KABOBS

The two surest ways to get to know somebody are by breaking bread or crossing swords. With the circles I run in, you get around to both eventually.

Figures, then, I can't see any kind of skewer, kabob, or other food gettin' run through without it reminding me of somebody—buddy or bastard—ending up on the wrong end of my claws. Eventually, crafted a few of my own as tributes. Hard to resist when a grill's fired up, and I'm already packin' six adamantium spit-roasters. But there's a world full of dishes that get impaled. And I've been just as many places, exploring local cuisine and cutting down local creeps. So don't be surprised next time a fresh memory gets unlocked by a shishkabob, bub.

# KUZURI NA KUSHIKATSU

Grub in the Land of the Rising Sun ain't all any one way. They got plenty of mixed-up, deep-fried gut-punches that could go toe-to-toe with any fierce appetite. I can't forget the extra-rich kushikatsu served up one time at the estate of Kenuichio Harada: the original Silver Samurai. Juicy pork loin, tender veggies, and quail eggs—each one wrapped in crispy, golden fried batter and dunked in that sweet, tangy katsu sauce. Every skewer's got its own thing going on, so you're never getting the same bite twice. The whole thing was just as complex as our host, who's aimed to kill me and aid me in almost equal measure. Of course, one joke about how a bite gettin' stabbed through looked a lot like *him* and I'm right back on his bad side. I guess the joke's on me, see he started calling it Kuzuri Na Kushikatsu, which I'm told means "Wolverine-Style" Kushikatsu.

**Origin:** Japan • **Servings:** 4 to 6 • **Type:** Main • **Difficulty:** Average • **Prep Time:** 45 minutes • **Cook Time:** 30 to 40 minutes • **Rest Time:** None • **Pairs well with:** *Pickled Daikon* (pg 111)

**FOR THE KATSU SAUCE:**

¼ cup Worcestershire sauce

¼ cup ketchup

2 tablespoons dark brown sugar

3 tablespoons oyster sauce or hoisin

1 to 2 teaspoons water, or as needed

**FOR THE SKEWERS:**

1 pound boneless pork loin or 1 package extra firm tofu, cut into 1-inch cubes

4 green onions, cut into 1-inch pieces

1 small lotus root or 1 medium zucchini, sliced into ½-inch-thick slices

1 cup cubed kabocha squash or sweet potato

1 cup broccoli florets

6 cooked, peeled quail eggs, optional

½ cup pickled ginger, drained, optional

2 teaspoons salt, or to taste

1 teaspoon black pepper, or to taste

**татку MAKE THE KATSU SAUCE:** In a small mixing bowl, whisk together the sauce ingredients. Cover and set aside.

**TO MAKE THE SKEWERS:** Season the meat and veggies with salt and pepper. If you'd like, pound the pork with a meat tenderizer.

Thread the pork and green onions onto 4 to 6 skewers, alternating between the two. Skewer the rest of the ingredients, including the ginger, making sure like stays with like, to ensure consistency in cooking times.

SNIKT!: SKEWERS AND KABOBS

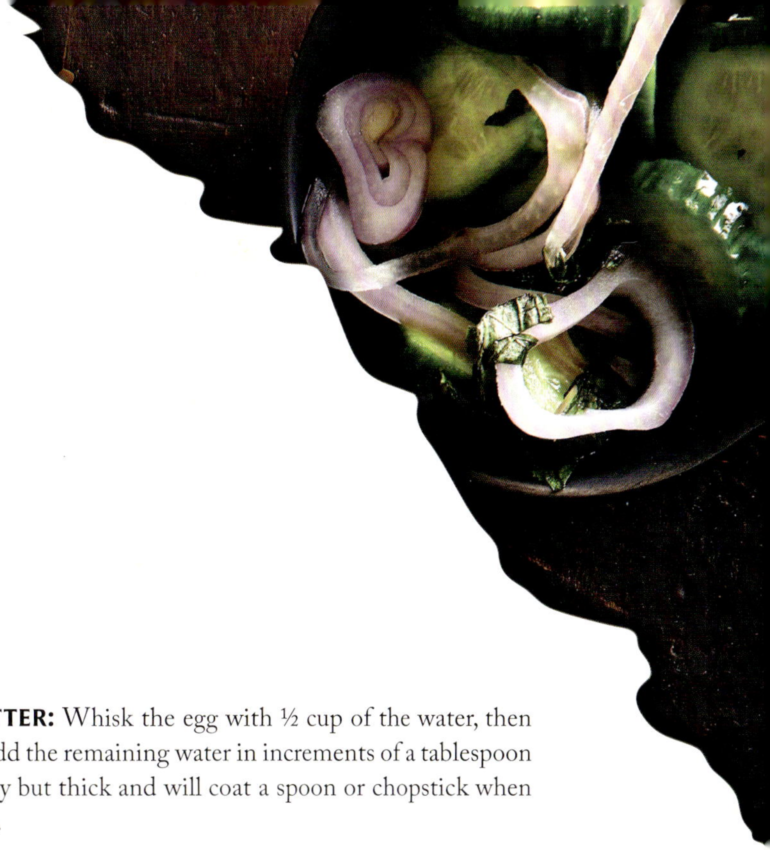

**FOR BATTERING, BREADING, AND FRYING:**

½ cup all-purpose flour

1 large egg, lightly beaten

¾ cup water, or as needed

2 cups panko breadcrumbs, or more as needed

Neutral oil such as peanut or canola oil, for frying

**SPECIAL EQUIPMENT:**

15 to 20 pre-soaked bamboo skewers

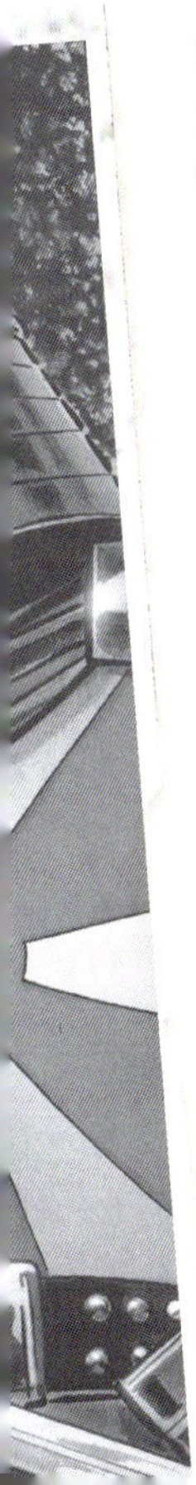

**TO MAKE THE BATTER:** Whisk the egg with ½ cup of the water, then whisk in the flour. Add the remaining water in increments of a tablespoon 'til the batter is runny but thick and will coat a spoon or chopstick when one is dipped into it.

Pulse the panko a few times in a blender 'til closer to a breadcrumb consistency, then place it in a shallow bowl.

In a cast-iron skillet or wok, add 2 to 3 inches of oil and heat to 340°F to 360°F. Dredge the ingredients on the skewers in the batter, making sure they are thoroughly coated in batter. Once battered, roll them in the panko 'til well-coated. You might want to do this just when you're ready to fry those skewers, and not batter everything all at once.

Once the oil is hot, fry the vegetables first, because they have the most neutral taste and won't flavor the cooking oil, then the eggs and ginger, then the pork skewers. Do this in batches of 4 to 6 skewers at a time to not overcrowd the pot. Flip the skewers as necessary 'til they are browned on all sides. In between batches, fish out bits of loose panko with a slotted spoon so the oil doesn't start to brown too much, and taste burnt.

Serve the skewers hot or warm, with the katsu sauce on the side for dipping or drizzled over the skewers.

# LOWTOWN SATAY

I got plenty of memories of Madripoor, and Lowtown, in particular. But after my own flesh-and-blood clawed his way to the top of the island's criminal underworld—profiting off the pain of the regular folks there—seeing these skewers at every street food stand only reminds me of Daken. It seems like every time I try to get through to my son, one of us gets killed. So as much as these sweet, smokey, and nutty flavors please the palette, I find I'd rather be sharing 'em than dining on my own …

**Origin: Madripoor • Servings: 4 to 6 • Type: Main or Appetizer • Difficulty: Average**
**Prep Time: 30 minutes • Cook Time: 15 minutes • Rest Time: 2 hours • Dietary Considerations: GF**
**Pairs well with:** *Ragin' Radishes* **(pg 120),** *Mystique's Mei Fun* **(pg 124)**

### FOR THE PEANUT SAUCE:

¾ cup creamy peanut butter

½ cup coconut milk

1 tablespoon lime juice

1 tablespoon sambal oelek, optional

1 tablespoon brown sugar

1 tablespoon lemongrass paste

1 tablespoon toasted sesame oil

1 tablespoon *Dagger Bay Blend* (pg 30) or curry powder

½ teaspoon salt, or to taste

### FOR THE SATAY:

2 pounds boneless skinless chicken thighs

2 teaspoons salt, or to taste

1-inch piece ginger, peeled

5 cloves garlic

2 tablespoons lemongrass paste

2 large shallots or 1 medium red onion, roughly chopped

1 tablespoon soy sauce or coconut aminos

⅓ cup brown sugar

2 tablespoons *Dagger Bay Blend* (pg 30) or curry powder

2 teaspoons toasted sesame oil

2 tablespoons neutral oil such as peanut oil

Cooking spray, for greasing

**TO MAKE THE PEANUT SAUCE:** Stir the ingredients together 'til smooth, adding water as needed to loosen things up. Taste and adjust seasonings. Set aside 'til serving time.

**TO MAKE THE SATAY:** On a clean surface, pound the chicken thighs with a meat tenderizer. Cut into 1-inch pieces and set aside.

Add the remaining satay ingredients (aside from the cooking spray) to a blender. Blend on high speed 'til fairly smooth. Add more oil as needed, in increments of a teaspoon, if the blender gets stuck.

Pour the marinade into a large non-reactive food storage container. Add the chicken pieces and stir to coat. Cover and let marinate in the fridge for at least 2 hours or up to overnight.

Preheat the grill to medium, or 400°F. Thread the chicken pieces on the bamboo skewers. You can shake off any excess marinade but there's no need to rinse. Discard the remaining marinade.

Grill the skewers over direct heat, turning once or twice, for about 4 to 5 minutes per side, 'til the chicken is nicely browned and the juices run clear. The internal temperature should be at least 170°F and the chicken should have no pink remaining inside.

**TO MAKE THE SALAD:** Add the cucumber, onions, herbs, vinegar, and sugar in a small bowl and toss to combine. Serve the skewers with the peanut sauce and cucumber salad on the side. Garnish with chopped mint or cilantro and crushed peanuts.

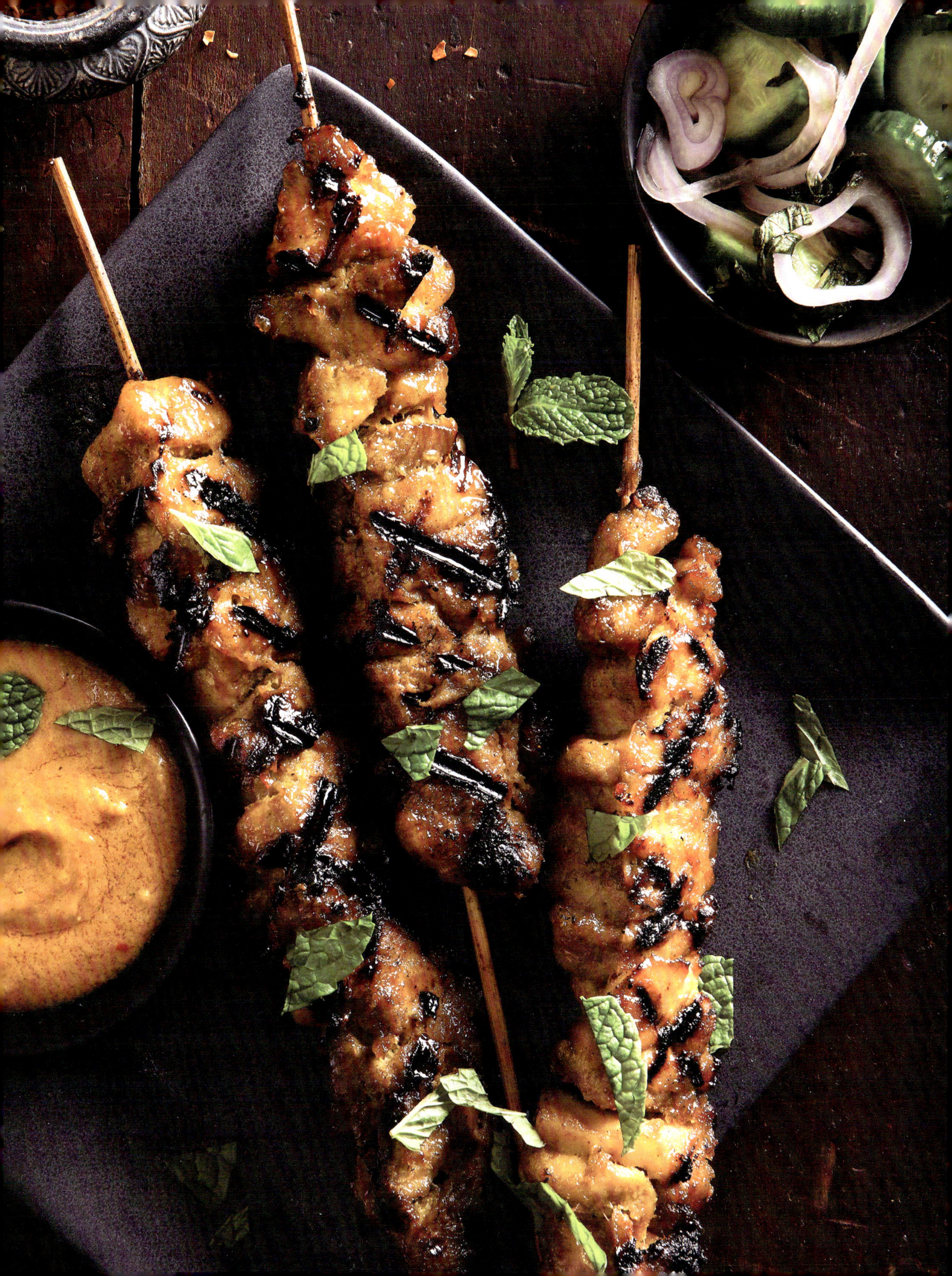

**FOR THE OPTIONAL SIDE SALAD AND GARNISH:**

½ cucumber or 2 baby cucumbers, sliced

⅓ cup sliced shallot or red onion

1 to 2 tablespoons chopped fresh mint and/or cilantro, plus more for garnish

1 tablespoon lime juice or rice vinegar

2 teaspoons granulated sugar

Pinch of salt, or to taste

1 tablespoon crushed peanuts

**SPECIAL EQUIPMENT:**

12 bamboo skewers, soaked

Baking sheet, for alternative method

Aluminum foil, for alternative method

Grill rack, for alternative method

**Alternative Method:** Instead of grilling, set the oven to broil on 500°F. Line a baking sheet with aluminum foil and place a grill rack on top. Grease the grill rack with oil or cooking spray. Place the marinated kebabs on the greased grill rack on the top rack of the oven. Broil for 5 to 7 minutes on each side 'til the chicken is nicely browned and the juices run clear. The internal temperature should be at least 170°F and the chicken should have no pink remaining inside.

# TSARINA'S SHASHLIK

Black Widow earned herself a reputation as hard-edged as anybody in the game. It's almost impossible to picture her as that scared kid I helped rescue so long ago. I was workin' to drive the Hand out of Madripoor at the time. And those ninja creeps kidnapped the young Natasha Romanov, believin' her to be the lost heir of the Russian Czars.

No one really knows if she is (not even Nat herself). But when she busts out traditional Russian cuisine, you may as well be at a royal banquet. In particular, these sharply seasoned, succulent roasted pork bites of hers evoke two great memories: stickin' claws into the Hand, and becoming the honorary "Little Uncle" to my always impressive "Tsarina."

**Origin: Russia • Servings: 4 to 6 • Type: Main • Difficulty: Easy • Prep Time: 15 minutes • Cook Time: 20 minutes • Rest Time: 3 hours • Dietary Considerations: GF**

2 pounds boneless pork shoulder, cut into 1½-inch cubes

1 tablespoon salt

1 teaspoon black pepper

1 tablespoon chopped fresh dill or 1 teaspoon dried dill

2 teaspoons paprika

1 teaspoon allspice

1 teaspoon coriander

1 teaspoon ground bay leaf

1 white onion, sliced

1 cup kefir or 1 cup sparkling water

Yellow onion (optional)

**SPECIAL EQUIPMENT:**

6 to 12 skewers

Season the pork with half the salt and pepper.

In a bowl, stir together the other spices.

Add all the remaining ingredients aside from the skewers to a nonreactive bowl (ideally glass) or a sealable bag and massage to thoroughly coat the pork pieces in the marinade. Cover or seal and marinate in the refrigerator for at least 3 hours, or up to 2 days.

Preheat the grill to 400°F or medium-high heat. Thread the marinated pork pieces onto the skewers, shaking off the white onion any excess marinade (no need to rinse). Option: alternate the pork with slices of yellow onion. Ditch the marinade.

Grill the pork skewers to your desired doneness, about 5 to 8 minutes on each side or 'til the pork is nicely browned and internal temperature reaches at least 145°F. Serve hot!

**OVEN INSTRUCTIONS:** To cook the skewers in the oven, preheat the oven to 400°F (200°C) and line a baking sheet with aluminum foil, placing a wire rack on top. Arrange the skewers on the rack and bake for 20 to 25 minutes, flipping halfway, then broil for 2 to 3 minutes for a charred finish. Let rest for 5 minutes before serving.

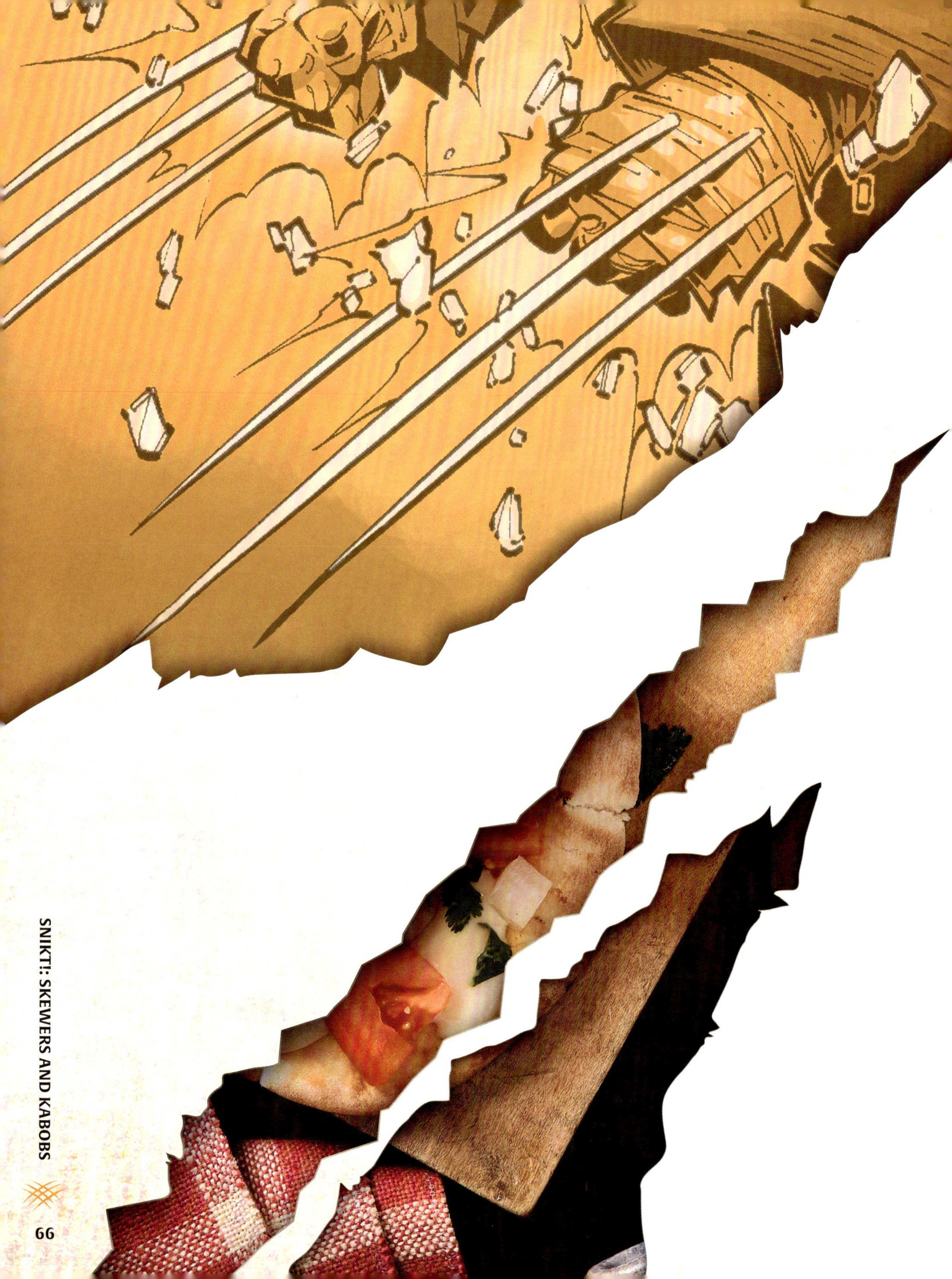

## HOW TO
# SKEWERING LIKE A PRO

Not sure why, but skewered foods just taste better. 'Course, that's only if you know what you're doing. You want that meat seared exactly right, veggies with a bite, and flavors that punch you in the face. Stick to these tips, and you'll be skewering like the best there is.

- **EVEN CUTS:** Whether it's meat or veggies, make sure everything's cut to about the same size. Even pieces mean even cooking—no one wants raw chicken sitting next to burnt onions.
- **SOAK WOODEN SKEWERS:** While metal like adamantium is best most of the time, some skewers just don't taste right unless they're grilled on bamboo skewers, like satay (pg 62) and yakitori (pg 84). But if you're using wooden skewers, you need to soak them in water for at least 30 minutes before grilling. This prevents the wood from burning to a crisp.
- **DON'T OVERCROWD:** If you have a variety of ingredients on the skewers, leave a little space between each piece. Overcrowding leads to uneven cooking and steamed food instead of a nice char.
- **PREHEAT THE GRILL:** Get your grill hot—real hot—before you start cooking. A blazing grill sears better, locks in flavor, and helps your food not stick to the grates.
- **GREASE THE GRATES:** Before layin' those skewers on the grill, brush or spray the grates with oil or cooking spray to prevent sticking. Don't skip this step unless you like scraping burnt food off the grates.
- **ROTATE:** Rotate the skewers to ensure even cooking. You're aiming for a good sear and caramelization on all sides while the inside cooks through.
- **DONENESS:** Poultry like chicken should hit 165°F, the juice should be clear and the meat should not have any pink inside. Beef and lamb should hit around 145°F for medium-rare, which means a red center that's slightly pink toward the edges. With seafood, you just wanna cook it 'til it's opaque and not a minute longer.
- **RESTING:** If there's meat on the skewers, let them rest for at least 10 to 15 minutes after grilling to give the meat time to settle and keep those juices from leaking out.

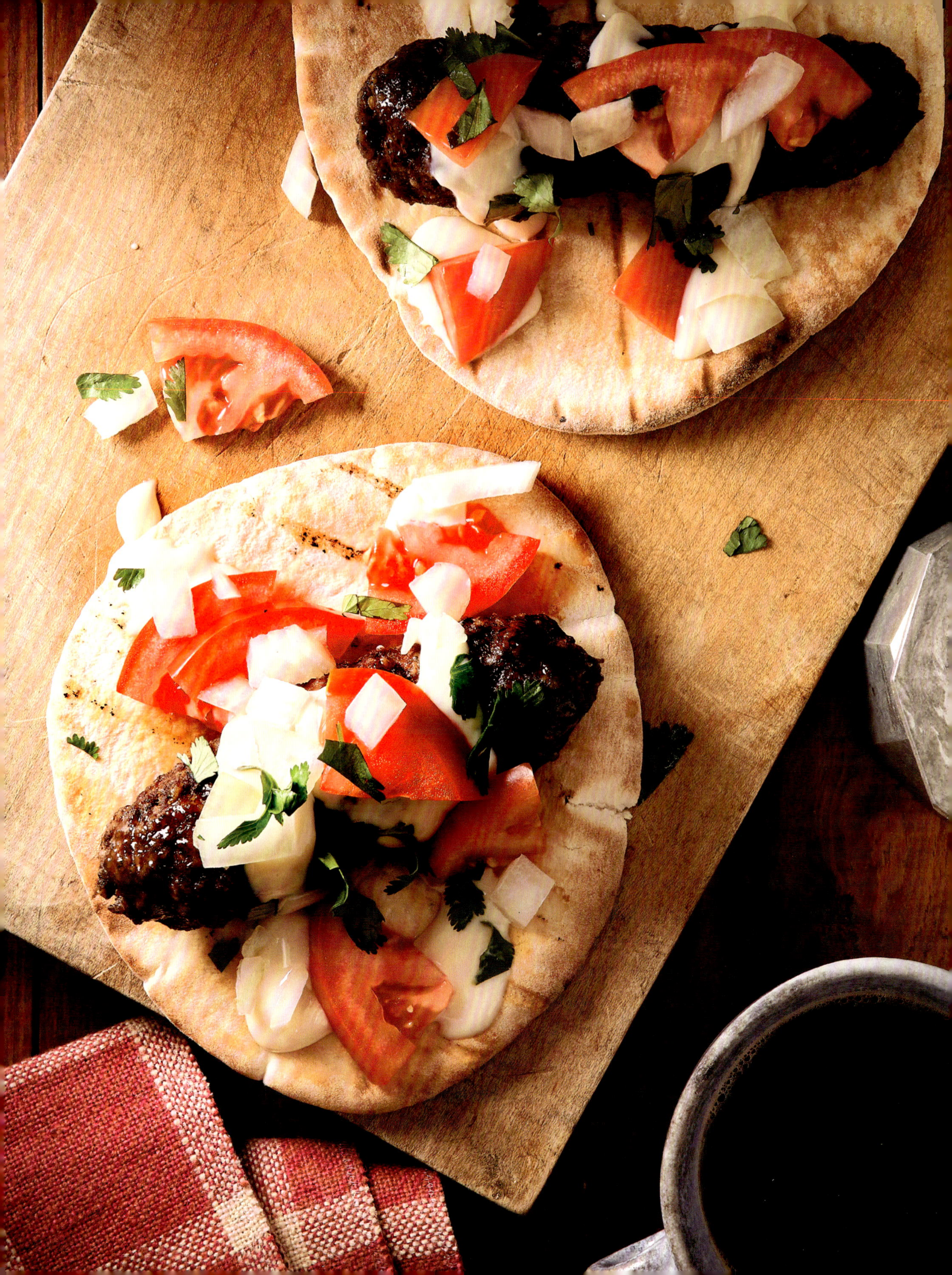

# BISON DONAIR KEBABS

The smell of this sweet, tangy donair sauce carries me back to the street food slingers in Halifax. And this bison-based twist on the classic brings up even older memories: Once the juicy, savory flavor of the meat hits, I snap further back to wild memories of hunting buffalo alongside a wolf pack. Miss your shot and a one-ton stack of beef might just stampede over you. Lookin' back, it was good practice for going up against Juggernaut … But unlike playing matador with Cain Marko, taking down one of those big bovines means you got a lean but hearty start on some comfort food for your recovery.

**Origin: Canada • Servings: 6 • Type: Main • Difficulty: Average • Prep Time: 30 minutes**
**Cook Time: 10 minutes • Rest Time: 1 hour • Dietary Considerations: GF***
**Pairs well with:** *Poutine* (pg 94)

## FOR THE DONAIR SAUCE AND TOPPINGS:

½ cup sweetened condensed milk

2 teaspoons garlic powder, or to taste

2 tablespoons white vinegar

1 large tomato, diced

½ white onion, medium diced

Finely chopped fresh parsley, optional for garnish

Warm pita bread, optional for serving

## FOR THE DONAIR KEBABS:

2 pounds ground bison or ground sirloin

¼ cup plain breadcrumbs

1½ teaspoons salt, or to taste

1 tablespoon *Mutant Medley* (pg 30)

2 teaspoons dried oregano

1 teaspoon ground coriander

1 teaspoon dried thyme

1 teaspoon baking soda

½ teaspoon red pepper flakes, optional to taste

1 teaspoon ground black pepper, or to taste

Oil or cooking spray, for greasing

## SPECIAL EQUIPMENT:

12 skewers, metal recommended

Plastic wrap

Baking sheet, for alternative method

Aluminum foil, for alternative method

Grill rack, for alternative method

**TO FIX UP THE DONAIR SAUCE:** whisk together the condensed milk, garlic powder, and white vinegar in a large bowl or small mixing bowl. Cover with plastic wrap and refrigerate 'til you need it. Try to give at least an hour to meld. Extra sauce can be stored in the fridge for up to 2 weeks.

**TO MAKE THE DONAIR KEBABS:** Combine the meat, breadcrumbs, and all the seasonings thoroughly. You can do this with a stand mixer with a dough hook on slow speed or using your hands in a large mixing bowl. If using your hands, knead the meat roughly for 5 minutes or so to break it down.

Divide the mixture into 12 balls roughly the same size, and mold each ball into a cylinder 'bout 1 inch in thickness. Insert the skewers into the kebabs and mold 'em onto the skewers a bit more, if you need. Cover loosely with plastic wrap and store in the refrigerator for at least 1 hour, or overnight, to allow the flavors to meld and the meat to firm up on the skewers.

Preheat the grill to 450°F, spray or brush the grates with oil. Grill the kebabs over direct heat 'til brown all over, about 8 to 12 minutes, turning 2 to 3 times for more even browning.

Set the kebabs on a serving platter and drizzle generously with the Donair sauce. Sprinkle with the diced tomatoes and chopped onions and garnish with chopped fresh parsley.

For the last 5 minutes, turn the oven to broil at 500°F. Broil 'til kebabs are nicely browned. Set the kebabs on a serving platter and drizzle generously with the Donair sauce. Sprinkle with the diced tomatoes and chopped onions and garnish with chopped fresh parsley.

**Alternative Method:** Instead of preheating your grill, preheat the oven to 350°F. Line a baking sheet with aluminum foil and place a grill rack on top. Grease the grill rack with oil or cooking spray. Place the kebabs on the greased grill rack. Bake for 15 to 20 minutes, turning halfway through, 'til cooked through.

## HOW TO
# PERFECTLY COOKED MEAT

When it comes to red meat like beef, venison, or lamb, you gotta know when it's cooked just right. Overcook it, and you're just wasting a prime cut—undercook it, and you're not doing it any favors either. But when you nail it, there's nothing better. Here's how to hit your mark every time:

**RARE:** The internal temperature for the meat should reach 120°F to 125°F. Red, cool center. Barely warmed up, raw as a rookie on their first trip to the Danger Room. Press it with your finger, it's like poking the fleshy part of your cheek—not much resistance, still cool inside. Only the brave or the reckless go here.

**MEDIUM-RARE:** The internal temperature for the meat should reach 130°F to 135°F. Warm, red center. Perfect balance of flavor and juiciness. A bit of bounce, like pressing your chin just under your lip—soft, but firming up. This is where pros like me live.

**MEDIUM:** The internal temperature for the meat should reach 140°F to 145°F. Pink center. Still juicy, still tender, but toein' the line. Feel like pressing on the end of your nose. You're playin' it safe, but at least you're still in the game.

**MEDIUM-WELL:** The internal temperature for the meat should reach 150°F to 155°F. Little pink left in the center. Feels like pressing the space between your eyebrows. Things are getting a bit tough now, like a stubborn brawl.

**WELL-DONE:** The internal temperature for the meat should reach 160°F and above. No pink—insides are dark like an alternate timeline, and tough as Colossus in battle mode. If you're here, make sure your blades are sharp.

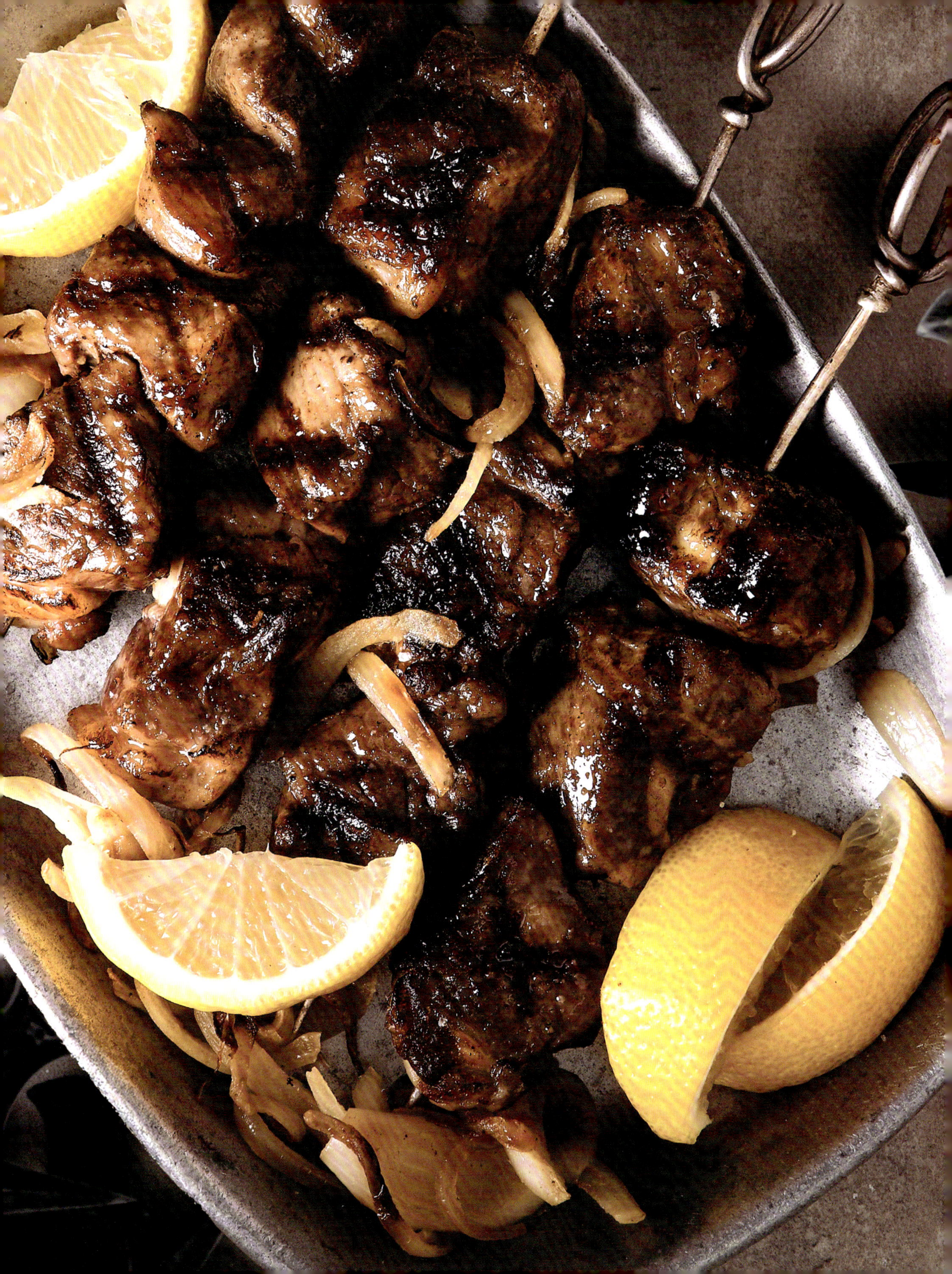

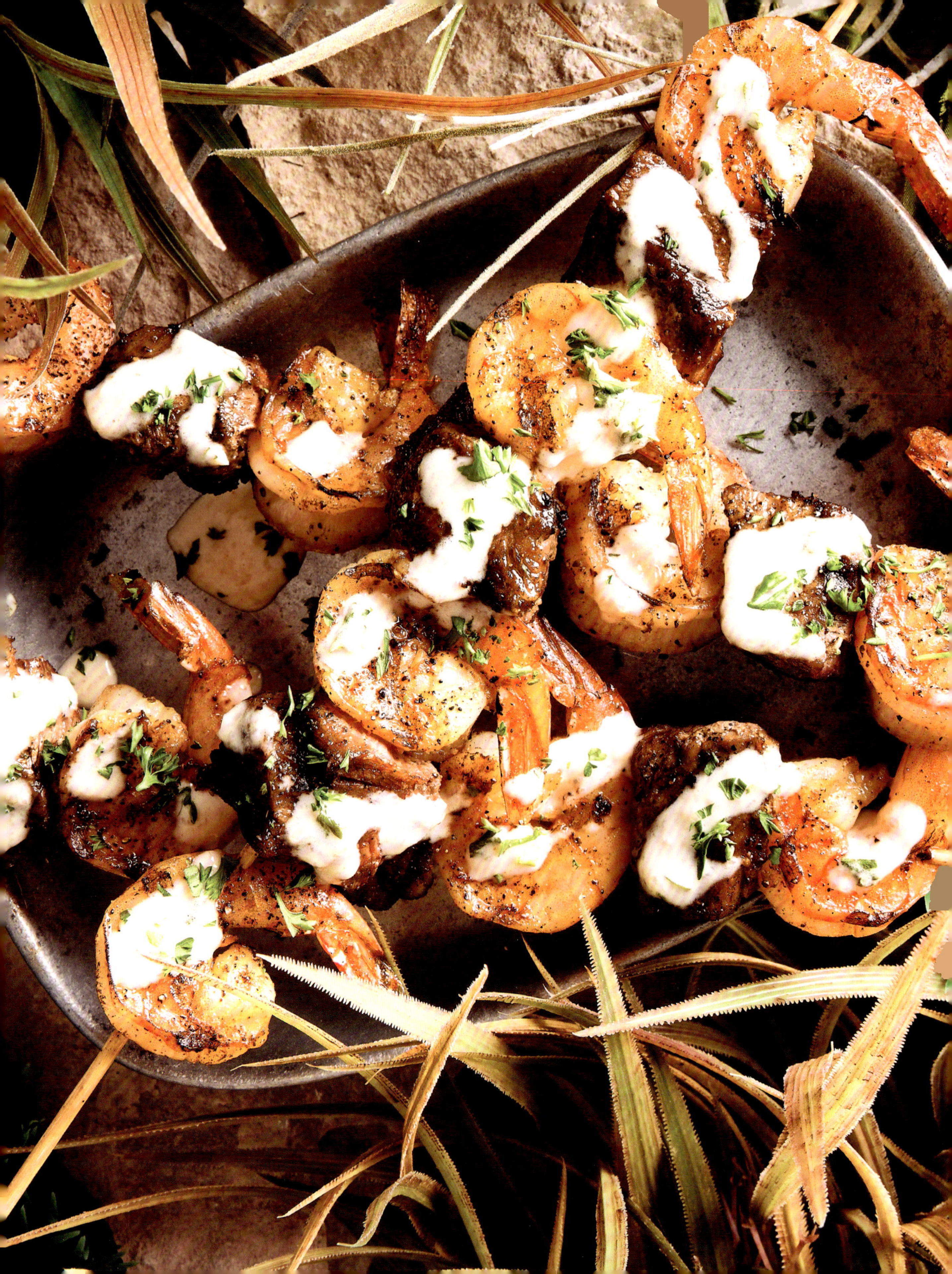

# SKEWERED SURF 'N TURF

This is a low-key legend straight from Australia, which also pretty much describes the man I'd grill 'em with: Gateway. After the world thought the X-Men dead, it gave some of us (including a longer-than-usual stay from Dazzler and Longshot) a chance to lay low "down under" and do some good without an anti-mutant bullseye on our backs. We still don't know Gateway's real name, but that sage-silent-type fella was a mutant teleporter from a nearby Indigenous tribe in the Outback. We only got to where we needed to go thanks to him. And I'd repay the kindness as often as I could with this "reef and beef": fresh-caught shrimp and juicy seasoned steak drenched in garlic cream sauce. Because when someone don't wanna talk, you don't *say* thanks. You *show* it.

**Origin: Australia • Servings: 4 to 6 • Type: Main • Difficulty: Average • Prep Time: 30 minutes Cook Time: 30 minutes • Rest Time: None**

### FOR THE SKEWERS:

1 pound large shrimp or prawns, deveined and shells removed

1 pound sirloin steaks or tri-tip, cut into 1-inch cubes

1 teaspoon *Mutant Medley* (pg 30) or other all-purpose seasoning

1 teaspoon *Weapon X* (pg 30) or other steak seasoning

1½ teaspoons salt, or to taste

½ teaspoon black pepper, or to taste

### FOR THE GARLIC CREAM SAUCE:

¼ cup unsalted butter

6 garlic cloves, minced

2 heaping tablespoons all-purpose flour

1 cup whole milk

½ cup heavy cream

½ teaspoon smoked paprika, or to taste

1 teaspoon salt, or to taste

Black pepper, to taste

½ cup grated parmesan cheese

½ cup fresh flat-leaf parsley, chopped

### SPECIAL EQUIPMENT:

10 to 15 skewers

Baking sheet, for alternative method

Aluminum foil, for alternative method

Grill rack, for alternative method

Season the shrimp and steak pieces with Mutant Medley, Weapon X, salt and pepper and set aside.

While the meat absorbs the seasoning, start the sauce. In a medium saucepan, melt the butter over medium heat. Add the garlic and sauté 'til fragrant, about 1 minute. Stir in the flour and cook for 1 more minute 'til lightly golden. Gradually whisk in the milk 'til smooth, then add the cream. Season with paprika, salt, and pepper. Simmer on low heat for 2 to 4 minutes, stirring to remove any lumps, 'til the sauce thickens and coats the back of a spoon. Stir in the Parmesan and parsley, then turn off the heat. Cover and set the sauce aside.

Preheat the grill to medium-high, or 425°F. Skewer the meat, alternating the steak and shrimp. Lay the surf 'n turf skewers on the preheated grill and grill for 3 to 5 minutes per side, 'til the shrimp is pink and opaque, and the steak is nicely browned and done to your preference inside, 130°F to 135°F for medium-rare and 140°F to 145°F for medium.

Serve the skewers with the sauce on the side and/or drizzled directly over the skewers.

**Alternative Method:** Instead of grillin', set the oven to broil on 500°F. Line a baking sheet with aluminum foil and place a grill rack on top. Grease the grill rack with oil or cooking spray. Place the kebabs on the greased grill rack on the top rack of the oven. Broil for 5 to 6 minutes on each side, 'til the beef is nicely browned and the shrimp is cooked through. The shrimp should be pink and opaque and the internal temperature of the beef should be 130°F to 135°F for medium-rare and 140°F to 145°F for medium.

# HOW TO
# STEAK CUTS

Here's the lowdown on steak cuts: just like Sentinels over the years, each's got its own flavor and specialty—but it's our job to make sure they're sliced up right. Get to know 'em and you'll be grilling like a pro in no time.

## RIBEYE

**WHAT IT IS:** A juicy, marbled cut from the rib section.

**WHY IT'S GREAT:** This one's packed with flavor and tenderness—perfect for throwing on the grill or searing in a pan. You want a steak that's both juicy and rich, this is it.

**TIP:** This cut's marbling means you don't need to overdo it with fat or butter—just a hot grill or pan to sear it up nice.

## NEW YORK STRIP

**WHAT IT IS:** A great cut for grilling, offering a balance of tenderness and flavor.

**WHY IT'S GREAT:** Not as tender as ribeye, but packs more of a punch in the flavor department.

**TIP:** It's leaner than ribeye, so a little extra butter or a quick sear in a hot pan helps enhance its flavor.

## FILET MIGNON

**WHAT IT IS:** Cut from the tenderloin, known for its exceptional tenderness.

**WHY IT'S GREAT:** This cut's top-notch for special occasions when you want to impress. You'll see this one on menus in Hightown a lot.

**TIP:** Cook it gently, it's delicate. A simple seasoning, even just salt and pepper, is often all it needs. Sear in a hot pan and finish in the oven if needed.

## SIRLOIN

**WHAT IT IS:** Cut from the rear back of the cow, leaner than ribeye.

**WHY IT'S GREAT:** It's got a solid balance of flavor and tenderness without burning a hole in your wallet. Ideal for skewers.

**TIP:** Try the "sirloin cap," also known as picanha. This cut comes from the top part of the sirloin and features a delicious fat cap that adds rich flavor and keeps the meat juicy.

## ROUND STEAK

**WHAT IT IS:** Lean cut from the rear leg of the cow.

**WHY IT'S GREAT:** It's versatile and easy on the budget—ideal for grilling or pan-frying. Get your flavor without breaking the bank.

**TIP:** Tenderize this one before cooking. It's great for marinating and quick grilling or stir-frying. Best in recipes that call for thin slices or chunks.

## TRI-TIP

**WHAT IT IS:** A versatile cut, great for roasting, grilling, or smoking.

**WHY IT'S GREAT:** It's not too pricey, offers a great flavor and can be cooked in multiple ways.

**TIP:** The grain can run in different directions with this cut so be sure to slice against the grain in each direction to ensure maximum tenderness.

## HANGER STEAK

**WHAT IT IS:** A flavorful cut from the diaphragm, hangin' between the rib and loin.

**WHY IT'S GREAT:** Known for its rich, beefy flavor and tenderness when cooked just right. It's been called the "butcher's steak" because butchers used to keep it for themselves.

**TIP:** Like tri-tip, this cut has a grain running in two directions, so make sure you slice in the right direction (against the grain).

## T-BONE

**WHAT IT IS:** Combines a portion of the tenderloin and strip steak, separated by a T-shaped bone.

**WHY IT'S GREAT:** You get the best of both worlds here—tenderloin on one side, strip steak on the other.

**TIP:** Since it has both a strip steak and tenderloin, it's best to monitor the temperature carefully to avoid overcooking the more delicate tenderloin side.

## PORTERHOUSE

**WHAT IT IS:** Similar to the T-bone but with a larger tenderloin portion.

**WHY IT'S GREAT:** Perfect for sharing, and it's a real winner on the grill.

**TIP:** Like the T-Bone, it's a pretty big piece of meat, sear on high heat and finish cooking slowly, either in the oven or on the cooler side of the grill to ensure even doneness.

## TOMAHAWK

**WHAT IT IS:** A bone-in ribeye with an extra-long bone, giving it that impressive "tomahawk" appearance.

**WHY IT'S GREAT:** This cut is essentially a ribeye with the rib bone left in, making it a real stunner for those special occasions.

**TIP:** The long bone makes it easy to handle and flip, but it also means you'll need a big grill or pan for this beauty.

## FLANK STEAK

**WHAT IT IS:** A long, flat cut from the lower chest or abdominal area.

**WHY IT'S GREAT:** Marinate it, grill it—great for fajitas, stir-fries, and other quick-cooking dishes.

**TIP:** Always slice against the grain to keep it tender. Marinate it well for a flavorful kick and grill it over high heat for a nice sear.

## SKIRT STEAK

**WHAT IT IS:** Flavorful, thin cut from the diaphragm muscle.

**WHY IT'S GREAT:** Ideal for quick cooking methods like grilling or stir-frying.

**TIP:** Marinate and cook quickly over high heat. Slice against the grain to keep it tender.

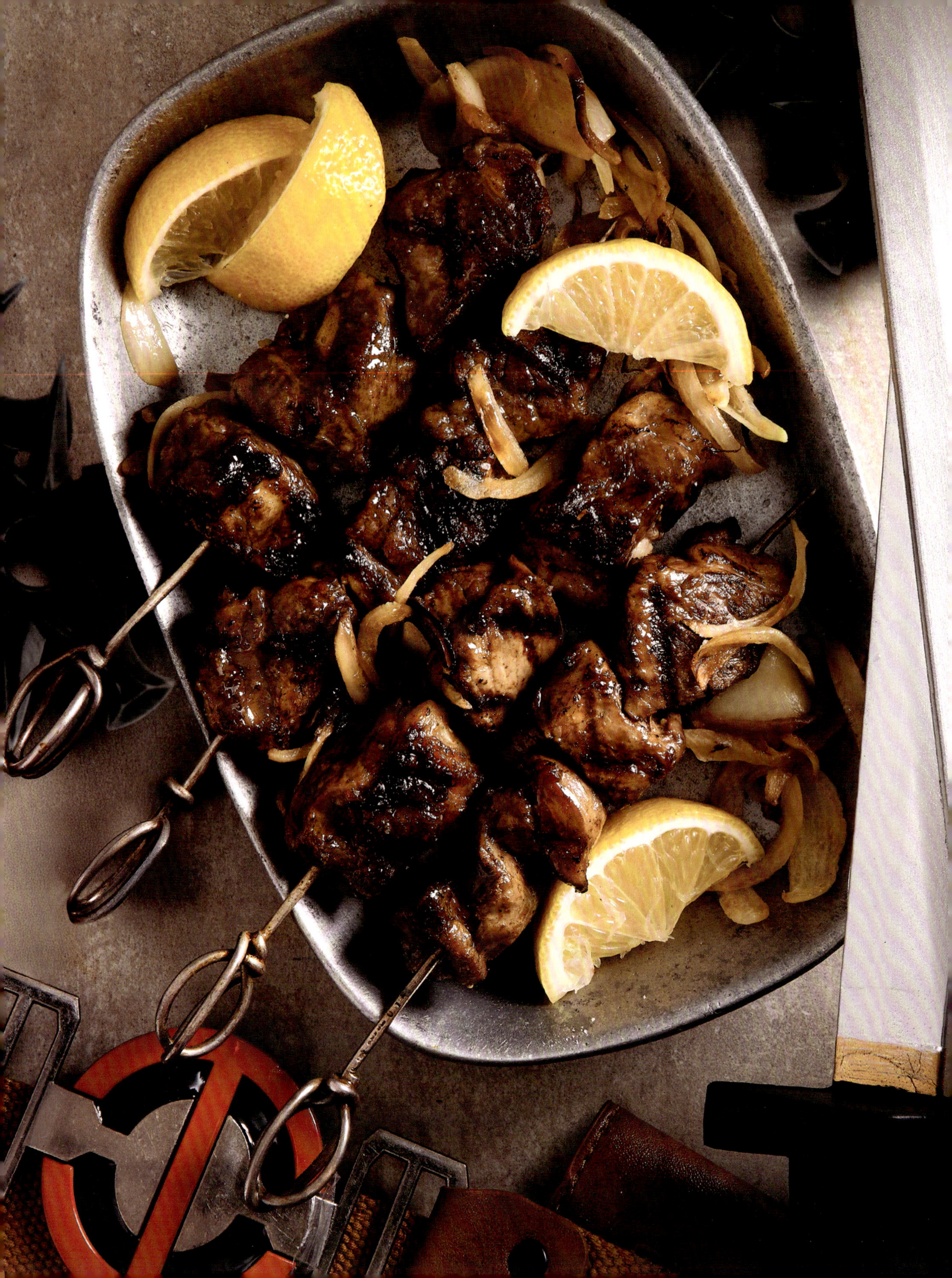

# STABBY SHISHLIKI

Well pop my pouches. The big, bad Wolverine is secretly scribbling a cookbook?!? And here I thought this journal I found snooping through your stuff would just be filled with doodles of **HOT ANIME GIRLS** or, given your age, the cave painting equivalent. But I think I get the gist—so, here's a hot little number that reminds me of **YOU**! It's meaty, greasy, salty, Canadian, and it's got **MUTTON CHOPS**! (Plus, I've jammed my swords through both and roasted you.)

P.S. I'm not mad you stole the idea of doing a cookbook from me. But we should either do some savvy cross-promotion synergy or Marvel and Insight Editions might make what Weapon X did to us look like a spa day.

Origin: Canada • Servings: 6 to 8 • Type: Main • Difficulty: Easy • Prep Time: 15 minutes
Cook Time: 10 to 15 minutes • Rest Time: 24 hours • Dietary Considerations: GF

2 pounds lamb shoulder or boneless lamb leg meat, cut into 1½-inch cubes (see Note)
2 teaspoons salt
¾ teaspoon black pepper
2 medium white onions, thinly sliced
1 lemon, cut into wedges, optional, for serving
Oil or cooking spray, for greasing

### Special Equipment:

6 to 12 skewers, metal recommended
Baking sheet, for alternative method
Aluminum foil, for alternative method
Grill rack, for alternative method

Place the meat in a large mixing bowl and generously season with salt and pepper, rubbing it in with your hands to ensure even coverage. Add the onions and mix well so they are evenly combined with the lamb.

Transfer the mixture to a heavy-duty storage bag, pressing out as much air as possible before sealing. Place the bag in the refrigerator to marinate for at least 24 hours, ideally for 2 to 3 days.

Thread the meat pieces onto the skewers, removing pieces of onion as you go. Try to position any particularly fatty bits toward the outside of the skewer. Discard the onions, or sauté them separately, if you like.

Preheat the grill to 450°F to 550°F. Grill on direct heat, rotating the skewers regularly, for about 7 to 10 minutes or 'til nicely browned outside and done to your preference inside.

Alternative Method: Instead of preheating a grill, set the oven to broil on 500°F. Line a baking sheet with aluminum foil and place a grill rack on top. Grease the grill rack with oil or cooking spray. Place the kebabs on the greased grill rack on the top rack of the oven. Broil for 5 to 6 minutes on each side or 'til the kebabs are nicely browned and done to your preference inside.

Note: If lamb isn't your thing, use a tri-tip or sirloin cap. Maximum effort!

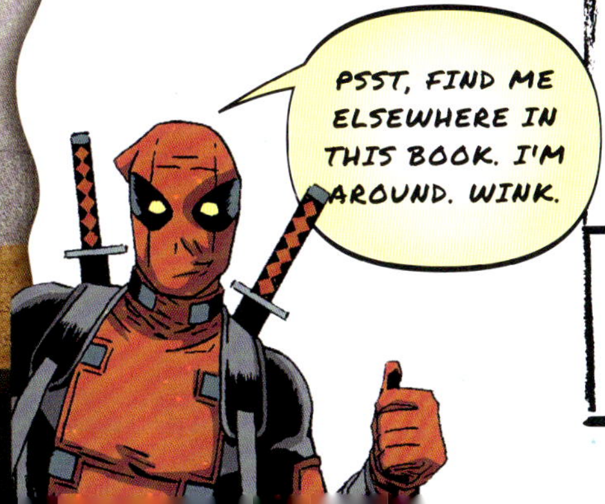
PSST, FIND ME ELSEWHERE IN THIS BOOK. I'M AROUND. WINK.

# KRAKOAN KABOBS

Hard to forget my first mission with the rag-tag "new" X-Men was a rescue of the original team from the living mutant island Krakoa. Not just 'cause those were my first impressions of folks who'd go on to be like family, but because we'd spend a good hunk of time with Krakoa as our *home*. And when every fruit, root, and seasoning folks harvest has a connection to the island's consciousness, it makes for a memory in every bit of this light, sweet, and spicy combo. Even if you make 'em with store-bought produce, they will make ya feel like you're on an island excursion.

**Origin: Krakoa • Servings: 6 • Type: Main • Difficulty: Average • Prep Time: 30 minutes • Cook Time: 20 minutes • Rest Time: 1 hour • Dietary Considerations: GF, V, V+***

## FOR THE TEMPEH OR FISH:

4 tablespoons olive oil, divided

1 lime, zest and juice

2 cloves garlic, minced

2-inch piece fresh ginger, minced

1 tablespoon honey or brown rice syrup

1½ teaspoons salt, divided

¾ teaspoon pepper, divided

1 tablespoon jerk seasoning, divided

2 blocks (16 ounces) tempeh or 1 pound firm white fish (like swordfish or mahi mahi), cut into 1-inch cubes

## FOR THE KABOBS:

½ medium pineapple, peeled and cored, cut into 1-inch pieces

1 large red onion, cut into 1-inch pieces

2 medium red bell peppers, cut into 1-inch pieces

Roasted macadamia nuts, crushed, optional

**TO MAKE THE TEMPEH OR FISH:** In a mixing bowl, stir together two tablespoons of the oil, lime juice and zest, garlic, ginger, honey, and half the salt, pepper, and jerk seasoning. Add the tempeh or fish and gently toss to coat. Cover and refrigerate for at least 1 hour to marinate, up to overnight.

**TO MAKE THE KABOBS:** In another bowl, pile in the pineapple, red onion, red bell peppers, remaining 2 tablespoons of oil, and the remaining salt, pepper, and jerk seasoning. Toss 'til well mixed.

**TO MAKE THE SAUCE:** Stir together the ingredients in a bowl. Serve this alongside the skewers, if you like. Set aside 'til serving time.

Assemble skewers by alternating a mix of tempeh or fish, pineapple, red pepper, and onion onto skewers, using 3 to 4 pieces of tempeh or fish per skewer. Reserve the marinade for brushing.

Preheat the grill to 375°F or medium heat. Brush the skewers with the leftover marinade. Grill for 4 to 5 minutes on all four sides or 'til grill marks are prominent and veggies tender, brushing on more marinade each time you flip the skewers. If using fish, make sure it is cooked through; it should be white, opaque, and flaky.

Serve the skewers hot, sprinkled with crushed macadamia nuts, with the dipping sauce on the side.

**Alternative Method:** Instead of grilling, set the oven broiler to 450°F. Line a baking sheet with aluminum foil and set a grill rack on top. Spray or brush the rack with oil. Place the skewers on the baking sheet and brush them generously with the leftover marinade. Roast the skewers in the top rack of the oven for about 15 to 20 minutes, flipping halfway through and brushing with more marinade. If using fish, ensure it is cooked through. It should look white, opaque, and flaky. Once done, sprinkle the skewers with crushed macadamia nuts and serve with the dipping sauce on the side.

**FOR THE OPTIONAL DIPPING SAUCE:**

½ cup plain coconut yogurt

2 teaspoons sriracha hot sauce, or to taste

2 teaspoons lime juice

1 teaspoon soy sauce or tamari

**SPECIAL EQUIPMENT:**

6 to 12 skewers, wood or metal

Baking sheet, for alternative method

Aluminum foil, for alternative method

Grill rack, for alternative method

Cooking brush, for alternative method

*Note: This recipe can be made vegan if you use tempeh instead of fish and brown rice syrup instead of honey.*

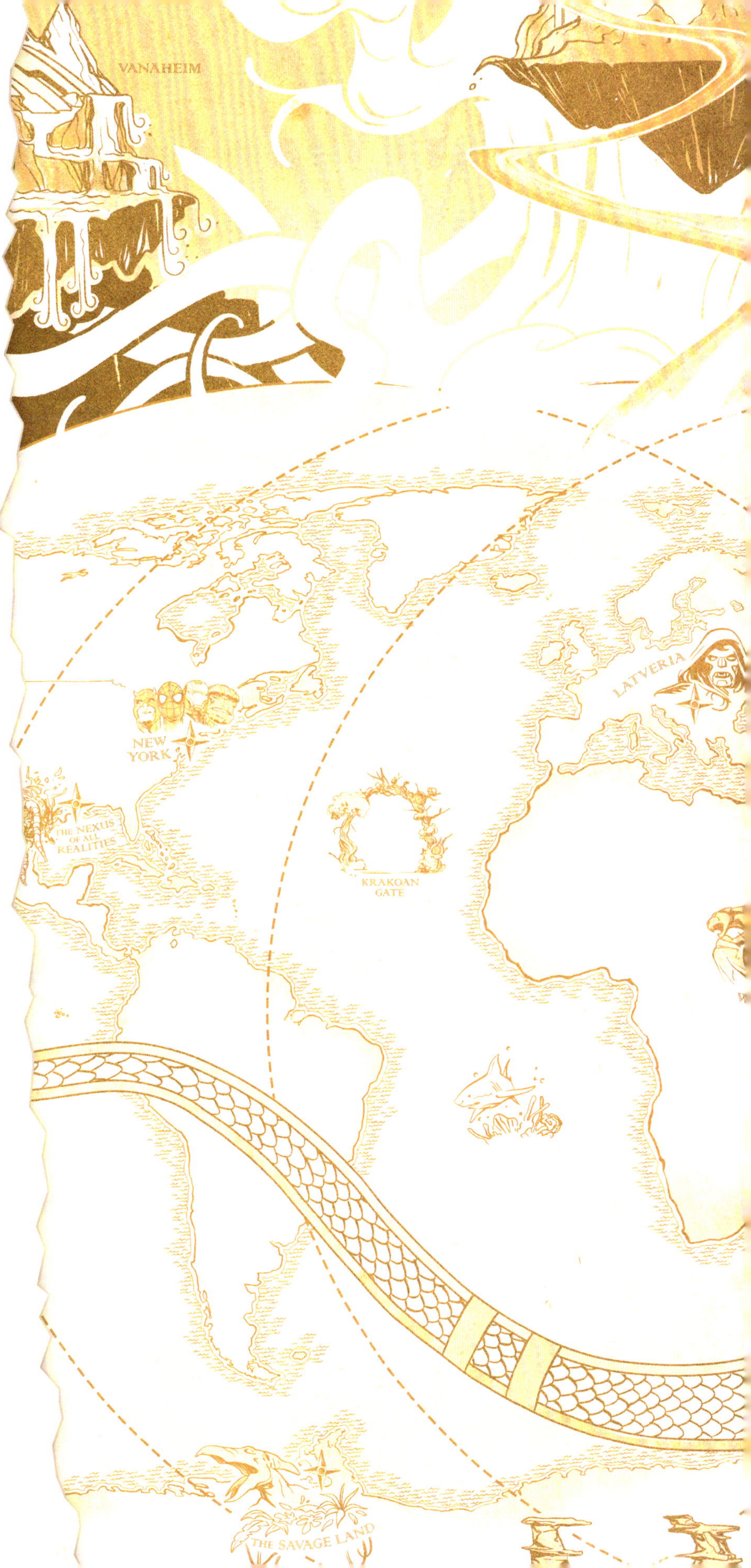
VANAHEIM
LATVERIA
NEW YORK
THE NEXUS OF ALL REALITIES
KRAKOAN GATE
THE SAVAGE LAND

# TORNADO POTATO

I've scarfed down all kinds of New York City street food in between punch-ups with Kree invaders, Mole Man monster hordes, or Limbo-dimension demon attacks. All the pizza slices or bodega bagels with Luke Cage, Ben Grimm, and the Web-Head were startin' to run together, when Laura dragged me to the depths of Queens to get "tornado potatoes." I'd seen spuds served up like this in Korea, but had always veered toward something meatier.

Figures that daughter o'mine would refuel with something as stabby and surprising as she is. Said she got a taste for this (vegetarian!) cheap snack in her dark days livin' with a few other runaway kids in the city. Ain't no way some poor girl cloned off *me* could turn out entirely normal. But after getting brainwashed into work as a kiddie assassin, it's a relief her kind of weird is takin' two trains to get mixed-flavor, spiral-cut, fried spuds. Eventually, we hacked out this recipe ourselves—some proprietary spices tusslin' with the parmesan, salts, and sugars. Didn't turn out the same as the original. But in my experience, clones never do.

**Origin: New York • Servings: 3 • Type: Snack • Difficulty: Average • Prep Time: 15 minutes • Cook Time: 10 minutes • Rest Time: None • Dietary Considerations: GF, V, V+***

3 yukon gold potatoes, peeling optional

Neutral oil, such as avocado or canola, for frying or greasing

¼ cup grated parmesan cheese (see Note)

1 tablespoon gochugaru powder or *Danger Room Rub* (pg 30)

1 tablespoon granulated sugar

1 tablespoon *Mutant Medley* (pg 30)

1 teaspoon flaky salt

Chopped parsley, optional for garnish

### SPECIAL EQUIPMENT:

3 skewers, wood or metal
Air fryer, optional

Slice off one end of the potato, placing the flat side down on a cutting board. Insert a skewer through the center of the potato. Holding a paring knife or other small sharp knife at an angle, cut while slowly rotating the potato in the opposite direction, creating a continuous spiral. You can also use the ribbon blade or a spiralizer for this, if you've got one. Gently slide the potato up the skewer, straightening the spiral to create the "tornado" shape. Make sure the potato is secure on the skewer.

In a small bowl, stir together the parmesan, gochugaru, sugar, and Mutant Medley. If you are using Danger Room Rub instead of gochugaru, you may want to skip or reduce the granulated sugar.

In a deep fryer or thick-bottomed pot, heat 4 or 5 cups of oil to 350°F. Fry the potatoes in two batches 'til they are golden brown all over. If you're able to submerge the potatoes in the oil completely, that's about 5 to 7 minutes total. If you can't submerge the potatoes completely, that's about 3 to 5 minutes per side. Set aside to drain on a paper towel–lined plate.

While the potatoes are still piping hot, season with the salt and sprinkle all over with the cheese mixture to taste. Garnish with chopped parsley, if you like.

**Alternative Method:** If you've got an air fryer handy, preheat it to 375°F. Place the potatoes in the air fryer basket and cook for 22 to 25 minutes 'til the potatoes are crispy and golden.

*Note: This recipe can be made vegan by using vegan parmesan cheese.*

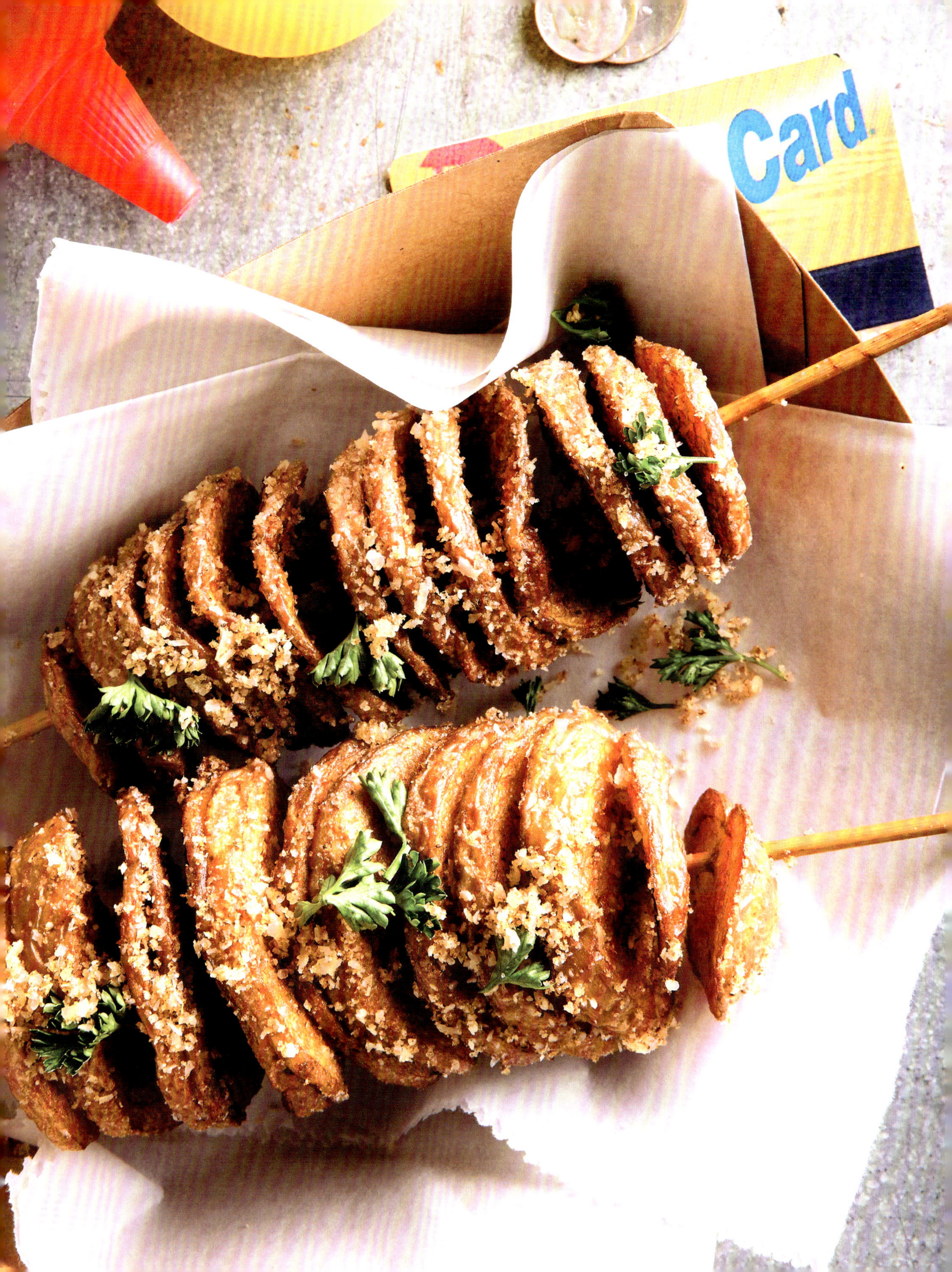
Card

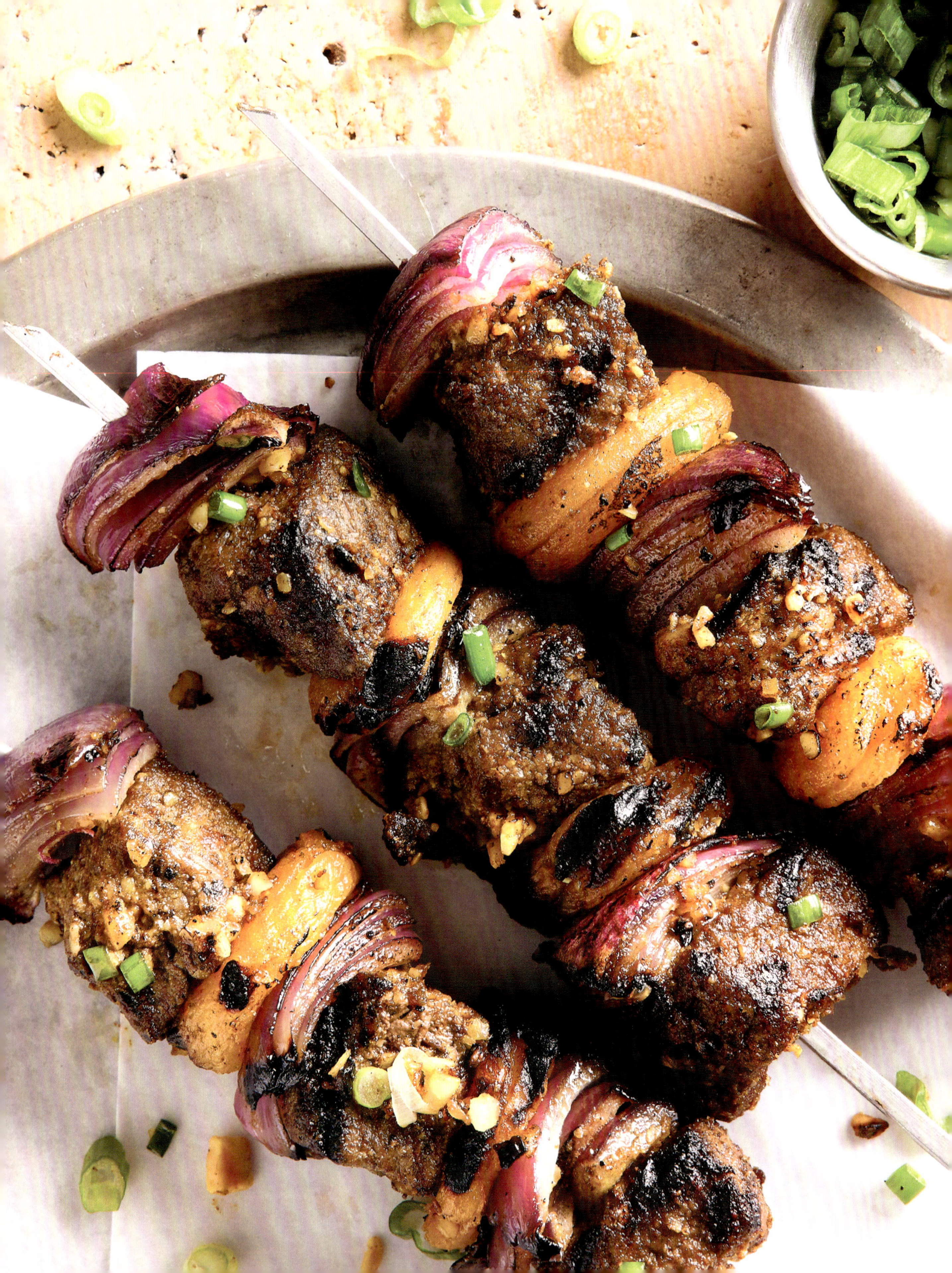

# HAMMER BAY BBQ

The first taste I had was on the short-lived mutant haven of Genosha, where Magneto forged his own homeland for our kind off the coast of Africa. Whether it was just proximity, or maybe mutants from the region bein' among the first to set up new lives and businesses, these sweet, apricot and peanutty–spiced beef combos might've been to Genosha what hot dogs are to the States. One of the few times ol' Magnus left a *good* taste in my mouth.

**Origin: Genosha • Servings: 6 • Type: Main • Difficulty: Average • Prep Time: 30 minutes • Cook Time: 15 minutes • Rest Time: 1 hour • Dietary Considerations: GF**

### FOR THE SKEWERS:

2 pounds top sirloin or tri-tip, cut into 1-inch cubes

1½ teaspoons salt, or to taste

5 ripe apricots, sliced or 12 to 15 dried apricots

½ medium red onion, cut into 1-inch slices

1 tablespoon chopped chives or green onion, for garnish

### FOR THE CRUST:

2 cups dry roasted peanuts (see Note)

1 tablespoon brown sugar

1 tablespoon *Mutant Medley* (pg 30) or all-purpose seasoning

1 tablespoon *Dagger Bay Blend* (pg 30) or curry powder

2 teaspoons smoked paprika

2 teaspoons allspice

2 teaspoons cinnamon

1 teaspoon ginger

### SPECIAL EQUIPMENT:

6 to 12 skewers

Season the beef pieces evenly with the salt and set aside. If using dried apricots, start soaking them in hot water to soften them.

**TO MAKE THE CRUST:** Blend the peanuts in a blender 'til you have coarse crumbs. Tie the peanuts up in a kitchen towel and squeeze out as much oil as you can. Transfer the ground peanuts to a bowl, add in the sugar and spices and stir together 'til well-combined.

**TO MAKE THE SKEWERS:** Pat the meat dry thoroughly with paper towels. Sprinkle the peanut mixture generously over a clean surface. Firmly but gently roll the meat pieces in the peanut mixture to coat. Let sit at room temperature for 30 minutes to 1 hour.

Thread the crusted meat, apricots, and onions onto the skewers, alternating between them so you have onions and apricots in between each piece of meat. Use about 3 to 4 pieces of meat per skewer.

Grease the grates with cooking spray or oil and preheat the grill to medium-high, or 425°F. Lay the skewers on the preheated grill and grill for 4 to 6 minutes per side, 'til nicely browned and the meat is done to your preference inside.

Garnish with green onions or chives and serve hot.

**Alternative Method:** Preheat the oven to 400°F. Line a baking sheet with aluminum foil and place a grill rack on top. Grease the grill rack with oil or cooking spray. Place the skewers on a baking sheet and roast for 12 to 15 minutes, turning halfway through, until the meat is cooked to your preferred doneness. Garnish with chopped chives or green onion and serve.

*Note: Got a peanut allergy? Swap 'em out for some roasted pistachios—after you shell 'em, of course. Keeps that crunch.*

# YAKITORI NEGIMA

Lean and mean. Focused but powerful. Tried and true. Everything I aim to be, Master Ogun honed in me as my Sensei. His training calmed my mind and taught me to conquer the beast inside. But his own goal to conquer death took him down a dark, mystic path. Still, I hold onto the lessons and values he taught—especially in returning to a little ritual of making these lightly sweet, lean but impactful skewers as some perfect protein for training.

**Origin: Japan • Servings: 4 to 6 • Type: Main or Appetizer • Difficulty: Easy • Prep Time: 20 minutes Cook Time: 12 minutes • Rest Time: None • Dietary Considerations: GF\***
**Pairs well with:** *Mixed Veggie Kushiyaki* **(pg 87)**

## FOR THE YAKITORI SAUCE (TARE):

½ cup soy sauce or tamari

½ cup mirin

¼ cup light brown sugar

2 cloves garlic, minced

1-inch piece fresh ginger, minced

## FOR THE SKEWERS:

2 pounds boneless skinless chicken thighs, cut into 1-inch pieces

8 medium green onions, cut into 1-inch pieces

Neutral oil, for greasing

Sesame seeds, optional for garnish

## SPECIAL EQUIPMENT:

12 pre-soaked bamboo skewers

Baking sheet, for alternative method

Aluminum foil, for alternative method

Grill rack, for alternative method

**TO MAKE THE YAKITORI SAUCE:** Add the soy sauce or tamari, mirin, sugar, garlic, and ginger to a small saucepan. Bring to a boil over high heat, then reduce to a simmer and cook 'til the sauce thickens slightly, 10 to 12 minutes. Remove from the heat and divide into two separate containers, one for basting and one for serving on the side. Set aside.

**TO MAKE THE SKEWERS:** Thread the chicken and green onions onto the skewers, alternating between the two.

Preheat the grill to medium, or 400°F. Spray or brush the grates with oil.

Set the skewers on the grill and baste them generously with yakitori sauce. Grill 'til the chicken is cooked through and there's no pink remaining, turning and basting once or twice, about 8 to 12 minutes total, or 4 to 6 minutes per side.

Serve hot with the remaining yakitori sauce on the side. Sprinkle with sesame seeds, if you like.

**Alternative Method:** Instead of grilling, set the oven broiler to 425°F. Line a baking sheet with aluminum foil and set a grill rack on top. Grease the grill rack with oil. Lie the skewers on the grill rack, making sure there's at least a half inch of space in between each skewer. Bake for 4 to 6 minutes, then flip the skewers and brush them with yakitori sauce. Bake for another 4 to 6 minutes, until the chicken is cooked through and there's no pink remaining. Serve hot.

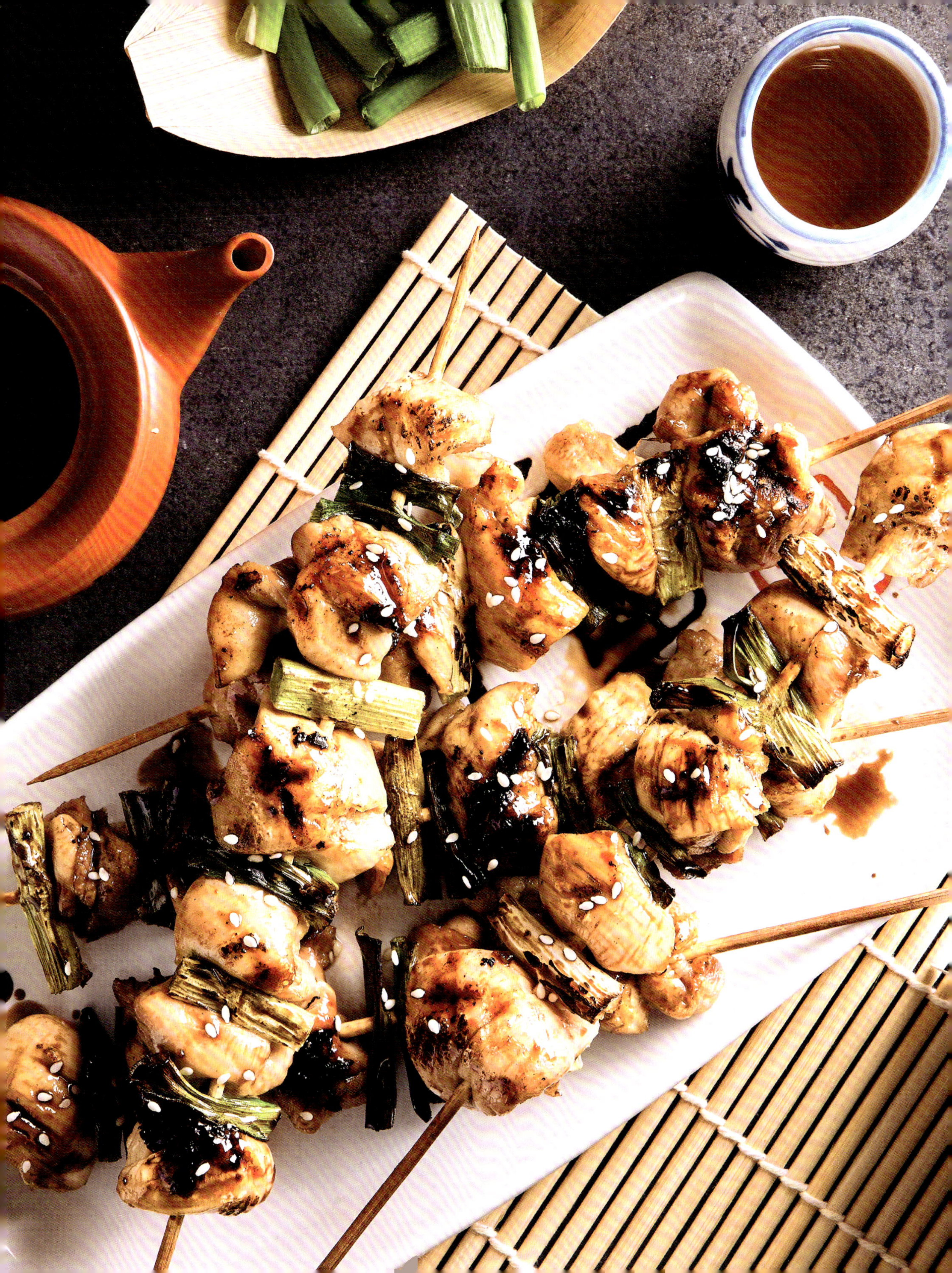

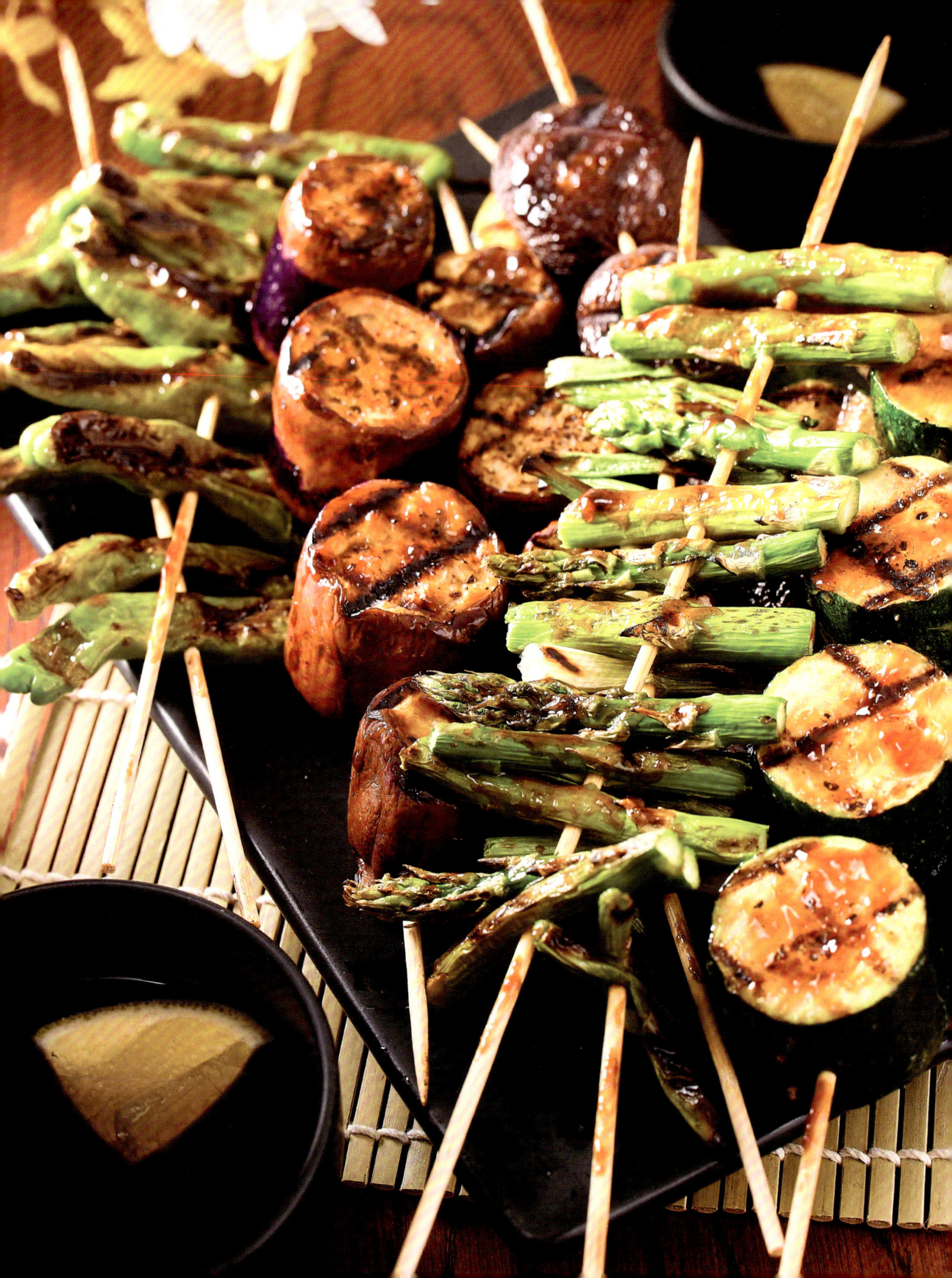

# MIXED VEGGIE KUSHIYAKI

My times in Japan include some of the greatest joys and deepest pains of all my years. But the ghost that haunts me whenever I return is Mariko. Despite bein' born into one of the country's most ruthless crime families—the Yashida clan—she was as gentle, hopeful, and radiant a woman as I'd ever met. The violence and machinations of her father and their rivals tore us away from each other more than once, but we kept finding our way back together. Then one of 'em slipped poison to her, and … only thing that stops the hurt is to remember the good. She fed my soul and made me a better man. All I can do now is try and take care of myself the way she'd want me to—feeding the body as thoughtfully as the spirit. Fresh vegetables, traditionally seasoned, for a vibrant taste. Her recipe here is how I like to restore myself with something real, and whole, and *good*.

**Origin:** Japan • **Servings:** 4 to 6 • **Type:** Appetizer/Vegetarian Main • **Difficulty:** Easy
**Prep Time:** 30 minutes • **Cook Time:** 20 minutes • **Rest Time:** None
**Dietary Considerations:** GF*, V, V+ • **Pairs well with:** *Yakitori Negima* (pg 84)

*Yakitori Sauce* (Tare) (pg 84)

8 shiitake mushrooms, stems removed

2 Japanese or Chinese eggplants, cut into 6 pieces

2 large or 4 medium green onions, cut into 2-inch pieces

2 medium zucchinis, cut into 1-inch rounds

4 large spears asparagus, cut into 2-inch pieces

12 shishito peppers

Neutral oil or cooking spray, for greasing

Flaky sea salt, to taste

Black pepper, to taste

Shichimi togarashi or sesame seeds, optional

### SPECIAL EQUIPMENT:

12 pre-soaked bamboo skewers

Baking sheet, for alternative method

Aluminum foil, for alternative method

Grill rack, for alternative method

Prepare the Yakitori Sauce according to the instructions on page 84. Divide into two bowls, one for brushing the veggies as they grill and one for serving.

Thread the vegetables onto the skewers, grouping veggie types together. Add as many pieces as will comfortably fit onto each skewer. Avoid overcrowding and make sure to leave enough space at the bottom of the skewer to grip. On each skewer of the same type of veggie, aim to have a similar number of vegetables per skewer.

Preheat the grill to 400°F or medium heat and spray or grease the grates with oil.

Sprinkle the veggies with salt and pepper. Grill for 5 to 10 minutes over indirect heat, rotating and brushing with the yakitori sauce 2 to 3 times. Some of the veggies will take longer than others, so transfer the finished skewers from the grill to a serving platter as they finish. The peppers, tomatoes, and green onions will take the shortest amount of time, and the mushrooms, eggplant, and zucchini will take the longest. The asparagus will likely be sometime in between.

Sprinkle the finished veggies with more salt and pepper. Option: add shichimi togarashi or sesame seeds, while still hot. Serve with a side of the remaining yakitori sauce.

# CHOCO BANANA

Some things really are simple: after half the world's heroes fought off a Skrull invasion in Central Park, when I hit the streets, a grateful li'l kid holding two Choco Bananas handed me one. No idea why I got the prize. But it's real good. And I'm not one to question a good thing. 'Course hunting down the recipe took a whole lot of following my nose …

**Origin: Japan • Servings: 10 • Type: Dessert • Difficulty: Average • Prep Time: 20 minutes
Cook Time: 5 minutes • Rest Time: 1 hour • Dietary Considerations: GF, V**

5 large bananas

1 cup white chocolate candy melts or yellow candy melts

1 to 2 drops yellow gel food coloring, optional for if you're using white chocolate

¼ cup chocolate sprinkles

¼ cup blue sprinkles

1 cup dark or milk chocolate candy melts

½ cup rainbow sprinkles, candies, and/or crushed nuts

**SPECIAL EQUIPMENT:**

Ten 6-inch skewers, wood recommended

Peel the bananas and cut them in half crosswise. Skewer the bananas on the cut end with the blunt end of the skewer. Ensure the bananas are skewered deep enough to be secure on the stick.

Line a standard baking sheet with parchment paper and place the bananas on the baking sheet and freeze 'til firm, about 1 hour.

Make sure you have all your ingredients easily accessible, place the toppings in separate small bowls. Line a separate baking sheet with parchment paper for finished bananas. The candy melts can harden quickly so it's good to work fast.

Place the white chocolate or yellow candy melts in a microwave-safe bowl and melt it in 25-second increments, stirring in between, 'til they are melted and smooth. If your candy melts have other directions on the back, go ahead and use those. Stir in the yellow food coloring 'til they are a bright yellow color. Once the candy has melted and your toppings are ready, remove 4 or 5 of the frozen banana skewers from the freezer.

Hold one of the bananas over the bowl of melted candy. Using a large spoon or a small ladle, generously drizzle the yellow chocolate over the banana, rotating it to ensure even coverage. Do this as quickly as you can, the chocolate will begin to set upon contact with the cold banana. Allow any excess chocolate to drip back into the bowl. Immediately sprinkle the coated banana with the blue and chocolate sprinkles. Place the coated banana on the baking tray and repeat the process 'til all 4 or 5 bananas are covered in yellow chocolate and sprinkles.

Repeat this process with the chocolate candy melts, rainbow sprinkles, or other toppings of your choice, and the remaining 5 or 6 bananas.

The frozen bananas are ready to serve once the chocolate sets up a bit, which happens pretty quick. If you're not planning to eat the choco-bananas immediately, store them in an airtight container or zip-top plastic bag in the freezer. Let them sit at room temperature for 10 to 15 minutes before serving (if serving from the freezer).

SNIKT!: SKEWERS AND KABOBS

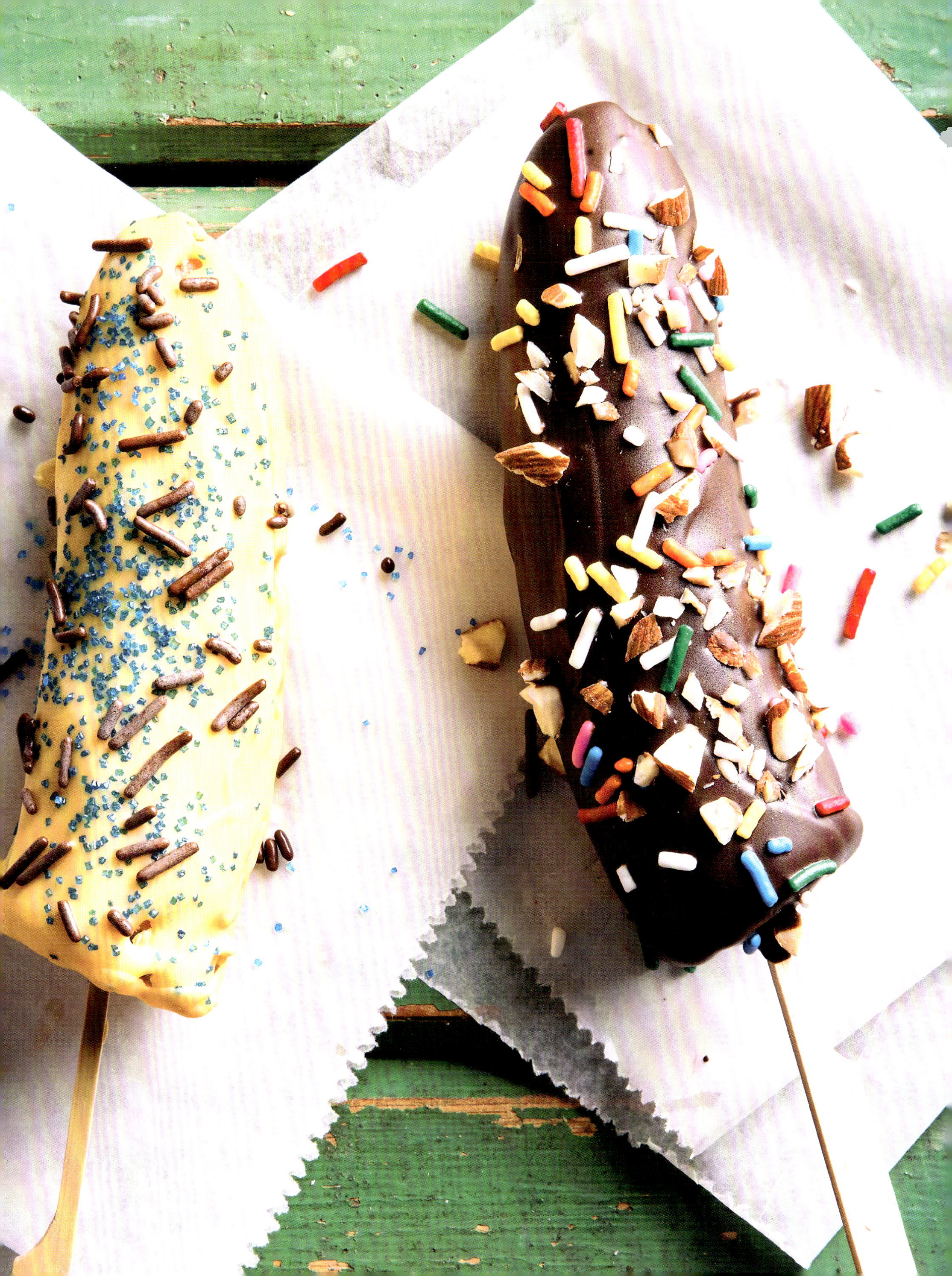

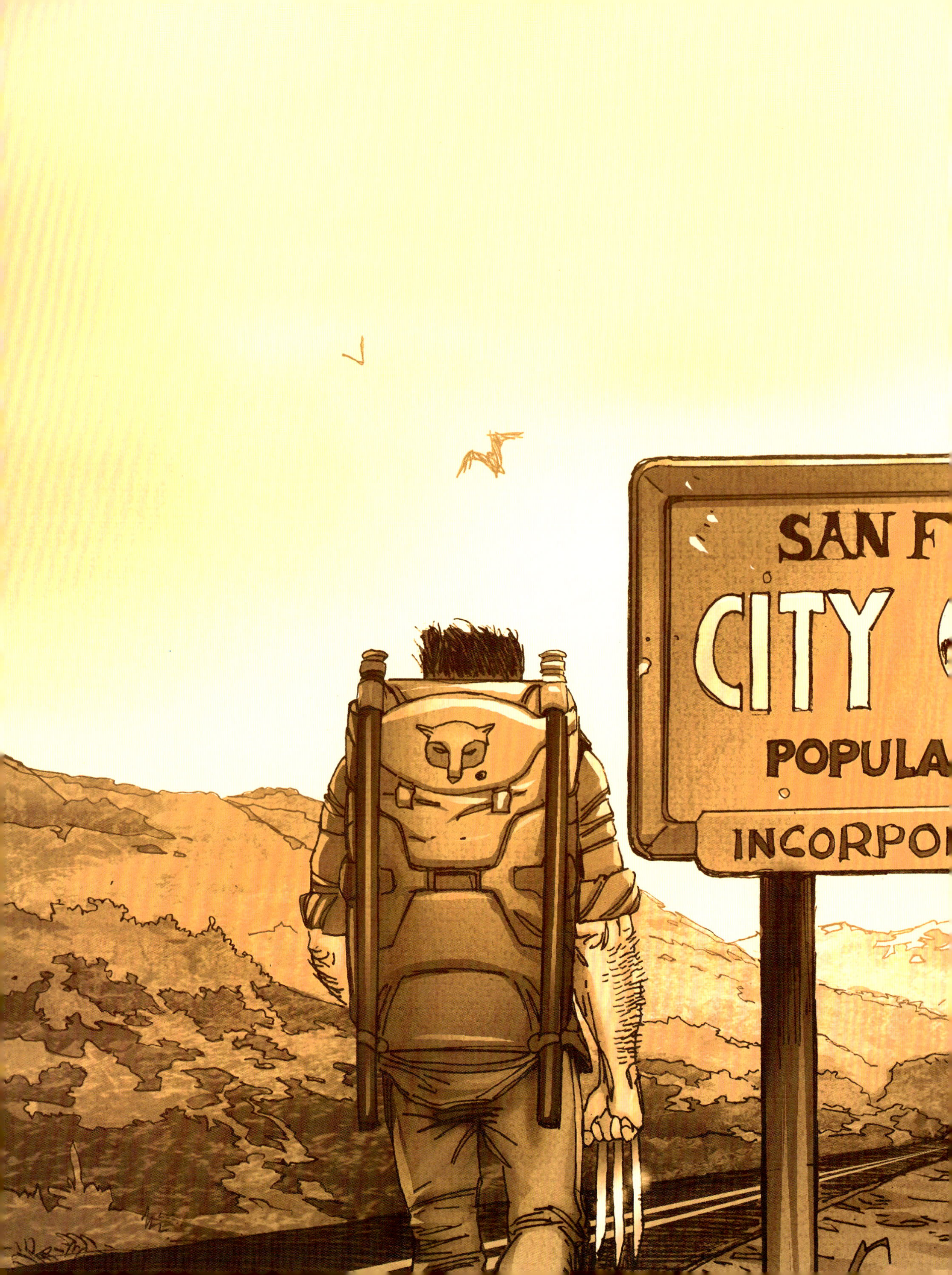
SAN F
CITY
POPULA
INCORPO

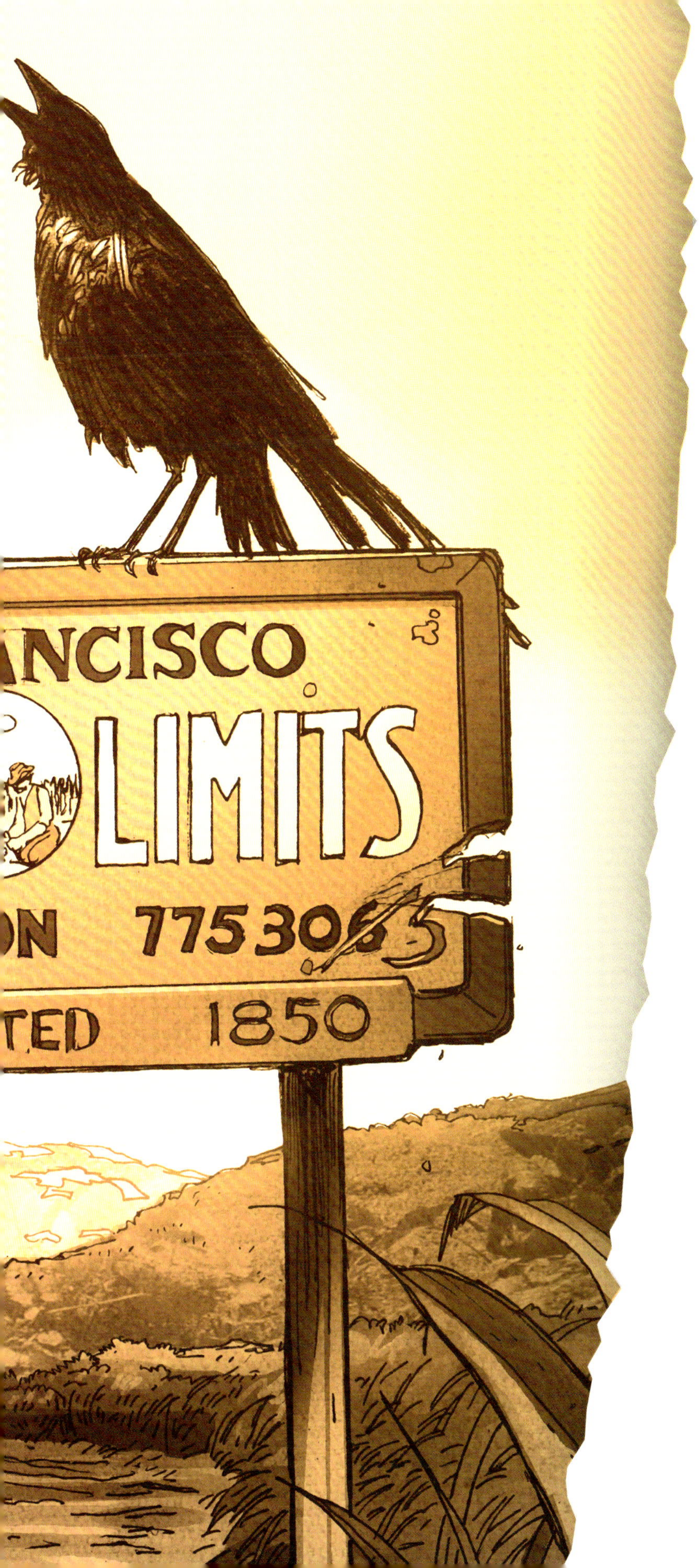
ANCISCO
LIMITS
ON 775306
TED 1850

# 4

## ON THE ROAD: STREET EATS AND TAVERN BITES

It's a great big world (hell, Multiverse) and I've been lucky enough to see more of it than most. But for every incredible experience that adds to more than you thought possible, there's just as many ways you get burned. (For one thing, seems like damned near every place has mutant-hunting Sentinels at this point.)

You stick around long enough and you might start feelin' like you're home. At least for a while. Countries here are ones I've s`pent some real time in, learning the ins-and-outs. You wouldn't necessarily call me a local, but let's say I know where the locals eat. Places like Canada, Japan, Madripoor, and the United States.

I figured it might help to round up some go-to favorites—either to look out for, or to cook up yourself whenever you're feelin' homesick. (Whichever home that may be.) Plus, I jotted down some reminders about culture and expectations. Knowin' how to *not* ruffle feathers sure helps when it comes to keeping a low profile. After all, can't catch a flight to the *next* great adventure if you get yourself locked up (again).

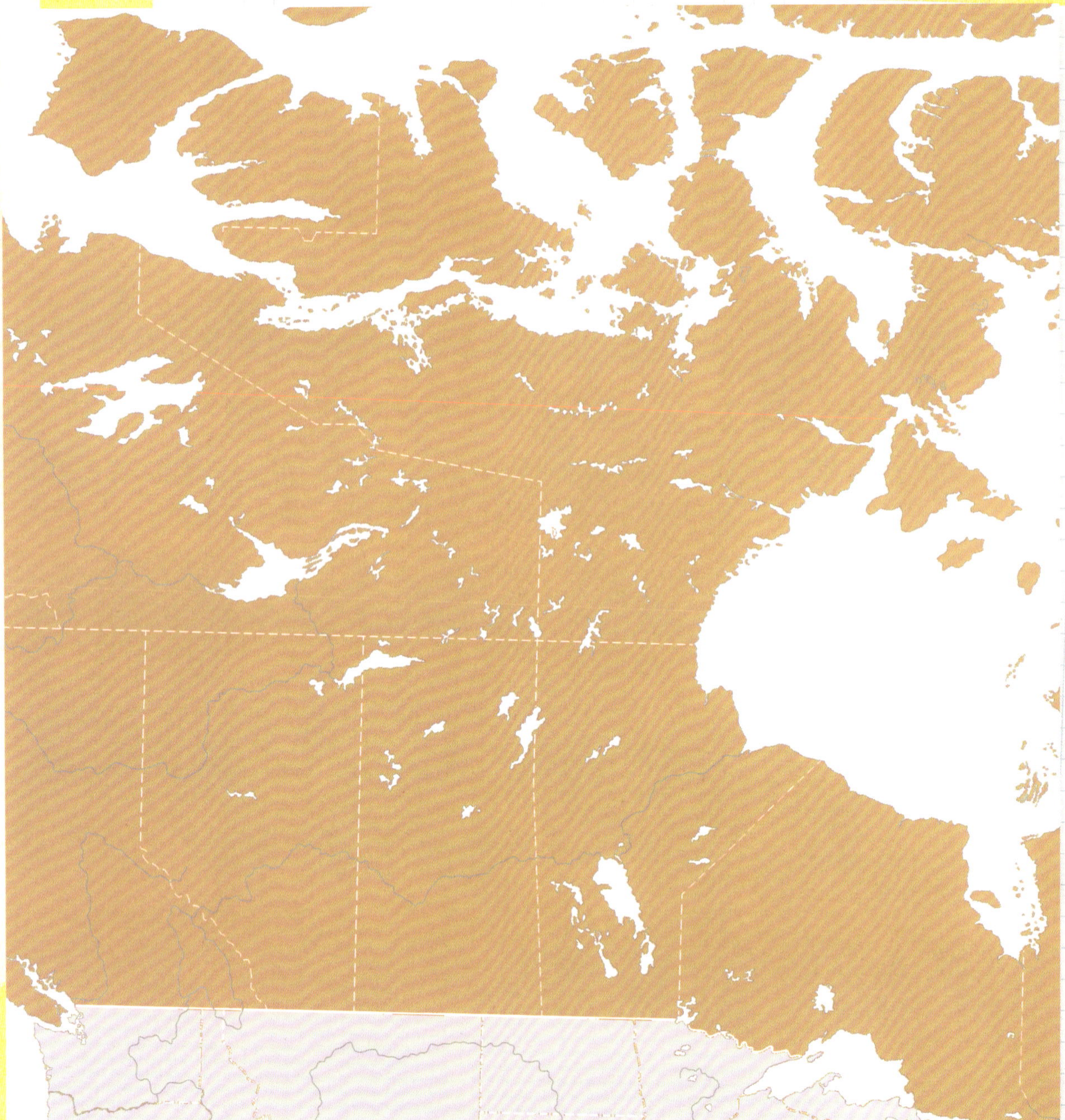

# FROM TIME SPENT IN
# CANADA

## HOW TO
# A POUTINE EXPLORATION

I may be Canadian, but I ain't precious about following anyone's rules about making poutine. Unlike Deadpool, whose always goin' on about his classic recipe. Far as I'm concerned, anything goes—long as the potatoes are crispy, drenched in a good sauce, and topped with some kind of melty cheese, it's good poutine. Jubilee's chili fries (pg 154)? Yeah, that's just American poutine.

### JAPANESE-STYLE POUTINE:

- **SWAPS:** Swap the gravy for Japanese curry sauce. Keep the cheese curds as is or swap them with fresh mozzarella.
- **TOPPINGS:** Add a drizzle of Japanese mayo, bonito flakes, and sliced green onions.

### SMOKEY BBQ POUTINE

- **SWAPS:** Add 1 tablespoon *Danger Room Rub* (pg 30) or other salt-free BBQ seasoning to the gravy along with the other seasonings, and a couple tablespoons of barbecue sauce with the broth. Swap the cheddar cheese curds for pepperjack curds.
- **TOPPINGS:** Add BBQ pulled pork, barbecue chicken, or burnt ends brisket. Lightly drizzle some ranch dressing or BBQ sauce over the top and sprinkle with french fried onions.

### PATCH'S MADRIPOORIAN POUTINE

- **SWAPS:** Instead of gravy, use a double serving of the peanut sauce on pg 62 warmed up in a saucepan or microwave.
- **TOPPINGS:** Add chopped fresh cilantro, crispy fried shallots, and dry roasted peanuts. Add a little sambal oelek or some chopped thai chiles if you like things spicy.

### X-23'S NACHO POUTINE

- **SWAPS:** Use red enchilada sauce or salsa roja instead of gravy. Swap out cheese curds for oaxaca cheese, chihuahua cheese, or taco flavored cheese curds.
- **TOPPINGS:** Add guacamole, sour cream, pico de gallo, and a sprinkle of chopped cilantro.

### RAGIN' CAJUN POUTINE

- **SWAPS:** To the gravy, add 1 chopped bell pepper with the veggies and at least 1 tablespoon of *Gambit's Magic* (pg 30) or other Cajun seasoning to the spices. Stir some gumbo file into the gravy at the end, if you want.
- **TOPPINGS:** Add slices of fried andouille sausage and cooked shrimp and/or chicken, and a sprinkle of chopped parsley.

### BREAKFAST POUTINE

- **SWAPS:** You don't have to change the foundation of fries-gravy-curds at all for this one, but if you want to, swap the fries for home fries, tater tots, or hash browns.
- **TOPPINGS:** Add 1 or 2 poached or sunny-side-up eggs, crumbled bacon or sausage, and some extra chopped chives.

*SERIOUSLY?! YOU'RE NOT EVEN GONNA HAVE THEM START WITH MY CLASSIC RECIPE ON PG 94?!*

# POUTINE

WHAT THE PUCK, LOGAN?!? YOU'RE WRITING ABOUT THE SIXTH-MOST POWERFUL GUY IN ALPHA FLIGHT BEFORE ME?!?! I THOUGHT WE HAD SOMETHING SPECIAL.

UNLESS THIS IS JUST ABOUT KEEPING UP YOUR CANADIAN CRED? WELL, I'M CANADIAN!! (I THINK. CURRENTLY? WE'VE BOTH HAD A LOT OF RETCONS.) AT THE VERY LEAST, I WATCH A TON OF CANADIAN TEEN DRAMAS ON TV. AND BACK WHEN WE WERE BOTH TRAPPED IN WEAPON X, THEY HAD A VOCAL COACH GET ME TO STOP PRONOUNCING IT "A-BOOT."

PLUS, I LOVE POUTINE! ASIDE FROM ITS NAME BEING PUNCHLINE GOLD, CRISPY GOLDEN FRENCH(-CANADIAN?) FRIES SMOTHERED IN DECADENT GRAVY-SOAKED CHEESE CURDS ARE A PERFECT EVERYDAY SNACK. AND IF WE'RE COMPARING RECIPES TO PEOPLE, TRY THIS OUT: THIS POUTINE'S AS HOT, POPULAR, BEEFY, GREASY, DELIGHTFULLY EXCESSIVE, AND MESSY AS ME ... OR YOUR CONTINUITY!

SERVINGS: 4 · TYPE: SIDE OR APPETIZER · DIFFICULTY: AVERAGE · PREP TIME: 45 MINUTES

COOK TIME: 30 MINUTES · REST TIME: NONE · DIETARY CONSIDERATIONS: · N/A

PAIRS WELL WITH: BERSERKER BURGER (PG 134), BISON DONAIR KEBABS (PG 67)

## FOR THE GRAVY:

2½ CUPS BEEF BROTH

1 TABLESPOON KETCHUP

1 TABLESPOON WORCESTERSHIRE SAUCE

1 TEASPOON SALT, OR TO TASTE

½ TEASPOON PEPPER, OR TO TASTE

¼ CUP UNSALTED BUTTER

1 SHALLOT, MINCED

2 CLOVES GARLIC, MINCED

⅓ CUP ALL-PURPOSE FLOUR

2 TEASPOONS DARK BROWN SUGAR

1 TEASPOON BEEF BOUILLON PASTE

2 TEASPOONS MUTANT MEDLEY (PG 30)

## FOR THE FRIES (SEE NOTE):

5 MEDIUM RUSSET POTATOES, PEELING OPTIONAL

2 TABLESPOONS CORNSTARCH OR RICE FLOUR

1 TABLESPOON SALT, OR TO TASTE

NEUTRAL OIL, SUCH AS CANOLA OR PEANUT OIL, FOR DEEP FRYING

## TO SERVE:

2 CUPS CHEDDAR CHEESE CURDS

1 TO 2 TABLESPOONS CHIVES, CHOPPED, FOR GARNISH

START PREPARING THE FRIES: CUT THE POTATOES INTO ½-INCH-THICK BATONS USING THE BATONNET METHOD (PG 18).

SOAK THE FRIES IN ICE WATER FOR 25 TO 30 MINUTES. THIS WILL REMOVE EXCESS STARCH AND HELP THE FRIES CRISP UP.

WHILE THE FRIES SOAK, BEGIN THE GRAVY: IN A MEDIUM MIXING BOWL, WHISK TOGETHER THE BEEF STOCK, KETCHUP, BROWN SUGAR, BEEF BOUILLON PASTE, WORCESTERSHIRE, MUTANT MEDLEY, AND A PINCH OF SALT AND PEPPER.

MELT THE BUTTER IN A LARGE SAUCEPAN OVER MEDIUM-HIGH HEAT. ADD THE SHALLOT AND GARLIC AND SAUTÉ UNTIL THE SHALLOTS HAVE SOFTENED, ABOUT 3 TO 4 MINUTES. SPRINKLE IN THE FLOUR AND COOK THE ROUX, STIRRING CONSTANTLY, 'TIL GOLDEN BROWN, ABOUT 6 TO 7 MINUTES.

SLOWLY ADD THE BEEF STOCK MIXTURE AND BRING TO A BOIL. SIMMER, STIRRING OCCASIONALLY, UNTIL THICK ENOUGH TO COAT THE BACK OF A SPOON BUT STILL POURABLE, ABOUT 6 TO 8 MINUTES. KEEP ON VERY LOW HEAT, COVERED, WHILE YOU FRY THE POTATOES.

TO FRY: ADD THE OIL TO A DEEP THICK-BOTTOMED POT ABOUT 3 TO 4 INCHES DEEP. BRING THE OIL UP TO 350°F OVER MEDIUM-HIGH HEAT.

DRY THE POTATOES THOROUGHLY WITH A KITCHEN TOWEL. TOSS THEM IN THE CORNSTARCH OR RICE FLOUR AND SPRINKLE WITH SALT.

ONCE THE OIL REACHES 350°F, ADD THE POTATOES IN 2 TO 3 BATCHES. FRY THE POTATOES IN THE OIL FOR 3 TO 5 MINUTES UNTIL GOLDEN AND CRISPY.

REMOVE THE COOKED FRIES FROM THE OIL USING A SLOTTED SPOON AND TRANSFER TO A PAPER TOWEL—LINED BAKING SHEET. SPREAD THEM IN A SINGLE LAYER AND TOSS WITH MORE SALT TO TASTE. REPEAT WITH THE REMAINING BATCHES 'TIL ALL THE FRIES ARE COOKED.

IF YOU LIKE YOUR FRIES EXTRA CRUNCHY, LET THEM COOL TO ROOM TEMPERATURE THEN FRY THEM ONE MORE TIME 'TIL THEY ARE A DARKER GOLDEN BROWN.

DIVIDE THE FRIES BETWEEN 4 SERVING PLATES. SPRINKLE ½ CUP OF THE CHEESE CURDS OVER EACH SERVING AND TOSS WITH THE HOT POTATOES. LADLE THE HOT GRAVY OVER EVERYTHING AND ALLOW THE CHEESE TO MELT FOR A FEW MINUTES. GARNISH WITH CHIVES AND SERVE HOT!

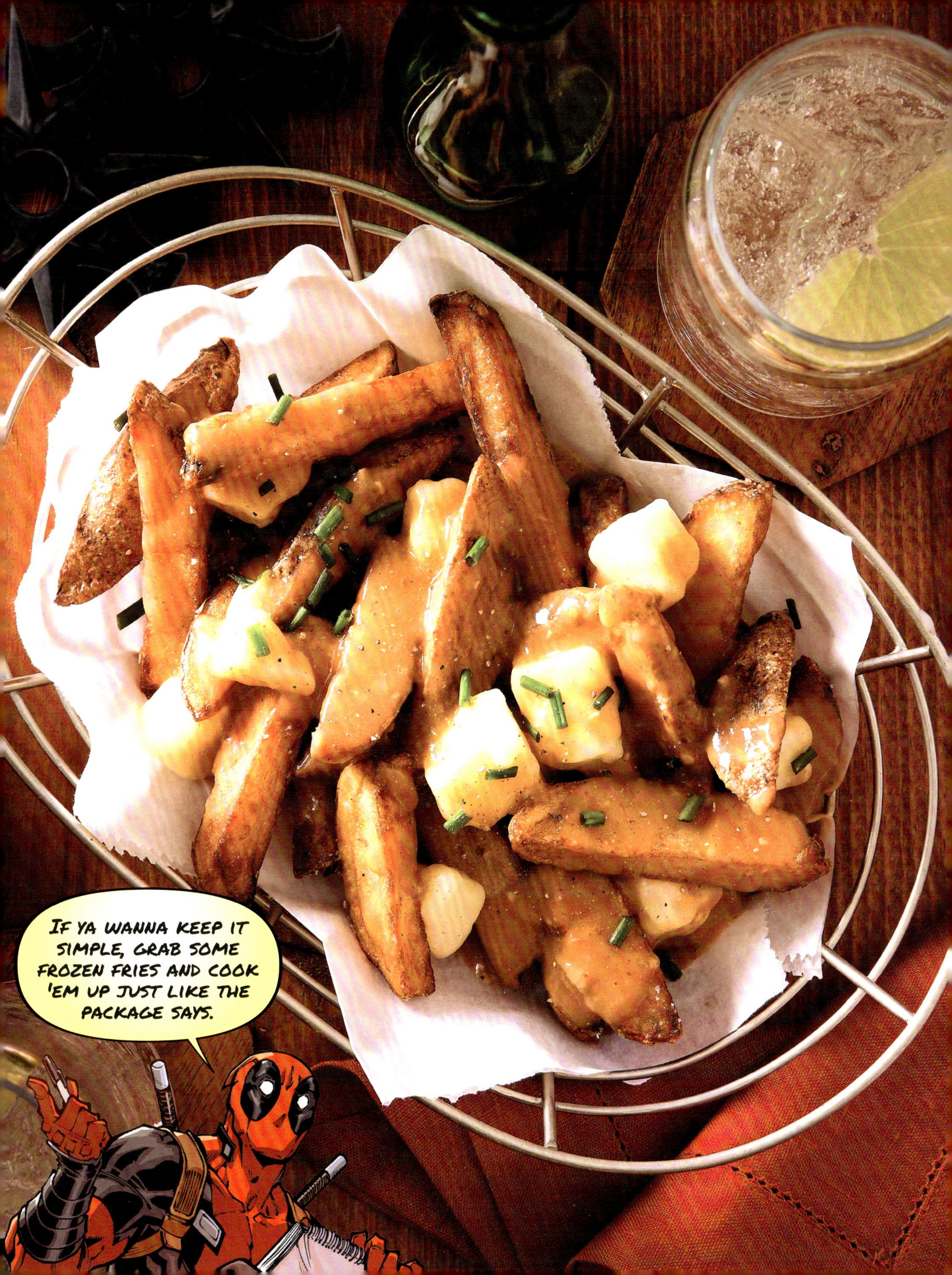
IF YA WANNA KEEP IT SIMPLE, GRAB SOME FROZEN FRIES AND COOK 'EM UP JUST LIKE THE PACKAGE SAYS.

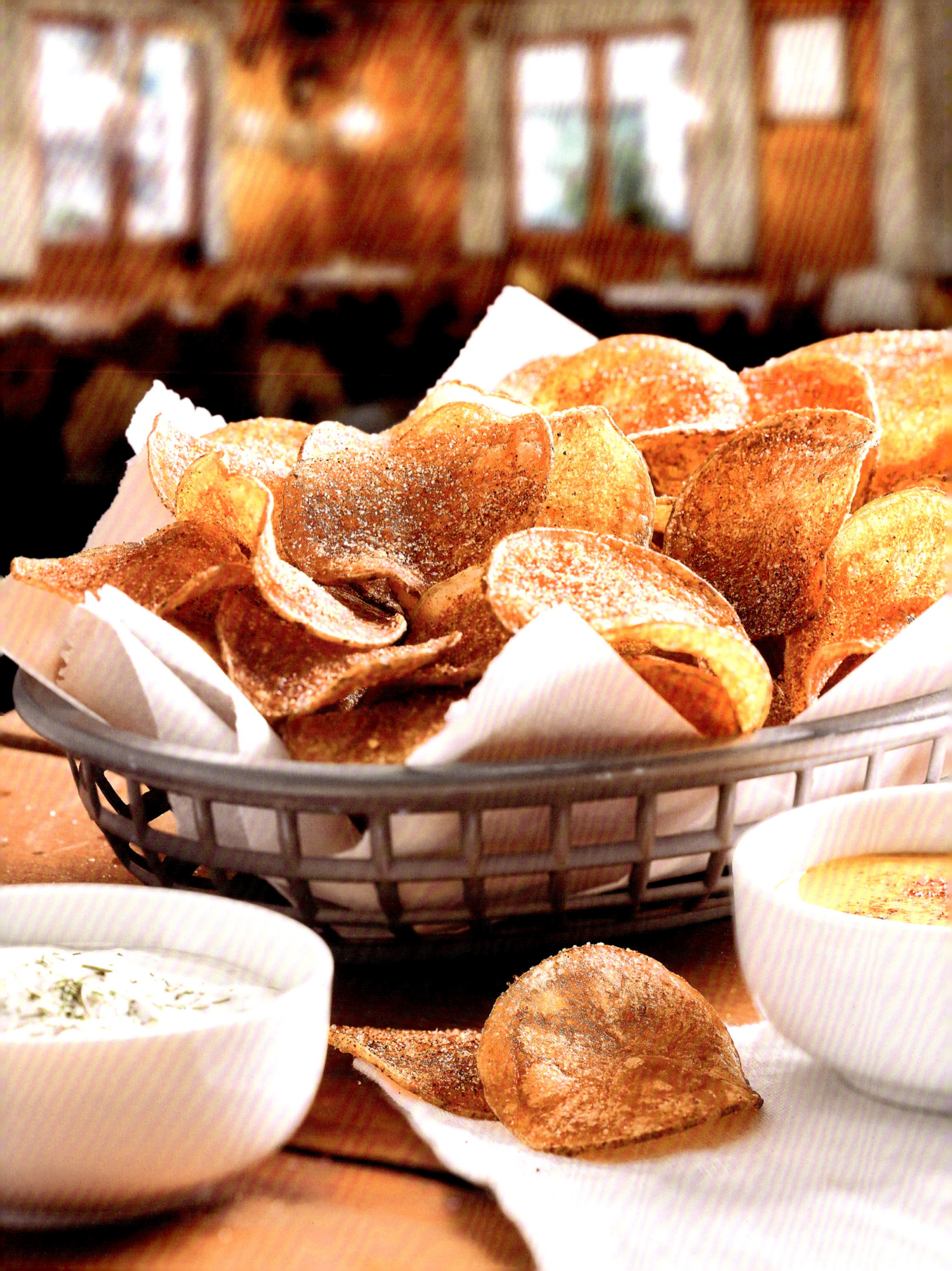

# ALL-DRESSED CHIPS

I'll just say it: there are a few all-time greats from home that just don't turn up much in the States. Two in particular go hand-in-hand: this style of 'tater chips and Alpha Flight's own bite-sized brawler, Puck. The team's had plenty of good eggs in the pack, but me and Eugene Judd have always been particularly *simpatico*. Two under-average stature Canadians who spent their over-average lifespans as mercs, world-travelers, and super-folk. We've had plenty to bond about over plenty of meals. Anytime he can, Puck balances out his stories with big bowls of these Canadian-style super-seasoned crispy spuds. The few times I can lure my buddy to visit, I gotta make 'em myself—so bust out the sharp mustard and onion powders, earthy paprika seasoning, plus garlic, cayenne, and vinegar for kick. Might as well make a double batch—us little guys got big appetites. Just don't call us that to our faces …

**Servings: 4 to 6 • Type: Snack • Difficulty: Average • Prep Time: 30 minutes**
**Cook Time: 40 minutes • Rest Time: 30 minutes • Dietary Considerations: GF, V, V+**

### FOR THE ALL-DRESSED SEASONING:

1 teaspoon smoked paprika

2 teaspoons sweet paprika

1 teaspoon garlic powder

1 teaspoon onion powder

1 teaspoon mustard powder

2 teaspoons milk powder or nutritional yeast

½ teaspoon citric acid or 1 teaspoon vinegar powder, or to taste

2 teaspoons granulated sugar

Pinch of cayenne, optional

### FOR THE CHIPS:

4 medium russet or 4 large yellow potatoes, peeling optional

Neutral oil, such as peanut oil, for greasing or frying

### SPECIAL EQUIPMENT:

Air fryer, optional

Cooling rack or paper-lined plate

**TO MAKE THE ALL-DRESSED SEASONING:** Mix the paprikas, powders, sugar, and cayenne in a small bowl. Set aside.

**TO MAKE THE CHIPS:** Fill a medium mixing bowl halfway with ice and water. Slice the potatoes as thin as possible. It's fastest and easiest to use a mandolin for this, if you've got one, but it can be done with a sharp knife and some patience. After the potatoes are cut, toss them immediately into the ice water. Keep them in the ice water bath for at least 30 minutes, or overnight.

After at least 30 minutes, rinse the potato slices in a colander and shake off as much water as possible. Arrange the slices in a single layer on a towel–lined surface. Pat the chips dry with another clean towel.

If you have an air fryer, this is the best option for chips at home—less potential for sogginess. Preheat your air fryer to 325°F and spray both the chips and the basket with oil. Spread the chips evenly in the basket, no more than two layers deep at a time. Air fry for 20 minutes, tossing every 5 to 7 minutes 'til crisp and golden. Remove any chips that finish early and repeat 'til all the chips are fried.

If frying the chips in oil, heat 2 inches of oil in a large, deep skillet 'til it reaches 350°F to 375°F. Working in batches, add the potato slices to hot oil in one layer and cook for 3 to 4 minutes, stirring occasionally with a slotted spoon, 'til they begin to brown slightly and crisp up.

Transfer the chips to a cooling rack or paper towel–lined plate. While the chips are still hot, sprinkle them evenly with the seasoning powder on both sides. You could also put them in a big mixing bowl and toss them in the seasoning.

Serve immediately or store in an airtight container at room temperature.

# JAPANESE-STYLE HOT DOG

Not too long ago I was up in Vancouver helpin' Maverick with a ghost from our Cold War mercenary days on "Team X," and we were struck by just how much had changed. Where I remember wooden shacks sellin' beaver-pelt boot liners and fresh-cut venison, there were now towering office buildings and storefronts filled with cellphones and every kind of international grub a belly could hope for. One offerin' that caught our eyes were street carts serving Japanese-style hot dogs. This recipe particularly hit the spot: a mix of spicy, sweet, and tart on top of juicy beef. But they've got all kinds of flavors, ingredients, and techniques—from sushi, tempura, nimono, you name it—transforming the ol' street meat. Me and Nord couldn't help but relate, the way mixin' it up around the world has changed these old dogs—I think for the better.

**Servings: 5 • Type: Sandwich • Difficulty: Easy • Prep Time: 10 minutes**
**Cook Time: 30 minutes • Rest Time: None • Dietary Considerations: V***
**Pairs well with:** *All-Dressed Chips* (pg 97), *Tornado Potato* (pg 80)

2 tablespoons unsalted butter

1 large yellow onion, thinly sliced

1 tablespoon wasabi paste

4 hot dogs (your favorite kind, see Note)

4 hot dog buns

10 small, seasoned nori sheets (like from a nori snack pack, optional)

¼ cup Japanese-style mayonnaise

¼ cup katsu sauce (pg 60), okonomiyaki sauce (pg 116), or teriyaki sauce

2 green onions, shredded or sliced on a bias

4 tablespoons pickled ginger and/or finely chopped *Pickled Daikon* (pg 111)

Furikake and/or shichimi togarashi, optional or to taste

Melt the butter in a large skillet over medium-high heat. Add the onions and sauté 'til tender and semi-translucent, about 5 minutes, then add the wasabi paste and stir to coat the onions. Continue to sauté for 8 to 10 minutes 'til the onions have browned. If you like your onions caramelized, cook them on low heat for 40 to 50 minutes 'til caramelized. Remove the onions from the heat and set aside.

Cook the hot dogs using your preferred method (boiling, broiling, grilling) and keep them warm 'til you're ready to assemble. Lightly grill the hot dog buns facing down or toast them in a toaster oven.

Line each hot dog bun with 2 strips of nori. Spread the onions evenly along the bottom of the buns. Place a cooked hot dog in each bun, sprinkle it with pickled ginger or chopped pickled daikon, then drizzle generously with mayonnaise and katsu sauce.

Sprinkle the hot dogs with green onions and furikake and/or shichimi togarashi to taste.

*Note: This recipe can be made vegetarian if you use meatless hot dogs.*

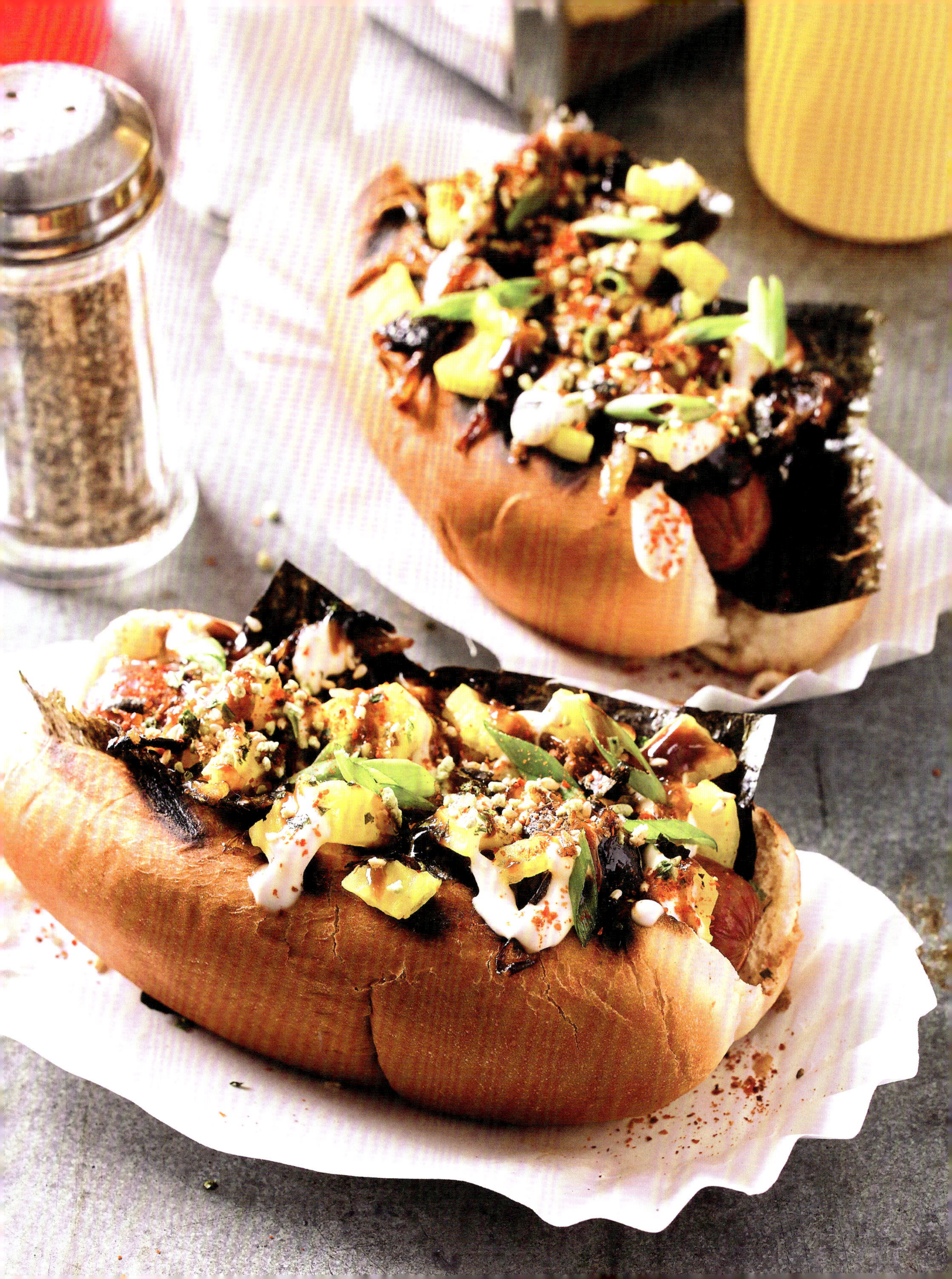

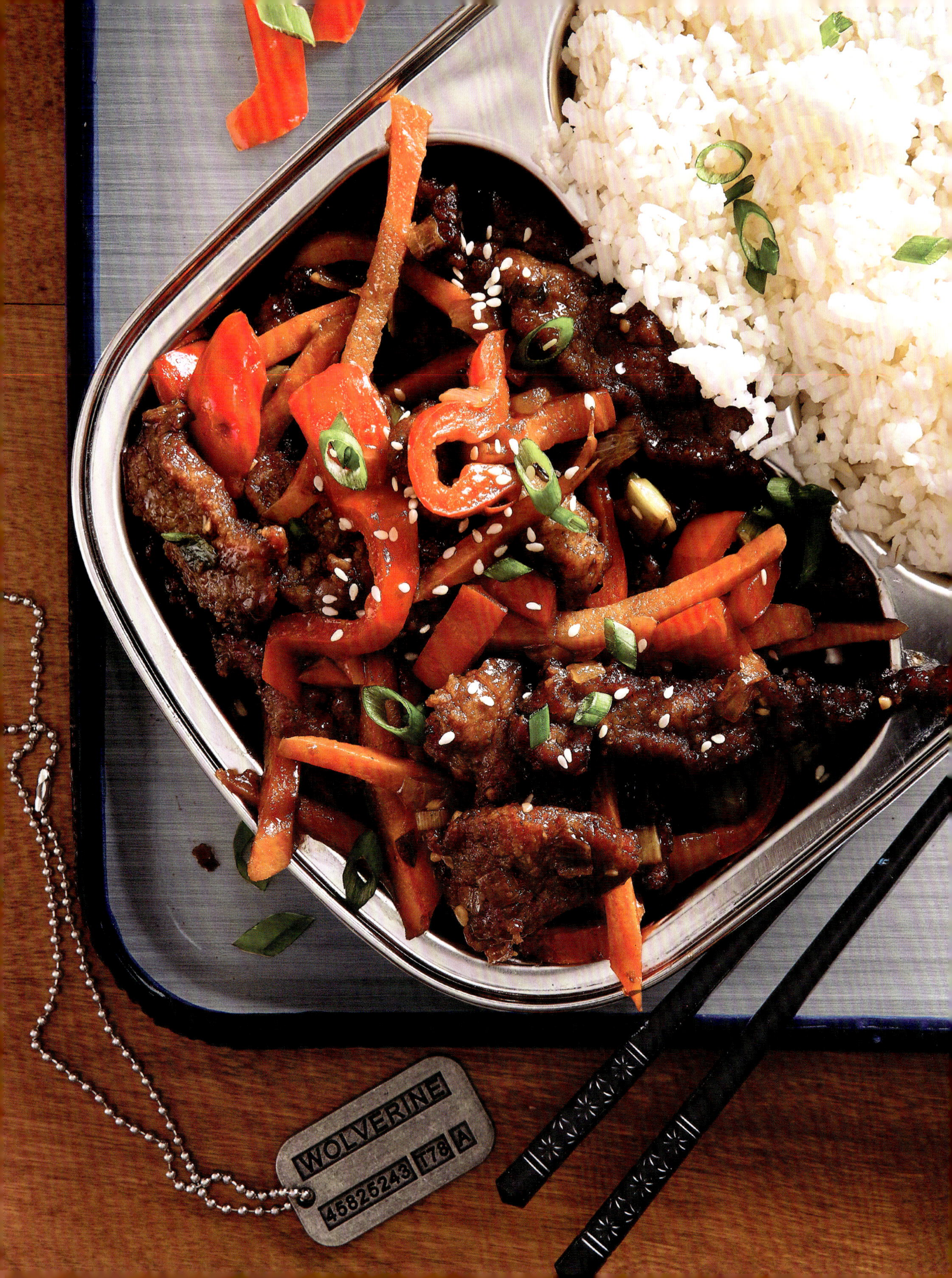
WOLVERINE
45825243 T78 A

# GINGER BEEF

Some days you just want a meal from back home that tastes exactly how you remember it. So, when I'm in Canada, this is the savory, full-flavor meal I order up immediately. It takes the kind of beef-rice-vegetable formula that I remember of utilitarian meals from certain Intelligence mess halls—'cept it combines Chinese-style cooking with a special, sweet sauce straight outta Alberta. This is what I eat when I want to take it all in: I'm not under mind control, takin' orders, or being manipulated by some master villain—just a man from Canada with a past I'm learnin' to make peace with.

**Servings: 4 • Type: Main • Difficulty: Average • Prep Time: 20 minutes**
**Cook Time: 30 minutes • Rest Time: None**

1 pound skirt steak or flank steak

1 teaspoon baking soda

1 cup cornstarch or tapioca starch

Neutral oil, such as canola or peanut oil, divided, for frying

1 large white onion, finely chopped

4 cloves garlic, minced

2 medium carrots, julienned

1 red or green bell pepper, sliced

1 bird's eye chile, sliced (or use red pepper flakes, to taste)

2-inch piece fresh ginger, minced or grated

4 green onions, thinly sliced, light and green parts separated

¼ cup low-sodium soy sauce, or to taste

2 tablespoons Chinese red vinegar, black vinegar, or rice vinegar

1 tablespoon toasted sesame oil

½ teaspoon black pepper

½ cup dark brown sugar, packed

1 tablespoon sesame seeds, plus more for garnish

Steamed rice, for serving, optional

Sprinkle the steak all over with the baking soda and pound it thoroughly using the spiky side of a meat tenderizer. Cut the steak into thin strips and toss the strips in the cornstarch. Set aside.

Heat 2 tablespoons of the oil in a wok or large cast-iron skillet over medium-high heat. Add the onions and sauté for 2 minutes 'til translucent. Add the garlic, carrots, bell pepper, and chile. Sauté for another 3 to 4 minutes 'til the veggies are slightly tender. Add the ginger and the white parts and most of the green part of the green onion, stirring them into the veggies and cooking for another 1 to 2 minutes.

Add the soy sauce, vinegar, sesame oil, black pepper, brown sugar, and sesame seeds, stirring everything together thoroughly. Reduce the heat to very low and let the sauce reduce slightly while you fry the beef.

Meanwhile, in a separate wok or cast-iron skillet, heat 1 inch of oil to 350°F to 375°F. Shake off any excess cornstarch from the beef, then fry the pieces in batches 'til crispy, about 3 to 4 minutes per batch. Transfer the fried beef pieces to a paper towel–lined plate or other surface to drain.

Once all the beef has been fried, add it into the sauce mixture and toss to coat. Garnish with the remaining green onions and serve immediately.

ON THE ROAD: STREET EATS AND TAVERN BITES

# NANAIMO BARS

This is a recipe I almost lost for good—and found again in the middle of Scarlet Witch's chaos magic. When she reshaped reality, makin' the "House of M" for "proud papa" Magneto to rule, she managed to put back all the stuff scrambled up in my head and unlock some real memories of my own past. One bit of sweetness, amid the tragedy of my early years, was a rare time my momma seemed to come out of her withdrawn state to bake up a special surprise. Bein' before my mutation kicked in, senses weren't what they are now. But when this recipe got popular through Canada mid-century, it felt like I got back whatever it was I savored all those years earlier. Densely layered with nuttiness, lightness, and darker tones—but all together sweet. Just like life, when you can look back at it.

**Yield:** 9 to 16 bars • **Type:** Dessert • **Difficulty:** Average • **Prep Time:** 40 minutes
**Cook Time:** None • **Rest Time:** 2 hours • **Dietary Considerations:** V

### FOR THE BASE COOKIE LAYER:

- ¾ cup unsalted butter
- ¼ cup granulated sugar
- 6 tablespoons unsweetened cocoa powder
- ½ teaspoon salt
- 1 large egg, lightly beaten
- 2 cups graham cracker crumbs
- ½ cup shredded coconut
- ½ cup crushed walnuts or almonds

### FOR THE MIDDLE CUSTARD LAYER:

- ½ cup unsalted butter, softened
- ¼ cup heavy cream, or more if needed
- 2 heaping tablespoons vanilla custard powder or vanilla pudding mix
- 2 cups powdered sugar, or more if needed
- Pinch of salt

### FOR THE CHOCOLATE TOPPING:

- 1¼ cup semi-sweet chocolate chips
- ½ cup unsalted butter

Line an 8-by-8-inch baking dish with parchment paper, letting some parchment overhang on the sides. You'll use this to lift the bars out later.

**TO MAKE THE BASE COOKIE LAYER:** Melt the butter in a double boiler or a saucepan over medium-low heat. Add in the sugar, cocoa powder, and salt and mix well. Slowly add in the beaten egg and stir 'til the mixture thickens.

Take the mixture off the heat and stir in the graham cracker crumbs, shredded coconut, and crushed nuts 'til well-combined.

Firmly press the mixture into the bottom of the prepared baking dish, using the bottom of a cup if needed. It should fill about half the pan. Chill in the fridge while you prepare the middle layer.

**TO MAKE THE MIDDLE CUSTARD LAYER:** In a large mixing bowl, cream together the butter, heavy cream, custard powder (or pudding mix), powdered sugar, and salt, using a stand mixer or hand mixer. Whip 'til pale and fluffy. The texture should be thick yet smooth, spreadable but firm enough to hold its shape, like a thick custard or pudding. Add more cream, a teaspoon at a time, if the mixture is too thick, or more powdered sugar if it's too runny.

Spread the middle layer evenly over the cooled bottom layer. Chill in the freezer for 20 to 30 minutes before you make the top layer.

**TO MAKE THE CHOCOLATE TOPPING:** Microwave the chocolate chips and butter in a microwave-safe bowl, heating in 20-second intervals and stirring between each, 'til smooth and shiny.

Spread the chocolate mixture evenly over the chilled middle layer. Place the dish in the fridge to set for 1 to 2 hours.

Once set, lift the whole dessert out of the pan using the overhanging parchment paper. Cut into bars (9 to 16 squares) with a sharp knife, wiping the blade between cuts.

Store in an airtight container in the refrigerator for up to 1 week or freeze for up to 2 months. Let bars come to room temperature before serving.

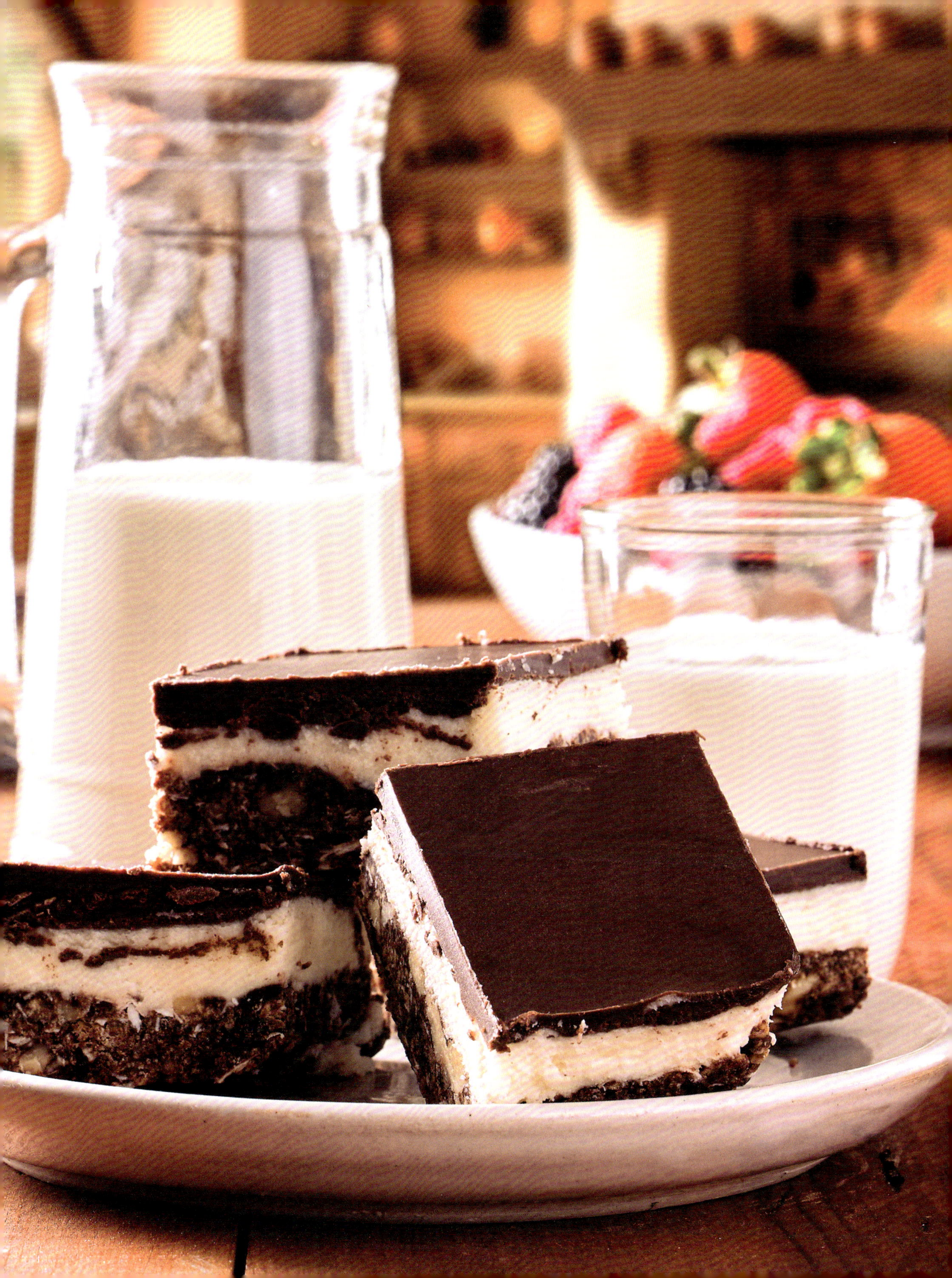

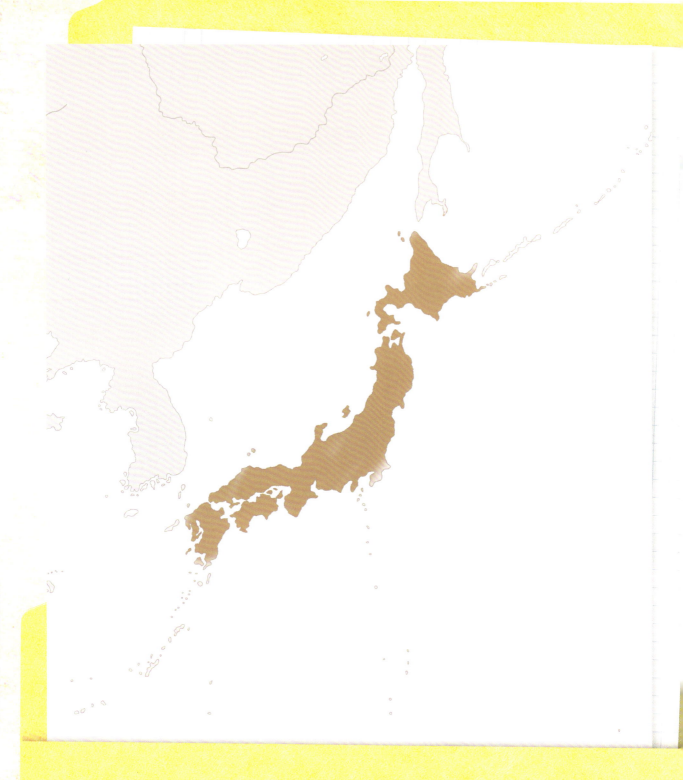

ON THE ROAD: STREET EATS AND TAVERN BITES

# FROM TIME SPENT IN
# JAPAN

## HOW TO
# JAPANESE CONVENIENCE FOOD

When you're out on the road, convenience stores are your best friend. They're always there for you when you need a quick bite, a caffeine boost, or just a break from the drive. But not all of 'em are cut from the same cloth. And let me tell you, the ones you find in Japan, called konbini, do it right.

**ABOUT KONBINI:** These ain't your average convenience stores. They've turned grab-and-go grub into a fine art. Loaded with fresh, top-notch eats, they've often got Wi-Fi, ATMs, and printers, too.

Tips to remember:
- If you want something hot, you can ask the staff there to microwave your food. The phrase is "Atatamete moraemasu ka?" It means, "Can you heat this up for me?" Comes in handy if you aren't lucky enough to be travelin' with Idie Okonkwo.
- Don't forget to grab a chopstick or spoon, at least if you want to keep your claws clean. These are usually kept by the register. If they're not within reach, you can try this with the clerk: "Ohashi o kudasai." It means, "Please give me chopsticks."
- You can chow down on your meal inside, if you see a chair. If not, it's okay and even common to crouch and eat right outside. My kinda place!

## HOW TO
# HOLDIN' CHOPSTICKS

Here's how you handle chopsticks whether you're out in the wild or at some fancy sushi joint. Once you get the hang of it, you'll be grabbin' everything from noodles to steak like a pro. You can even use them for cooking your food, they're great for stirring or you can use 'em like tongs.

Start with one chopstick resting in the crook of your thumb, lettin' it balance on your ring finger. This chopstick stays steady, doesn't move—think of it like an anchor.

Now take the second chopstick like you're gripping a pencil, positioning it between your thumb, index, and middle finger. This is the one that does the heavy lifting.

Move the top chopstick to pinch your food between the two. Once you get that motion down, you can snatch up anything—slippery noodles, thick cuts of steak, doesn't matter, you'll be handling chopsticks like they're an extension of your own claws.

*One thing to keep in mind: You'll find chopsticks in plastic, porcelain, bamboo, palmwood, and stainless steel—it all depends on where in the world you're dinin'. You might say they work the same way. 'Course you might also say bone and adamantium-*bonded* bone work the same way. But you don't want to come out on the wrong end of things if you misjudge the weight …

# TOMAGO SANDO

Y'ever take care of a kid, it's your job to make sure they eat. I learned that one *years* back, when Kitty Pryde hauled me to Tokyo to save her pops from Yakuza trouble. She couldn't have been more than a teen then and as worried as I'd ever seen her. Too upset to eat. 'Course, you ever take care of a teen, you learn they don't tend to like help when you offer it directly. So, I ordered up a Tomago Sando for myself, knowin' Kitty would like it. A konbini classic, soft and fluffy, with an extra creamy savory-sweet egg salad. I mean, right? Instead of offering her any, I just chowed down. Eventually, the Kitten got famished enough to sneak a bite of my lunch. The sandwich calmed her nerves and hit the spot. 'Course, then it was all she wanted to eat for days.

**Yield: 2 sandwiches • Type: Sandwich • Difficulty: Easy • Prep Time: 15 minutes • Cook Time: 10 minutes • Rest Time: 15 minutes • Dietary Considerations: V**
**Pairs well with:** *All-Dressed Chips* (pg 97)

6 large eggs

3 tablespoons Japanese-style mayonnaise

1 teaspoon milk

¾ teaspoon granulated sugar

½ teaspoon salt

¼ teaspoon finely ground black pepper

1 tablespoon unsalted butter

4 slices shokupan or another thick fluffy white bread, crusts trimmed

Set a pot of water to boil. Prepare an ice bath in a medium mixing bowl. Once the water is boiling, gently add the eggs. Remove 2 of the eggs after 7 minutes and put them in the ice bath. After a minute, transfer them to a separate small bowl, so they don't get confused with the other eggs. Transfer the other 4 eggs to the ice bath after 9 to 10 minutes (total) of boiling, or 2 to 3 minutes after the first 2 eggs were removed.

Unshell the 4 hard-boiled eggs from the second batch and separate the yolks from the whites. Thoroughly mash the yolks with a fork. Chop the egg whites to your desired thickness.

Add the yolks, whites, mayonnaise, milk, sugar, salt, and black pepper to a small mixing bowl and stir to combine.

Lay out 2 slices of the bread and spread each slice with half of the butter. Cut one of the soft-boiled (7 minutes) eggs in half lengthwise and place the halves face down onto the center of one piece of bread, either diagonally or horizontally depending on how you plan to cut the sandwich. Add half the egg salad on top of the eggs and spread it on top of the eggs and around the bread. Place the other bread slice on top and gently push down.

Place the sandwich on a long piece of plastic wrap and cover it tightly, pressing down firmly but gently to seal. If you want, use a sharpie to mark a line where to cut (wherever the eggs are placed). Repeat this step for the other sandwich, using the remaining bread, egg, and egg salad.

Let the sandwiches rest for at least 15 minutes in the refrigerator, up to overnight, then slice the egg sandwich in the same direction as the soft-boiled eggs and dig in.

# RAMEN NOODLES FROM SCRATCH

Making ramen noodles from scratch ain't for the faint of heart, but if you're up for the challenge, the payoff's worth every minute. You'll get noodles with a good bite and a flavor that'll take your ramen game to the next level. Traditional ramen noodles use an alkaline solution called kansui, but you can just use some baking soda mixed with warm water.

### Servings: 2 to 3

2 cups all-purpose flour

1 teaspoon kansui or 2 teaspoons baking soda

½ cup warm water

1 teaspoon salt

Mix the baking soda or kansui into the warm water 'til fully incorporated. This mixture created an alkaline water that gives the noodles their classic chewy texture.

In a large bowl, combine the flour and salt. Gradually add the alkaline water, stirring 'til the mixture starts to come together. If the dough is too dry, add regular water a tablespoon at a time 'til it's just moist enough to hold together. The dough should be a bit crumbly but manageable.

Dump it onto a floured surface and knead for 8 to 10 minutes 'til you've got a smooth, elastic dough that doesn't stick.

Cover the dough with plastic wrap or a damp towel and let it rest for 1 hour.

Roll out the dough on a floured surface to about ⅛ inch thick. Use a sharp knife or pasta cutter to slice the dough into thin strips, approximately ⅛ inch wide.

Bring a large pot of water to a rolling boil. Boil the noodle strips for 2 to 3 minutes, or 'til tender but still slightly firm.

Drain the noodles and rinse briefly under cold water to stop the cooking process and remove excess starch.

Use immediately or store in an airtight container or zip-lock bag in the refrigerator for up to 3 days or in the freezer for up to 1 month.

# GAIJIN'S RAMEN

Okay, Logan:

I told you I was taking mental notes of your culinary prowess in Japan. But after tasting your signature savory chicken ramen, I really needed to jot it all down. One change: no way I'm gonna make my own noodles from scratch. But I admit, it's extra impressive when you do.

Yukio said that some folks refer to you as the gaijin. But that even if you are a foreigner, you show respect for the traditions, the food, even the people (as much as you respect anybody, I guess) in Japan. I like that about you. And I like that it feels like home wherever we sit down to a meal together. With that in mind, I wanted to make sure you preserve your ramen recipe. So ... how'd I do?

Xo Kitty

Servings: 2 to 3 • Type: Soup/Stew • Difficulty: Average • Prep Time: 20 minutes

Cook Time: 40 minutes • Rest Time: None • Pairs well with: Pickled Daikon (pg 111)

2 to 3 large eggs

3 chicken thighs, deboned with skin on, or use boneless skinless chicken thighs

2 teaspoons salt, divided, or to taste

½ teaspoon pepper, or to taste

1 tablespoon unsalted butter

1 tablespoon sesame oil

4 cloves garlic, minced

1-inch piece fresh ginger, peeled and minced

6 green onions, sliced on a bias, white and green parts separated

1 teaspoon Mutant Medley (pg 30), or to taste

2 tablespoons soy sauce

3 tablespoons mirin

1 to 2 teaspoons toasted sesame oil

5 to 6 cups chicken broth

1 ounce dried or 1 cup fresh shiitake mushrooms

6 ounces dried ramen noodles or 16 ounces fresh (pg 107)

Shichimi togarashi and/or crunchy garlic chile oil, to serve, optional

Fill a pot with enough water to cover the eggs and bring it to a boil over medium-high heat. Carefully lower the eggs into the boiling water with a slotted spoon or a pair of tongs, and simmer for 7 minutes for a slightly runny yolk, or 8 minutes for a jammy yolk. While the eggs cook, prepare an ice bath by filling a large bowl with ice water. As soon as the eggs are done, transfer them immediately to the ice bath. When they are cool enough to handle, peel them and slice them in half lengthwise. Set aside.

Season the chicken with 1 teaspoon of the salt and pepper to taste. In a Dutch oven or large pot, melt the butter over medium heat. Place the chicken skin-side down in the skillet and cook for 5 to 7 minutes, 'til nicely browned on the bottom. Flip the chicken and cook for another 4 to 5 minutes 'til the other side is golden and the chicken is cooked through with no pink remaining in the center. Remove from the pot and set aside.

In the same pot, heat the sesame oil over medium heat 'til it shimmers. Add the garlic, ginger, the white part of the green onion and most of the green parts (save some for topping). Season with Mutant Medley and cook 'til softened, about 2 to 3 minutes. Stir in the soy sauce, mirin, and sesame oil and let it cook for another 1 minute. Scrape any remaining browned bits from the bottom of the pot.

Pour in the chicken stock, add the mushrooms, cover the pot, and bring it to a boil. Turn heat to medium-low and continue simmering for another 8 to 12 minutes 'til the mushrooms are done to your liking. Season the broth with more salt and Mutant Medley to taste.

Cook the noodles according to the package or recipe directions. While the noodles cook, slice the chicken and the mushrooms (assuming they are not already sliced) into thin strips.

Divide the noodles between 2 large bowls. Arrange the sliced chicken and mushrooms on top of the noodles, ladle the ramen broth over, and garnish with the remaining green onions, the soft-boiled egg halves, and shichimi togarashi or chile oil. Serve hot.

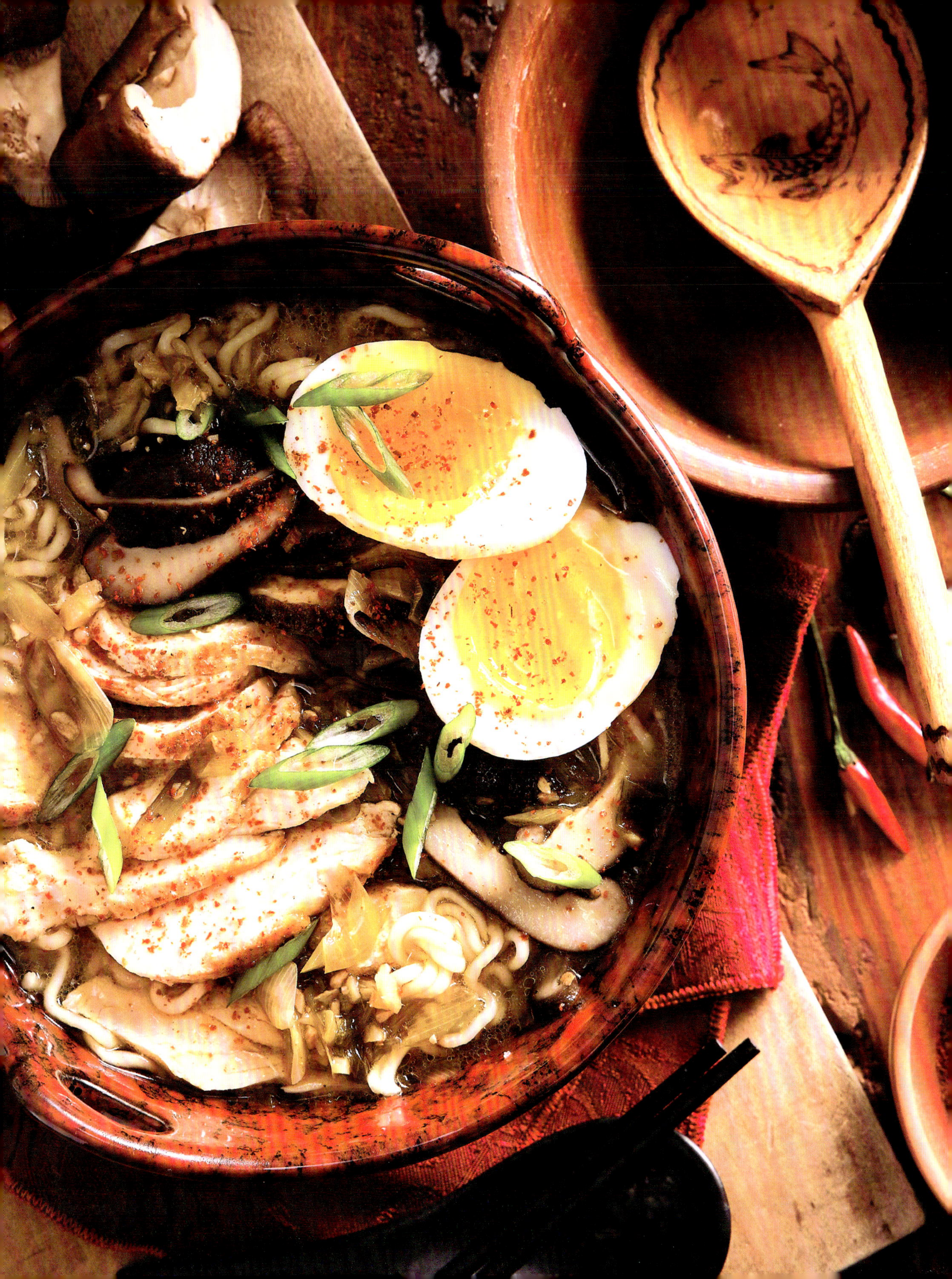

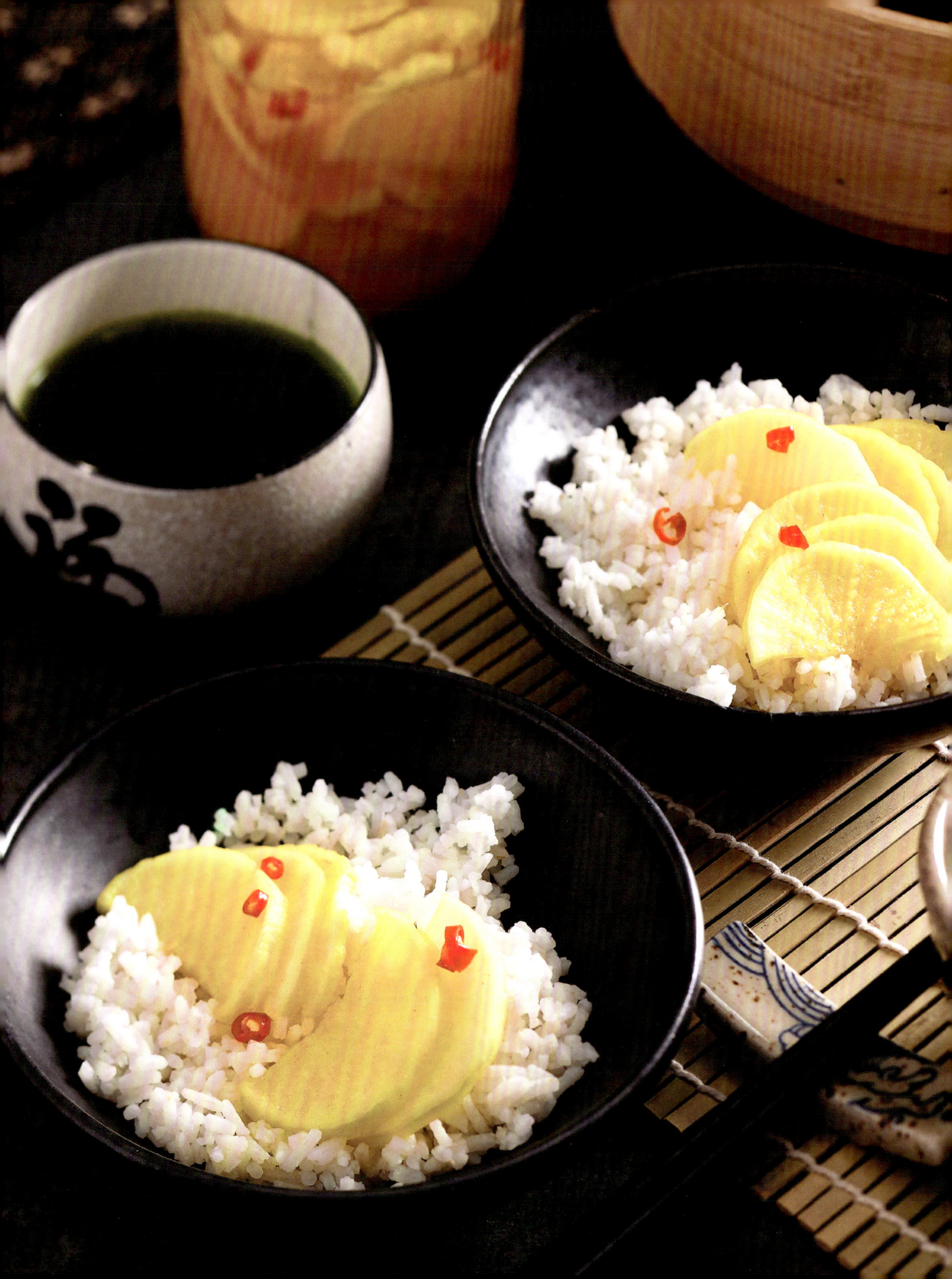

# PICKLED DAIKON

Pickled daikon radish turns up all across Japan. But when you go skulkin' through the dicier parts of Tokyo, and catch its scent mixed with gun oil and fresh-poked tattoos, you're in Yakuza territory. Not sure if those gangster boys got a side hustle making the stuff, or if they just buy it in bulk for the clubhouse. But just like their slightly sweet / slightly tangy snack, this flavor of trouble comes all kinds of ways—on their own or in support of something bigger. (And for me, at least, both go down just as easy.)

**Servings:** 8 to 12 • **Type:** Snack/Condiment • **Difficulty:** Easy • **Prep Time:** 10 minutes • **Cook Time:** 10 minutes • **Rest Time:** 24 hours • **Dietary Considerations:** GF, V, V+

**Pairs well with:** *Japanese-Style Hot Dog* (pg 98), *Kuzuri Na Kushikatsu* (pg 60)

½ medium daikon radish, peeled

2 teaspoons salt

⅔ cup rice vinegar

2 tablespoons mirin

1½ cups granulated sugar

2 teaspoons turmeric, for color, optional

1 bird's eye chile pepper, sliced, optional or to taste

Cut the daikon in half lengthwise, then slice it crosswise into half-moon slices about ¼ inch thick.

Add the daikon to a large colander and sprinkle it with the salt and toss them to evenly coat in the salt. Let brine for 2 to 4 hours. They will be too salty after this, and that's good, with the vinegar and sugar marinade, everything will even out.

In a small saucepan, add the vinegar, mirin, and sugar. Bring the mixture to a low simmer over medium heat. As soon as all the sugar has dissolved, turn the heat off, whisk in the turmeric, and let it cool to room temperature.

After the daikon has brined, drain and squeeze out the excess water. Add the daikon and the sliced chile to 2 mason jars or other sealable glass containers.

Pour the vinegar mixture over the daikon slices in the jar. Seal the jar, shake to make sure all of the daikon is in the brine.

Refrigerate overnight or up to 72 hours before serving. Goes great with fried foods!

# SALMON MAYO ONIGIRI

Salmon, rice, mayo—could easily be ingredients for a dish back in Canada. But all balled up with vinegar and seaweed finishings—the stuff I knew gets transformed into a Japanese stalwart. Those necromancing ninjas, the Hand, tried to re-mold yours truly into their attack dog pretty much the same way. ('Cept with demonic magic and mind control instead of the earthy-salty tang of furikake.) At least after my friends got me straightened out, I got to enjoy a few of these on my revenge tour.

**Servings: 6 • Type: Snack • Difficulty: Easy • Prep Time: 15 minutes • Cook Time: None • Rest Time: None • Dietary Considerations: GF**

6 ounces canned or leftover cooked salmon

2 to 3 tablespoons Japanese-style mayo

2 to 3 teaspoons sriracha hot sauce, optional or to taste

3 cups steamed short-grain rice, cooled

2 tablespoons rice vinegar

2 tablespoons mirin

3 small seasoned nori sheets, cut lengthwise

3 to 4 tablespoons furikake and/or shichimi togarashi, to taste

If your fish has bones and skin, remove as much of that as you can.

In a small mixing bowl, flake the salmon into small pieces using a fork. Add the mayo and sriracha sauce and mix 'til well-combined. Add more mayo and hot sauce to taste, just make sure it doesn't get so wet it won't hold together.

In a separate medium mixing bowl, add the rice, vinegar, and mirin. Fold 'til well-combined.

With wet hands, take a handful of the seasoned rice and place it in your palm. Create a well in the center for the filling. Add about a tablespoon of the filling into the well. Encase the filling with the rice and shape it into a thick triangle-shape with your hands, wetting them as necessary. You can also do this with an onigiri mold. Fill the molds halfway with the rice, then create a well in the centers. Spoon the salmon filling inside each, packing it in as much as possible. Add the rest of the rice on top, then press the mold according to the manufacturer's instructions.

Take a strip of nori and wrap it around the bottom center of the onigiri. The strip of nori not only adds flavor, it acts as a barrier between your fingers and the sticky rice while you eat.

Add a generous amount of furikake to a plate or shallow bowl. Lightly press the sides of the onigiri into the furikake. Repeat 'til you have 6 onigiri.

Wrap extras tightly in plastic wrap and store in the fridge, pull them out whenever you want a quick satisfying snack.

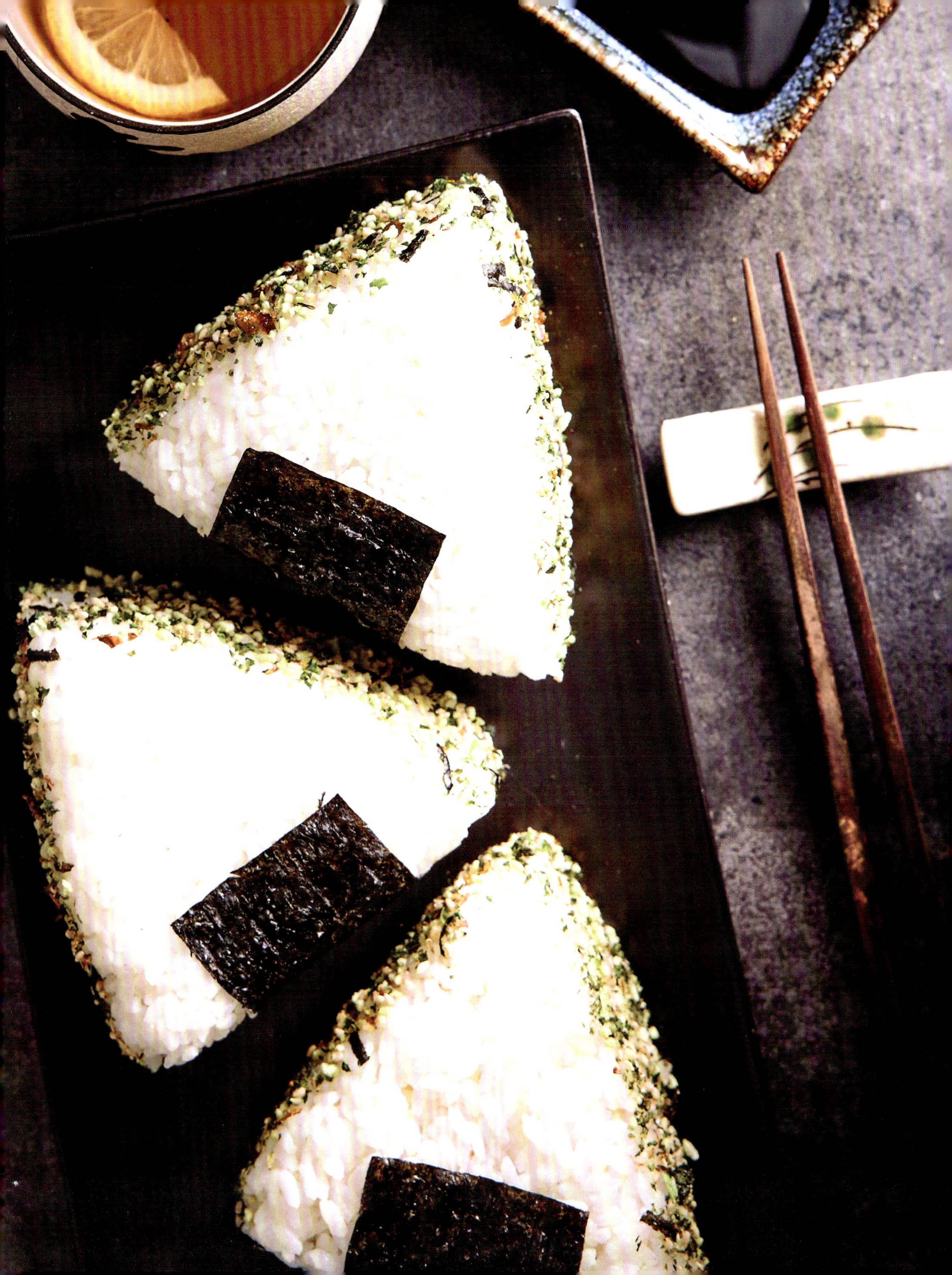

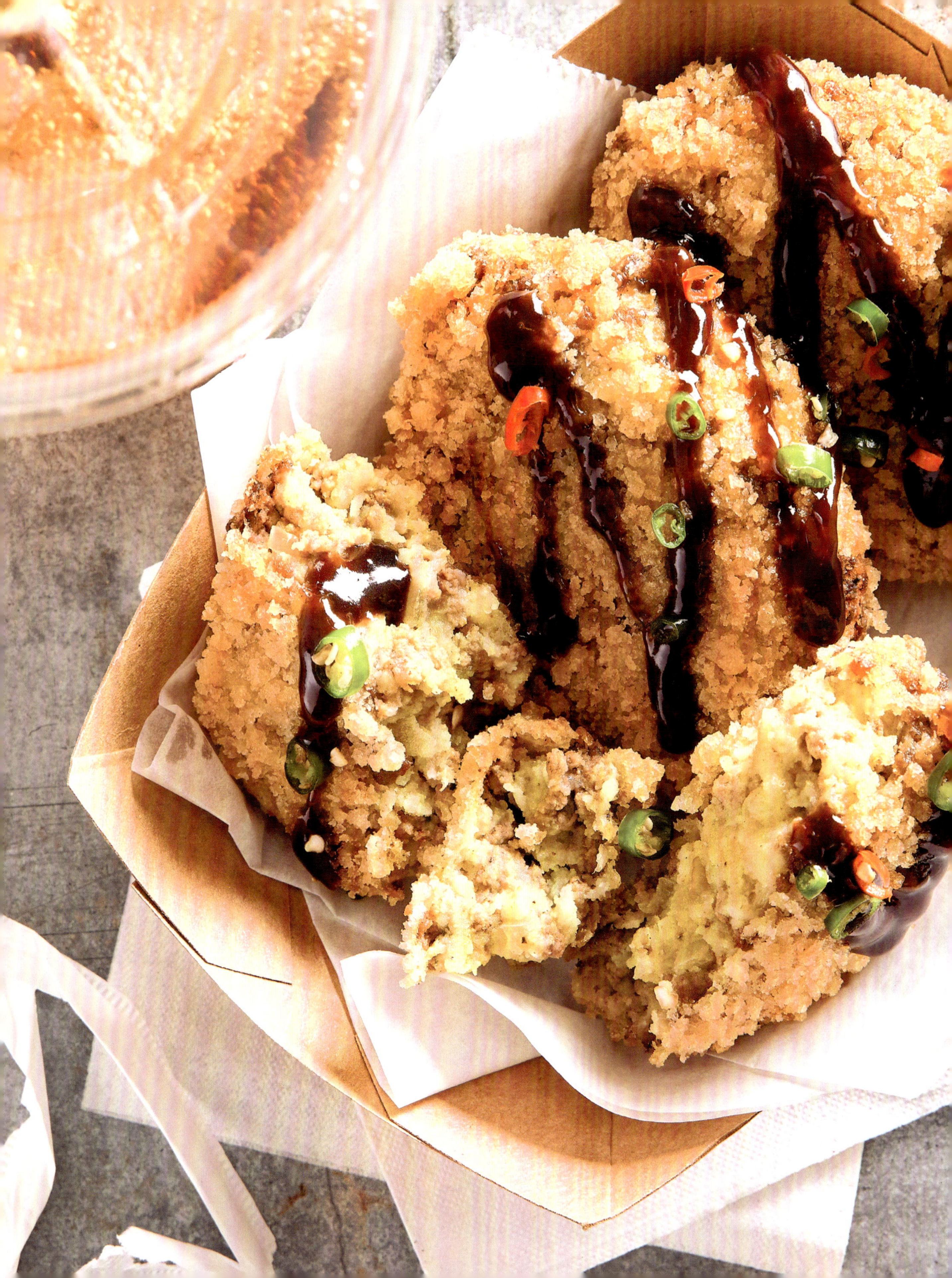

# KOROKKE

Another grab-and-go favorite in Japanese storefronts or automats. Chopped and smashed up bits of potato and meat, with curry seasoning, crunchy panko, and sweet katsu sauce forge it into something to slay the hunger. I must've wolfed down a couple dozen of these tryin' to fuel the ol' healing factor into gear after a back alley tussle with Lady Deathstrike. That hellacious adamantium manicure of hers had left me just as shredded as the stuff inside these dense and savory mini-bites.

**Yield:** 12 to 16 croquettes • **Type:** Snack • **Difficulty:** Average • **Prep Time:** 30 minutes • **Cook Time:** 30 minutes • **Rest Time:** 30 minutes • **Dietary Considerations:** V*
**Pairs well with:** *Pickled Daikon* (pg 111)

4 large russet potatoes, peeled and quartered

2 teaspoons salt, or to taste

1 teaspoon black pepper, or to taste

1 tablespoon Japanese curry powder or *Dagger Bay Blend* (pg 30)

1 tablespoon *Mutant Medley* (pg 30)

Neutral oil (such as peanut or canola)

1 medium yellow onion, minced

1 pound ground beef or vegetarian substitute (see Note)

¼ cup cornstarch or tapioca starch

2 eggs, lightly beaten

1½ cups panko breadcrumbs

Katsu sauce (pg 60) (for serving, optional)

Boil the potatoes for 15 to 18 minutes 'til fork-tender. Once done, strain the potatoes in a colander and place them into a large mixing bowl. Add 1 teaspoon of salt and half a teaspoon of black pepper, curry powder, and Mutant Medley. Mash the potatoes with a fork or a potato masher, ensuring they are thoroughly mashed with no large pieces remaining and the seasonings have been distributed evenly.

Sauté the onions in a skillet over medium-high heat with 1 tablespoon of the neutral oil, 'til nicely browned, about 6 to 8 minutes. Add the ground beef to the onions and cook 'til there's no more pink, breaking up large pieces with a wooden spoon, about 5 to 7 minutes. Season with the remaining salt and pepper. Thoroughly drain the excess fat with colander, then transfer the beef and onions to the mixing bowl with the potatoes. Stir to combine. Taste and adjust seasonings.

Form the potato mixture into 12 to 16 oval-shaped patties of roughly equal size, compressing them as tightly as possible so there is no trapped air. Place the patties on a parchment-lined baking sheet, cover with plastic wrap, and refrigerate for at least 20 to 30 minutes. This step is crucial so don't skip it, it'll make coating and frying them much easier.

Add the cornstarch to a shallow bowl. Have the beaten eggs available in a separate shallow bowl nearby. In a third separate shallow bowl, add the panko breadcrumbs. Coat each potato ball first in the cornstarch 'til evenly coated. Then coat it in the beaten egg, and finally roll it in the panko breadcrumbs 'til covered completely.

Heat 2 inches of neutral oil to 350°F (give or take 10 degrees) in a wok or large cast-iron skillet. In batches of 2 to 3 at a time (depending on the size of your wok or skillet, but avoid overcrowding), fry the croquettes for 2 to 3 minutes per side 'til golden brown on both sides. Fish out the cooked croquettes with a slotted spoon and set them on a paper towel–lined plate to drain.

Serve the croquettes warm with katsu sauce on the side for dipping or drizzled lightly over the top.

*Note: This recipe can be made vegetarian by using tofu or other meatless ground beef alternative.*

# OKONOMIYAKI

Not every stand-out taste or aroma triggers memories of something else. In fact, what was special about first tryin' one of these in Osaka was that it felt *new*. Folks call it a "savory pancake." But with the complex and tangy mix of Worcestershire and oyster sauces, plus cabbage and made-to-order piles of any favorite regional toppings, the closest comparison might be a pizza and this flavor's a world away. If anything, Okonomiyaki reminds me why I'm always on the move. It ain't just bein' restless. It's knowing that even after all my years, there's still new experiences out there. And when you find one, that's something to savor.

**Yield: 6 to 8 pancakes • Type: Main or Breakfast • Difficulty: Average • Prep Time: 15 minutes
Cook Time: 30 minutes • Rest Time: None • Dietary Considerations: N/A**

### FOR THE PANCAKES:

8 bacon slices, chopped

1½ tablespoons dashi powder

1 cup warm water

4 large eggs

1½ cups all purpose flour

¼ cup cornstarch

1 teaspoon baking powder

½ green cabbage, sengiri-cut or finely shredded

6 green onions, sliced on a bias, whites and greens separated

¼ cup tenkasu or crushed crispy fried onions

2 to 4 tablespoons vegetable oil or bacon fat

### FOR THE OKONOMIYAKI SAUCE:

¼ cup ketchup

¼ cup Worcestershire sauce

2 tablespoons oyster sauce or stir fry sauce

2 tablespoons light brown sugar

### FOR TOPPINGS:

Japanese-style mayonnaise, to taste

Okonomiyaki sauce, to taste

Furikake and/or shichimi togarashi, to taste

Bonito flakes, to taste

Sliced green onions (reserved green parts from the pancakes mix), to taste

Pickled ginger or *Pickled Daikon* (pg 111), to taste

To make the okonomiyaki sauce, whisk together the sauce ingredients in a small mixing bowl. Cover and set aside 'til it's time to serve.

In a large skillet, fry the bacon pieces over medium-high heat 'til crispy, about 5 to 7 minutes. Transfer them to a paper towel–lined plate to drain and cool. Reserve the bacon fat for frying the pancakes or for another use.

In a medium mixing bowl, dissolve the dashi powder in warm water, then whisk in the eggs. In a separate large mixing bowl, stir together the flour, cornstarch, and baking powder. Pour the egg mixture into the flour mixture and whisk 'til a smooth, runny batter forms.

Add the shredded cabbage, green onion (save most of the green parts for topping), tenkasu, and cooked bacon to the batter. Fold everything together, making sure all the ingredients are coated in the batter.

Preheat a large skillet or griddle to medium-low heat. Brush some of the oil or bacon fat over the surface.

Once the pan is hot, scoop ⅓ to ½ cup of the mixture onto the pan and spread it out into a 4- to 5-inch circle. Cook each pancake for 3 to 4 minutes per side, 'til the veggies are cooked through and the pancakes are golden brown on both sides. You can cook multiple pancakes at once depending on the size of your pan. Add more oil or fat as needed in between batches.

Transfer the cooked pancakes to serving plates. Drizzle generously with mayo and okonomiyaki sauce. Add green onions and additional toppings to taste. Serve warm.

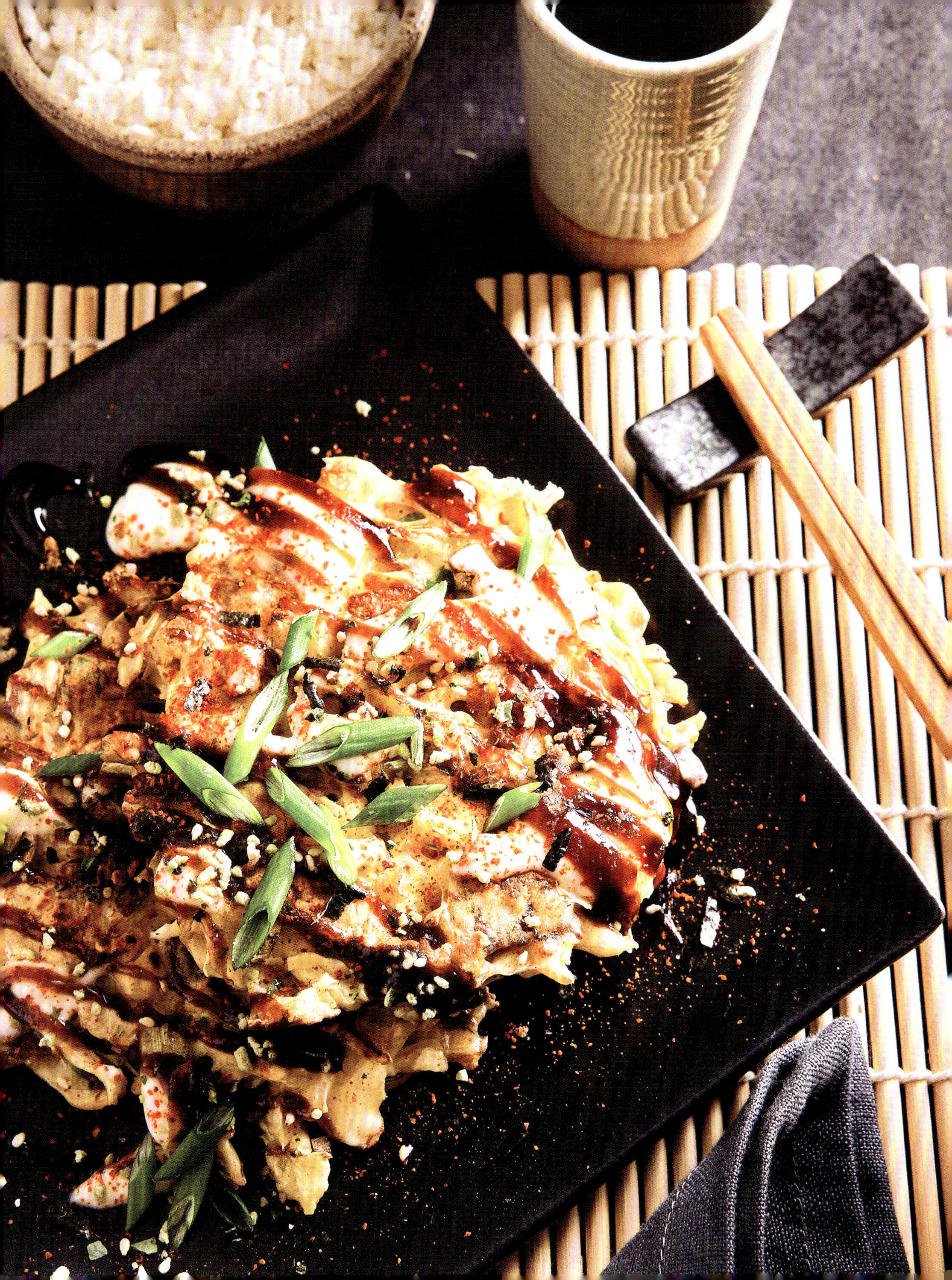

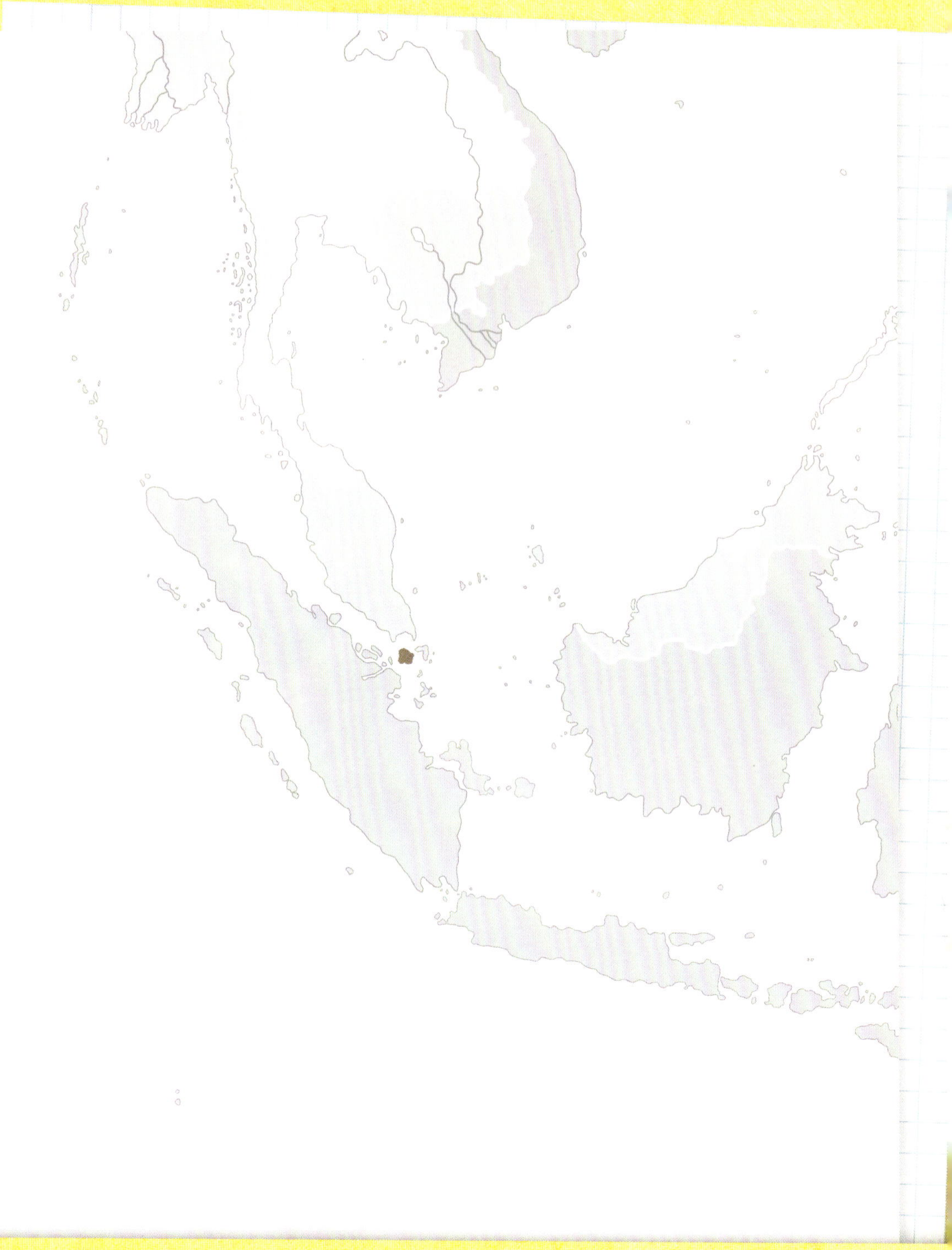

## FROM TIME SPENT IN
# MADRIPOOR

# HOW TO
# MADRIPOOR DINING AND SURVIVAL GUIDE

With one of the richest tourist industries in the world, Madripoor's cuisine is naturally top notch. Hightown's where the wealthy and powerful live it up in luxury, dining on gourmet meals with price tags as high as the skyscrapers. You'll usually find me in Lowtown, where the meals are cheap and the fights are dirty.

## HIGHTOWN

In Hightown, the food is fancy, the drinks are pricey, and the hoity-toity folks you're rubbing elbows with are usually plottin' something …

Spots to check out:

- **KING'S IMPRESARIO RESTAURANT:** This is the fanciest joint in town and the food's as rich as the clientele. You'll see business deals being made over lobster laksa and beluga caviar, but don't let the fine dining lull you into a false sense of security, this place is just as dangerous as anywhere else on Madripoor.
- **THE HOTELS:** A collection of luxury hotels catering to the wealthy and powerful, they've got everything from shopping malls to indoor amusement parks inside those flashy walls. The Madripoor Pearl alone boasts more than 10 upscale restaurants. Whether it's rooftop sushi bars with views of the harbor or extravagant buffets under diamond chandeliers, you're in for the dining experience of a lifetime. Which is good, because it'll probably cost you your life's savings.

## LOWTOWN

Lowtown's a cesspool of crime, corruption, and just about every vice under the sun. It's also where you'll find the real flavors of the island, in my opinion. If you've got guts and some pocket change, the street vendors and hole-in-the-wall joints dish out some of the best food you'll ever eat.

Spots to check out:

- **THE PRINCESS:** My old haunt and a Lowtown staple. You'll find all sorts in here—mercs, smugglers, and maybe the occasional super hero hiding out. If you're looking for information, or just a place to lay low, this is where you wanna be. Plus, it's got a kitchen that serves up some top-notch grub. Ask for Patch's special.
- **LOWTOWN CENTRAL BAZAAR & MARKETPLACE:** A chaotic, bustling marketplace where you can find everything from experimental tech to ancient alien relics. It's also a food lover's paradise. The Bazaar's packed with hawkers selling everything from grilled skewers of mystery meat to piping-hot bowls of noodle soup. The smells alone are enough to make your mouth water, but keep an eye on your wallet—pickpockets love a distracted mark.
- **THE BRONZE MONKEY:** This place is more dangerous than a viper backed into a corner. It's where you go when you want to disappear, or when you've got a score to settle. Don't be surprised if a fight breaks out while you're enjoying the puffer fish sashimi.

119

# RAGIN' RADISHES

**BEST THERE IS WARNING**

For a tiny island, there's no shortage of incredible food across Madripoor. There's also no shortage of thieves and cutthroats—so when you eat, keep one eye peeled. 'Course, most my time there, one eye was my max, as I made a name for myself as Patch. (Spy supreme Nick Fury once told me, while workin' intel ops after the war, that giving folks one thing to notice usually meant they forgot the rest of the face.) While digging into the underworld there, I based myself outta the Lowtown district's Princess Bar. Despite the highfalutin name, the chow was pure street food—my favorite bein' this specialty. Crispy on the outside, soft on the inside, cooking this mix mellows the daikon radishes' usually sharp flavor. Makin' these takes quite a bit of time, but the savory end result is good enough to satisfy unsavory characters.

**Servings: 2 • Type: Main/Side • Difficulty: Hard • Prep Time: 45 minutes**
**Cook Time: 90 minutes • Rest Time: 2 hours • Dietary Considerations: V\*, GF\***

### FOR THE RADISH CAKES:

½ large daikon radish, grated

1 cup plain rice flour (see Notes)

2 tablespoons tapioca starch

1½ cups prepared dashi stock, chicken broth, or vegetable broth

1 tablespoon neutral oil, such as peanut or canola, plus more for greasing

2 cloves garlic, minced

Salt, to taste

### FOR THE SCRAMBLE:

2 tablespoons neutral oil, such as peanut or canola

1½ cups cubed radish cakes (see Notes)

4 cloves garlic, minced

4 green onions, sliced on a bias, whites and green separated

1 cup bean sprouts, optional

1 tablespoon fish sauce or 1 tablespoon of your favorite vegetarian alternative

1 tablespoon light soy sauce or tamari

1 tablespoon sambal oelek, or to taste

1 tablespoon granulated sugar

6 large eggs

1 bird's eye chile, sliced, optional

**TO MAKE THE RADISH CAKES:** Bring 4 to 6 cups of water to a boil in a medium pot. Boil the daikon for 5 to 7 minutes 'til soft, then drain the daikon in a colander and let it cool a little. After it's cool enough to handle, squeeze as much water out as you can.

In a medium mixing bowl, whisk together the rice flour and tapioca starch. Whisk in the stock 'til smooth. Add the cooked daikon and stir to combine.

Heat the oil in a wok over medium heat. Cook the garlic in the oil for 1 to 2 minutes 'til fragrant. Add the daikon batter and stir constantly 'til the mixture thickens up. The mixture should look like a slightly thick cake batter.

Prepare a large steamer, or a wok with a steaming rack. If you don't have this, you can use smaller heat-proof bowls or ramekins and steam the cakes individually in a smaller stovetop steamer (most cookware sets will have a pot with a small, fitted steamer basket) or a smaller bamboo steamer. Whichever way you are steaming, line the cooking vessel(s) with parchment on the bottom and grease the sides with oil or cooking spray. Transfer the batter to the parchment-lined round cake pan or divide into the smaller prepared ramekins. If using a cake pan, steam the cake for 50 to 60 minutes, or 'til a chopstick or fork inserted in the center comes out clean. If using the ramekins, this will take closer to 20 to 25 minutes per batch.

Transfer the cake(s) to the fridge and let set for at least 2 hours, or overnight. Once set, remove from the pan or ramekins and cut into 1-inch cubes or pieces.

**TO MAKE THE SCRAMBLE:** Heat the oil in a wok or large skillet over medium-high heat. Once the oil is hot add the cubes of radish cake and fry, stirring occasionally, 'til every side has been browned, about 5 to 7 minutes.

Lower the heat to medium and add the garlic, the white parts of the green onion, bean sprouts (if using). In a small bowl, whisk together the fish sauce, soy sauce, sambal oelek, and sugar. Add to the wok and stir fry for 1 to 2 minutes 'til everything is coated in the sauce.

Add the eggs and allow them to cook for 1 or 2 minutes undisturbed, then break apart the eggs. Once the eggs are cooked through, flip everything onto a serving plate. Garnish with the remaining green onion and sliced chile.

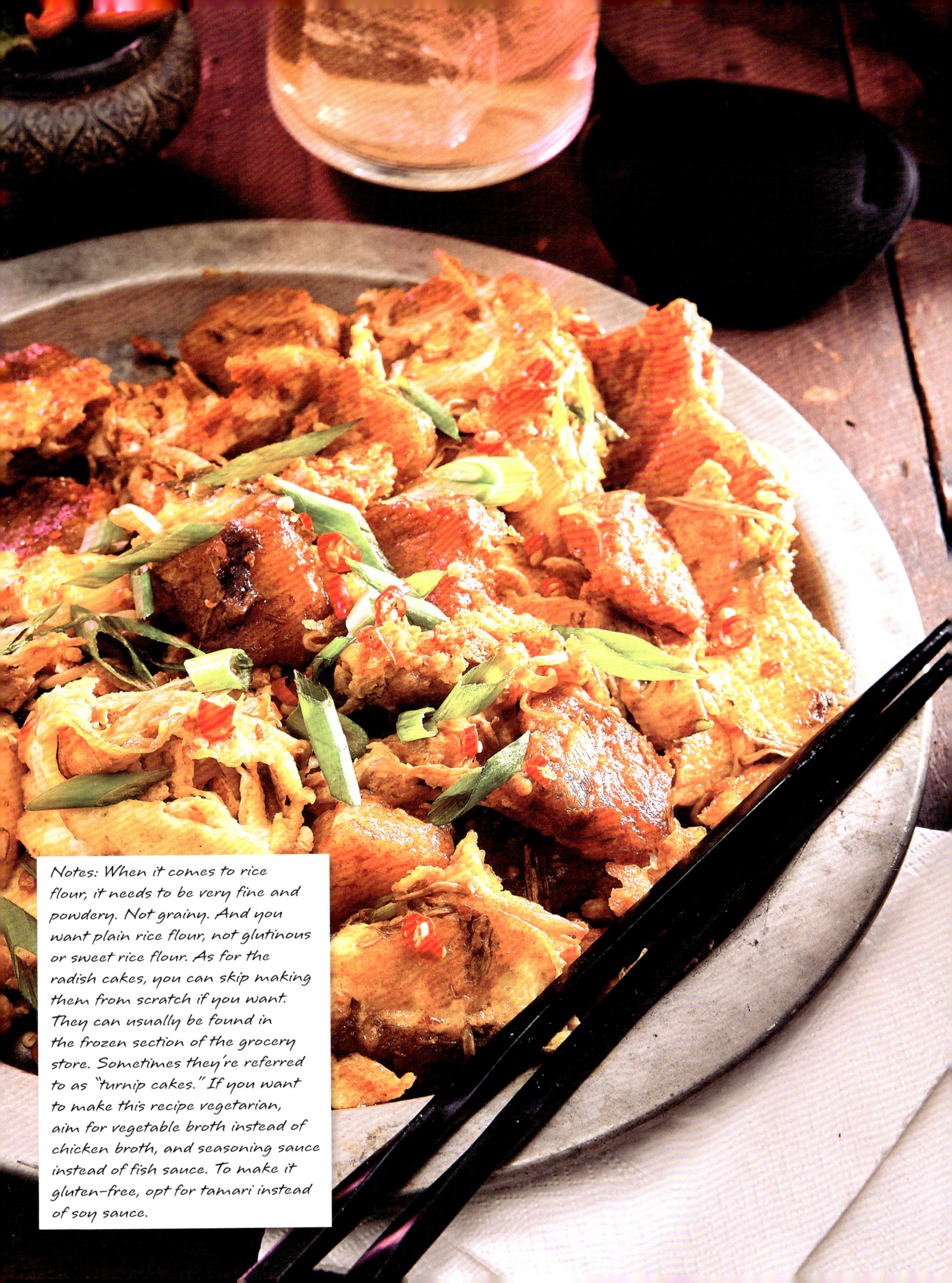

Notes: When it comes to rice flour, it needs to be very fine and powdery. Not grainy. And you want plain rice flour, not glutinous or sweet rice flour. As for the radish cakes, you can skip making them from scratch if you want. They can usually be found in the frozen section of the grocery store. Sometimes they're referred to as "turnip cakes." If you want to make this recipe vegetarian, aim for vegetable broth instead of chicken broth, and seasoning sauce instead of fish sauce. To make it gluten-free, opt for tamari instead of soy sauce.

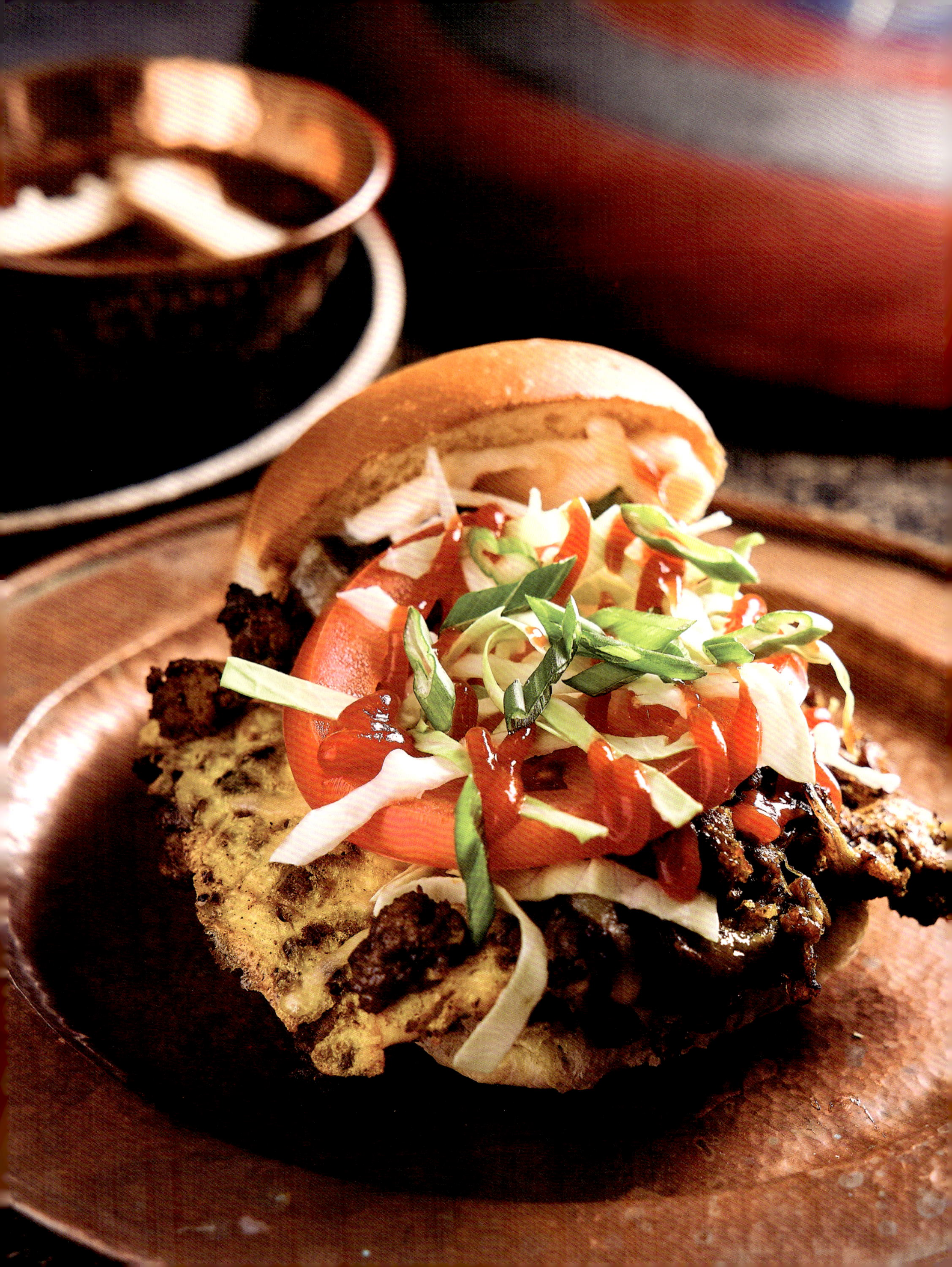

# ROTI ~~JOHN~~ *STEVE*

Story goes this famous sandwich was the result of a chef in Singapore tryin' to make a cheeseburger for a tourist on the fly, just based off the tourist's description. I imagine it would be like trying to describe meeting Captain America in the slums of Madripoor, fighting off Hand ninjas. I made my own snap judgment of Cap—wearin' his red-white-and-baby-blue spandex. And I'm the first to admit I was off base (mostly.) My opinion on ol' Steve Rogers improved once we stopped fighting long enough to pick up some Madripoorian Roti John. Now, I can say he's as reliable as they come, in addition to packing a helluva punch. With so many of the same qualities, they prob'ly coulda named this sandwich Roti Steve.

**Yield: 2 sandwiches • Type: Sandwich • Difficulty: Average • Prep Time: 15 minutes • Cook Time: 20 minutes • Rest Time: None • Pairs well with:** *Tornado Potato* **(pg 80),** *Poutine* **(pg 94)**

### FOR THE OMELET:

1 tablespoon neutral oil, such as peanut or canola

½ large red onion, thinly sliced

2 cloves garlic, minced

½ pound ground beef

1 teaspoon *Dagger Bay Blend* (pg 30) or curry powder

½ teaspoon cumin

Pinch of turmeric

1 teaspoon salt, or to taste

½ teaspoon black pepper, or to taste

2 large eggs, lightly beaten

### FOR THE SANDWICHES:

2 sandwich rolls, halved

Grated mozzarella cheese

Japanese-style mayonnaise

Ketchup

Sriracha hot sauce and/or sambal oelek

Shredded cabbage or lettuce

Sliced tomatoes and/or cucumber

Green onions, sliced on a bias

To make the omelet, heat the oil in a large non-stick skillet or griddle over medium-high heat. Add the onions and garlic and sauté 'til the onions have browned, about 5 to 7 minutes. Add the ground beef and continue to cook 'til the beef has browned and there's no more pink, breaking up any big pieces with a wooden spoon, about 6 to 8 minutes. Drain out any excess fat. Season the beef with Dagger Bay Blend, cumin, turmeric, salt, and pepper, stirring to mix in the spices.

Turn the heat to low and spread the meat around the pan into a single layer. Add in the beaten eggs so they flow in between the meat. Take the bottom halves of the sandwich rolls and place them facedown onto the eggs, pressing them in gently so they absorb some of the eggs and juices. Push any eggs on the side under the sandwich slices. Allow to cook 'til the eggs have set and cooked into the sandwich bottoms, about 1 to 3 more minutes.

Flip everything onto a plate so the filling (egg) side is facing up. Or use a spatula to transfer and flip the sandwich bottoms individually, if that's easier. If adding shredded cheese, add it immediately so it melts onto the egg filling.

Add the fixings to taste, drizzling on the condiments last. If you like, pan fry the top halves of the sandwich rolls in the skillet so they are lightly browned, or lightly toast them for a minute or two in a toaster, then add them on top.

ON THE ROAD: STREET EATS AND TAVERN BITES

# MYSTIQUE'S MEI FUN

There was a little while where Mystique set up shop in Madripoor, runnin' a ring that levered MGH—Mutant Growth Hormone—to try and create her own mutie-friendly utopia. Like most things Raven does, I can get behind the goal, just not how she goes about it. Girl's shown a lot of faces to me: ally, enemy, up close and personal … guess it makes sense of a shapeshifter. But I might've been most surprised by her turn as "executive chef." Part of her network in Madripoor included taking over an endurin' restaurant that'd always been *good* but never great. Next time I came in on business, the shop had a line out the door. When I tried this fully loaded curry stirfry, I could taste the excitement. Mystique knew what buttons to push, what secrets to deploy, and where to cut—just like she always does. But her plans clicked perfectly into place for once with this Mei Fun. Probably 'cause for once, I wasn't tryin' to stop her.

**Servings: 6 to 8 • Type: Main/Side • Difficulty: Average • Prep Time: 30 minutes • Cook Time: 40 minutes Rest Time: None • Pairs well with: *Lowtown Satay* (pg 62)**

**FOR THE SAUCE:**

1½ cups chicken broth, or more as needed

2 tablespoons soy sauce

2 tablespoons oyster sauce

2 or 3 teaspoons *Dagger Bay Blend* (pg 30) or other curry powder

½ teaspoon black pepper, or to taste

1 tablespoon brown sugar

1 teaspoon toasted sesame oil

**FOR THE MEI FUN:**

2 to 3 tablespoons neutral oil (such as peanut or canola)

2 large eggs, lightly beaten

½ pound shrimp, peeled and deveined

2 shallots, sliced

4 cloves garlic, minced

4 green onions, chopped into 1-inch pieces

1-inch piece ginger, minced or grated

2 large carrots, julienned or shredded

½ medium head napa or savoy cabbage, shredded

14 ounces mei fun noodles or rice vermicelli

½ pound cooked char siu or BBQ pork

Calamansi or lemon wedges, for serving, optional

**TO MAKE THE SAUCE:** Whisk together the ingredients 'til well-combined and set aside.

**TO MAKE THE MEI FUN:** Heat a tablespoon of the oil in a wok over medium-high heat 'til smoking hot. Pour in the eggs and fry 'til cooked completely, about 2 to 3 minutes. Break it into smaller pieces with a spatula and transfer to a plate. Set aside.

In the same wok, sear the shrimp for 1 to 3 minutes. As soon as they turn pink, transfer them to the plate with the eggs.

Check your pack of noodles. If the directions say to soak them, do so for the amount of time recommended on the package.

While the noodles soak, add another 1 to 2 tablespoons of oil into the wok. Add the shallots, garlic, green onion pieces, ginger, and carrots. Sauté 'til the carrots are slightly softened but still crunchy, about 5 to 6 minutes, then add the cabbage and cook for another minute or two 'til just wilted.

To the wok, add the sauce and bring to a boil, then add the noodles. Stir 'til all the noodles are coated with the sauce. Keep on stirring and cooking 'til the noodles are tender, about 3 to 5 minutes. Add more broth as needed if the things are drying up before the noodles are tender. Just watch the salt content, make sure it's staying where you want it and switch to water if necessary.

Toss in the char siu, eggs, and shrimp. Cook for another minute or two to allow everything to meld together, then transfer to a serving tray or serving plates. Serve with calamansi or lemon wedges on the side.

*Note: Can't track down mei fun noodles? No big deal. Swap in whatever you've got. Flat rice noodles, glass noodles, even angel hair if you have to. Gets the job done just fine. Just make sure to follow the package directions.*

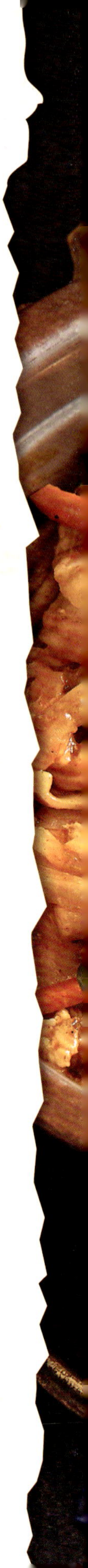

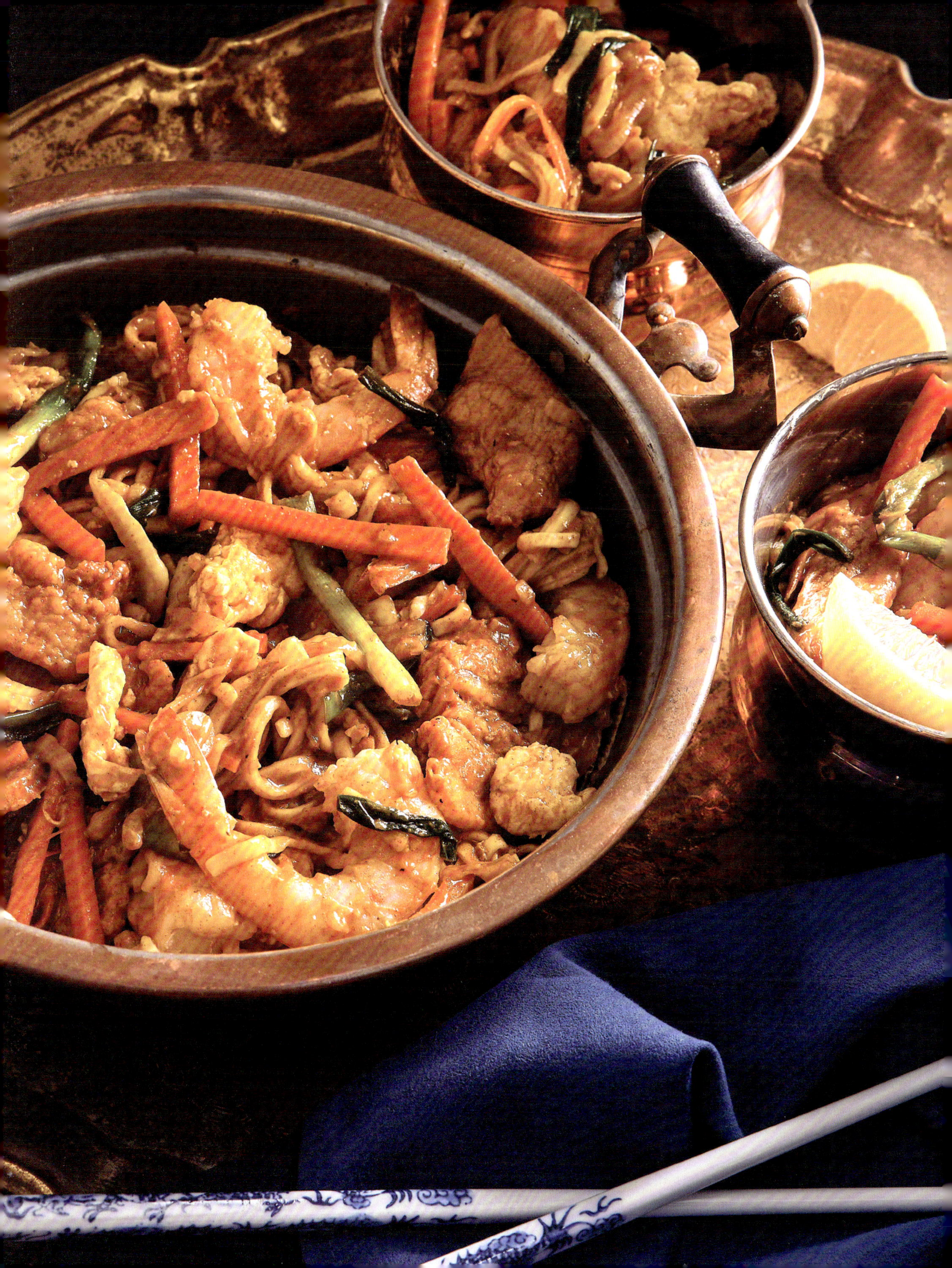

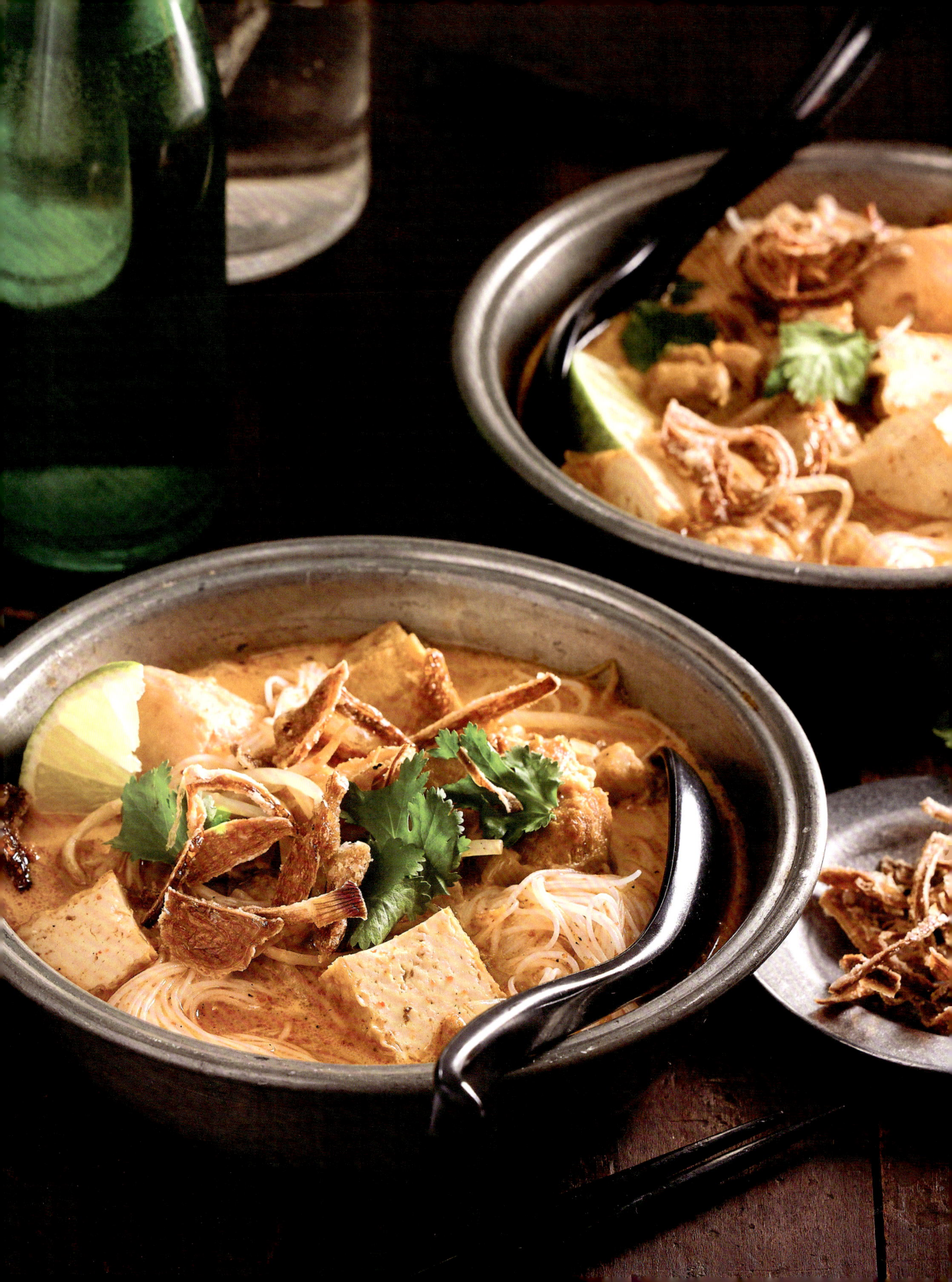

# LOWTOWN LAKSA

Given the country's location in Southeast Asia, Madripoor menus got more than their fair share of curry. But it became a scent I'd always sense on super villain and snake in the grass Viper. When we were mercenaries on the island, long before we were *married* (long story, quick divorce) the ex–Madame Hydra loved her expensive Hightown versions (curries sportin' fresh lobster, imported truffles and the like). Me? I always preferred to skip the penguin-waiter show and slurp down a bowl of sweet and salty Lowtown Laksa. The fragrant, dense spices now call to mind the one who gladly got away.

**Servings: 4 • Type: Soup/Stew • Difficulty: Average • Prep Time: 15 minutes**
**Cook Time: 30 minutes • Rest Time: None**

### FOR THE LAKSA:

1 to 2 tablespoons vegetable oil

1 pound boneless skinless chicken thighs, cut into 1-inch pieces

1 package laksa or rice vermicelli noodles

1 large shallot, minced

2 cloves garlic, minced

1-inch piece ginger, minced or grated

2 tablespoons laksa paste or Thai red curry paste

2 cups canned coconut milk

3 to 4 cups chicken broth

2 tablespoons coconut palm sugar or light brown sugar

¼ cup fish sauce or use 2 tablespoons soy sauce

1 to 3 teaspoons salt, or to taste

6 store-bought fish balls, optional

6 to 8 fried tofu puffs, optional

1 cup bean sprouts, optional

### TOPPINGS:

Lime wedges

Crispy fried onion or shallots

Chopped fresh cilantro

Chile crisp oil or sambal oelek

Heat 1 tablespoon of oil in a wok or Dutch oven. Cook the chicken pieces in the oil over medium heat 'til lightly browned and cooked through, stirring occasionally. Remove the chicken and set it aside in a bowl or a large plate.

Cook the noodles according to package directions and set aside.

Add the remaining oil if needed to the wok or dutch oven (there may already be enough fat leftover from the chicken). Cook the shallots, garlic, and ginger 'til fragrant and the onions become translucent. Add the laksa or curry paste and continue to cook for a minute or two, then add the coconut milk, chicken broth, sugar, fish sauce, and salt to taste.

Turn the heat up to medium-high and bring to a simmer. Add the fish balls, tofu puffs, bean sprouts to taste (if using), along with the cooked chicken and any juices. Cook for 1 to 3 more minutes 'til the bean sprouts have softened and the flavors come together. Taste and adjust salt.

Divide the noodles into serving bowls. Ladle the broth and other ingredients into the serving bowls. Top with lime wedges, crispy onions, cilantro, and chile crisp oil to taste.

# LEPAT PISANG

Madripoor is so bustlin' with its modern convenience—and assassins—that it's easy to forget the island's been a major international shipping port for hundreds of years. So in addition to all the illicit business comin' in and out, it's a haven for freshly harvested fruits and spices from all 'round the world. Even the cheap street treats skip the artificial stuff to lean into the natural sweetness of overripe bananas and coconut. In Madripoor, chopped nuts (you name the type) and warm spices like cinnamon and nutmeg give a fuller flavor and a few darker notes to the taste. This particular recipe was a hit with both California mallrat Jubilee and English heiress (and ninja), Betsy Braddock. I'd call that an international success.

**Yield: 16 • Type: Dessert • Difficulty: Easy • Prep Time: 30 minutes • Cook Time: 30 minutes • Rest Time: None • Dietary Considerations: V, V+**

16 banana leaves (see Note)

⅓ cup coconut palm sugar or light brown sugar

1 cup all-purpose flour

¼ cup plain rice flour

¼ teaspoon salt

½ teaspoon cinnamon

¼ teaspoon allspice and/or nutmeg

7 or 8 ripe or slightly overripe bananas, thoroughly mashed

1 tablespoon coconut oil, melted

Shredded coconut or chopped nuts, optional

Caramel sauce or sweetened condensed milk, for serving, optional

Blanch or steam the banana leaves for 30 seconds or 'til they are pliable enough to fold.

In a medium mixing bowl, stir together the sugar, flour, rice flour, salt, and spices. Add the mashed banana and stir 'til well-combined.

Lay out a softened banana leaf square on a work surface and brush it with coconut oil. Scoop about 2 heaping tablespoons of banana mixture into the center of the banana leaf square. Sprinkle on a generous pinch of shredded coconut or chopped nuts (if using). Fold the banana leaf around the filling, then fold up the ends to secure. Repeat 'til there's no more filling. You should have about 16 cakes.

Prepare a steamer. Steam the wrapped lepat pisang for 25 to 30 minutes, in batches if necessary, 'til they are cooked through and firm.

Serve warm or at room temperature. Drizzle with caramel sauce or sweetened condensed milk, if you like.

*Note: If you can't find banana leaves in the frozen section of your grocery store, and you're in a bind, you could substitute corn husks, grape leaves, or parchment paper. But the flavor will be a little different.*

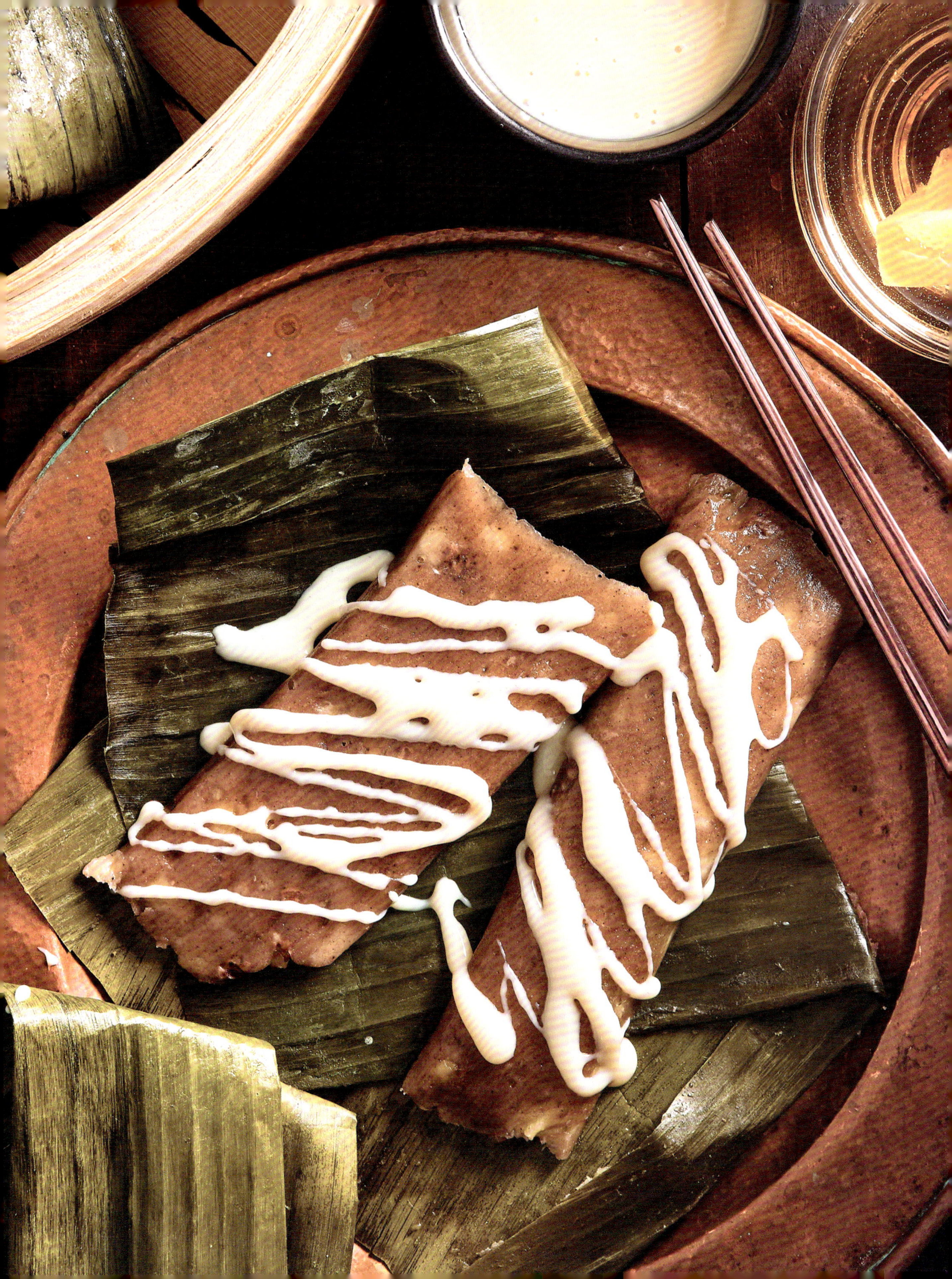

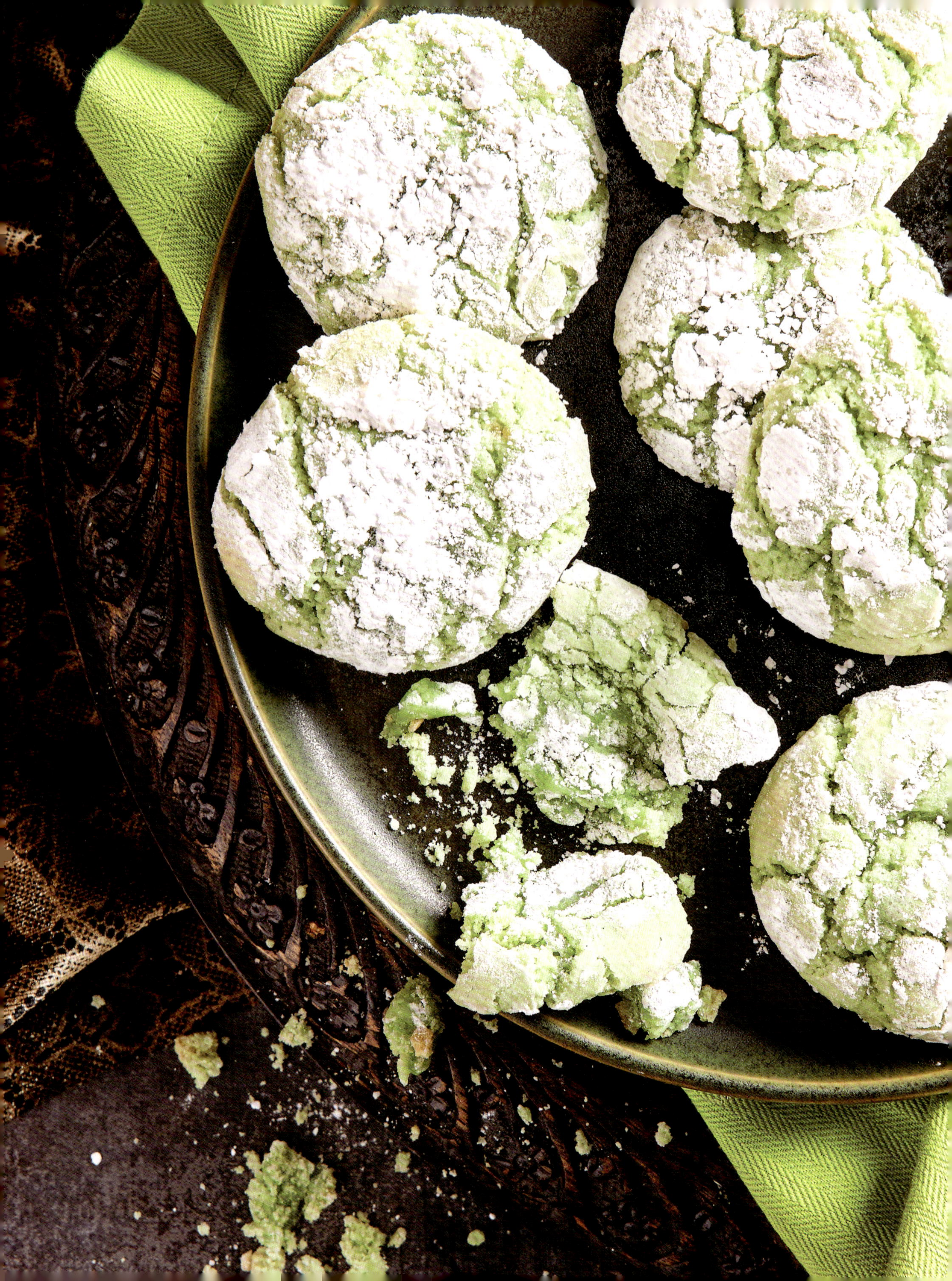

# JADE GIANTS

It's common knowledge: you wouldn't like the Hulk when he's angry. But what some poor souls forget is that the big guy gets hangry, too. I'll never forget seeing him smash down a few hundred of these cookies back in Madripoor. Banner may've been gray and callin' himself "Joe Fixit" at the time, but his hotel clearly knew not to let him get too hungry. Everytime Hulk stomped through their doors, the terrified staff rushed out with platters and stacks of these sugary, pillowy treats. So, I bribed staff for the recipe. Because I've *already* learned the hard way that it's better to stay on his good side …

**Yield: 24 • Type: Dessert • Difficulty: Easy • Prep Time: 20 minutes • Cook Time: 10 minutes**
**Rest Time: 10 minutes • Dietary Considerations: V**

½ cup unsalted butter, softened

½ cup light brown sugar

½ cup granulated sugar, plus more for rolling

2 large eggs

1 tablespoon pandan extract

2 to 3 drops green food coloring, optional for brighter color

2 cups all-purpose flour

⅓ cup sweet or glutinous rice flour

1½ teaspoons baking powder

¾ teaspoon salt

1 cup powdered sugar, for rolling

Preheat the oven to 350°F. Line two baking sheets with parchment paper.

In a large mixing bowl, use a hand mixer or a stand mixer to cream together the butter, brown sugar, and granulated sugar 'til the mixture is light and fluffy. Add the eggs one at a time, beating well after each addition and scraping down the sides of the bowl to ensure everything is fully combined. Mix in the pandan extract and food coloring 'til well incorporated.

In a separate mixing bowl, sift together the all-purpose flour, glutinous rice flour, baking powder, and salt. Add this into the butter mixture in 2 to 3 additions, blending 'til just combined.

Prepare 2 shallow bowls—fill one with granulated sugar and the other with the powdered sugar. Use an ice cream scoop to portion the dough and roll it into balls. Place the dough balls onto the baking sheets and refrigerate for 10 to 15 minutes.

Remove the dough balls from the fridge and roll each ball first in the granulated sugar, then in the powdered sugar to coat thoroughly. You can't use too much powdered sugar here, you want to get as much onto the cookies as you can.

Place the dough balls back on the prepared baking sheets, leaving a 2-inch gap in between each cookie to allow the cookies to expand. Bake for 10 to 12 minutes, 'til the cookies have a crackled top and are slightly soft in the center.

Let the cookies cool on the trays for 5 minutes, then transfer to a cooling rack. Allow them to cool completely before serving.

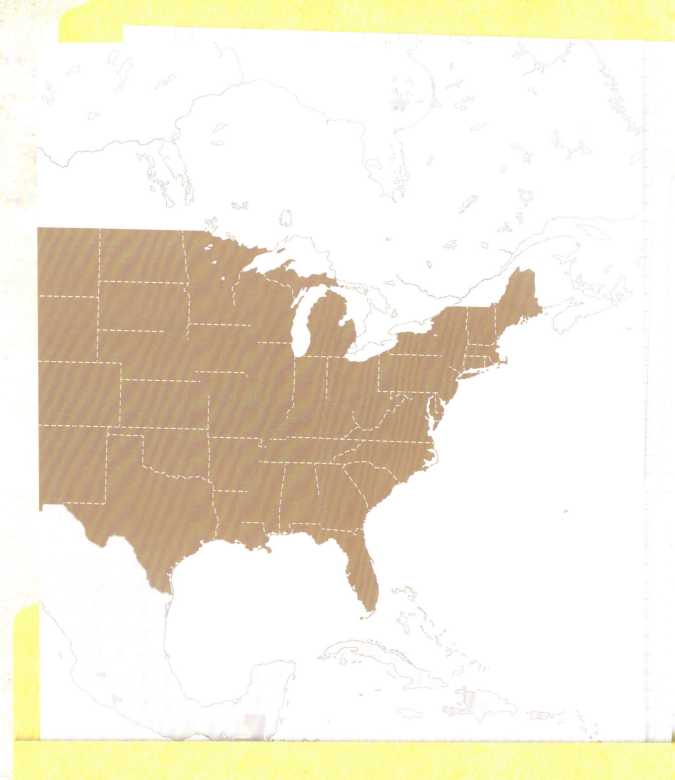

# FROM TIME SPENT
# STATESIDE

## HOW TO
# ROADSIDE DINERS, DIVES, AND OTHER PLACES OPEN 24/7

One of my favorite things about traveling in the States: almost nothing beats a stack of pancakes after driving all night, or a juicy burger after changing a tire or tunin' up your bike. Here's what I know about the truest havens there are for us mere (sorta)mortals:

**WHAT TO EXPECT:**
- **AMBIANCE:** Old booths, maybe some faded neon or old photos on the wall … all good signs. The no-frills, laid-back vibe can't be faked and must be appreciated.
- **NAMES:** The folks here are usually friendly and the servers often know the regulars by name. So pick your alias carefully. And be prepared to remember it.
- **MENUS:** Simple, hearty grub. You'll find plenty of classic American comfort food—fries and milkshakes. And, of course, breakfast. Plus, they don't skimp on portions, so come hungry.

**FINDING THE BEST SPOTS:**
- **ASK THE LOCALS:** Wanna know where to eat? Ask the locals. Gas station clerk, hardware store guy, old lady at the bus stop, doesn't matter. The locals know where the good stuff's hiding. And they'll even hide you, if they like you enough. So show some respect, bub.
- **LOOK FOR CROWDS:** A packed parking lot is always a good sign. If a place is busy, it's probably because the food is good and the prices are easy on the wallet. If not, well it's still easier to blend in with the masses.
- **ROADSIDE SIGNS:** Keep your eyes peeled for signs pointing you off an interstate exit. Sometimes the best joints are a little out of the way.

- **DON'T JUDGE A BOOK:** Some of the best places look a little run down. So what? That's how you know it's been around long enough to get it right. Dives and truck stops, in particular, can seem a little rough around the edges, but that's what gives 'em character.

**WHAT TO ORDER:**
- **SIGNATURE DISHES:** Every place has something they do best. Could be a burger, a pie, or a plate of pancakes that'll blow your mind. Trust folks when they say they're the best they are at what they do. On the off chance they're right, well, it's better to believe 'em.
- **DAILY SPECIALS:** Ask first; don't go ordering on a whim. Sometimes you're getting' whatever extra ingredients the cook's trying to get rid of, but other times you're looking at a seasonal dish that's a real winner. Your waiter's reaction will tell you everything you need to know.
- **ALL-DAY BREAKFAST:** Pancakes, eggs, and bacon aren't just for mornings.

**\*CASH-ONLY SPOTS\*:** Some spots only accept cash. It's good to have some on hand, just in case. And it's even better when you're trying to stay off the grid.

133

# BERSERKER BURGER

Whenever I'm back in the States for the usual life stuff, I know odds are wherever I go I can get one of my favorite foods: a burger. All the better when I can get that burger in my custom order: onions, jalapeños, chile sauce, pickles, and cheese. A horrified Havok called it "Berserker-style." Whenever I see one of *those* burgers in the vicinity, I grab it. Maybe it's too intense for the likes of Alex Summers—but that just means more for me, bub.

**Yield: 4 burgers • Type: Sandwich • Difficulty: Average • Prep Time: 20 minutes • Cook Time: 20 minutes • Rest Time: None • Pairs well with: *Tornado Potato* (pg 80), *Jubilee's Food Court Chili Fries* (pg 154), *Poutine* (pg 94)**

1½ pounds 80% lean ground beef

1 teaspoon olive oil

1 large yellow onion, thinly sliced

1 jalapeño, thinly sliced

1½ teaspoons salt, divided

1 teaspoon black pepper, divided

8 pepperjack and/or cheddar cheese slices

4 hamburger buns

½ cup chile sauce or a spicy ketchup

8 spicy pickle chips

Divide the ground beef into 8 equal portions and shape each portion into a ball. Place the meatballs on a plate, cover with plastic wrap, and let chill in the refrigerator 'til it's time to go in the skillet.

Cut 8 squares of parchment paper, each about 3 inches wide, and set aside.

Heat a large cast-iron skillet or griddle over high heat. Once hot, drizzle evenly with olive oil. Add the onions and jalapeños, cooking for 4 to 6 minutes 'til softened and lightly browned.

Arrange the onions and jalapeños into 8 small roughly equal mounds in the skillet, leaving at least 2 inches of space between each mound. If your skillet is too small for this, remove half of the onion mixture and cook the burgers in batches of 2 or 4 at a time.

Sprinkle each onion mound evenly with ⅛ teaspoon salt and a generous pinch of black pepper.

Place a ball of meat on top of each onion mound. Cover with a square of parchment paper and press down firmly with a burger press or metal spatula, flattening the meat into a thin 4-inch-wide patty. Remove the parchment paper.

Season the patties with the remaining salt and pepper. Cook undisturbed 'til the edges of the patties begin to brown, about 2 to 3 minutes.

Flip the patties so the onion-jalapeño mixture is on top. Add a slice of cheese to each patty and cook for another 2 minutes, 'til the patties are well-browned and the cheese is melted.

Stack the patties into 4 double stacks. If you like, lightly toast the buns on the skillet or in a toaster oven.

Place each burger stack on the bottom half of a burger bun, top with pickle chips, and spread 1 tablespoon of chile sauce (or to taste) on each top bun. Place the top bun and serve hot.

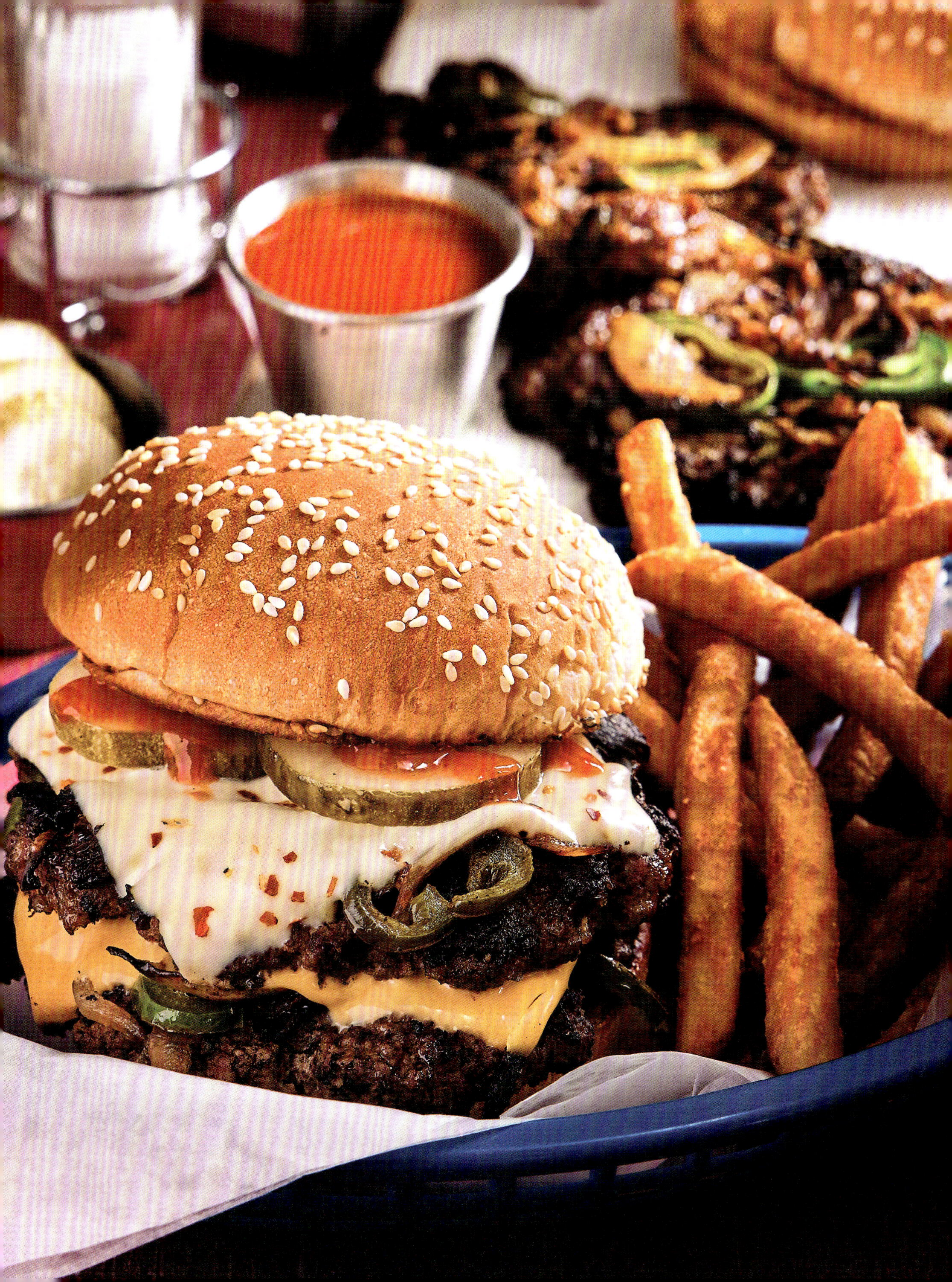

# SHREDDED HERO

Back before she was Captain Marvel, me and Carol Danvers actually teamed-up a few times on the spy circuit. Even without cosmic energy, that woman was a powerhouse, and more than earned being called American *Intelligence*. So of course she cracked the code for a better sammich. Flying to a Russian air drop with her, I was griping about the big slices of meat and tomato hangin' off every bite of my lunch. She suggested a new tactic. Been hackin' up my deli haul her way ever since. Sure, she's saved the world a dozen times over (and probably the universe by now). But this Shredded Hero's pretty great, too.

**Servings:** 2 to 3 • **Type:** Sandwich • **Difficulty:** Easy • **Prep Time:** 15 minutes • **Cook Time:** None **Rest Time:** None • **Dietary Considerations:** N/A • **Pairs well with:** *All-Dressed Chips* (pg 97)

**FOR THE DRESSING:**

¼ cup mayonnaise

2 tablespoons red wine vinegar

2 tablespoons Italian dressing or vinaigrette of choice

1 tablespoon Italian seasoning and/or salad seasoning

1 tablespoon grated parmesan cheese

Salt and pepper to taste

**FOR THE SANDWICH:**

2 cups shredded iceberg and/or romaine lettuce

1 large tomato, sliced

¼ of a large red onion, sliced

⅓ cup sliced banana peppers

4 slices smoked honey ham

4 large or 8 small slices salami

4 large or 8 small slices pepperoni

4 slices provolone cheese

2 or 3 sandwich rolls, toasting optional

**TO MAKE THE DRESSING:** In a small mixing bowl, whisk together the ingredients. Set aside.

**TO MAKE THE SANDWICH:** Stacked in approximately this order, place the lettuce, tomato, onion, banana peppers, ham, salami, pepperoni, provolone, on a large cutting board.

Using a very sharp knife, chop all the ingredients horizontally, then vertically. Continue to chop up ingredients 'til everything is in bite-sized pieces of roughly equal size. Alternatively, you can slice up everything separately.

Add everything to a large mixing bowl and toss with the dressing to taste. Taste filling and adjust seasonings, then scoop the filling into the sandwich rolls.

HIGHER, FARTHER, FASTER!

# CUBANO SANDWICH

My favorite classic Cubano outside of Havana was an easy pick-up in Greenwich Village. But once mutants decamped from New York to Krakoa, I started farming out the retrieval mission to Marauders, Hellions, X-Terminators—anybody runnin' ops back to NYC. Might seem like overkill, but a perfectly balanced mix of juicy roast pork, melted swiss, and zesty kick of mustard and pickles is worth a side-quest. Once Emma Frost caught wind that the missions she'd been funding were getting side-tracked though … the White Queen plucked this how-to from the kitchen crew's minds and made it clear I'd have to work my own sandwich press from then on.

**Yield: 4 sandwiches • Type: Sandwich • Difficulty: Average • Prep Time: 15 minutes Cook Time: 30 minutes • Rest Time: 2 hours**

### FOR THE PORK TENDERLOIN:

1½ teaspoons salt

¼ cup olive oil

¼ cup orange juice

2 tablespoons lime juice

¼ cup chopped fresh cilantro

4 cloves garlic, minced

2 teaspoons dried oregano

2 teaspoons ground cumin

1 pound pork tenderloin (not pork loin!)

### FOR THE SANDWICH:

1 loaf Cuban or Italian bread

2 tablespoons mustard

8 slices swiss cheese

8 ounces sliced smoked ham

8 roasted pork tenderloin slices

1 cup sliced dill pickles

2 to 3 tablespoons butter

**TO MAKE THE PORK TENDERLOIN ROAST:** Add the marinade ingredients to a sealable bag or other food storage container, ensuring the marinade is well-combined and completely covering the pork. Marinate for at least 2 hours, up to overnight.

Preheat the oven to 375°F. Line a rimmed baking sheet with foil and set a wire rack on top. Place the pork tenderloin on the rack and bake, uncovered, on the top rack for 25 to 35 minutes or 'til the pork is a nice brown outside and has reached an internal temperature of 145°F for medium-rare, or up to 155°F for medium-well. Let the tenderloin rest for 15 minutes before slicing it into ½-inch-thick medallions. Set aside to cool, or it can be stored in an airtight container in the fridge for up to 1 week.

**TO MAKE THE SANDWICHES:** Slice the loaf of bread in half lengthwise. Slather the mustard generously all over the cut side of the bread. Place half of the cheese on the bottom layer of the bread. Layer on the smoked ham, sliced pork, and pickles, then top with the remaining cheese. Cut it into 4 sandwiches of roughly equal size.

If you have a panini press or double-sided electric grill, preheat it 'til hot. Slather the butter generously on the outsides of the sandwiches and grill for 3 to 5 minutes 'til the cheese is melty and the outsides are golden brown and crisp.

**Alternative Method:** If you don't have a panini press, preheat a skillet or a griddle over medium heat. Butter one side of the sandwiches generously, then add the sandwiches to the skillet, butter-side down. Place a burger press or another heavy skillet, such as a cast-iron pan, on top to press them down. Once the bottom is toasted (it should make that nice scraping sound when a blade is gently dragged across), and the cheese is starting to melt, about 3 to 4 minutes, quickly butter the tops and flip the sandwich over and cook for another 3 to 4 minutes. Serve hot!

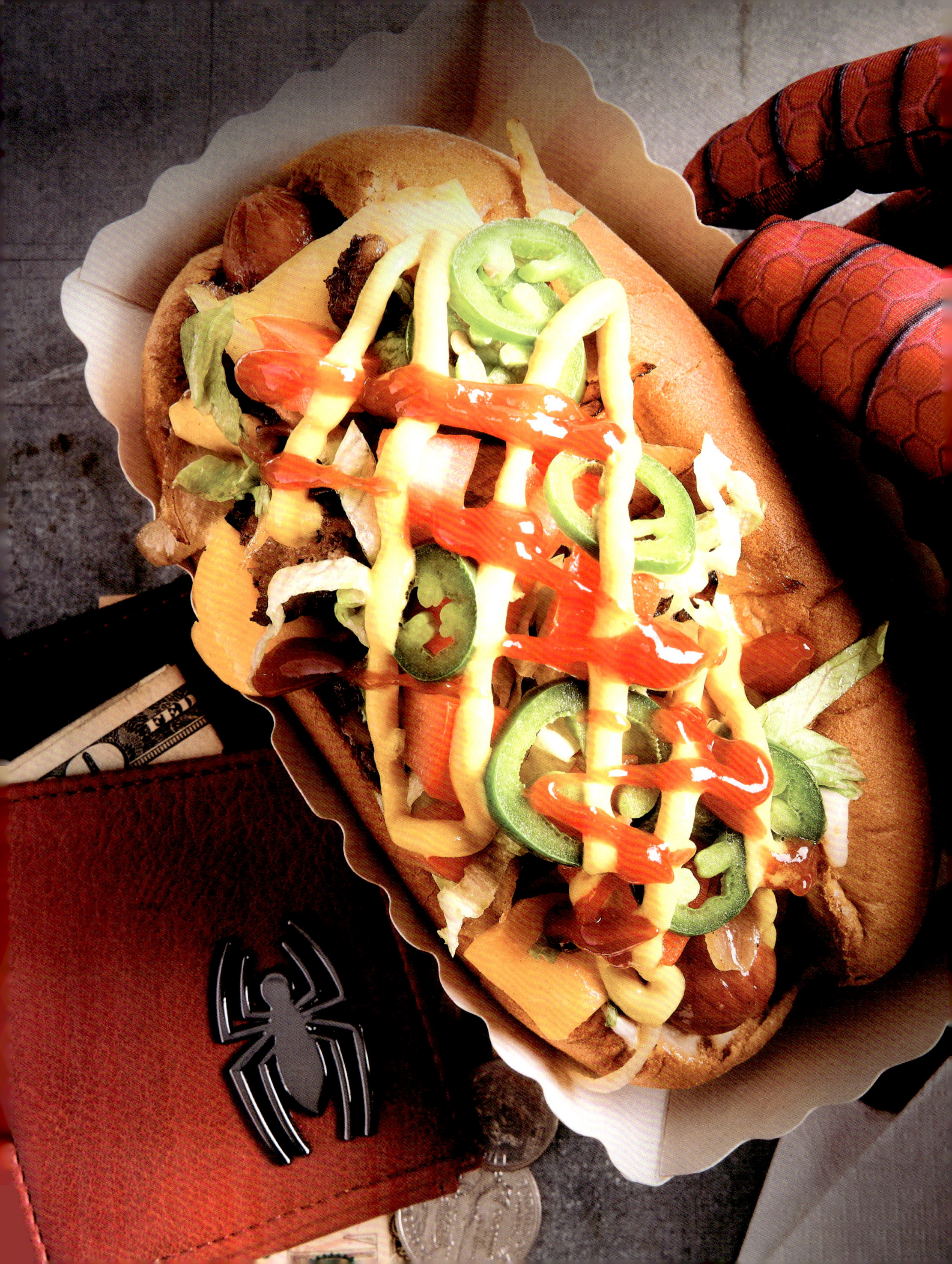

# SLINGIN' CHOPPED CHEESE DOGS

When you're in New York City, seems like you can't go a few blocks without bumpin' into two things: hot dog carts and Spider-Man. Often, together. At first, neither of 'em were really my taste. Mostly 'cause the kid can't stop running his mouth. Once me, him, Banner, and Ghost Rider were filling in for the FF, and I slashed up one of his 'furters in hopes of shuttin' him up. Instead, the Web-Head just picked up the pieces and made *this* majorly upgraded and flavor-packed bun-buster. It's a perfect example of how I've come to see him—Spidey's a guy who gets dealt a rough hand and lets it drive him to make things *better*. That, I got a lot of respect for.

**Servings: 4 • Type: Sandwich • Difficulty: Easy • Prep Time: 20 minutes • Cook Time: 40 minutes**
**Rest Time: None • Dietary Considerations: GF\*, V\***

1 tablespoon unsalted butter

1 large sweet onion, thinly sliced

1 pound ground beef

1 teaspoon salt, or to taste

½ teaspoon pepper, or to taste

2 to 3 teaspoons *Mutant Medley* (pg 30)

8 slices cheddar or American cheese

4 long beef franks

4 large hot dog buns or sandwich rolls

¼ cup mayonnaise, or to taste

**FOR THE TOPPINGS:**

1 cup iceberg lettuce, chopped, optional

1 roma tomato, chopped

Pickled jalapeños, chopped, optional or to taste

Ketchup and mustard, to taste

Melt the butter in a skillet or on a griddle over medium heat. Once melted, add the onion and cook 'til the onions start to brown, about 6 to 8 minutes. Push the onions to one side. Add the ground beef and do not break apart. Season with salt, pepper, and Mutant Medley. Sear for 3 to 4 minutes 'til browned on the bottom, flip, and cook for a further 2 to 3 minutes.

Break apart the beef then fold in the grilled onions. Once there is no more pink in the beef, divide into 4 equal sized portions and top each with 2 slices of cheese. Let cook for another 2 to 3 minutes, then remove from the heat.

Meanwhile, in a separate skillet or griddle, or in the same one if there's room, brown the hot dogs for 2 to 3 minutes per side 'til browned and slightly blistered. This is a good time to lightly grill or toast the buns, while the hot dogs cook.

Spread the toasted buns with about a tablespoon of mayo each. Add a hot dog to each, then scoop one of the four portions of beef, onions, and cheese on top of each one. Top with lettuce, tomato, and pickled jalapeños. Drizzle with ketchup and mustard to taste. Serve immediately.

*Note: Many ketchups, mustards, and mayonnaises are gluten free. To take this one the whole way, just grab a gluten-free hot bun or roll. If you're angling for a vegetarian dish, they've got all sorts of meat-free hot dogs and ground meat alternatives these days.*

ON THE ROAD: STREET EATS AND TAVERN BITES

# LAYERED CAKE: ASSEMBLE!

**BEST THERE IS WARNING**

I might need to start myself a second book just for all the food that reminds me of my time with the New Avengers. Tony Stark would lay out quite a spread whenever they'd have us assemble. By the time the unbreakable Luke Cage was leading the team, the meets became something of a potluck. Not sure if was outta necessity, since he and Jessica Jones were jugglin' freelance work and a baby, too. But it made a real shuffled deck of "hero" types (the Thing, Mockingbird, Iron Fist, Spidey …) feel like a reunion with old friends. While I was bustin' out lots of the recipes here, I started to realize nobody was bringing dessert. Maybe we're not the "sweetest" crowd in a conventional sense.

But bein' an Avenger means not backing down, no matter how daunting the odds. Getting *this* delicate mission right was trickier than stoppin' a super villain escape from the Raft prison. But that made cutting up this fluffy, melt-in-your-mouth case more *satisfying* too … until I find out the whole damn team assumed the Web-Head's *aunt* made it.

**Servings: 8 to 12 • Type: Dessert • Difficulty: Hard • Prep Time: 1 hour • Cook Time: 35 minutes
Rest Time: None • Dietary Considerations: V**

### FOR THE CHERRY–WHITE CHOCOLATE GANACHE:

24 ounces white chocolate

½ cup maraschino cherry juice or other cherry juice

¾ cup heavy whipping cream

1 teaspoon almond and/or vanilla extract

1 or 2 drops red gel food coloring, for brighter pink, optional

### FOR THE FLUFFY BUTTERMILK CHIFFON CAKE:

6 large eggs, separated, at room temperature

½ teaspoon cream of tartar or lemon juice

1½ cups granulated sugar, divided

½ cup vegetable or canola oil

¾ cup cold buttermilk

2 teaspoons vanilla extract

2 cups cake flour (see Note)

1 tablespoon baking powder

**TO MAKE THE CHERRY–WHITE CHOCOLATE GANACHE:** Place the white chocolate, cherry juice, and cream in a microwave-safe bowl. Heat in 20-second intervals, stirring between each interval, 'til almost melted. Once smooth, mix in the extract and food coloring (if using). Cover with plastic wrap and refrigerate for about 1 hour.

**TO MAKE THE FLUFFY BUTTERMILK CHIFFON CAKE:** Preheat the oven to 325°F.

In a large mixing bowl, beat the egg whites and cream of tartar (or lemon juice) 'til soft peaks form. Gradually add ¼ cup of the sugar and continue beating 'til stiff peaks form. Set aside.

In a separate small mixing bowl, whisk together the egg yolks, oil, buttermilk, and vanilla.

In a separate bowl, sift together the flour, remaining sugar, baking powder, and salt. Make a well in the center and add the egg yolk mixture. Mix 'til the batter is smooth and light.

Gradually pour the batter over the beaten egg whites, folding gently with a large rubber spatula 'til just combined. You want to be very gentle in this step, don't stir or mix.

Line the bottom of two 8-inch round cake pans with parchment paper (cut to fit). Do not grease the sides. Divide the batter evenly between the pans.

Bake at 325°F for 30 to 35 minutes, or 'til a toothpick inserted into the center comes out clean and the cake springs back when touched.

Once baked, immediately invert the pans onto a cooling rack and let cool completely in the pans for about 45 minutes to an hour.

1 teaspoon salt

1 cup fresh fruit or fruit preserves, such as cherry or strawberry, optional

*Note: If you can't find cake flour, sift together 1¾ cups all-purpose flour with ¼ cup cornstarch.*

After chilling, the ganache should have a peanut butter–like consistency. If it's too stiff, gradually warm it in the microwave in 5- to 10-second bursts 'til spreadable. If too loose, refrigerate again 'til it firms up. Once it's the right texture, transfer to a mixing bowl and whip for 2 minutes 'til smooth and fluffy.

Once the cakes are cool, run a knife around the edges and carefully remove the cakes from the pans. If the tops of your cake layers are uneven, trim them flat using a cake leveler or a bread knife.

Spread a small amount of frosting on a cake plate or cake board, then place the first layer on the plate. Spread a ¼-inch-thick layer of frosting on top of the first cake layer using a rubber spatula. If you like, layer on some fresh fruit or fruit preserves. Place the second cake layer on top, then spread another layer of frosting on top. Spread a thin (¼-inch-thick) layer of frosting all over the cake for the crumb coat. You should have a little less than half the frosting left. Refrigerate for 10 to 15 minutes to set the crumb coat.

Once the crumb coat is set (you can refrigerate for 10 to 15 minutes to speed things up), spread the rest of the frosting over the whole cake. Decorate as desired, then serve!

ON THE ROAD: STREET EATS AND TAVERN BITES

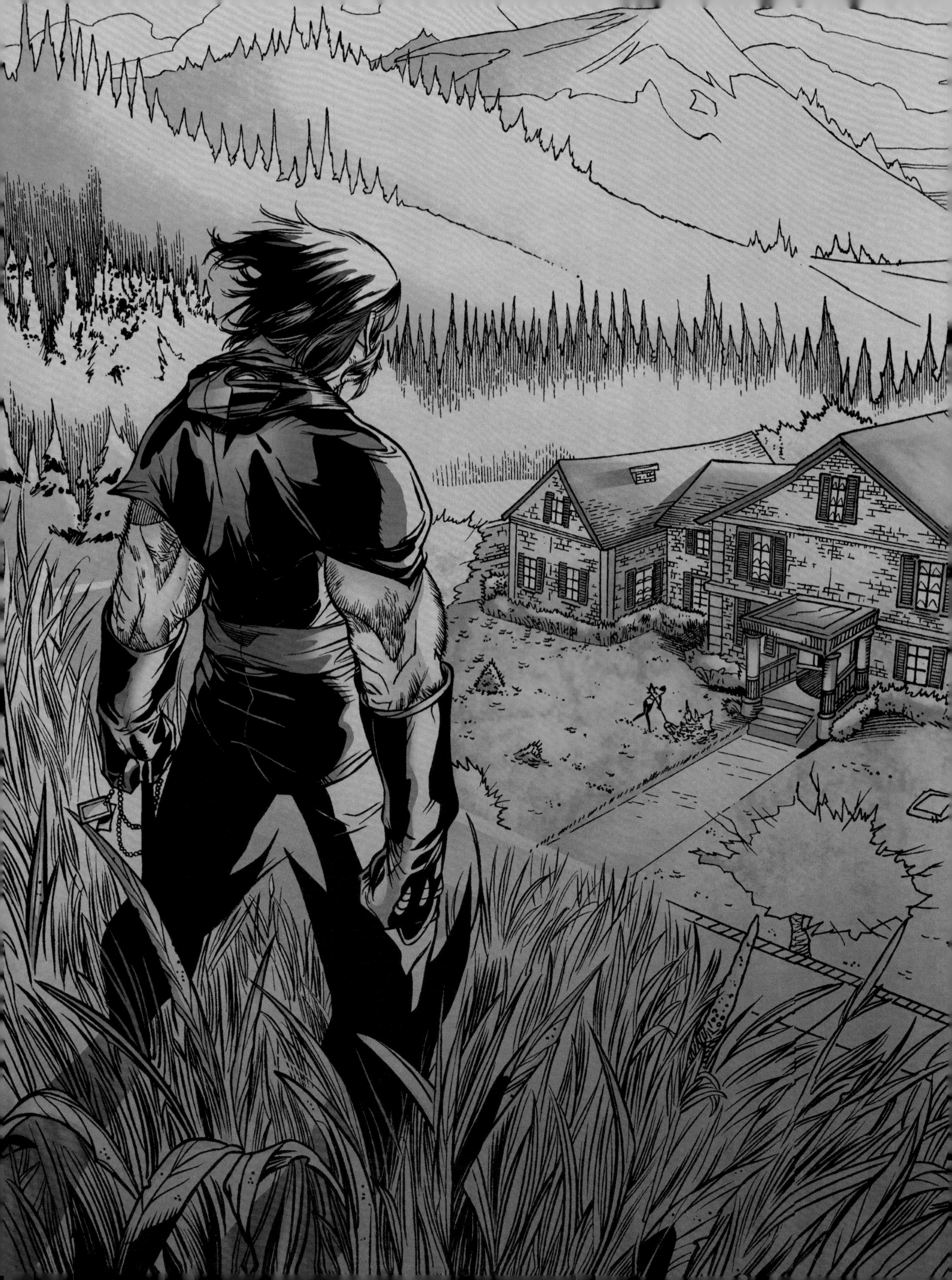

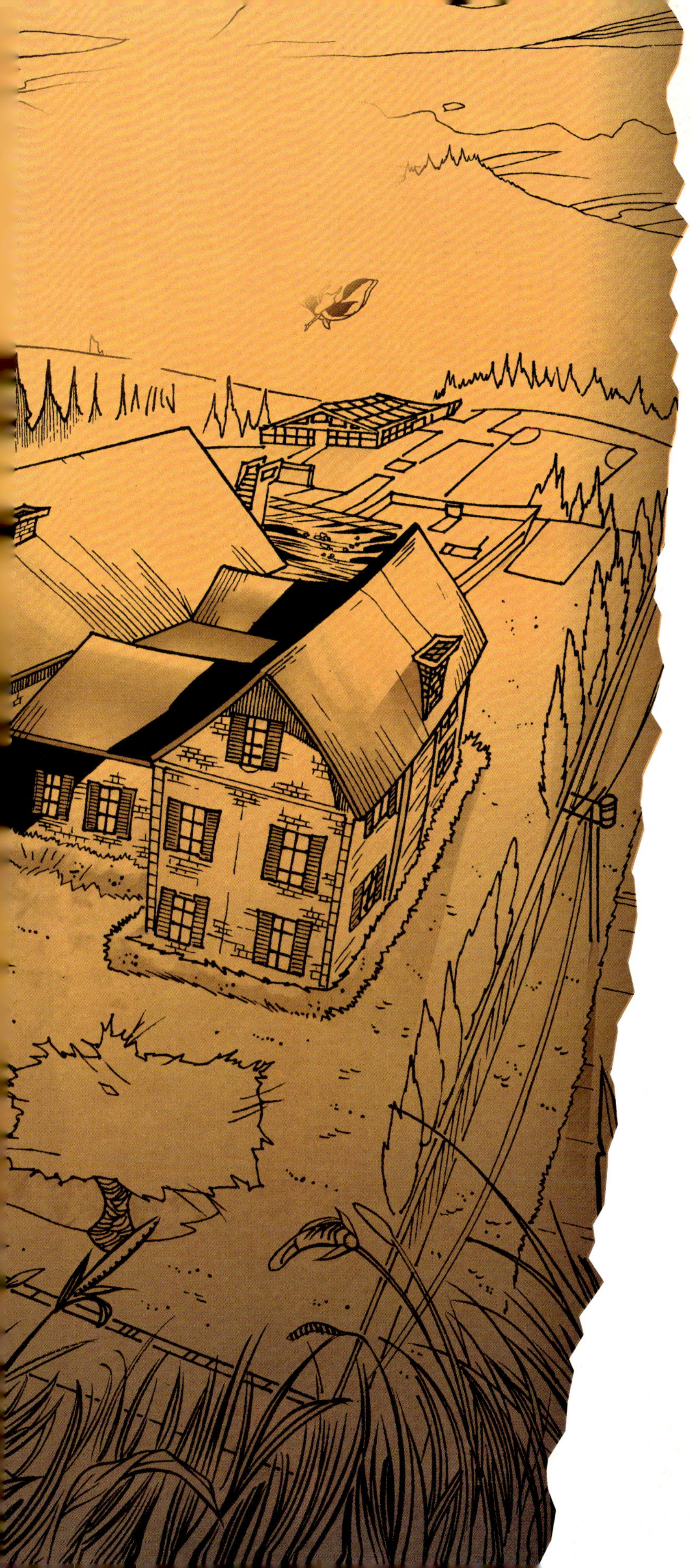

# 5

## HOME SWEET HOME: X-MEN FAMILY RECIPES

Mutation is a funny thing. A lifeform gets by for ages bein' one kinda thing—then a bolt from beyond hits, and changes everything. After more than a lifetime of kicking around the world, hitching up with other mutants in the X-Men finally gave me a place to put down roots. Bein' part of a team wasn't always an easy fit for me. But bit by bit, that funny thing happened. The folks around me mutated into more than a team—they became my *family*.

Over the years, we've shared countless holidays and "family dinners"—whether in the Professor's Mansion, the Australian outback, or wherever else we were callin' home. Those recipes, like X-Men themselves, come from all over the world—and plenty are just as memorable. 'Course, like any family, we've had our scrapes and falling-outs. And I've got some notes in here on how to survive that, too. But we always manage to patch things up because for most of us, this is the most we've ever felt at home.

# THE PROFESSOR'S CAMBRIC TEA

Charles Xavier changed my life. The man gave me a home. A family. More than anything, the Professor helped give me back my mind. After damn near a century of creeps screwin' with my brain, even the premiere mutant telepath had his work cut out for him. But despite my mess—and my rage—the man never ran outta patience, kindness, or *tea*.

Charles would start some sessions with a fresh mug, asking me to use my senses to comb through the blossoming flavors—leaves, herbs, and spices from all around the world blending and bleeding together. My first thought was that he wanted an excuse to take teatime like he did while going to school in England. But I will always give that man his due: the simple, alluring experience somehow cleared away the noise and relaxed my mind. Eventually, I graduated to makin' my own tea, with something of a ritual that brings its own calm and focus—to help me appreciate what I have. All thanks to Chuck.

**Servings: 2 • Type: Beverage • Difficulty: Easy • Prep Time: 5 minutes • Cook Time: 10 minutes Rest Time: None • Dietary Considerations: GF, V, V+**

**TEA RECOMMENDATIONS:**

**BLACK:** Earl Grey, Scottish or English Breakfast Tea, Assam, Lapsang Souchong

**HERBAL:** Lavender, Chamomile, Mint, Linden, Rose

**GREEN:** Jasmine, Matcha, Genmaicha, Houjicha

**SPICE:** Masala Chai, Cinnamon Spice, Ginger, Cardamom, Turmeric

**OTHER:** Rooibos, Pu'erh, Corn Tea, Flavored Teas

**FOR THE DRINK:**

1 or 2 tea bags or 1 or 2 tablespoons loose leaf tea*

1 cup whole milk or full-fat oat milk

Pinch of salt

½ vanilla bean, split or ½ teaspoon vanilla extract (optional)

1 tablespoon honey (or to taste)

In a small saucepan, combine the tea, milk, salt, and vanilla bean.

Heat the mixture over low heat 'til it becomes steamy, but be careful not to let it boil.

Remove from heat and strain into a teapot using a mesh strainer.

Stir in the honey, adjusting the sweetness to your liking.

Pour into teacups and serve hot.

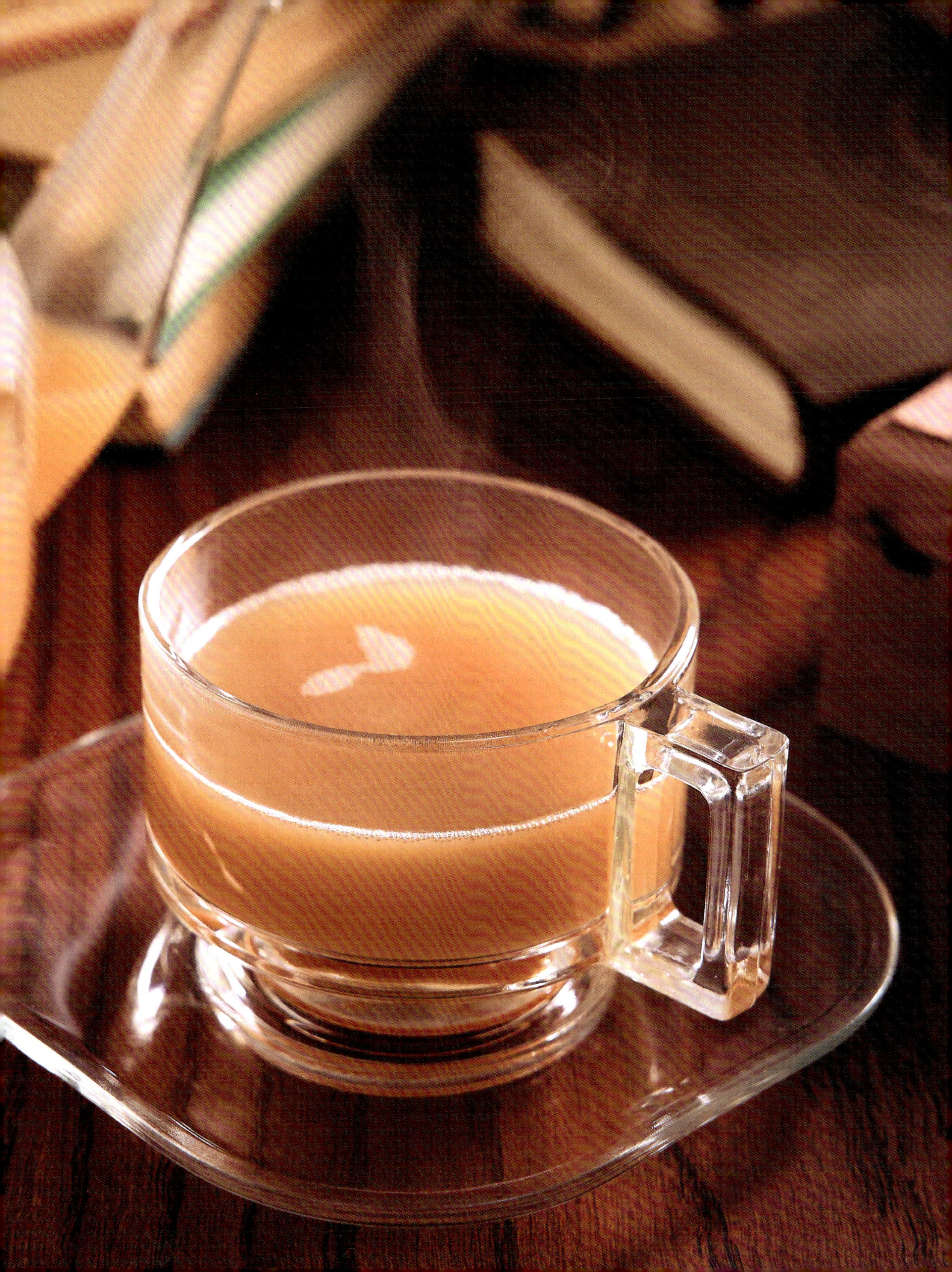

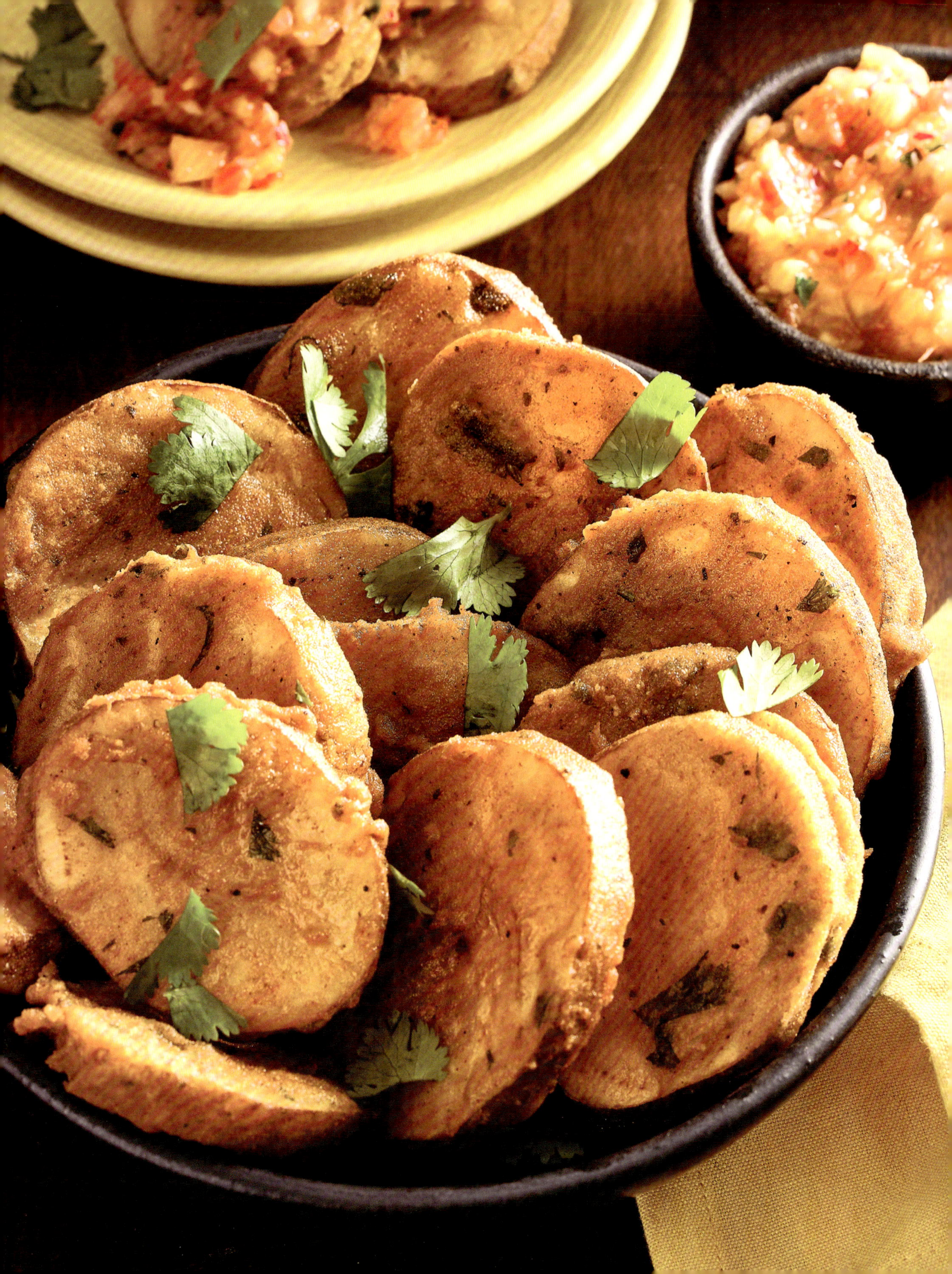

# STORM'S BAJIAS

Seeing the goddess she is now, it's easy to forget Ororo grew up orphaned, scrappin' her survival together through the streets and alleys of Cairo. That is, till you get a glimpse of her *savvy*—or her *cooking*. To put all the swirling, electrifying spices and flavors she rains onto a dish like this, she's gotta know her way around the market stalls. This recipe came from her mother's family in Kenya, so it means a lot when she makes it for the X-Men. Each crispy, bright, and dynamic bite shows you're dealing with a chef who knows spices, like found family, make a dinner table amazing.

**Servings: 4 to 6 • Type: Appetizer/Snack • Difficulty: Average • Prep Time: 30 minutes • Cook Time: 1 hour • Rest Time: None • Dietary Considerations: V, V+, GF***

## FOR THE MANGO CHUTNEY (OPTIONAL):

2 ripe mangos, peeled and diced

1-inch piece ginger, chopped

½ medium red onion, chopped

2 cloves garlic, sliced

1 large tomato, chopped

¼ cup chopped fresh cilantro

½ large red bell pepper, roughly chopped

1 serenade, Fresno, or jalapeño chile, chopped

1 tablespoon white wine vinegar or lime juice

1 tablespoon olive oil

½ teaspoon salt, or to taste

## FOR THE BAJIAS:

1 cup besan or gram flour

½ cup all-purpose flour or rice flour

1 tablespoon *Dagger Bay Blend* (pg 30) or curry powder

1½ teaspoons garam masala

1 teaspoon ground ginger

1¾ teaspoons salt, or to taste, divided

¾ teaspoon black pepper, or to taste

1 cup water, or more as needed

¼ cup chopped fresh cilantro, plus more for garnish

3 large potatoes, peeling optional

Neutral oil, such as grapeseed or canola, for frying

**TO MAKE THE MANGO CHUTNEY:** Add all the ingredients except the salt to a food processor or blender and mix 'til a thick, chunky sauce forms, similar in consistency to salsa. Add salt and pepper to taste. Set aside in an airtight container in the refrigerator 'til ready to use.

**TO MAKE THE BAJIAS:** Combine the chickpea flour, all-purpose flour, Dagger Bay Blend, garam masala, ground ginger, 1 teaspoon of the salt, and black pepper in a large mixing bowl 'til evenly mixed. Stir in the water and chopped cilantro 'til you have a thick, smooth batter. The consistency of the batter should be thick enough to easily coat the potato slices without excessive dripping but not so thick that it's hard to dip the potatoes into it. Adjust the water or flour quantity as needed.

Using a mandolin or a sharp knife, slice the potatoes into ¼-inch-thick slices. Sprinkle the potato slices evenly with the remaining salt.

Add 1 inch of oil to a large skillet or deep frying pan. Heat over medium-high heat to about 375°F, or hot enough that a drop of batter sizzles immediately upon contact.

Dip each potato slice into the batter, making sure both sides are well-coated. Let any excess batter drip off before carefully dropping the slices into the hot oil. Fry the coated potato slices for about 3 minutes per side or 'til golden and crispy on both sides. You may need to do this in batches to prevent overcrowding.

Once the fritters are golden and crisp on both sides, remove them from the oil using a slotted spoon or a pair of metal tongs. Transfer them to a paper towel–lined plate to drain. Continue battering and frying the remaining potato slices in batches 'til all are cooked.

Serve the bajias warm or at room temperature with a side of the mango chutney for dipping or use another dipping sauce of your choice. Garnish with chopped fresh cilantro, if you like.

# NIGHTCRAWLER'S BAVARIAN CHEESE DIP

Guten Tag, mein Freund! Since you enjoyed it so much, here is how you can make my traditional cheese dip on your own the next time I've teleported off to rescue a damsel in distress. While you and I usually enjoy it with the Bavarian pretzels (washed down with a cheers to fond memories), it also makes for an x-cellent spread. Prost! —Kurt, your fuzzy elf

Servings: 4 to 6 • Type: Appetizer/Snack • Difficulty: Easy • Prep Time: 10 minutes • Cook Time: None • Rest Time: 2 hours (optional) • Dietary Considerations: GF, V • Pairs well with: Hard or soft pretzels, Colossus's Buckwheat Blinis (pg 151)

FOR THE OBAZDA:

1 large shallot or 1/2 medium red onion

8 ounces Camembert or Brie cheese, room temperature

6 ounces quark or other cream cheese, softened

4 tablespoons unsalted butter, softened

1 1/2 tablespoons sweet paprika

2 teaspoons caraway seeds, ground

1/2 teaspoon salt, or to taste

1/2 teaspoon black pepper, or to taste

1 tablespoon apple juice

1 teaspoon apple cider vinegar

1 tablespoon german mustard

Chopped fresh parsley or chives, for garnish

TO SERVE:

Pretzels (soft or hard)

Sliced radishes or other raw veggies

Toasted rye, pumpernickel, or vollkornbrot, optional

Slice 4 to 5 thin slices from the shallot or red onion to use for garnish, then finely chop the rest.

Add the camembert to a medium-sized mixing bowl and mash it thoroughly with a fork. Add the cream cheese, butter, spices, apple juice, vinegar, and mustard. Continue to mash 'til the mixture reaches a creamy consistency. Add salt to taste.

If you like, let the spread chill for 2 hours or overnight, and then stir in the onions just before serving. If serving immediately, go ahead and mix in the onions.

Garnish the onion slices from Step 1 and chopped chives. Serve with soft and/or hard pretzels, sliced radishes and/or other veggies for dipping. Alternatively, serve spread on top of toasted rye, pumpernickel, or vollkornbrot.

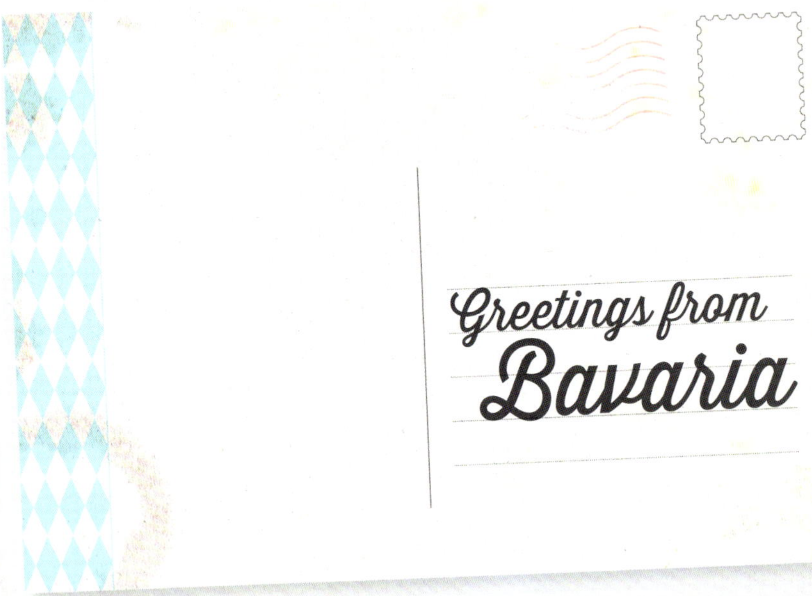
Greetings from
Bavaria

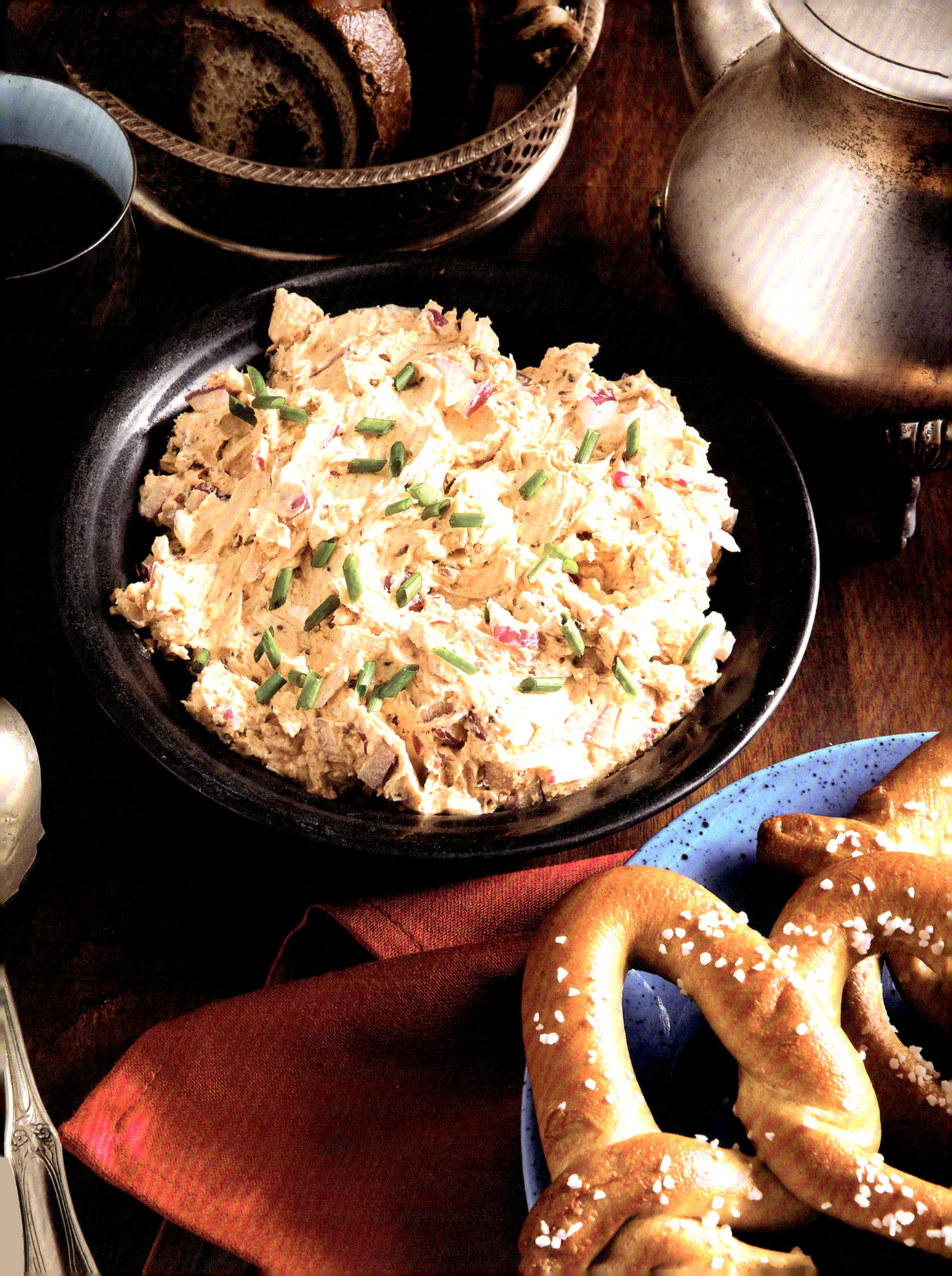

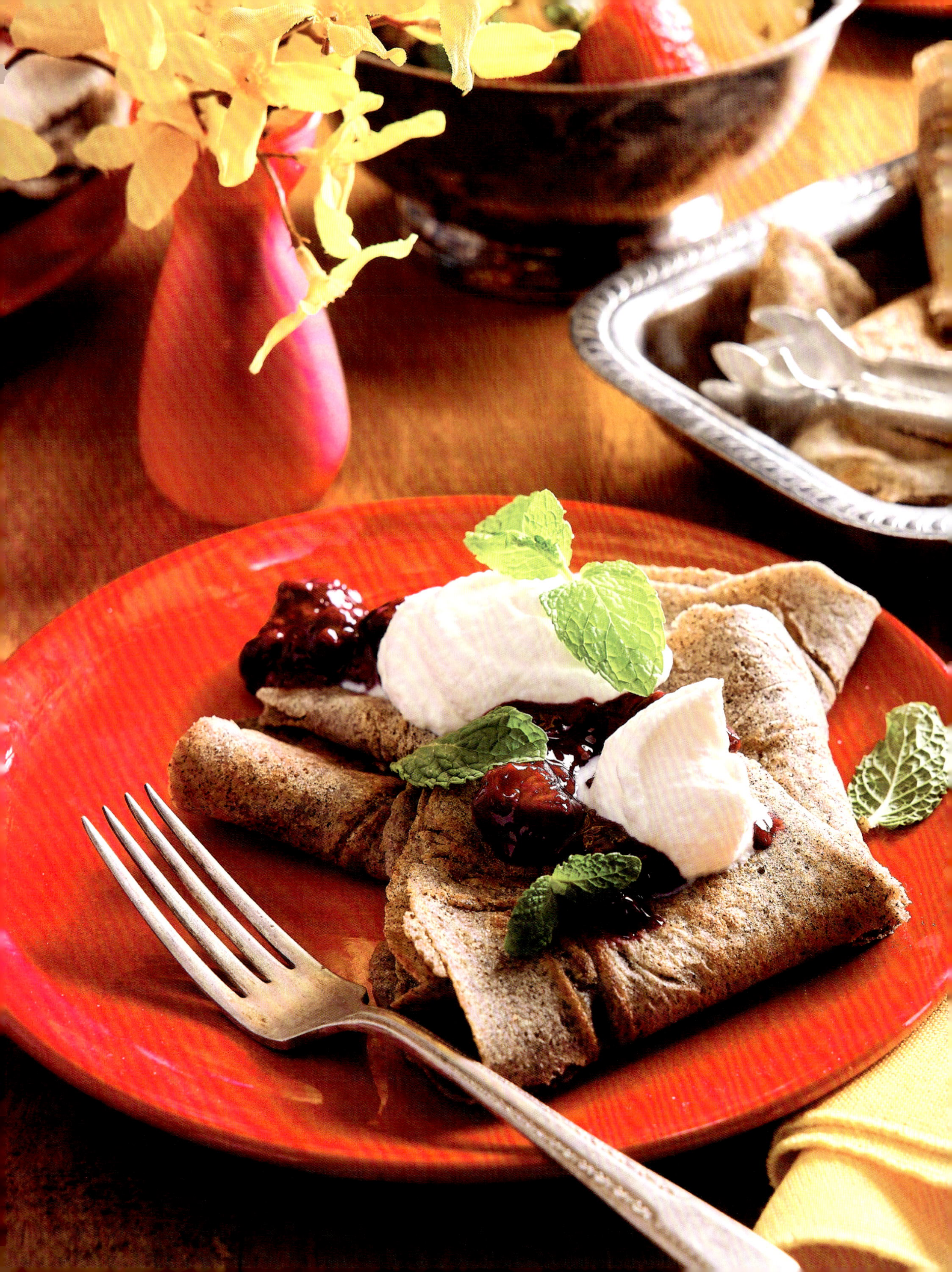

# COLOSSUS'S BUCKWHEAT BLINIS

Hearty—but delicate. Could describe Colossus's go-to team breakfast, or the ol' rusty Russian himself. No surprise a guy raised to work a communist wheat farm knows how to cook up (and put away) giant stacks of wheat cakes. But Piotr Rasputin's also a painter, a poet, and one of the most gentle souls I've ever known. So maybe it's no surprise his take on breakfast is something more like a fine crepe. And these blinis prove to be just as versatile as Pete himself—able to carry sweet or savory finishes just as easily as Colossus can throw a "fastball special."

**Servings: 4 to 6 • Type: Breakfast/Dessert/Appetizer • Difficulty: Average • Prep Time: 15 minutes
Cook Time: 30 minutes • Rest Time: None • Dietary Considerations: V
Pairs well with:** *Wojapi* **(pg 36)**

**FOR THE BLINIS:**

1 cup buckwheat flour
1 cup all-purpose flour
½ teaspoon baking powder
¼ teaspoon baking soda
1 to 2 tablespoons granulated sugar (savory or sweet)
¼ teaspoon salt
2 tablespoons unsalted butter, melted, plus more for greasing
1 cup kefir (more as needed)
3 large eggs, lightly beaten
1½ cups water

**TO SERVE (SAVORY OPTIONS):**

Cold smoked salmon
Sour cream or quark
Chopped fresh dill
Sliced veggies like cucumber or red onion (optional)
Caviar and/or capers

**TO SERVE (SWEET OPTIONS):**

Fresh fruit, fruit preserves, and/or *Wojapi* (pg 36)
Whipped cream, mascarpone, and/or chocolate hazelnut spread
Chocolate sauce, honey, or sweetened condensed milk (for drizzling)
Crushed nuts or mini chocolate chips

In a large mixing bowl, stir together the buckwheat flour, all-purpose flour, baking powder, baking soda, sugar, and salt. Set aside.

In a separate medium mixing bowl, add the butter, kefir, and eggs. Whisk to combine thoroughly.

Add the kefir mixture to the flour mixture and stir to combine. Add 1 cup of water and whisk to combine. Add the rest of the water a tablespoon at a time, adding just enough so you have a smooth but runny batter that's a bit runnier than pancake batter, almost like heavy cream.

Heat a skillet or griddle over medium heat. Once the pan is hot, grease it with butter.

**FOR LARGER CREPE-LIKE BLINI:** Pour in about ¼ cup of batter. As soon as the batter hits the pan, start tilting and rotating the pan to spread the batter evenly into a thin circle. If any holes appear, fill them in with a bit more batter. Cook for 1 to 2 minutes 'til set, then flip over and cook for another 30 seconds to 1 minute, or 'til the blini is browned on both sides. Repeat with the rest of the batter, stacking the finished blini on top of each other on a plate.

**FOR SMALLER BLINIS:** Add 1-tablespoon portions of batter to the pan, about 4 at a time, cooking for 1 to 2 minutes per side.

Serve immediately with either savory or sweet fillings spread in between each blini and/or on top to taste.

# SLIM'S CHEESESTEAK SANDWICHES

It's no secret Cyclops and me don't always see eye-to-eye. Even on his good days, Scotty can't help but seem a little bland. So, I was sure as hell skeptical when he kept goin' on about some damn cheesesteak bein' the best sandwich he had in ages. Third time he brought it up, I stole the Blackbird and flew to Philly just to bring a batch back to the mansion to prove him wrong. But damnit … they were GOOD. So good, I had to sniff out as many secret ingredients as I could to try and figure how to make my own. What can I say? Sometimes, Slim gets it right. Guess that's why everyone keeps lettin' him lead. (Not that I'd ever tell him he was right about the sandwiches.)

**Servings: 4 sandwiches • Type: Sandwich • Difficulty: Average • Prep Time: 20 minutes Cook Time: 30 minutes • Rest Time: None • Pairs well with: *All-Dressed Chips* (pg 97), *Poutine* (pg 94), *Jubilee's Food Court Chili Fries* (pg 154)**

1 pound ribeye or sirloin, shaved or very thinly sliced

1 tablespoon *Mutant Medley* (pg 30)

1 to 2 teaspoons *Weapon X* (pg 30) or other steak seasoning, optional

1 teaspoon salt, or to taste

¾ teaspoon black pepper, or to taste

4 sandwich rolls

6 tablespoons unsalted butter

1 large sweet onion, sliced

2 garlic cloves, minced

1 large red bell pepper, sliced

1 large yellow bell pepper, sliced

8 slices mild provolone or white American cheese

Season the meat evenly with Mutant Medley, Weapon X, salt, and pepper, and set aside.

Using a serrated knife, cut the sandwich rolls ¾ of the way through, so that the two halves easily open but are not completely separated. Spread about 1 tablespoon of butter evenly over the inside of each of the sandwich rolls. Toast the buns butter-side down on a large skillet or griddle 'til golden brown over medium heat. Set aside.

Turn the heat to medium-low and add 1 tablespoon of butter to the skillet or griddle. Add the onion, garlic, and bell peppers and cook, stirring occasionally, 'til the onions are browned and very tender, about 10 to 20 minutes. Transfer to a plate and set aside.

Turn the heat up to medium-high and melt the remaining tablespoon of butter on the skillet. Cook the meat in one layer for 4 to 5 minutes 'til no pink remains and they take on a nice browned, caramelized color. Depending on the size of your skillet or griddle, you may need to do this in batches to prevent overcrowding. You want the meat browned, not boiled. Once all the steak is cooked, add back the veggies and cook for 1 more minute together.

Turn off the heat, push the meat and veggies into 4 even portions, then add 2 slices of cheese on top of each. Let the cheese melt for a minute or two.

Once the cheese has melted, use a spatula to quickly scoop the cheesy beef into the toasted bun, cheese-side first. Serve immediately.

# LOGAN'S DRY-SMOKED RIBS

Might as well throw in my usual contribution to a mutant family cookout. Slightly sweet, tangy, and savory—these ribs take down even the most ferocious appetites. Sure, I got the skills to make delicate sashimi or vegan Madripoor curry, but a good teammate knows his role. And here, I'm the hunter, the one cuttin' to the bone—and the best there is at what I do.

**Servings: 4 • Type: Main • Difficulty: Average • Prep Time: 20 minutes**
**Cook Time: 4 to 5 hours • Rest Time: 4 hours**

### FOR THE RIBS:

1 rack baby back ribs

½ tablespoon salt

3 to 4 tablespoons *Danger Room Rub* (pg 30)

¼ cup honey, loosened

### FOR THE MOP SAUCE:

½ cup apple cider vinegar

½ cup apple juice

1 tablespoon garlic salt

### SPECIAL EQUIPMENT:

Baking sheet, for alternative method

Aluminum foil, for alternative method

Wire rack, for alternative method

Remove the membrane from the back of each rack of ribs by pulling it off with your fingers, using paper towels for grip, or with pliers.

Rub the salt and 2 tablespoons of the rub over the ribs on both sides, then transfer the ribs to a roasting pan. Cover with plastic wrap and let cure in the refrigerator for at least 4 hours, or overnight.

Prepare the mop sauce by mixing apple cider vinegar, apple juice, and garlic salt in a bowl. Set aside.

Prepare your smoker or grill for indirect heating by placing a drip pan in the center. Preheat the smoker to 230°F. Use hickory, apple, or pecan wood for smoking. Spray or brush the grill grates with oil to prevent sticking.

Smoke the ribs for 4 to 5 hours. Turn the ribs and baste them with the mop sauce every 50 minutes to keep them moist and flavorful. During the final basting session, sprinkle the remaining *Danger Room Rub* over the ribs. The ribs are done when the meat has pulled back from the ends of the rib bones by ¼ inch to ⅜ inch and twisting a bone causes it to come free from the meat.

Remove the ribs from the smoker or grill, then brush them with honey. Wrap the ribs in foil and let them rest for 15 to 20 minutes to allow the juices to redistribute.

Slice the ribs into one- or two-bone sections and serve.

**Alternative Method:** Instead of grilling, preheat the oven to 275°F. Line a baking sheet with aluminum foil and place a wire rack on top of the baking sheet. Place the seasoned ribs on the wire rack, bone-side down. Cook the ribs in the preheated oven for 2½ to 3 hours, brushing them with the mop sauce every 40 to 50 minutes, applying the remaining rub on the last baste. If you want, broil them at 500°F for the last 10 minutes for a nice char. Once the ribs are done, remove them from the oven, brush with honey, wrap in foil, and let rest for 15 to 20 minutes before slicing and serving.

# JUBILEE'S FOOD COURT CHILI FRIES

Dude. When my rhetorical clap-back is "Does a mall babe eat chili fries?"—you should know better than to try and pass your weird Canadian POO-teen off as my precious manna from food court heaven! But since you've been cool enough to teach me a few tricks over the years, I guess I can show the great and terrible Wolverine how to snikt-up some spuds into something totally killer.

Servings: 4 • Type: Side or Appetizer • Difficulty: Easy • Prep Time: 15 minutes • Cook Time: 45 minutes • Rest Time: None • Dietary Considerations: GF*

### FOR THE CHILI CON CARNE:

1 tablespoon olive oil

1 large sweet onion, finely chopped

1 pound lean ground beef

1 tablespoon tomato paste

1 heaping tablespoon chili powder

1 heaping tablespoon Mutant Medley (pg 30)

1 heaping teaspoon ground cumin

1 tablespoon brown sugar

2 cups tomato sauce

1 teaspoon salt, or to taste

1/2 teaspoon black pepper, or to taste

### FOR THE FRIES AND TOPPINGS:

1 pound frozen fries or use homemade fries (pg 94)

1 cup finely shredded cheddar cheese

1/2 cup sour cream

2 green onions, sliced on a bias

### SPECIAL EQUIPMENT:

Sparklers or firework cake toppers, optional

To make the chili sauce, heat the oil in a large skillet over medium-high heat. Add the onion and cook 'til starting to brown, about 5 to 6 minutes. Add the ground beef and cook 'til there's no more pink, breaking up any large pieces, about 8 minutes. Drain the excess fat, if necessary.

Stir in the tomato paste, chili powder, Mutant Medley, and cumin 'til thoroughly combined. Let cook for 2 to 3 minutes, then stir in the tomato sauce and brown sugar. Reduce heat to low and simmer uncovered for 12 to 15 minutes to allow the flavors to meld, and the sauce to reduce. Taste and adjust seasoning, then cover and set aside.

Cook the frozen fries according to the package directions or preheat an air fryer to 400°F and cook the fries in the air fryer basket for about 10 to 15 minutes 'til crispy.

To assemble the chili fries, add a layer of fries to the serving plate(s), then ladle on a generous amount of chili, followed by a generous dollop of sour cream and sprinkle of green onions. Garnish servings with firework cake toppers or sparklers and serve hot!

## HOW TO
# SURVIVING FAMILY DINNERS

Family dinners can be dangerous. If your kin's anything like mine, petty disagreements could end with the whole place leveled. That's why you gotta treat 'em like any combat scenario: stay sharp and be ready for anything. Here's some survival tips to help you get through it. Call it battle prep.

**PREPARATION** Before you step foot into the lion's den, prepare yourself mentally and physically. Hydrate. Practice your best "I'm interested in what you're saying" face in the mirror. Maybe grab a quick nap—you're gonna need all the energy you can get.

**THE ENTRANCE** When you step in, assess the situation. Who's in a good mood? Who's already startin' in on the Morlocks? I usually head straight for the snack table. Harder to get dragged into a conversation when you've got a mouth full of cheese dip. Just be careful not to choke if you have a family member like Kurt who appears outta nowhere.

**CONVERSATIONAL MINEFIELDS** Certain topics are like throwing a match into gasoline: politics, money, or whatever drama blew up at the last dinner. Dodge those like your life depends on it—at the mansion, sometimes it does. Stick to safe, boring stuff like the weather ... unless Ororo's around. In that case, DO NOT ENGAGE in weather talk.

**SEATING STRATEGY** This is key. If there's a kids' table, I say go for it. Less drama, more fun. But if you're stuck at the adult table, aim to sit next to someone who either doesn't talk much or has a tendency to doze off. And for the love of Peter Parker, do not sit directly across from any self-important schmucks with laser eyes.

**DODGING TOUGH QUESTIONS** "So, when are you settling down?" or "How're the kids?" I find that grunting and walking away gets my point across. If you feel like playing nice, throw out something vague like "It's a work in progress." But if you've got a family member who reads minds—figuratively or literally— well, good luck hiding anything from them. If things are getting too heated, say you need to "check on the casserole" and get outta there.

**THE FOOD CRITIC** There's always that one family member who thinks they're celebrity chef Chris Cosentino. If they start critiquing the mashed potatoes, just nod and grab a dinner roll to keep your mouth busy. But if they start trying to season the cranberry sauce, you might have to get physical. I'm watchin' you, Gambit.

**ESCAPE TACTICS** About halfway through dessert, start dropping hints about how early you gotta get up tomorrow. Gather your things, thank the host, and make your escape. Avoid eye contact with the chatty one—sorry, Jubes, I love ya, but I'm out.

**POST-DINNER RECOVERY** Once you've made it out alive, reward yourself. Kick back and treat yourself to some leftovers. You've earned it, bub.

# LOGAN'S "SOPHISTICATED" GRILLED CHEESE

Once I got good and settled at the mansion, I started teasin' the Professor about expecting a certain kind of *lifestyle* from here on out. And how he'd need to show me the ropes. He'd quip back about how he'd need to start with my table manners before he introduced me to "elevated dining." One day I got it into my head to make him the fanciest sandwich I could think of. Eat it *pinkies out* or something. If there's one thing I have a leg up on: there's no payin' for truffles when you've got a sense of smell like mine. So, I went hunting and here we are: The damn thing turned out great, with bitter honey, a rich and runny egg, and those perfumy truffles. I guess the good life's got its claws in me …

**Yield: 1 sandwich • Type: Main • Difficulty: Average • Prep Time: 15 minutes
Cook Time: 15 minutes • Rest Time: About an hour or so nap after eating this sandwich oughta do it, it's a rich one.**

2 slices sourdough bread

3 ounces unsalted butter

2.5 ounces Taleggio cheese

2 slices aged English cheddar

White or black truffles, to taste

1 duck or chicken egg

Sea salt, to taste

Fresh cracked black pepper, to taste

1 ounce bitter honey (buckwheat)

**SPECIAL EQUIPMENT:**

Truffle slicer

Put a sauté pan on medium heat. Butter the bread (both sides of each slice).

Place half the cheese on one slice of bread and add a layer of truffles on top. Put the rest of the cheese over the truffles and top with second slice of buttered bread.

Put the grilled cheese in the pan with some extra butter. Add more, as needed. Cook for about 4 to 5 minutes, 'til golden brown and crispy on one side.

Meanwhile, place a separate pan over medium-high heat and cook the egg sunny-side up. Season the egg with fresh black pepper and flakey salt.

Flip the grilled cheese to cook on the other side, another 4 or so minutes, so it's evenly golden brown on both sides and the cheese is fully melted. Remove the grilled cheese to a plate and place the sunny-side egg on top of the sandwich. Drizzle honey over the top, and rain down a few more shavings of truffles for good measure.

HOME SWEET HOME: X-MEN FAMILY RECIPES

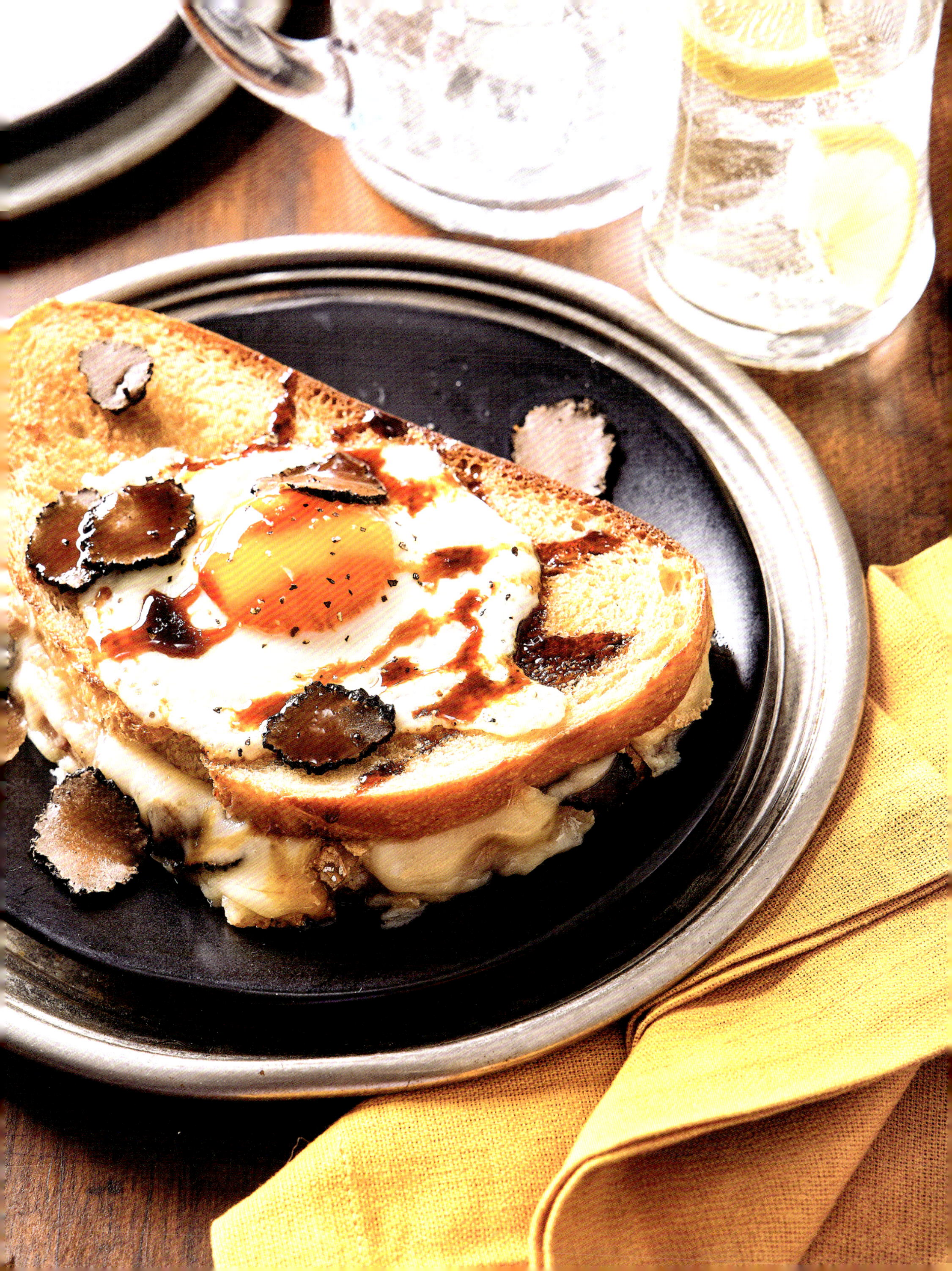

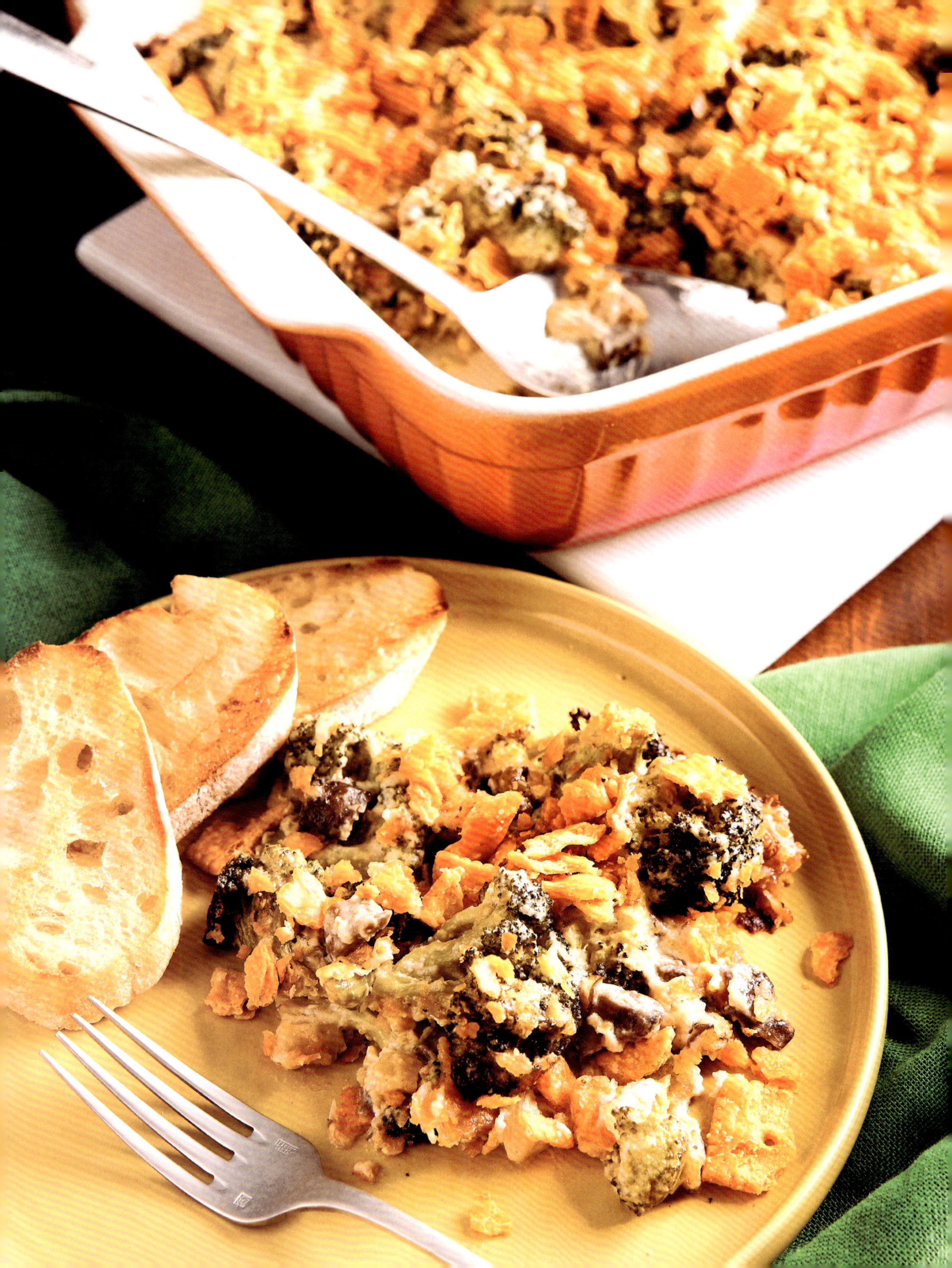

# JEAN'S HOLIDAY BROCCOLI CASSEROLE

Of all the things that make Jean Grey extraordinary—her cookin' *ain't* one of 'em. More than a few holiday dinners and team potlucks got spoiled by Gambit calling her contributions "bland." (Or just thinkin' it too loud for her telepathy to ignore.) But I always understood Red. People like us get more "extraordinary" than we can handle sometimes. Feared, attacked, dragged across space, killed, and resurrected a few times. After a while, it makes you hungry for a little *ordinary*. Sometimes a simple, warm, and creamy home-cooked meal can make life feel normal again. Come to think of it … might be the same thing she sees in Scott Summers. Now *that* boy's bland.

**Servings:** 8 to 10 • **Type:** Side • **Difficulty:** Easy • **Prep Time:** 20 minutes
**Cook Time:** 45 minutes • **Rest Time:** 20 minutes

### FOR THE CREAM OF MUSHROOM SOUP:

- 2 tablespoons butter
- 8 ounces baby bella mushrooms, chopped
- ¼ cup all-purpose flour
- ½ cup whole milk
- ¾ cup chicken or vegetable broth
- ½ teaspoon salt, or to taste
- ½ teaspoon black pepper, or to taste
- Pinch of nutmeg, optional

### FOR THE CASSEROLE:

- 1 tablespoon unsalted butter, plus more for greasing
- 1 medium yellow onion
- 2 cloves garlic, minced
- 1½ cups cream of mushroom soup
- ½ cup mayonnaise
- ½ cup sour cream
- 1½ cups grated sharp cheddar cheese
- 1 tablespoon *Mutant Medley* (pg 30)
- ½ teaspoon salt, or to taste
- 6 cups broccoli florets
- 1½ cups buttery and/or cheesy crackers, crushed

**TO MAKE THE CREAM OF MUSHROOM SOUP,** melt the butter in a medium saucepan over medium-high heat. Add the mushrooms and cook 'til they have released most of their liquid, about 5 to 7 minutes.

Stir in the flour 'til dissolved, then slowly stir in the milk. Stir in chicken or vegetable broth and bring to a simmer, simmer for 5 to 7 minutes 'til thick. Season to taste with salt and pepper. Let cool to almost room temperature before using, or store in the fridge for up to 1 week.

**TO MAKE THE CASSEROLE,** place the broccoli florets in a large steamer basket and set over a pot with 1 or 2 inches of boiling water. Let the broccoli steam for 5 minutes or 'til the broccoli is tender but still very green, then take off the heat and set aside. If you don't have a steamer, bring a large pot of salted water to a boil then add the broccoli and boil for 2 to 4 minutes 'til the broccoli is tender but still green, then strain with a colander and set aside.

Melt the butter in a medium skillet over medium-high heat. Add the onions and garlic and cook 'til the onions have softened, about 4 to 5 minutes. Set aside to cool.

Preheat the oven to 375°F. Grease a 9-by-13-inch casserole dish with butter.

In a large mixing bowl, combine the cooled cream of mushroom soup, mayonnaise, sour cream, shredded cheese, and seasonings. Mix well, then, once they are no longer hot, stir in the onions and garlic. Add the cooled steamed broccoli and stir to combine thoroughly. Taste and adjust seasoning.

Transfer the broccoli mixture to the greased casserole dish and smooth it out with a rubber spatula or a large spoon. Top with the crushed crackers.

Bake for 40 to 45 minutes or 'til the top is browned and the filling is bubbling. If you notice the top getting too brown or burnt in the last 20 minutes, loosely drape a sheet of aluminum foil over the top of the casserole dish.

Remove the casserole from the oven and let cool for 10 to 20 minutes before serving.

# KITTY'S KICKIN' KUGEL

All the way back from when she was "Sprite," the baby of the X-Men, to "Ms. Pryde" teachin' the new pups, Kitty's invited us to share in celebrations across the Jewish calendar. While she's made all kinds of "*kugel*"—sweet, savory, disastrous—this dessert-leanin' take on the creamy noodles especially hit the spot for me. And the darlin' must've noticed I took extra helpings 'cause she's stuck to making it this way ever since.

**Servings: 1 to 2 • Type: Side • Difficulty: Easy • Prep Time: 20 minutes • Cook Time: 1 hour Rest Time: 15 minutes • Dietary Considerations: V**

### FOR THE KUGEL:

½ cup unsalted butter, cut into tablespoons, plus more for greasing

1 cup dried or fresh blueberries

12 ounces wide egg noodles

2 cups milk

6 large eggs

2 cups cottage cheese

2 cups sour cream

½ cup light brown sugar

2 teaspoons ground cinnamon

1½ teaspoons vanilla extract

½ teaspoon salt

### FOR THE TOPPING:

2½ cups cornflakes, crushed (or used crushed graham crackers)

6 tablespoons butter, melted

¼ cup light brown sugar

½ teaspoon cinnamon

Preheat the oven to 350°F. Grease a 9-by-13-inch baking dish with butter.

If using dried blueberries, add them to a small bowl and cover with ¼ cup warm water. Let them soak for 10 to 15 minutes 'til they plump up and soften, then drain.

Cook the noodles according to the package directions, then drain and stir in the butter 'til it melts and coats the noodles.

In a large mixing bowl, whisk together the milk, eggs, cottage cheese, sour cream, sugar, cinnamon, vanilla, and salt.

Add the buttered noodles and blueberries to the mixing bowl and stir to combine, pour this into the prepared baking dish and smooth it out as best you can.

Add the topping ingredients to a medium mixing bowl and toss to combine. Sprinkle the topping evenly over the noodle mixture.

Bake for 1 hour or 'til the noodle mixture is set and the topping is crisp and nicely browned. If the topping is looking too brown or burning on the edges before the kugel is done, cover the dish loosely with foil for the rest of the cooking time.

Let the kugel rest for 10 to 15 minutes, then cut into squares and serve!

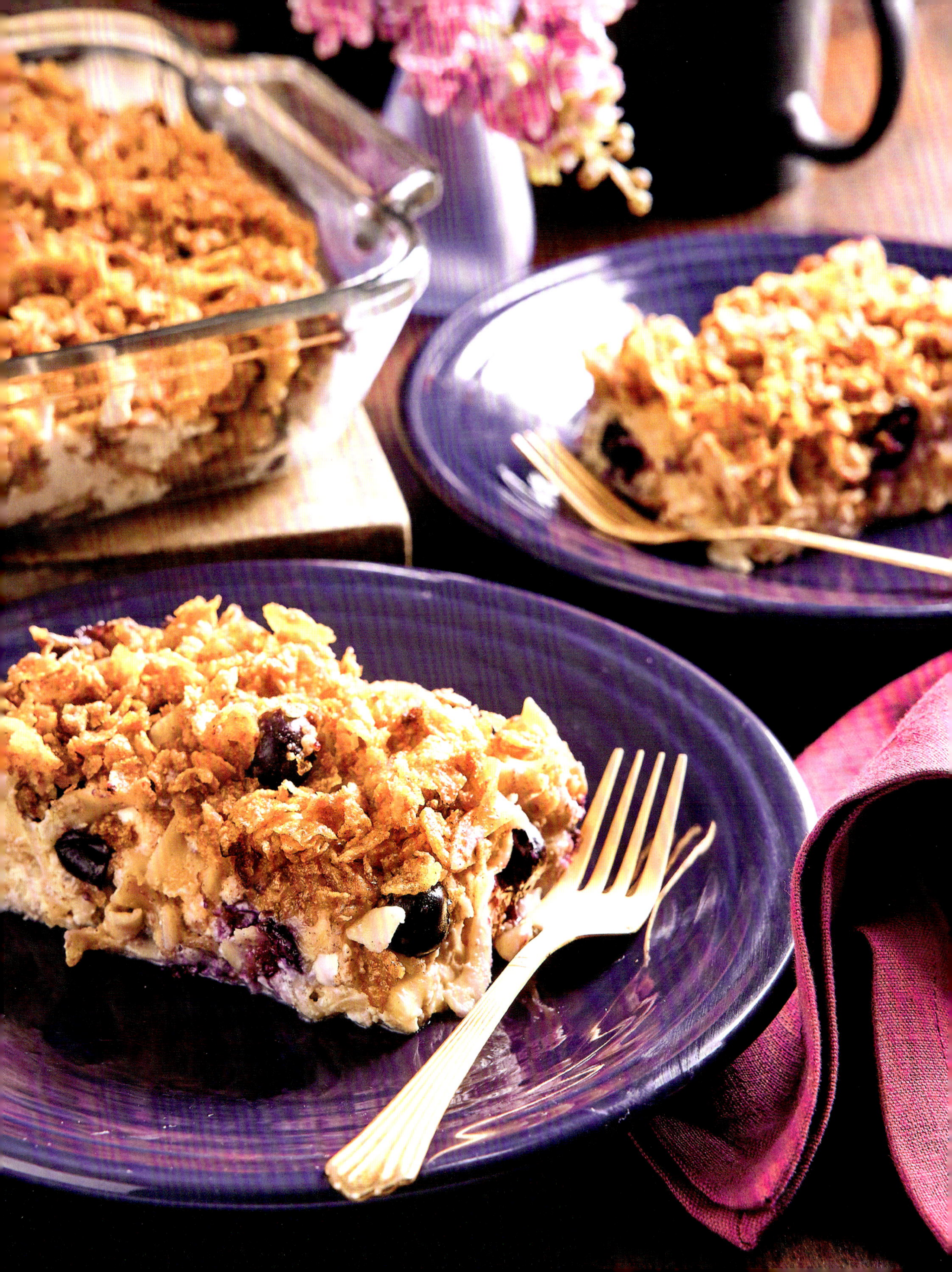

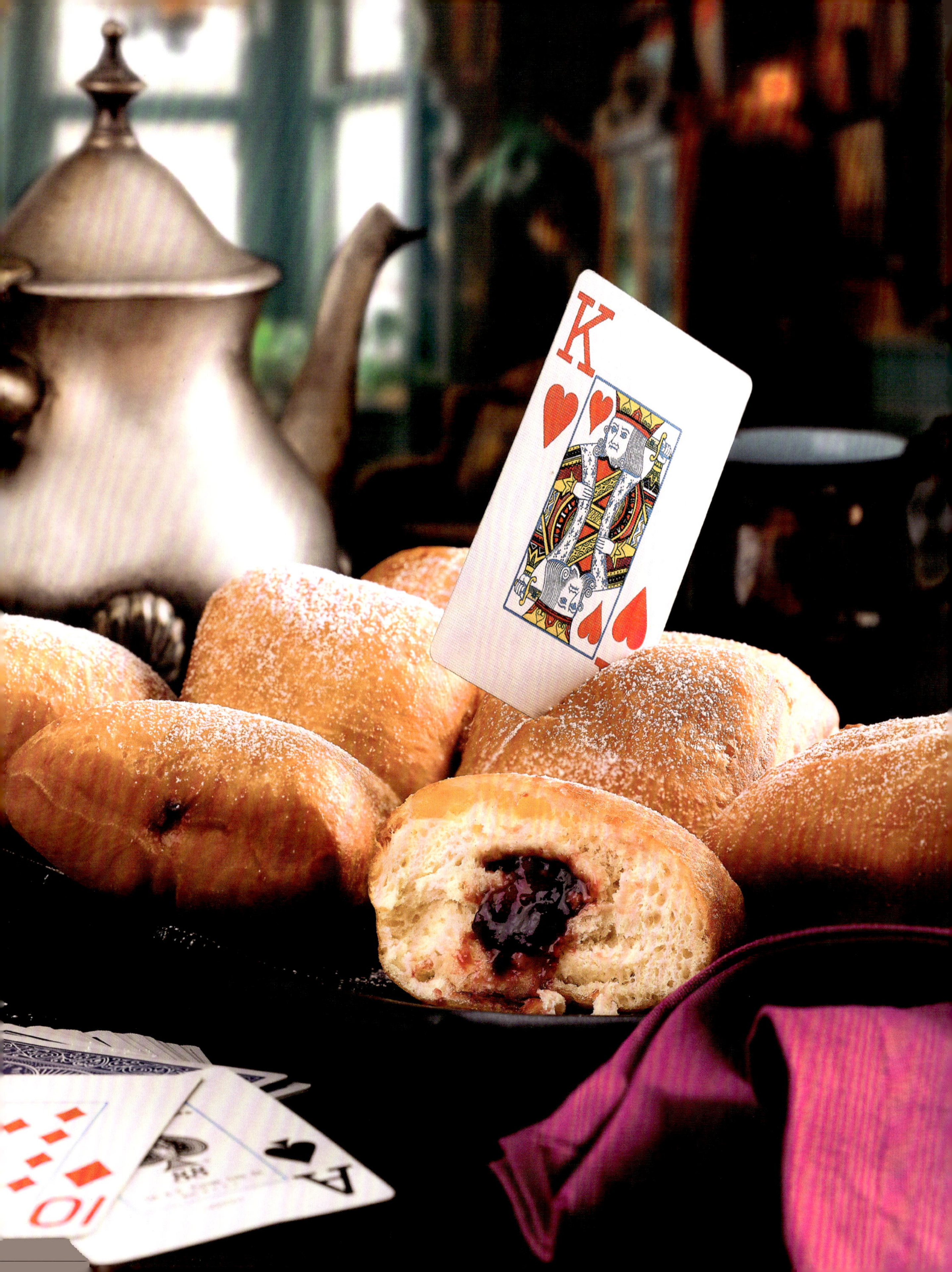
K

# GAMBIT'S "SCOUNDREL" BEIGNETS

Hard to say if Remy LeBeau is more proud of his skills as a thief or his Cajun heritage. Gambit's cockiness could be too much for some—until you taste his Louisiana cooking and realize the boy's right to brag. If it were just about keepin' record of great meals made in Xavier's mansion, Remy could fill a book all his own. But the perfect beignet requires precision, timing, and know-how—same things that make a proper heist. That's probably why he holds this recipe as the powder sugar–coated jewel in his crown. And that's why it was so satisfying to remember *I* stole it from *him*.

**Yield: 2 dozen • Type: Dessert/Snack • Difficulty: Hard • Prep Time: 45 minutes**
**Cook Time: 30 minutes • Rest Time: 2 hours • Dietary Considerations: V**

¾ cup warm water (105°F to 110°F)

2¼ teaspoons active dry yeast

⅓ cup granulated sugar

2 large eggs, room temperature

½ cup whole milk, room temperature

1 teaspoon vanilla extract

4 cups all-purpose flour, more as needed

½ teaspoon salt

3 tablespoons unsalted butter, melted and cooled

4 to 8 cups neutral oil, such as cottonseed or canola, for frying

1 cup seedless raspberry jam

1½ cups powdered sugar, or to taste

**SPECIAL EQUIPMENT:**

Piping bag

Add the warm water to a medium-sized mixing bowl. Use a kitchen thermometer to ensure the water temperature is between 105°F and 110°F. Whisk in the yeast and sugar, then let the mixture sit for 10 minutes 'til it becomes foamy.

Next, whisk in the eggs, milk, and vanilla extract. Add 2 cups of flour and the salt, followed by the melted butter, then gradually mix in the remaining flour. Knead the dough with your hands 'til it becomes smooth and elastic. If the dough is too sticky, add flour one tablespoon at a time 'til it pulls away easily from the sides of the mixing bowl. This step can be done in a stand mixer with a dough hook, if you have one.

Shape the dough into a ball and place it in a large, lightly oiled mixing bowl. Cover with plastic wrap or a damp towel and let the dough rise in a warm area 'til it has doubled in size, about 1 to 2 hours. The exact rising time may vary depending on the ambient temperature and your elevation.

Once the dough has risen, lightly flour your work surface and roll out the dough to a ½-inch thickness. Use a pastry cutter or a sharp knife to cut the dough into 2½-inch squares. Save any scraps, you can use them to test the oil temperature later.

In a large skillet or heavy-bottomed pot, heat 2 to 3 inches of oil to 370°F. If you don't have a thermometer, you can test the oil by dropping a small piece of dough into it; if it bubbles immediately and rises to the surface, the oil is ready.

Fry the beignets in batches to avoid overcrowding the pot or lowering the oil temperature too much. Spoon hot oil over the tops as the bottoms fry, and flip them to ensure both sides are golden and crisp, about 1 to 2 minutes per side.

Once cooked, drain the beignets on a paper towel–lined plate. Spoon the seedless raspberry jam into a piping bag with a small tip. Use a chopstick to make a hole in the side of the beignets. Place the tip of the piping bag into the hole and fill the beignets with 1 to 2 tablespoons of jam, then repeat 'til all the beignets are filled.

Generously dust the beignets with the powdered sugar and serve immediately.

# ICEMAN'S SNOWBALL SPECIAL

Funny how one of the oldest X-Men (at least in terms of joinin' ranks) can't help but seem like one of the kids. Don't get me wrong—Iceman is a helluva powerhouse when he wants to be. But just as often, Bobby's using his frost powers to get the new mutants into bobsled races or snowball wars. And just like a kid in a candy shop, he can't resist makin' a blizzard of these frozen concoctions outta thin air. I know the guy's mutant powers don't include summoning all the hot fudge, cookie pieces, or other treats to sprinkle on top … I'm pretty sure he just sneaks out with the Professor's credit card to stock up on those.

**Servings: 6 • Type: Dessert • Difficulty: Easy • Prep Time: 30 minutes • Cook Time: None Rest Time: 3 hours • Dietary Considerations: V**

1 pint vanilla ice cream or gelato

6 maraschino cherries or other cherries in syrup

1 pint other flavor ice cream or gelato (your choice!)

1 cup crushed cookies, cereal, or graham crackers

1 cup desiccated coconut and/or crushed nuts

½ cup prepared hot fudge or caramel sauce, for serving, optional

6 sprigs fresh mint, for garnish, optional

Allow the ice cream to thaw at room temperature for 10 minutes. Line 6 small (approximately 5- or 6-ounces) bowls or ramekins with plastic wrap.

Scoop some vanilla ice cream into each plastic-lined bowl 'til they're about half full.

Place a cherry in the center of each scoop.

Scoop enough of the other flavor of ice cream on top to fill the bowls and cover the cherry.

Tie the plastic wrap at the tops and freeze for 2 to 4 hours 'til hardened.

To a shallow bowl, or multiple shallow bowls if you want some variety, add the crushed cookies and/or other toppings. Line a baking sheet with parchment paper.

Working with one snowball at a time, unwrap the plastic and roll the snowballs in the toppings to coat, gently pressing them into the toppings to make them stick.

Place the finished snowballs on the parchment-lined baking sheet and freeze for 1 hour before serving. Or wrap each one individually in plastic wrap and store them in a large, airtight container in the freezer 'til ready to serve.

Serve in dessert bowls in shallow pools of fudge or caramel sauce to taste. Drizzle with more sauce, if you like, and garnish with a sprig of fresh mint.

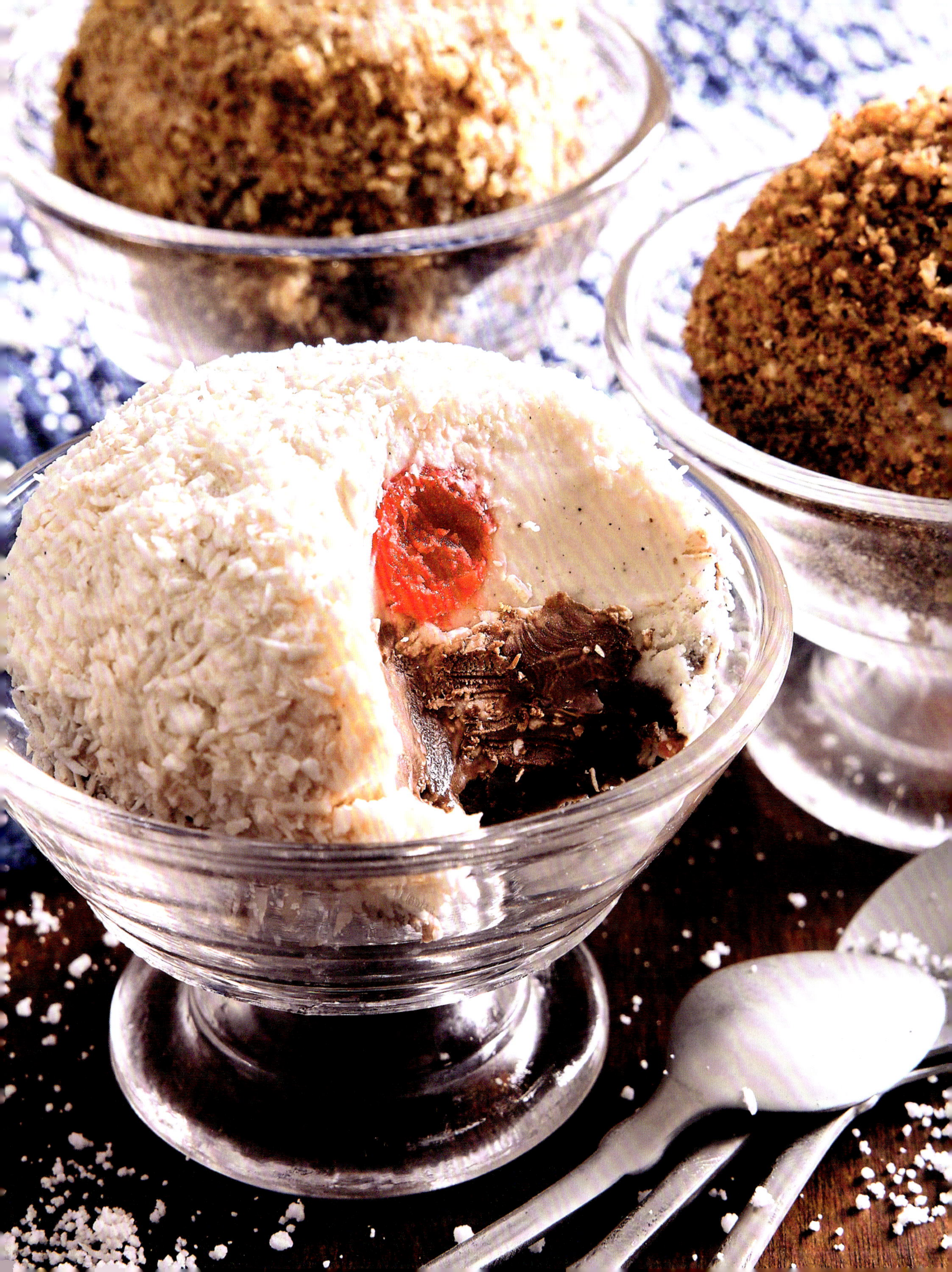

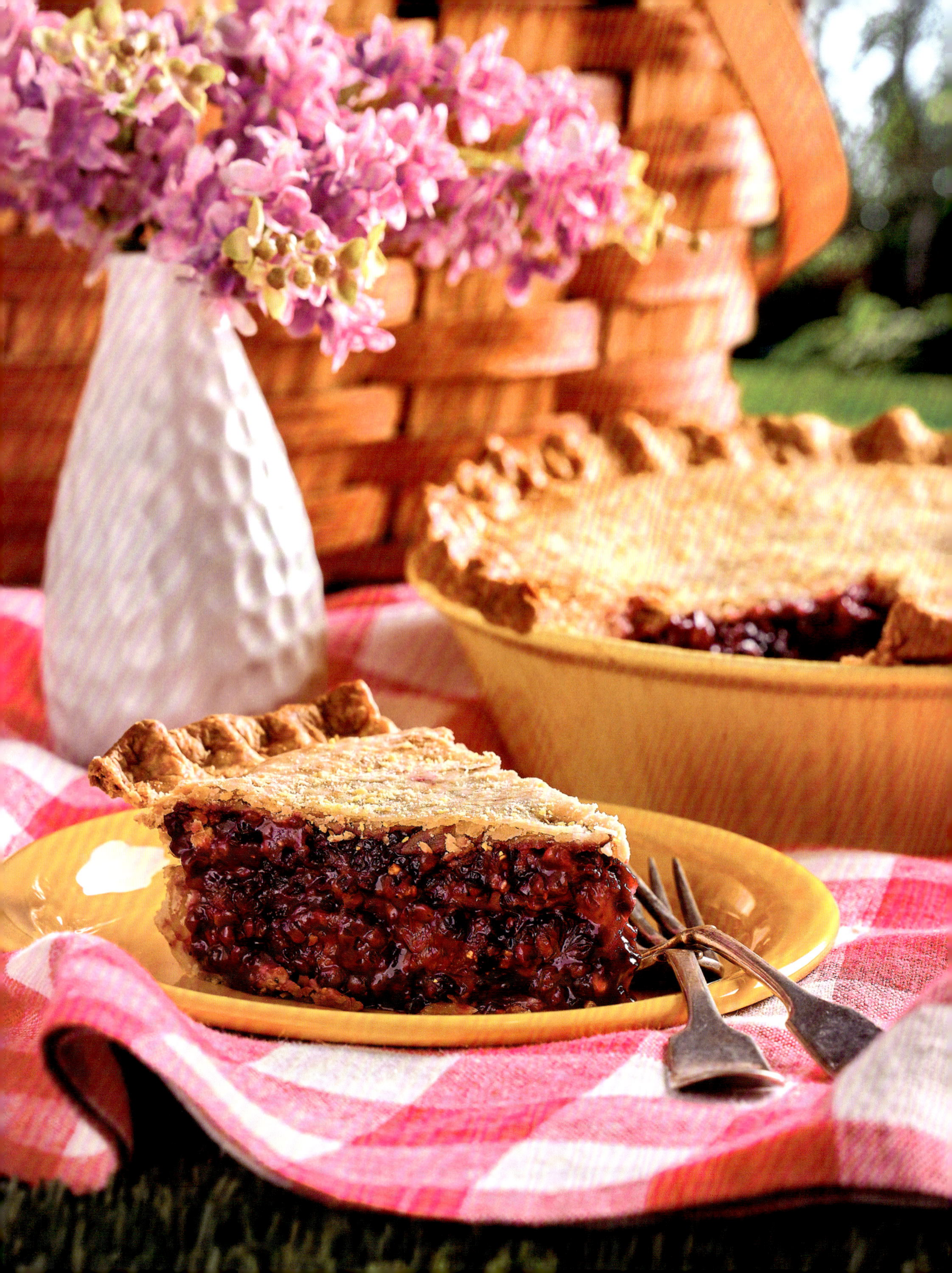

# ROGUE'S BOYSENBERRY PIE

There maybe ain't a single servin' of food in my years with the X-Men that caused as much hubbub as the "Boysenberry Pie Incident." For as tough a cookie as Rogue always proved to be, Gambit brought out her sweet side like no other. Bein' a proper southern girl, Anna Maria poured all that sweetness into an extra-buttery cornmeal crust and baked it to perfection. Us bein' the X-Men, though, no romantic picnic goes uninterrupted. So her perfectly spiced and seasoned boysenberry pie wound up a kinetically charged weapon in another fight between the Cajun and our combative time-traveler Bishop. The only thing more explosive was Rogue's temper when she wound up the one catching her labor of love right in the face.

**Servings:** 8 to 10 • **Type:** Dessert • **Difficulty:** Average • **Prep Time:** 40 minutes • **Cook Time:** 1 hour **Rest Time:** 3 hours • **Dietary Considerations:** GF

### FOR THE CRUST:

2½ cups all-purpose flour

¼ cup cornmeal, plus more for sprinkling

3 tablespoons granulated sugar

½ teaspoon salt

1 cup unsalted butter, plus more for greasing

4 to 6 tablespoons ice-cold buttermilk

1 egg, lightly beaten, for washing

### FOR THE FILLING:

6 cups boysenberries (see Note)

1 cup light brown sugar

½ medium lemon, zest and juice

1 teaspoon ground cinnamon

¼ teaspoon nutmeg, optional

1 teaspoon vanilla extract

½ teaspoon salt

6 tablespoons cornstarch or tapioca starch

2 tablespoons unsalted butter, room temperature, divided

**TO MAKE THE CRUST,** blend the flour, cornmeal, sugar, and salt in a food processor. Add the butter and pulse 'til the mixture resembles coarse crumbs. Gradually add tablespoons of buttermilk and blend 'til the dough begins to come together. Only add as much buttermilk as needed for the dough to hold and no more.

Divide the dough into 2 equal portions, shape each into a round disk, wrap in plastic wrap, and refrigerate for at least 2 hours.

To make the filling, add the berries, sugar, lemon zest, juice, cinnamon, nutmeg, vanilla, and salt to a large saucepan over medium heat. Simmer 'til warm and juicy, about 8 to 10 minutes, stirring occasionally (try not to smash the berries).

Spoon out about ½ cup of the juice from the pan into a small bowl. Whisk cornstarch into the juice 'til smooth. While simmering, slowly pour in the cornstarch slurry. Cook 'til thickened, stirring occasionally, for about 3 to 5 minutes, then remove the filling from the heat and let cool.

**TO PREPARE THE PIE,** preheat the oven to 400°F. Grease a 9-inch deep-dish pie plate with butter and sprinkle the bottom with cornmeal.

Take one of the portions of dough from the fridge. On a lightly floured surface, roll the dough out into a ⅛-inch-thick circle about 11 inches in diameter. Place the circle into the greased pie plate, pressing it evenly into the bottom and up the sides of the dish, trimming any excess. Set aside.

Reflour the surface and roll the second portion of dough into another 11-inch circle. Spoon the filling into the pie shell and sprinkle the filling with dollops of butter. Brush the edges with egg wash, then drape the top crust over the filled pie. Use your hands or a fork to crimp and seal the edges. With a sharp knife, cut 5 to 6 vents in the top of the pie. Brush thoroughly with the egg wash and sprinkle evenly with cornmeal.

Bake in the preheated oven for 15 minutes. Reduce the heat to 375°F and bake for another 30 to 35 minutes 'til the crust is golden brown and the filling is bubbling through the vents. Drape aluminum loosely over the crust if it ever starts to get too browned at the edges. Let cool completely before slicing, about 90 minutes.

*Note: If you can't find boysenberries, use a mix of blackberries and raspberries.*

# REMINISCIN' PORK SCHNITZEL

I don't know what it is about kids and war stories, but these new mutants ain't sittin' down at the table unless I'm telling tales about my time with the Howling Commandos. Nowadays, they know if I'm whipping up this schnitzel recipe, I'm about ready to *reminisce*. I picked it up fighting alongside Steve in Germany, and, well, maybe it's just the Cap they like hearin' about? Some things never change …

**Servings: 2 • Type: Main • Difficulty: Advanced • Prep Time: 40 minutes • Cook Time: 20 minutes**

## FOR THE SCHNITZEL:

Two 8-ounce pork loin portions

½ cup all-purpose flour

Kosher salt

Fresh black pepper

2 extra large eggs

1 cup panko breadcrumbs

4 tablespoons butter

1 sprig of thyme

## FOR THE SHREDDED CABBAGE:

2 cups chiffonade green cabbage

2 tablespoons flat-leaf parsley, fine chiffonade

2 tablespoons lemon juice

4 tablespoons extra virgin olive oil

Kosher salt, to taste

Fresh black pepper, to taste

## TO SERVE:

2 tablespoons whole grain mustard, to serve

2 lemon wedges

## SPECIAL EQUIPMENT:

Meat mallet

Mandoline, optional

Cooling rack, optional

**TO PREPARE THE PORK:** Place the pork loin inside of a freezer bag, and gently pound them out with the flat side of a meat mallet 'til they are an even ¼ inch thick. Remove from the bag and repeat with the second pork loin. You can prep as many as you want and bread and freeze them for an easy meal down the road.

Put the flour in a shallow dish and season with salt and pepper. Whisk the eggs in another shallow dish and season with salt and pepper. Put the panko in a third dish and again season with salt and pepper. Lightly dredge each piece of pounded pork loin in flour, then in the egg, and finally into the breadcrumbs, pressing the breadcrumbs onto the pounded pork cutlet gently so they have a nice even coating.

Lay the breaded pounded pork loin in a single layer on a plate lined with parchment and refrigerate, uncovered, for 10 to 12 minutes to allow the coating to dry out a little and adhere to the pounded pork loin.

**TO MAKE THE SCHNITZEL:** Heat the butter in a large nonstick skillet over medium-high heat. Add the thyme sprig and wait about 1 minute for it to infuse the oil. Remove the thyme sprig and reserve. Gently lay the pork into the pan and cook 'til golden brown and crispy, about 5 minutes per side, over medium-high heat. Remove from the pan and place on a cooling rack or paper towel.

Adjust the seasoning, adding salt and fresh ground black pepper as you like, then place the schnitzel on a plate.

**TO PREPARE THE SHREDDED CABBAGE:** Use a mandoline or a very sharp knife to shave the cabbage into really fine ribbons. Then cut the parsley leaves into a fine chiffonade. Combine in a small bowl with salt and pepper, lemon juice, and extra virgin olive oil. Mix gently, then divide and place on each plate with a lemon wedge and a dollop of mustard. Serve immediately.

# STUDENT'S DANGER ROOM X-MIX

New Mutants. Generation X. Young X-Men. We've had all kinds of names for all sorts of fresh-faced mutants looking for a place to belong, to figure out their powers and *themselves*. It's what bein' part of the X-Men did for me (though *this* face has stayed as fresh as the day I first showed up.) I'm proud to help do the same for them. Of course, part of that process is me kickin' their butts in the DANGER ROOM a thousand times. I try to keep their energy up with this signature mix that packs plenty of protein to keep 'em goin', sugar-rush to keep 'em happy, and a little bit of a kick to keep 'em sharp. Not every new recruit can be the next Shadowcat, Jubilee, Armor, or Pixie. But as long as I keep stockpiles of these snacks, they can always be at their best. (Except Quire. He's always the *worst*.)

**Servings: 10 to 12 • Type: Snack/Dessert • Difficulty: Easy • Prep Time: 15 minutes**
**Cook Time: 5 minutes • Rest Time: 20 minutes • Dietary Considerations: V**

1½ cups semisweet chocolate chips

¾ cup creamy peanut butter or sunbutter

⅓ cup unsalted butter

1 teaspoon vanilla extract

1 teaspoon chipotle pepper powder, or to taste

3 cups crispy corn or rice cereal squares

6 cups graham cereal, divided

1½ cups powdered sugar

1 cup mini marshmallows

1 cup pretzel sticks

1 cup dry roasted peanuts or other dry roasted nuts, optional

1 cup small candy-coated chocolates, optional

Place the chocolate chips, peanut butter or sun butter, and butter in a large microwave-safe bowl. Microwave on high for 20 seconds, then take the bowl out and stir the mixture. Return the bowl to the microwave and heat for another 20 seconds, then stir again. Continue this process, microwaving in 20-second intervals and stirring, 'til the chocolate has melted and mixture is completely smooth. Once smooth, stir in the vanilla extract and chipotle powder 'til well-combined.

Pour all the cereal squares and half (3 cups) of the graham cereal in a large mixing bowl. Pour the melted chocolate–peanut butter mixture over the cereal and gently stir with a rubber spatula 'til the cereal is evenly coated.

Transfer the coated cereal to a large sealable bag and add the powdered sugar. Seal the bag and shake 'til all the cereal is thoroughly coated. Spread the cereal out on parchment and let it sit 'til the chocolate has set, about 15 to 20 minutes.

If you like, skewer half the mini marshmallows with the pretzel sticks to make little marshmallow sticks.

Place the chocolate-coated cereal in a large mixing bowl, then add the remaining graham cereal, mini marshmallows, pretzel sticks, nuts, and candy-coated chocolates. Stir to combine, and serve.

Store leftover mix in an airtight container for up to 2 weeks at room temperature, or 3 to 4 weeks in the refrigerator.

# MEASUREMENT CONVERSIONS

## VOLUME

| US | METRIC |
|---|---|
| ½ teaspooon (tsp) | 1 ml |
| 1 teaspooon (tsp) | 5 ml |
| 1 tablespoon (tbsp) | 15 ml |
| 1 fluid ounce (fl. oz.) | 30 ml |
| ⅕ cup | 50 ml |
| ¼ cup | 60 ml |
| ⅔ cup | 80 ml |
| 3.4 fluid ounces (fl. oz.) | 100 ml |
| ½ cup | 120 ml |
| ⅔ cup | 160 ml |
| ¾ cup | 180 ml |
| 1 cup | 240 ml |
| 1 pint (2 cups) | 480 ml |
| 1 quart (4 cups) | .95 liter |

## TEMPERATURES

| Fahrenheit | Celsius |
|---|---|
| 200° | 93.3° |
| 212° | 100° |
| 250° | 120° |
| 275° | 135° |
| 300° | 150° |
| 325° | 163° |
| 350° | 177° |
| 400° | 205° |
| 425° | 218° |
| 450° | 232° |
| 475° | 246° |

## WEIGHT

| US | METRIC |
|---|---|
| 0.5 ounce (oz.) | 14 grams (g) |
| 1 pound (lb.) | 28 grams (g) |
| ¼ pound (lb.) | 113 grams (g) |
| ⅓ pound (lb.) | 151 grams (g) |
| ½ pound (lb.) | 227 grams (g) |
| 1 pound (lb.) | 454 grams (g) |

## ABOUT THE AUTHORS

Author **CASSANDRA REEDER** launched her blog, The Geeky Chef, in 2008, turning fictional food and drinks from a vast array of fandoms into reality with simple and fun recipes. Since then, a series of cookbooks based on the trailblazing blog have been published, including *The Geeky Chef Cookbook*, *The Geeky Bartender Drinks*, and *The Video Game Chef*. In 2024, she co-authored both *The Official Westeros Cookbook* and *Mass Effect: The Official Cocktail Book*. When not conjuring up recipes inspired by fiction and pop culture, Cassandra can be found perusing the food carts in Portland, Oregon, with her husband and two tiny agents of chaos.

**JAMES ASMUS** is a writer of books, theater, comedy, video games, and TV. His published work includes over a dozen Marvel Comics titles including *X-Men*, *Captain America*, and *Amazing Spider-Man*. Past projects with Insight Editions include *Rick and Morty: The Official Cookbook* and *Supernatural: The Official Cocktail Book*. He's written comics for *Rick & Morty*, *Transformers*, *My Little Pony*, and *Quantum and Woody* (which snagged five Harvey Award nominations, including Best Writer), and original series like apocalyptic buddy comedy *End Times of Bram & Ben*, action satire *Survival Street*, and the all-ages sci-fi dark comedy *Field Tripping*. He might just share Wolverine's mutant heightened sense of smell, but would've preferred the claws or healing factor. James lives outside Portland, Oregon, with his wife and two weirdly wonderful kids.

**CHRIS COSENTINO** is a passionate chef, author, cyclist, philanthropist, and a James Beard Award–nominated author. A graduate of Johnson & Wales University, his first executive chef position was at Incanto in San Francisco. There, he helped raise awareness about sustainability and utilizing the entire animal. He went on to create Boccalone, a celebrated cured-meat company. Cosentino is opening a new restaurant, Koast, to celebrate local ingredients and coastal cuisine in Wailea Village, on the island of Maui.

Cosentino is the author of *Offal Good: Cooking from the Heart with Guts*, *Beginnings: My Way to Start a Meal*, and a collaborator on write *Wolverine: In the Flesh*. Cosentino won BRAVO's "Top Chef Masters," earning over $140,000 for The Michael J. Fox Foundation.

## ACKNOWLEDGMENTS

First, a massive thank you to the friends and family who helped me test these recipes: My mom and #1 fan, Rolanda, and her very patient husband, Joe. My big brother, Nico, who found time in an endlessly chaotic schedule. My best friend, Jessica Garcia, and her husband, Wes, I honestly do not know what I'd do without you. And shout out to the rest of the Rausch clan for the love and support. Amanda and Brian Backur, you two are the absolute best! Big thanks to Alexis Sattler, and my co-author, James Asmus. Dream team! My everlasting gratitude to my husband, Jesk, and my babies, for being so patient as I cook and write and obsess. Love you always.

**CASSANDRA REEDER**

James would like to thank Cassandra for being an X-cellent partner on this, and Alexis for her uncanny leadership on this team-up. Thanks also to Justin Eisinger for my original orientation to the world of recipe writing, and to Desiree Wilson for your support, advice, and openness. A lifetime of appreciation to Nick Lowe for first bringing me into the Marvel fold, and for years of delightful collaborations and friendship. Thanks to my Dad for all those early trips to the comic shops. And eternal love to Mara, Devlin, and Irie.

**JAMES ASMUS**

# INDEX

## A

All-Purpose Seasoning, 30
Appetizers
Colossus's Buckwheat Blinis, 151
Jubilee's Food Court Chili Fries, 154
Lowtown Satay, 62–64
Mixed Veggie Kushiyaki, 87
Nightcrawler's Bavarian Cheese Dip, 148
Poutine, 94
Storm's Bajias, 147
Yakitori Negima, 84

## B

Bacon
Okonomiyaki, 116
X-Man's Brewis, 50
Bananas
Choco Banana, 88
Lepat Pisang, 128
BBQ Seasoning/Rub, 30
Beef
Berserker Burger, 134
Bison Donair Kebabs, 69
Ginger Beef, 101
guide to steak cuts, 74–75
Hammer Bay BBQ, 83
Healing Factor Pemmican, 28
Japanese-Style Hot Dog, 98
Jubilee's Food Court Chili Fries, 154
Korokke, 115
Moose Jerky, 31
Roti John Steve, 123
Skewered Surf N' Turf, 73
Skunk-Bear Venison Stew, 47
Slim's Cheesesteak Sandwiches, 152
Slingin' Chopped Cheese Dogs, 139

Beignets, Gambit's "Scoundrel," 163
Berries
Kitty's Kickin' Kugel, 160
Rogue's Boysenberry Pie, 167
Saskatoon Berry Crumble, 53
Wojapi, 36
Bison Donair Kebabs, 69
Blinis, Colossus's Buckwheat, 151
Blueberries
Kitty's Kickin' Kugel, 160
Boysenberry Pie, Rogue's, 167
Bread, Fried Bannock, 49
Breakfast
Colossus's Buckwheat Blinis, 151
Eggs Howlett, 27
Feral Flapjacks, 39
Okonomiyaki, 116
Broccoli
Jean's Holiday Broccoli Casserole, 159
Kuzuri Na Kushikatsu, 60–61
Buckwheat Blinis, Colossus's, 151
Burger, Berserker, 134

## C

Cabbage
Mystique's Mei Fun, 124
Okonomiyaki, 116
Reminiscin' Pork Schnitzel, 168
Cajun Seasoning, 30
Cake, Layered: Assemble!, 140–41
Campfires, preparing, 24
Carrots
Battuto, 48
Ginger Beef, 101
Mirepoix, 48
Mystique's Mei Fun, 124
Skunk-Bear Venison Stew, 47
Celery
Battuto, 48
Holy Trinity, 48
Mirepoix, 48

Cheese
Berserker Burger, 134
Cubano Sandwich, 137
Garlic Cream Sauce, 73
Jean's Holiday Broccoli Casserole, 159
Jubilee's Food Court Chili Fries, 154
Kitty's Kickin' Kugel, 160
Nightcrawler's Bavarian Cheese Dip, 148
Poutine, 94
Roti John Steve, 123
Shredded Hero, 136
Slim's Cheesesteak Sandwiches, 152
Slingin' Chopped Cheese Dogs, 139
Tornado Potato, 80
Chicken
Gaijin's Ramen, 108
Lowtown Laksa, 127
Lowtown Satay, 62–64
Yakitori Negima, 84
Chili Fries, Jubilee's Food Court, 154
Chocolate
Choco Banana, 88
Nanaimo Bars, 102
Student's Danger Room X-Mix, 169
Chopsticks, holding, 105
Chutney, Mango, 147
Coconut
Iceman's Snowball Special, 164
Lepat Pisang, 128
Nanaimo Bars, 102
Condiments
Mango Chutney, 147
Pickled Daikon, 111
Wojapi, 36
Cookies. See Jade Giants
Cubano Sandwich, 137
Curry Powder, 30

172

INDEX

## D

Dagger Bay Blend (Curry Powder), 30
Daikon
  Pickled Daikon, 111
  Ragin' Radishes, 120
Danger Room Rub (BBQ Seasoning/Rub), 30
Desserts
  Choco Banana, 88
  Colossus's Buckwheat Blinis, 151
  Gambit's "Scoundrel" Beignets, 163
  Iceman's Snowball Special, 164
  Jade Giants, 131
  Layered Cake: Assemble!, 140–41
  Lepat Pisang, 128
  Nanaimo Bars, 102
  Rogue's Boysenberry Pie, 167
  Saskatoon Berry Crumble, 53
  Snow Maple Taffy, 54
  Student's Danger Room X-Mix, 169
Dip, Nightcrawler's Bavarian Cheese, 148
Duck
  Ol' Canucklehead's Canard, 44

## E

Eggs
  Eggs Howlett, 27
  Gaijin's Ramen, 108
  Kuzuri Na Kushikatsu, 60–61
  Logan's "Sophisticated" Grilled Cheese, 156
  Mystique's Mei Fun, 124
  Ragin' Radishes, 120
  Roti John Steve, 123
  Tomago Sando, 106

## F

Family dinners survival guide, 155
Fish
  Cedar Plank Fish, 43
  how to fillet, 35
  Krakoan Kabobs, 78–79
  Salmon Candy, 32
  Salmon Mayo Onigiri, 112
  X-Man's Brewis, 50
Flapjacks, Feral, 39
Flavor bases, 48
Fries, Chili, Jubilee's Food Court, 154
Fruit. See also specific fruits
  Healing Factor Pemmican, 28
  Layered Cake: Assemble!, 140–41
Frying foods, 57

## G

Garlic
  Battuto, 48
  Garlic Cream Sauce, 73
  Garlic + Ginger + Onion, 48
  Sofrito, 48
Ginger
  Garlic + Ginger + Onion, 48
  Ginger Beef, 101
Greens
  Eggs Howlett, 27

## H

Ham
  Cubano Sandwich, 137
  Shredded Hero, 136
Hardtack, 50
Holy Trinity, 48
Hot dogs
  Japanese-Style Hot Dog, 98
  Slingin' Chopped Cheese Dogs, 139

## I

Ice cream
  Iceman's Snowball Special, 164

## J

Jade Giants, 131
Japanese convenience food stores, 105
Japanese-Style Hot Dog, 98
Jerky, Moose, 31

## K

Kabobs, Krakoan, 78–79
Katsu Sauce, 60
Kebabs, Bison Donair, 69
Knives
  chopping with, 16–17
  grips, 14
  Japanese knives, 12
  keeping blades sharp, 20
  slicing with, 17–18
  small, fine cuts with, 18
  square and cube cuts with, 18–19
  Western knives, 12
Kugel, Kitty's Kickin', 160
Kushiyaki, Mixed Veggie, 87

## L

Laksa, Lowtown, 127
Lamb
  Stabby Shishliki, 77

## M

Madripoor dining and survival guide, 119
Main dishes
  Cedar Plank Fish, 43
  Gaijin's Ramen, 108
  Ginger Beef, 101
  Hammer Bay BBQ, 83

INDEX

173

Krakoan Kabobs, 78–79
Kuzuri Na Kushikatsu, 60–61
Logan's Dry-Smoked Ribs, 153
Lowtown Laksa, 127
Lowtown Satay, 62–64
Mixed Veggie Kushiyaki, 87
Mystique's Mei Fun, 124
Okonomiyaki, 116
Ol' Canucklehead's Canard, 44
Ragin' Radishes, 120
Reminiscin' Pork Schnitzel, 168
Skewered Surf N' Turf, 73
Skunk-Bear Venison Stew, 47
Stabby Shishliki, 77
Tsarina's Shashlik, 65
X-Man's Brewis, 50
Yakitori Negima, 84
Mango Chutney, 147
Maple Taffy, Snow, 54
Meat. See also Beef; Bison; Lamb;
Pork; Venison
internal cooking temperatures,
70
Mirepoix, 48
Moose Jerky, 31
Mushrooms
Gaijin's Ramen, 108
Jean's Holiday Broccoli Casse-
role, 159
Mixed Veggie Kushiyaki, 87
Wild Mushroom Rice, 40
Mutant Medley (All-Purpose
Seasoning), 30

## N

Nanaimo Bars, 102
Noodles
Gaijin's Ramen, 108
Kitty's Kickin' Kugel, 160
Lowtown Laksa, 127
Mystique's Mei Fun, 124
Ramen Noodles from Scratch,
107

Nori sheets
Japanese-Style Hot Dog, 98
Salmon Mayo Onigiri, 112
Nuts
Hammer Bay BBQ, 83
Healing Factor Pemmican, 28
Iceman's Snowball Special, 164
Lepat Pisang, 128
Nanaimo Bars, 102
Student's Danger Room X-Mix,
169
Wild Mushroom Rice, 40

## O

Okonomiyaki, 116
Onigiri, Salmon Mayo, 112
Onions
Battuto, 48
Garlic + Ginger + Onion, 48
Holy Trinity, 48
Mirepoix, 48
Sofrito, 48

## P

Pancakes
Feral Flapjacks, 39
Okonomiyaki, 116
Peanut butter
Peanut Sauce, 62
Student's Danger Room X-Mix,
169
Peanuts
Hammer Bay BBQ, 83
Student's Danger Room X-Mix,
169
Pemmican, Healing Factor, 28
Peppers
Ginger Beef, 101
Holy Trinity, 48
Krakoan Kabobs, 78–79
Mixed Veggie Kushiyaki, 87
Slim's Cheesesteak Sandwiches,
152

Sofrito, 48
Pickled Daikon, 111
Pie, Rogue's Boysenberry, 167
Pineapple
Krakoan Kabobs, 78–79
Pork. See also Bacon; Ham
Cubano Sandwich, 137
Kuzuri Na Kushikatsu, 60–61
Logan's Dry-Smoked Ribs,
153
Mystique's Mei Fun, 124
Reminiscin' Pork Schnitzel,
168
Shredded Hero, 136
Tsarina's Shashlik, 65
Potatoes
All-Dressed Chips, 97
Jubilee's Food Court Chili
Fries, 154
Korokke, 115
Poutine, 94
Skunk-Bear Venison Stew, 47
Storm's Bajias, 147
Tornado Potato, 80
X-Man's Brewis, 50
Poutine
recipe for, 94
variations on, 93

## R

Radishes. See Daikon
Ramen
Gaijin's Ramen, 108
Ramen Noodles from Scratch,
107
Rice
Salmon Mayo Onigiri, 112
Wild Mushroom Rice, 40
Roti ~~John~~ Steve, 123

INDEX

174

# S

Salmon
　Cedar Plank Fish, 43
　Salmon Candy, 32
　Salmon Mayo Onigiri, 112
Sandwiches
　Berserker Burger, 134
　Cubano Sandwich, 137
　Japanese-Style Hot Dog, 98
　Logan's "Sophisticated" Grilled Cheese, 156
　Roti ~~John~~ Steve, 123
　Shredded Hero, 136
　Slim's Cheesesteak Sandwiches, 152
　Slingin' Chopped Cheese Dogs, 139
　Tomago Sando, 106
Saskatoon Berry Crumble, 53
Sauces
　Donair Sauce, 69
　Garlic Cream Sauce, 73
　Katsu Sauce, 60
　Okonomiyaki Sauce, 116
　Peanut Sauce, 62
　Wojapi, 36
　Yakitori Sauce (Tare), 84
Shrimp
　Mystique's Mei Fun, 124
　Skewered Surf N' Turf, 73
Sides
　Jean's Holiday Broccoli Casserole, 159
　Jubilee's Food Court Chili Fries, 154
　Kitty's Kickin' Kugel, 160
　Mystique's Mei Fun, 124
　Poutine, 94
　Ragin' Radishes, 120
　Wild Mushroom Rice, 40
Skewering foods, 67

Snacks
　All-Dressed Chips, 97
　Gambit's "Scoundrel" Beignets, 163
　Healing Factor Pemmican, 28
　Korokke, 115
　Moose Jerky, 31
　Nightcrawler's Bavarian Cheese Dip, 148
　Pickled Daikon, 111
　Salmon Candy, 32
　Salmon Mayo Onigiri, 112
　Storm's Bajias, 147
　Student's Danger Room X-Mix, 169
　Tornado Potato, 80
Snowball Special, Iceman's, 164
Snow Maple Taffy, 54
Sofrito, 48
Soups
　Gaijin's Ramen, 108
　Lowtown Laksa, 127
Spice blends, 30
Squash
　Kuzuri Na Kushikatsu, 60–61
　Mixed Veggie Kushiyaki, 87
Steak Seasoning, 30
Stews
　Gaijin's Ramen, 108
　Lowtown Laksa, 127
　Skunk-Bear Venison Stew, 47

# T

Taffy, Snow Maple, 54
Tare, 48
Tea, The Professor's Cambric, 144
Tempeh
　Krakoan Kabobs, 78–79
Tomatoes
　Donair Sauce, 69
　Sofrito, 48
Truffles
　Logan's "Sophisticated" Grilled Cheese, 156

# U

United States roadside diners and dives, 133

# V

Vegetables. See also specific vegetables
　Mixed Veggie Kushiyaki, 87
Venison
　Moose Jerky, 31
　Skunk-Bear Venison Stew, 47

# W

Weapon X (Steak Seasoning), 30
White chocolate
　Choco Banana, 88
　Layered Cake: Assemble!, 140–41
Wojapi, 36

# Y

Yakitori Negima, 84

# Z

Zucchini
　Kuzuri Na Kushikatsu, 60–61
　Mixed Veggie Kushiyaki, 87

PO Box 3088
San Rafael, CA 94912
www.insighteditions.com

 Find us on Facebook: www.facebook.com/InsightEditions
 Follow us on Instagram: @insighteditions

**MARVEL**

© 2025 MARVEL

All rights reserved. Published by Insight Editions, San Rafael, California, in 2025.

No part of this book may be reproduced in any form without written permission from the publisher.

ISBN: 979-8-88663-957-5

Publisher: Raoul Goff
SVP, Group Publisher: Vanessa Lopez
VP, Creative: Chrissy Kwasnik
VP, Manufacturing: Alix Nicholaeff
Publishing Director: Mike Degler
Editorial Director: Thom O'Hearn
Art Director: Stuart Smith
Senior Designer: Brooke McCullum
Editor: Alexis Sattler
Editorial Assistant: Gabrielle Cruz
Managing Editor: Shannon Ballesteros
Production Manager: Deena Hashem
Strategic Production Planner: Lina s Palma-Temena

MARVEL PUBLISHING
VP, Production and Special Projects: Jeff Youngquist
Editor, Special Projects: Sarah Singer
Manager, Licensed Publishing: Jeremy West
VP, Licensed Publishing: Sven Larsen
VP, Print & Digital Publishing: David Gabriel
Editor in Chief: C.B. Cebulski

Photography by Waterbury Publications, Inc.

Insight Editions, in association with Roots of Peace, will plant two trees for each tree used in the manufacturing of this book. Roots of Peace is an internationally renowned humanitarian organization dedicated to eradicating land mines worldwide and converting war-torn lands into productive farms and wildlife habitats. Roots of Peace will plant two million fruit and nut trees in Afghanistan and provide farmers there with the skills and support necessary for sustainable land use.

Manufactured in China by Insight Editions

10 9 8 7 6 5 4 3 2 1

GW01281555

# FIRST TECHNOLOGY
# Toys

Author: **John Williams**
Photography: **Zul Mukhida**

Dear Santa,
This year I've been good,
and so I wondered if you would
please bring me toys instead of socks.
(I really have got lots and lots!)

Thank you. Hope you get this letter,

Lots of love from

Henrietta

**Wayland**

# FIRST TECHNOLOGY

## Titles in this series

Machines

Energy

Tools

Toys

Wheels and Cogs

Packaging

Series editor: Kathryn Smith
Designer: Loraine Hayes

© Copyright 1993 Wayland (Publishers) Ltd

First published in 1993 by
Wayland (Publishers) Ltd
61 Western Road, Hove
East Sussex BN3 1JD, England

**British Library Cataloguing in Publication Data**

Williams, John
Toys – (First Technology Series)
I. Title II. Series
688.7

ISBN 0 7502 0780 9

Typeset by DJS Fotoset Ltd, Burgess Hill, Sussex.
Printed and bound in Turin, Italy, by Canale.

**Acknowledgements**
The publishers would like to thank Canterbury Bears and all their staff for their kind help and co-operation. All the photographs in this book were taken by Zul Mukhida, except for the following:
John Caldwell 6-11, 19, 20; Chapel Studios 18 (John Heinrich); GGS 6-7.

WARNING: Toys which are made badly can be dangerous. Make sure that children play with toys which have been rigourously tested and meet the appropriate safety standards.

Poem on page 1 © 1993 Catherine Baxter

Words printed in **bold** appear in the glossary on page 31.

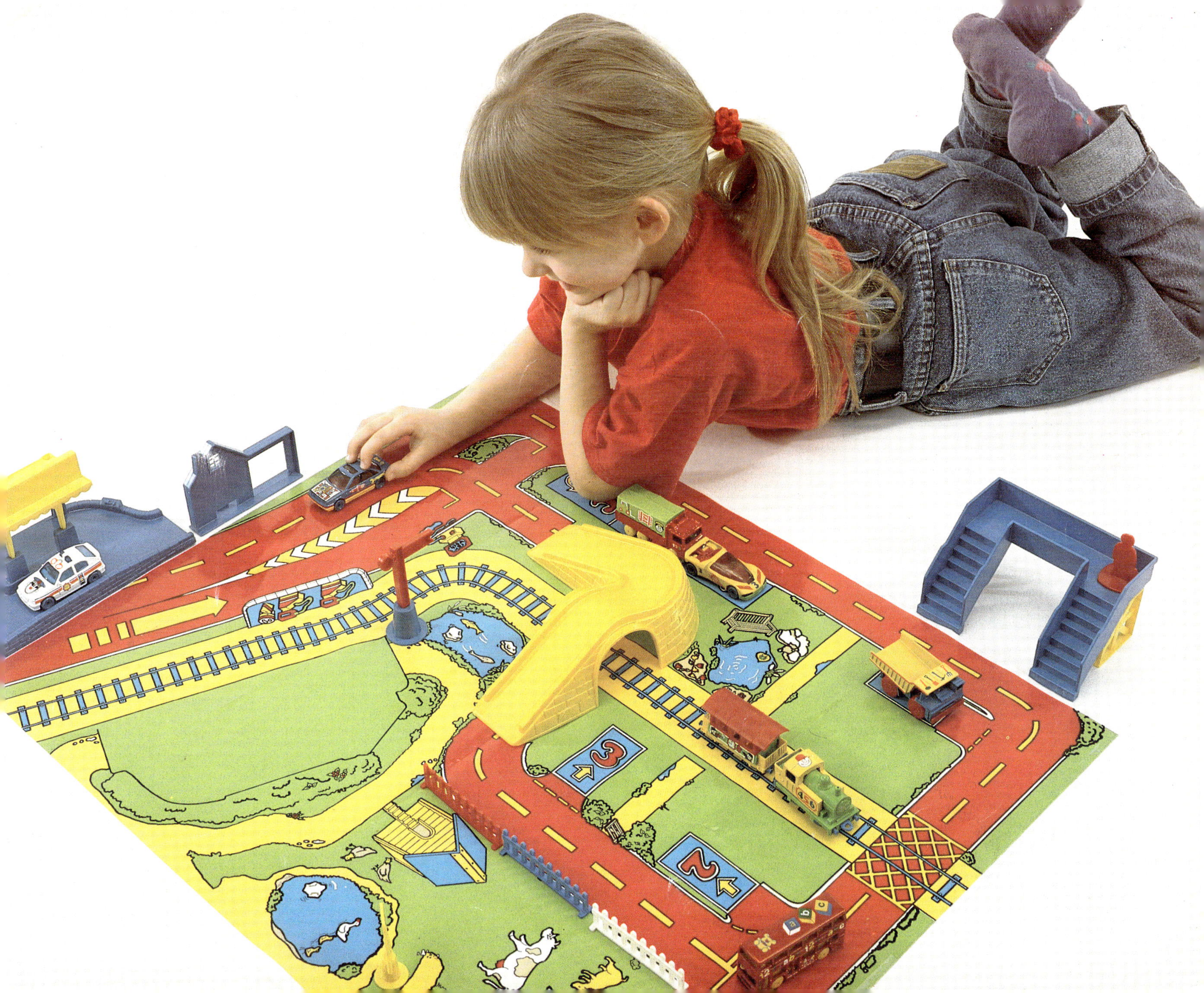

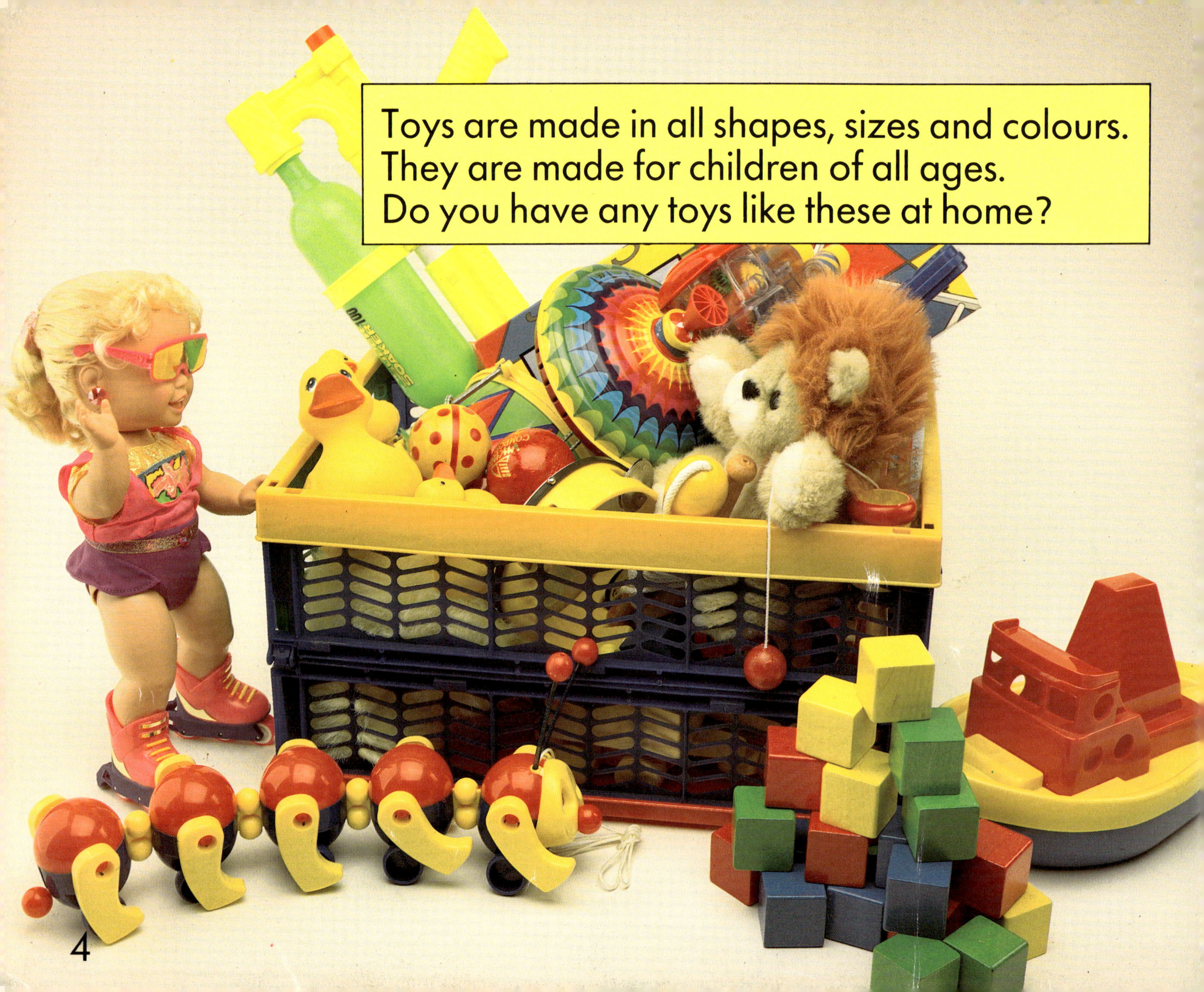

Toys are made in all shapes, sizes and colours.
They are made for children of all ages.
Do you have any toys like these at home?

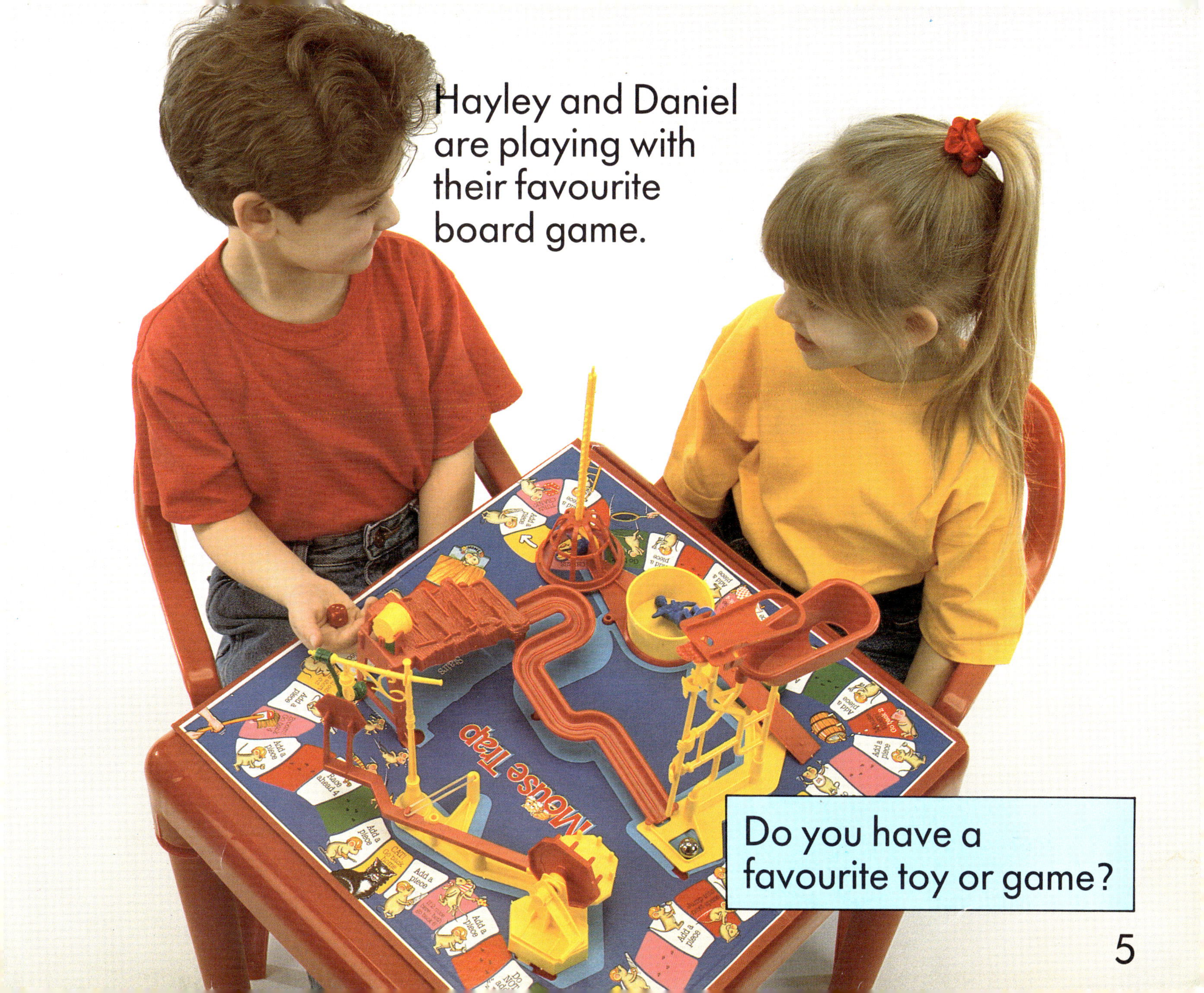
Mouse Trap

Hayley and Daniel are playing with their favourite board game.

Do you have a favourite toy or game?

Children have always played with toys.
These toys were made about 100 years ago.
Are they like the toys you play with?

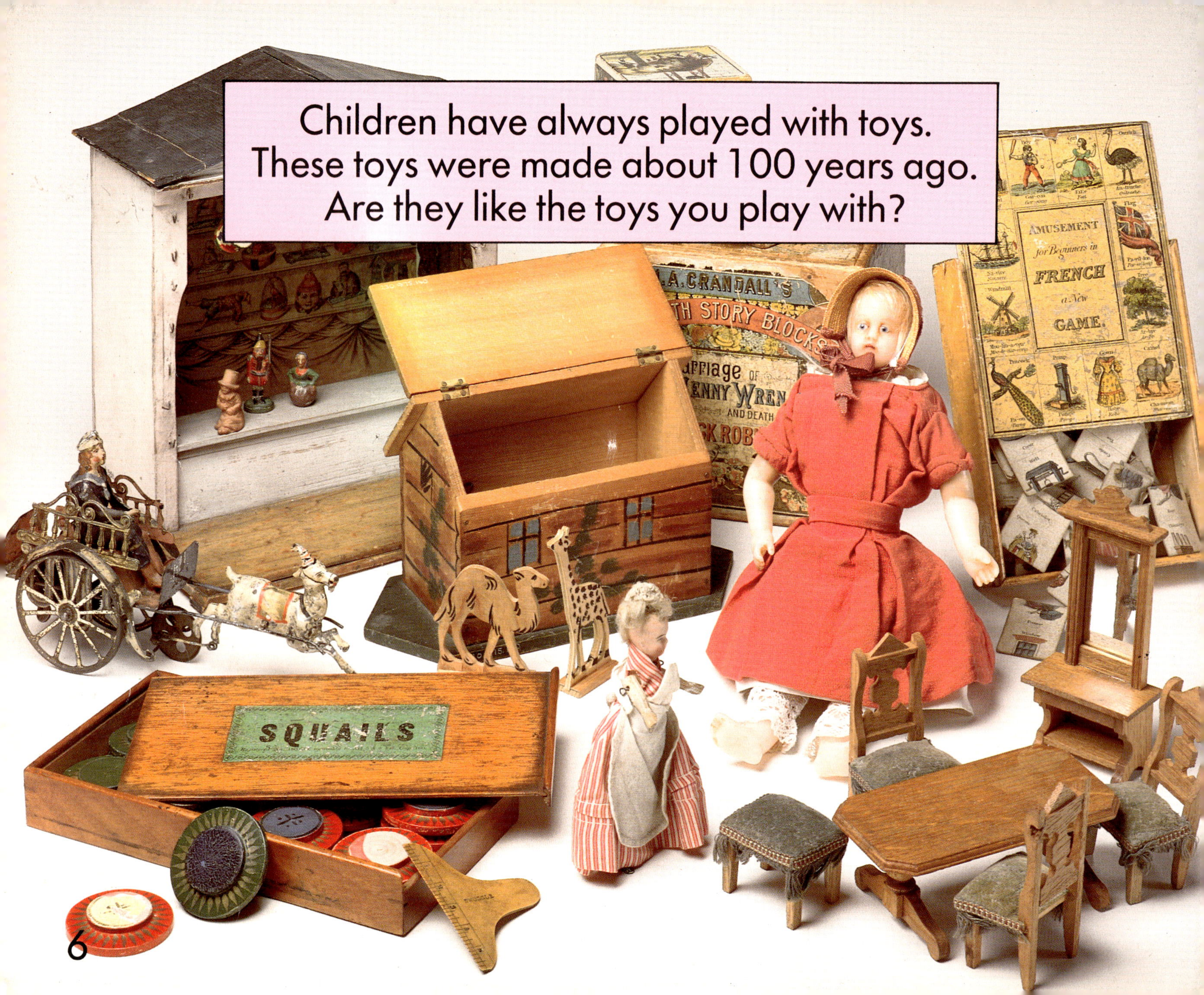
SQUAILS
AMUSEMENT
for Beginners in
FRENCH
a New
GAME.

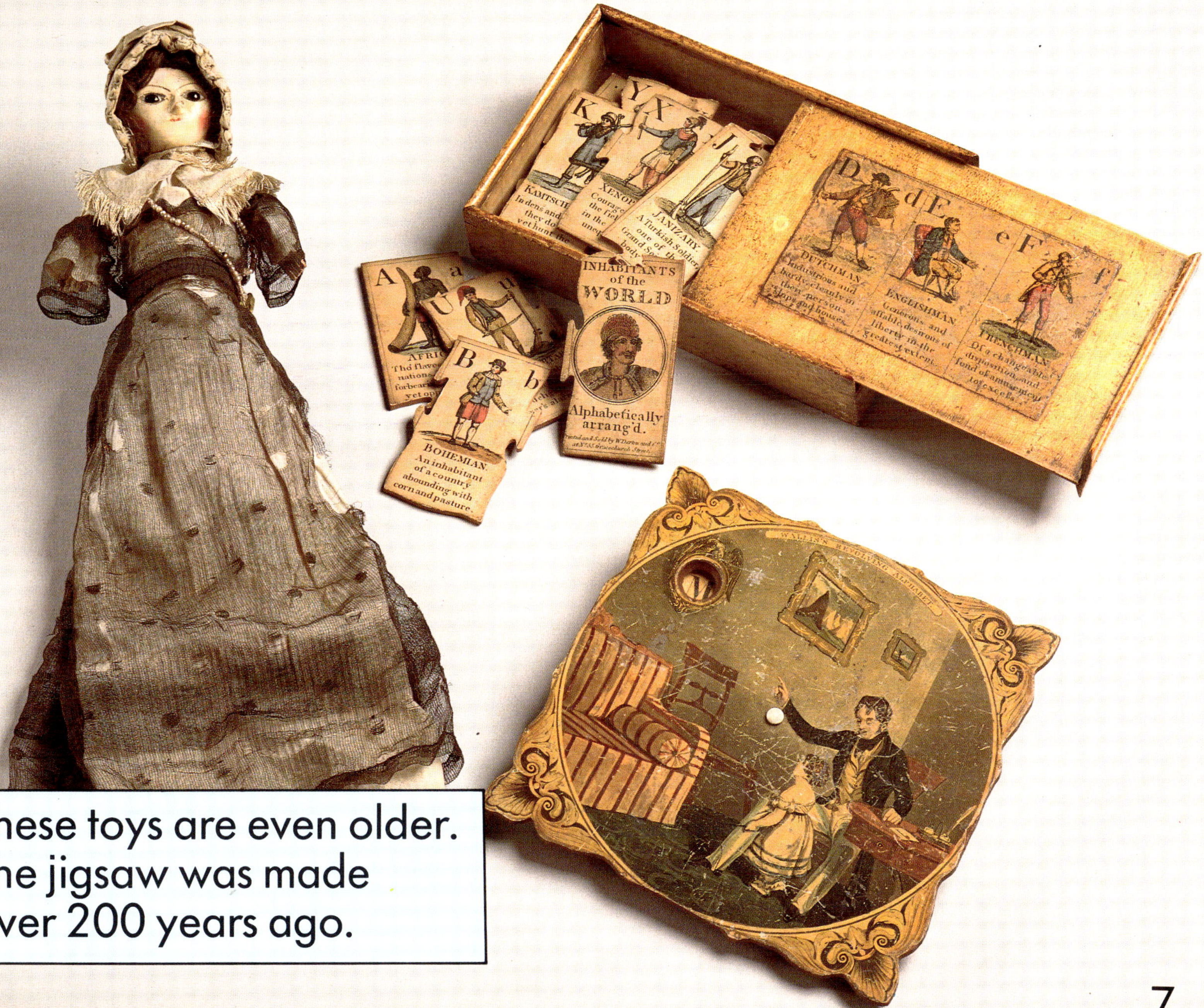
INHABITANTS of the WORLD
Alphabetically arrang'd.
BOHEMIAN. An inhabitant of a country abounding with corn and pasture.
DUTCHMAN
ENGLISHMAN


These toys are even older. The jigsaw was made over 200 years ago.

These metal cutters are used to cut pieces of cloth. The pieces are used to make a toy. Can you guess what the toy is?

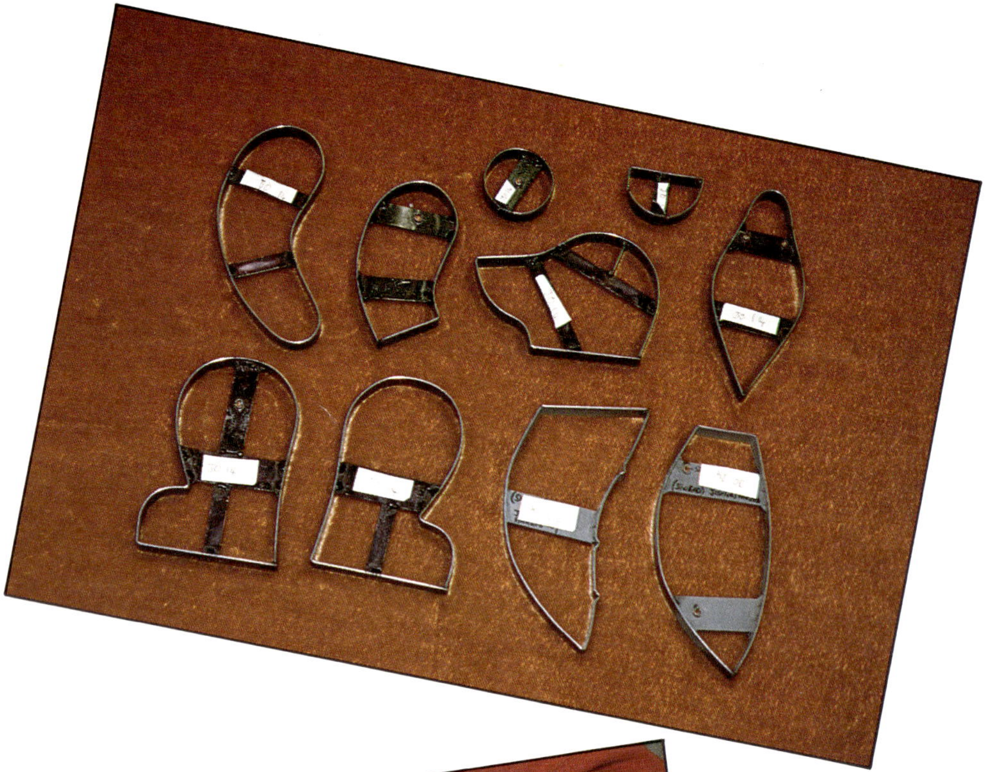

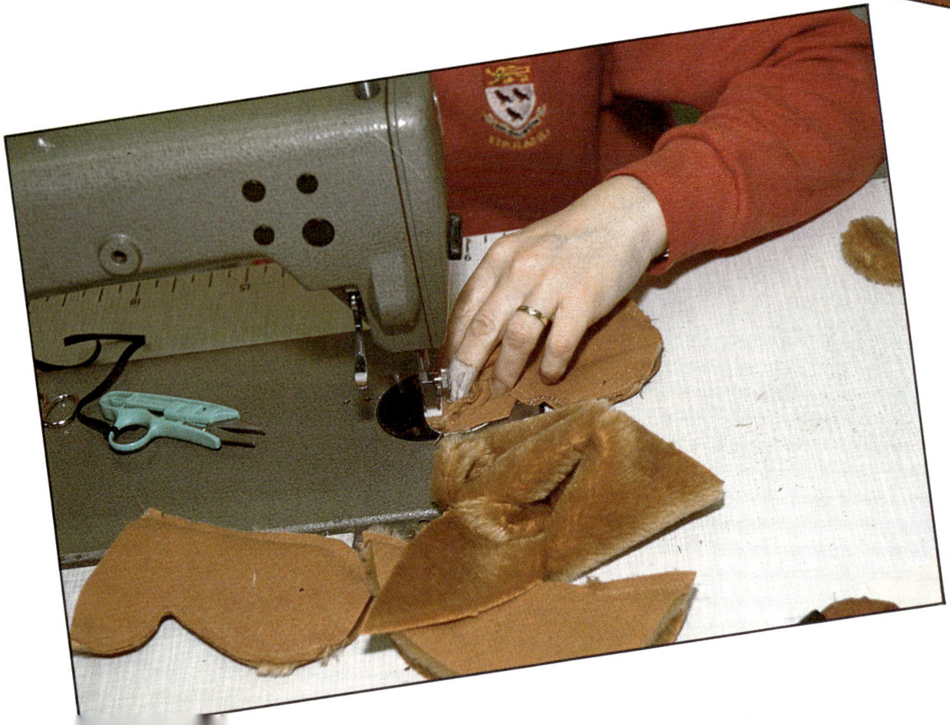

The pieces of cloth are stitched together to make a head, a body, arms and legs.

Special **joints** are put inside the arms and legs.

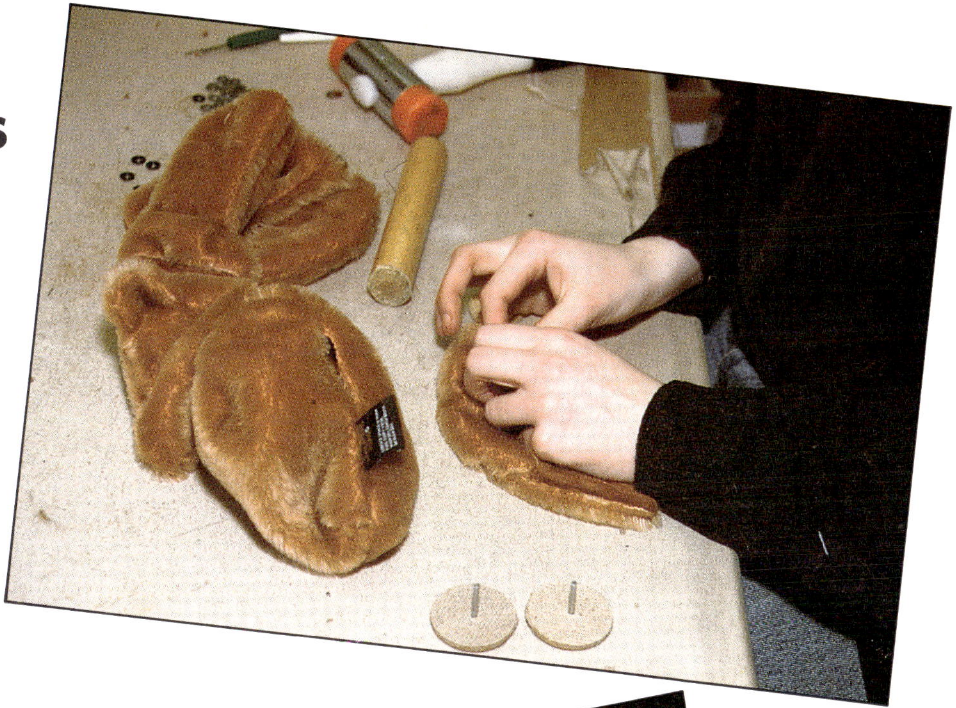

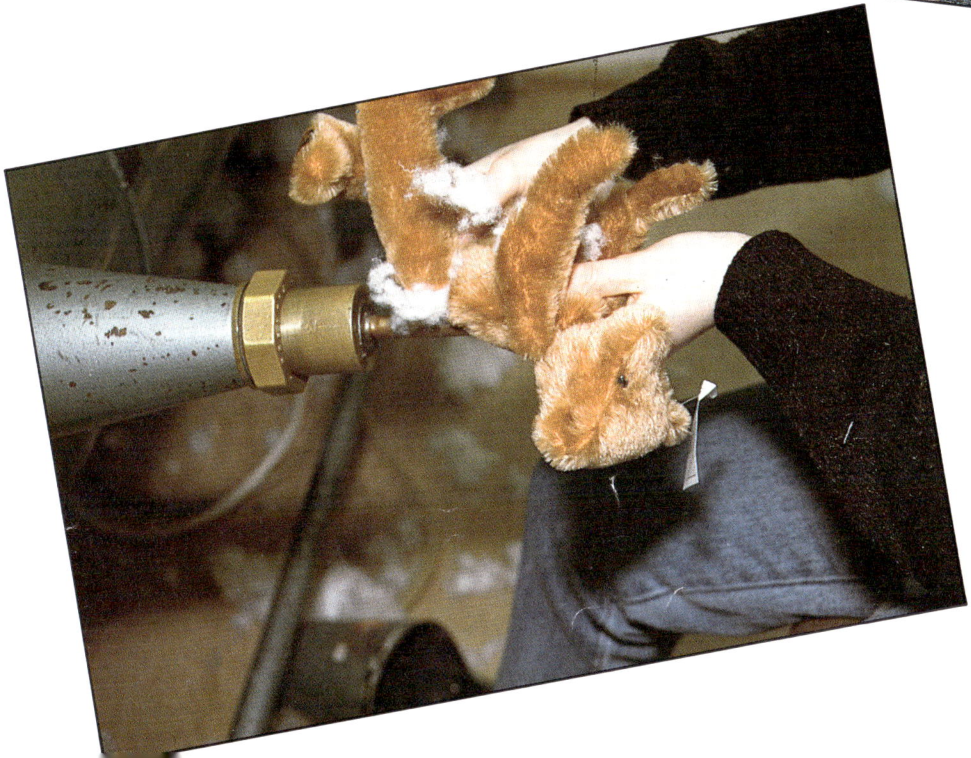

A machine blows **stuffing** into the toy.

All the holes
are sewn up
by hand.

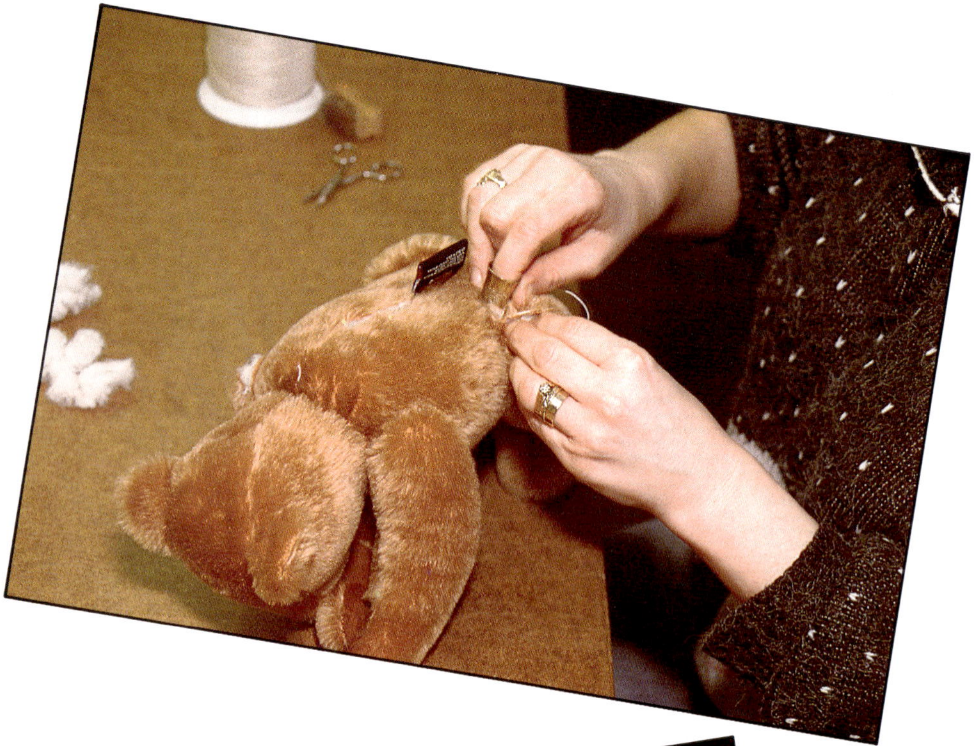

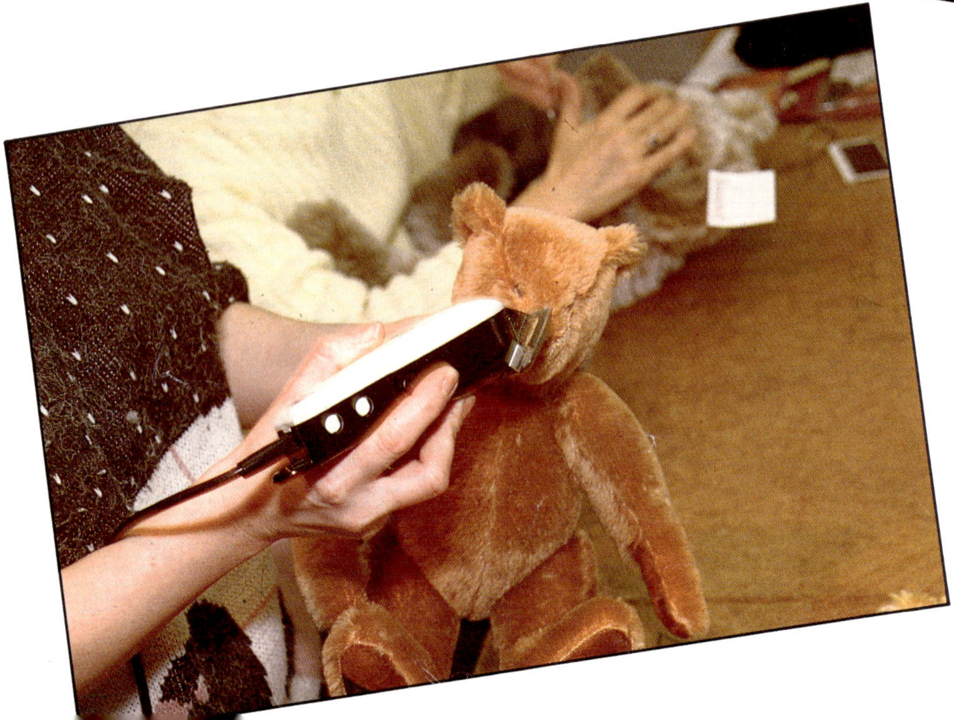

Fur is shaved
off the **face**.

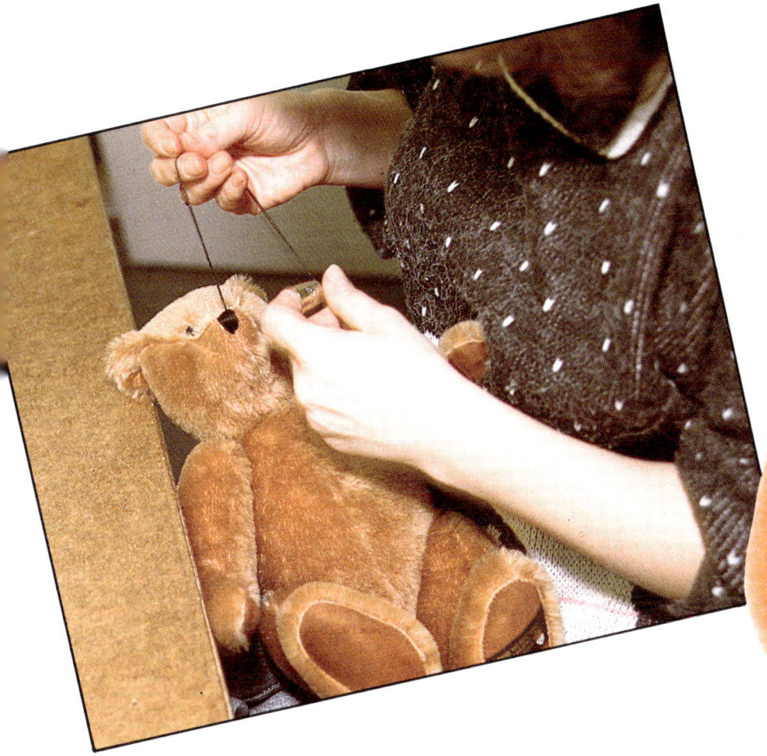

The nose is carefully sewn in place.

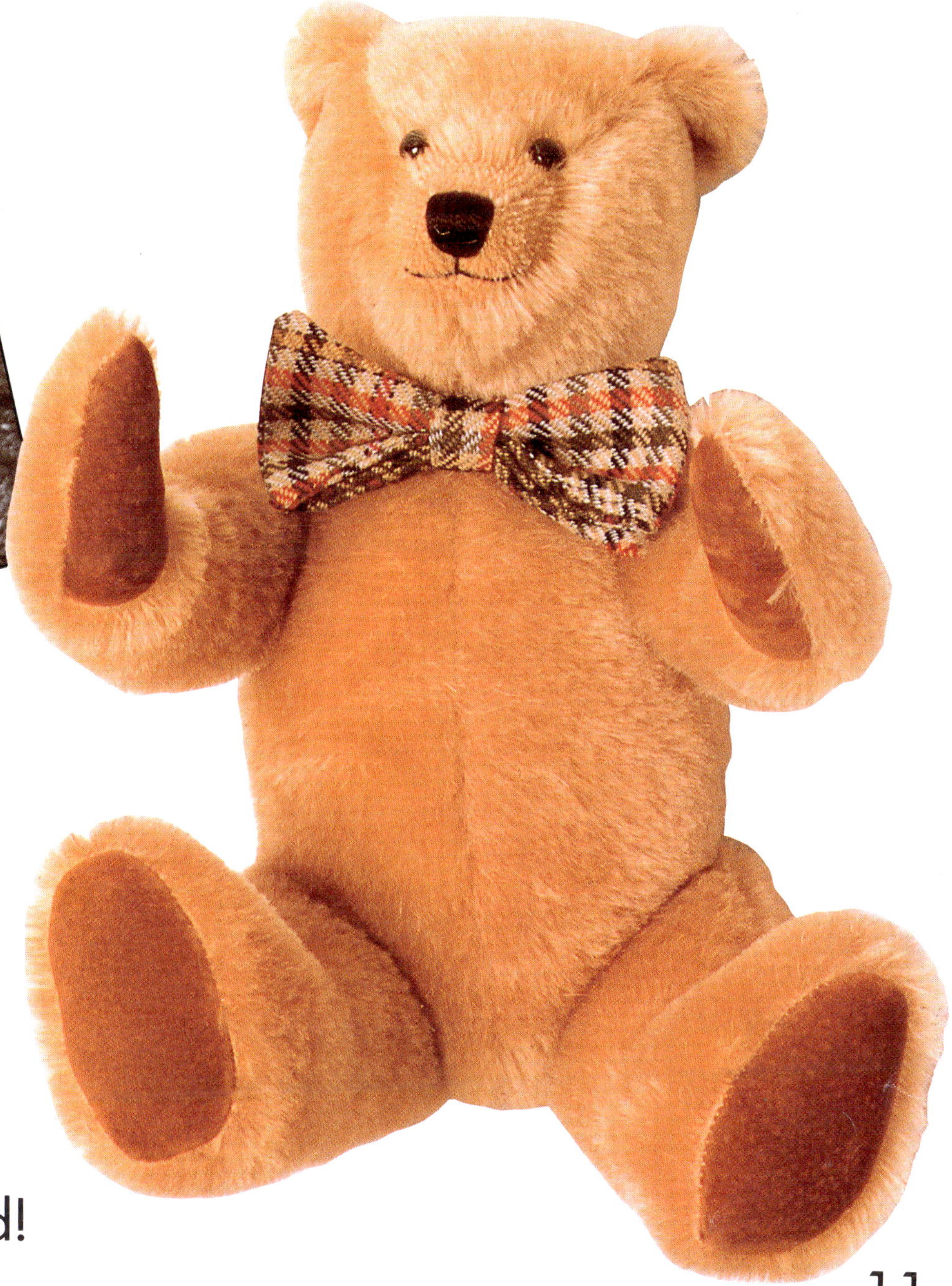

The teddy bear is finished!

Toys work in
different ways.
Hayley pushes
these cars
to make
them move.

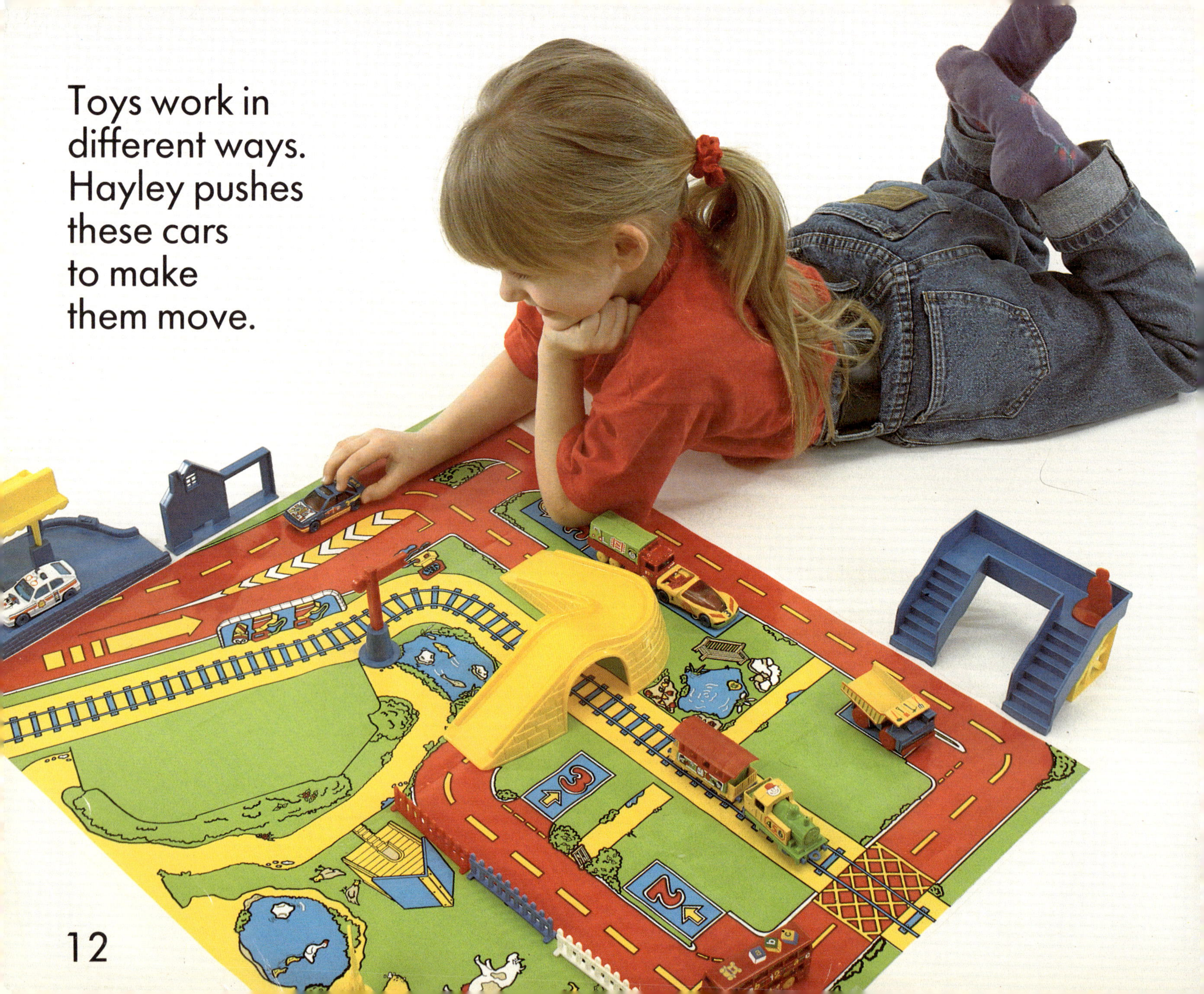

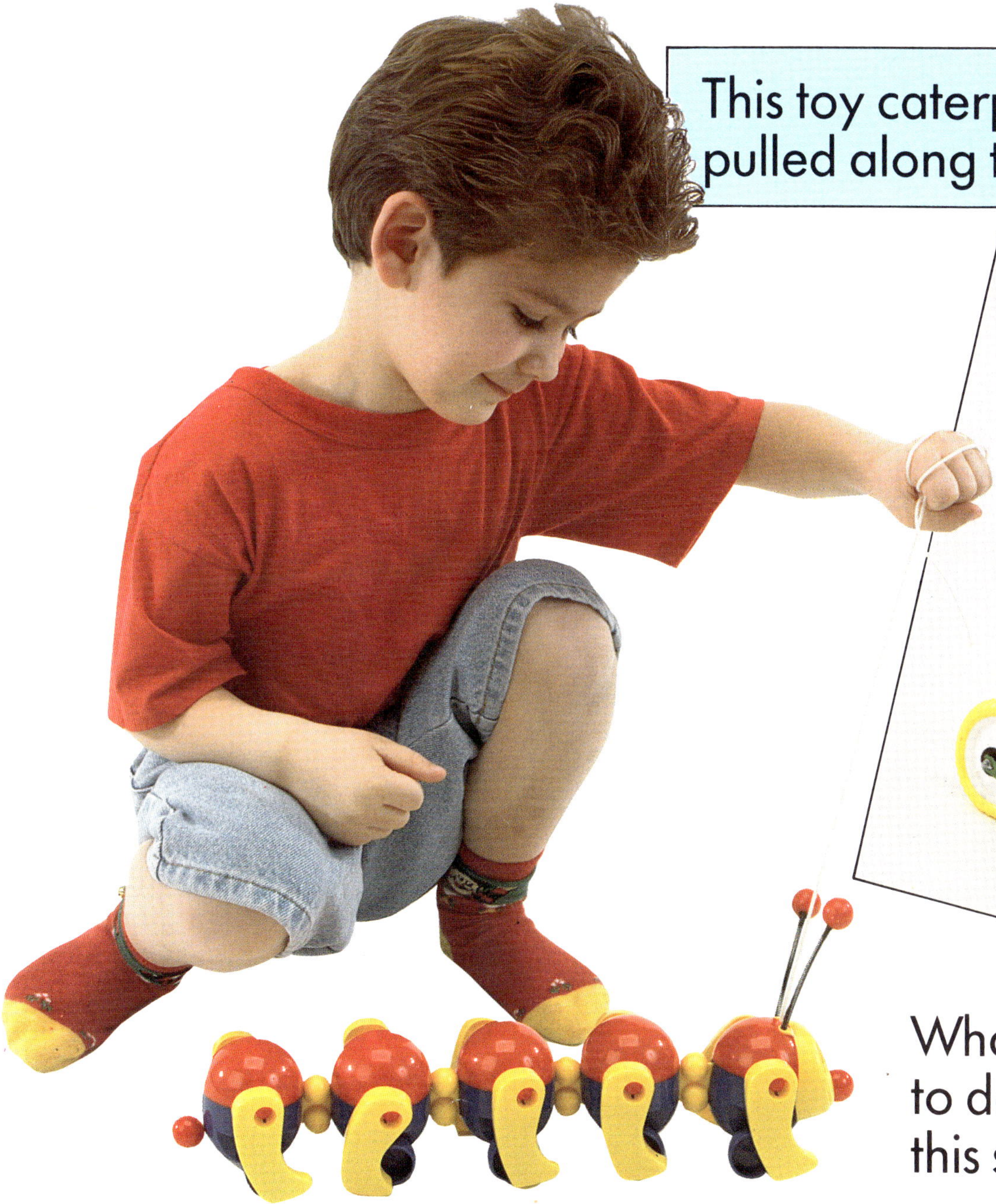

This toy caterpillar needs to be pulled along to make it move.

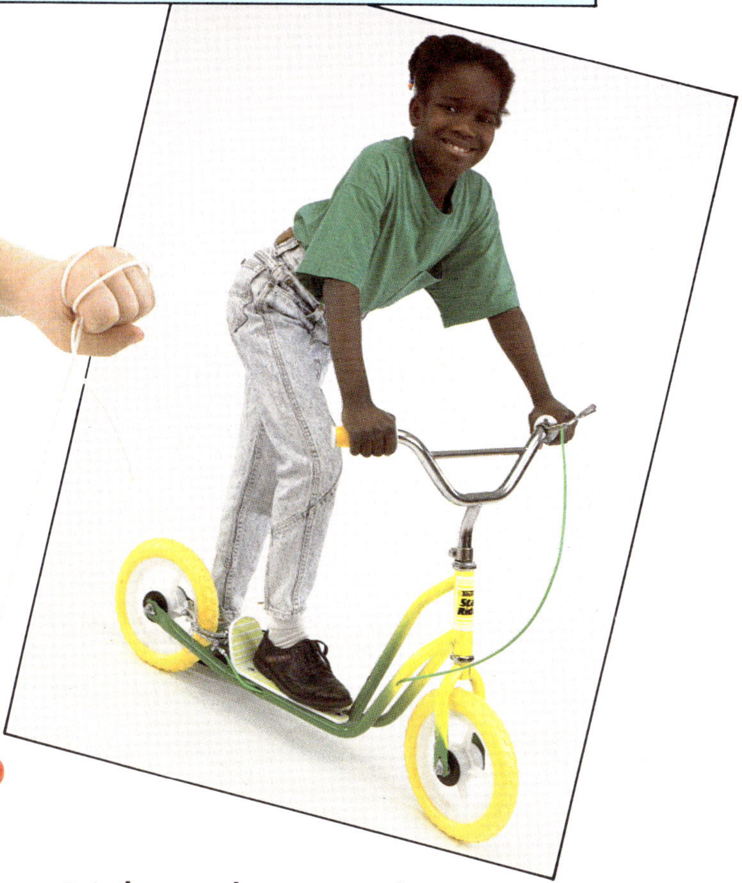

What do you have to do to make this scooter move?

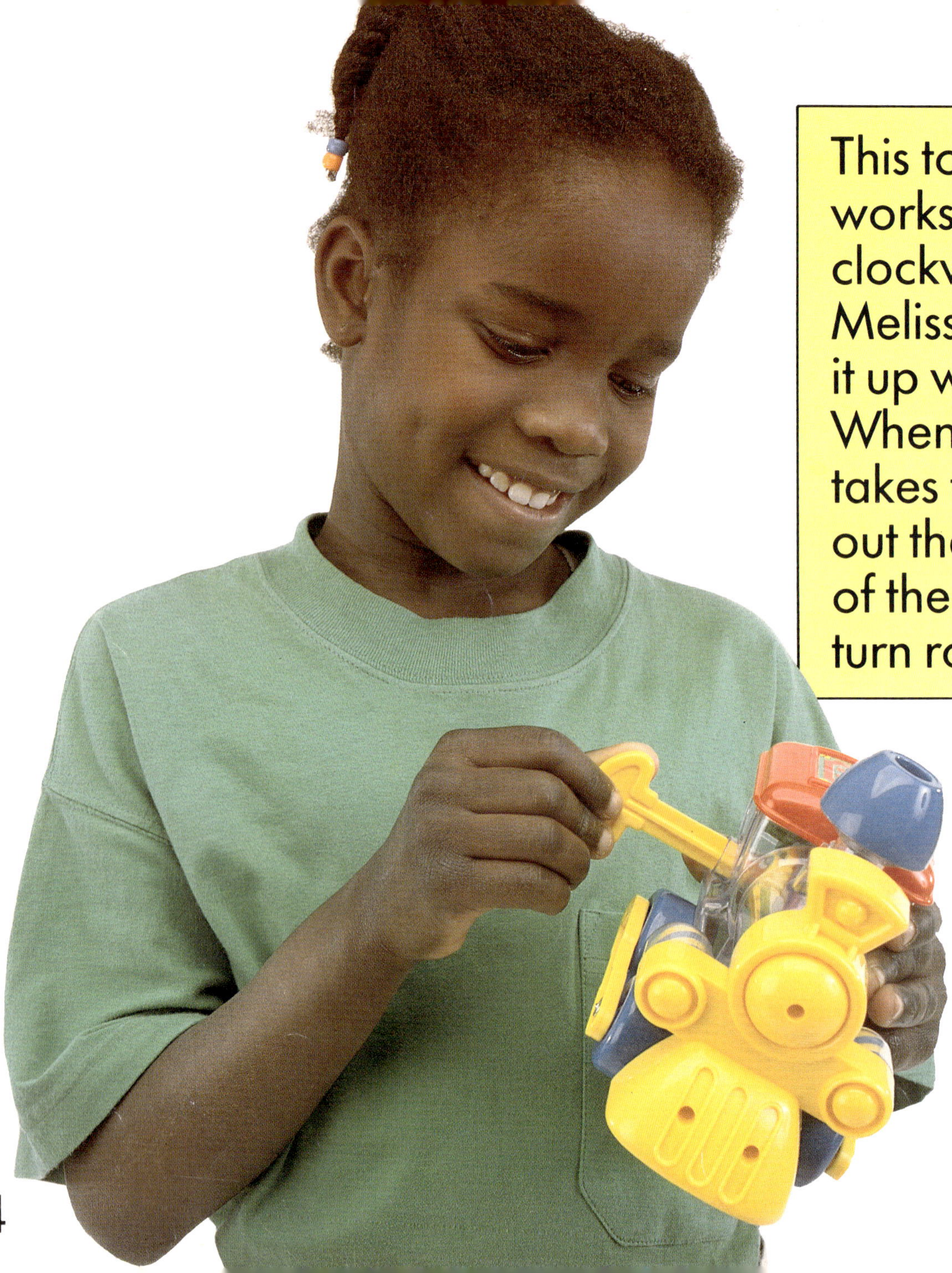

This toy train works by clockwork. Melissa winds it up with a key. When she takes the key out the wheels of the train turn round.

This remote-control car needs **electricity** to make it work.

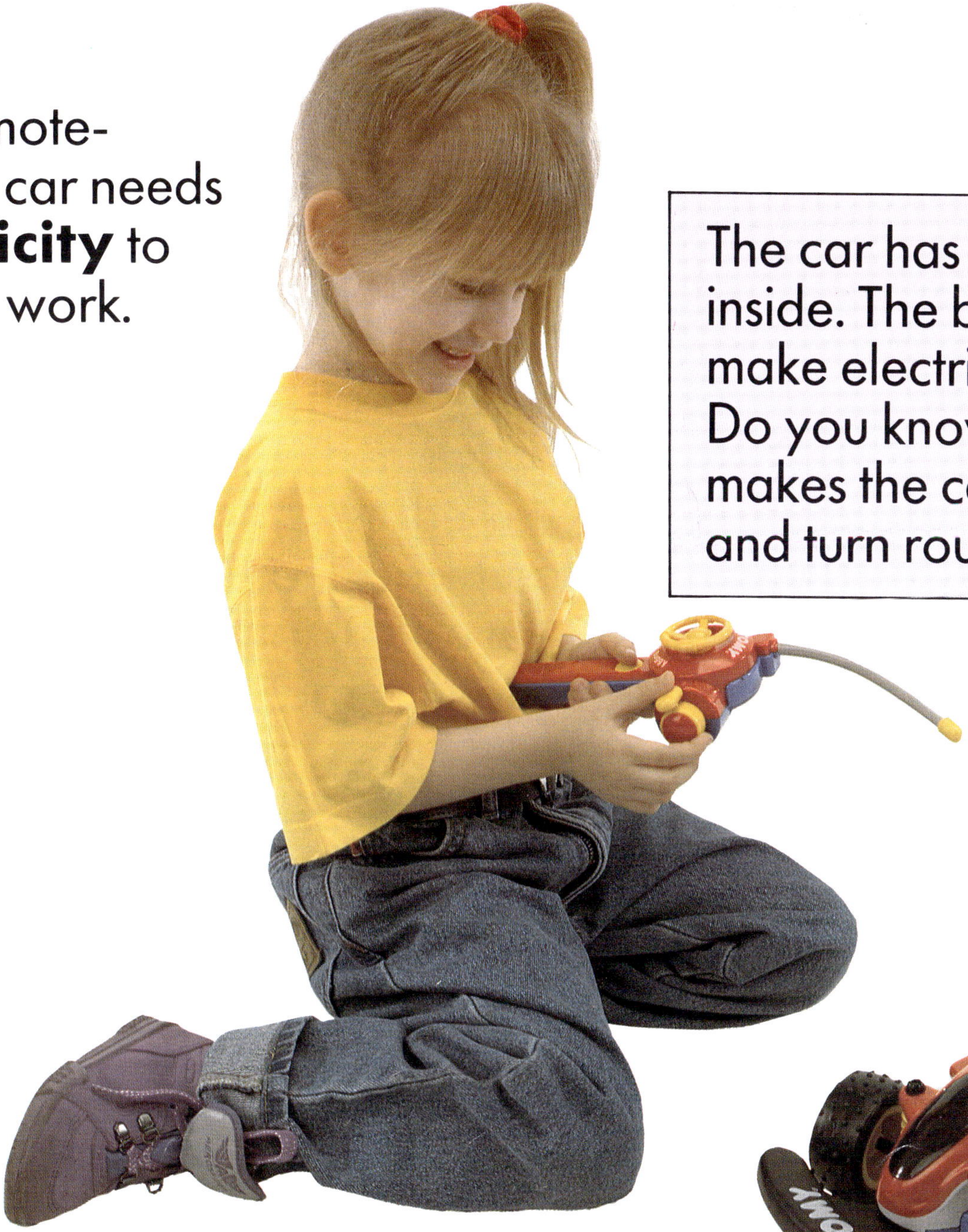

The car has **batteries** inside. The batteries make electricity.
Do you know how Hayley makes the car stop, start and turn round?

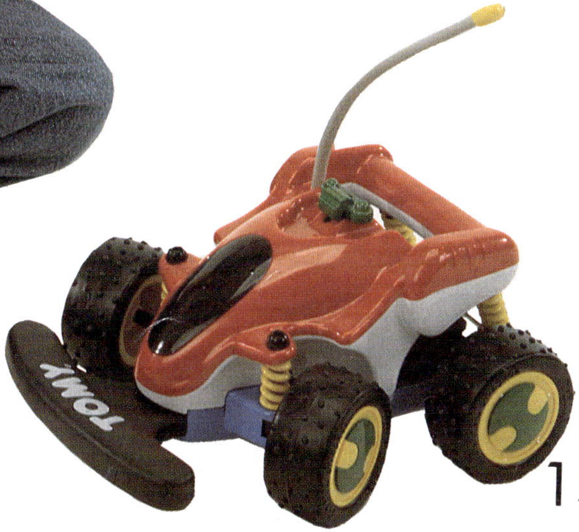
TOMY

This electronic game needs electricity to work too. Do you like playing with electronic games?

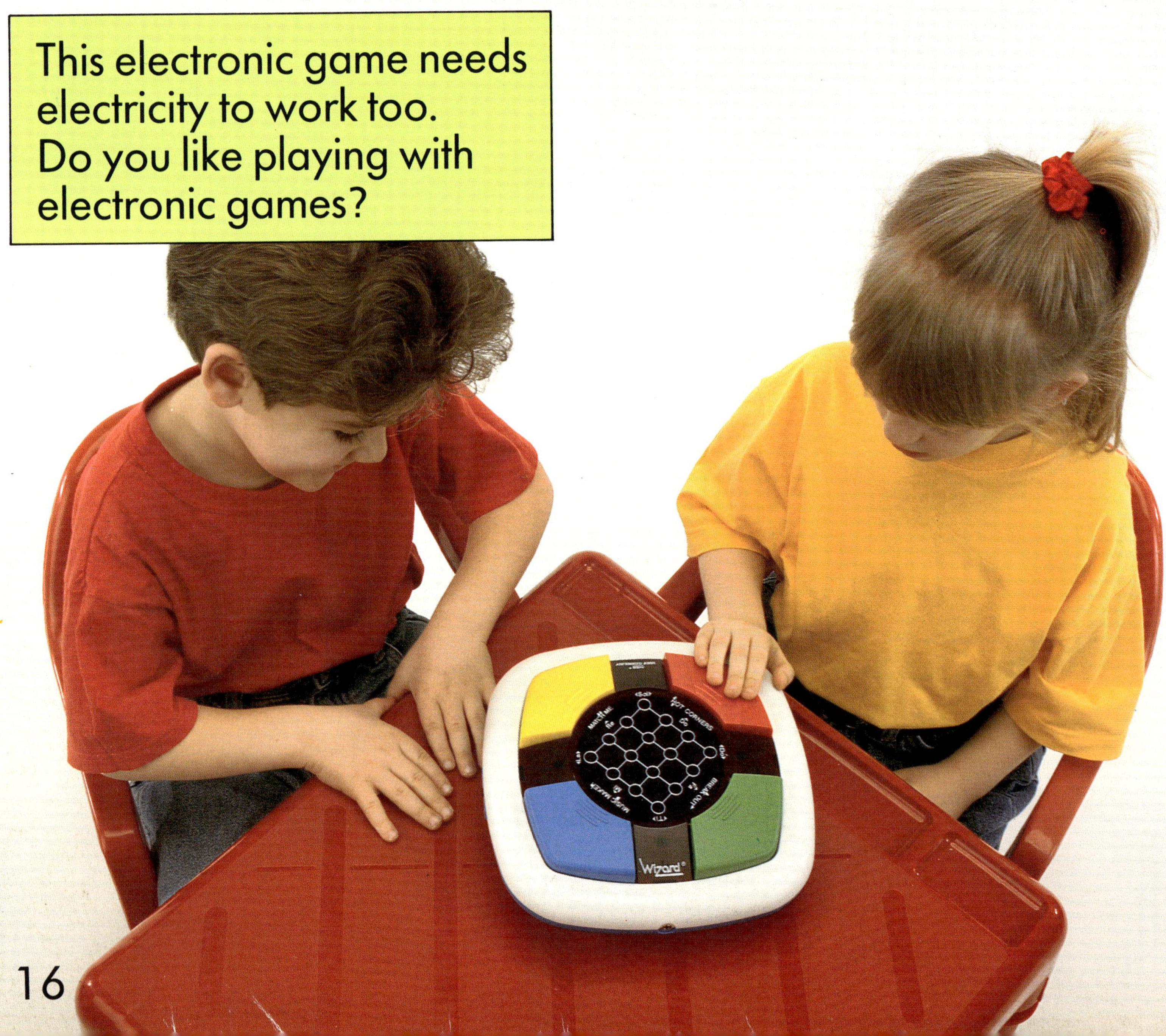

Wizard

Hayley pushes down with her hands on this top, to make it spin round. The top spins round very quickly.

These toys are puppets. You can make them move and dance by pulling on their strings.
Where are the people who make the puppets work?

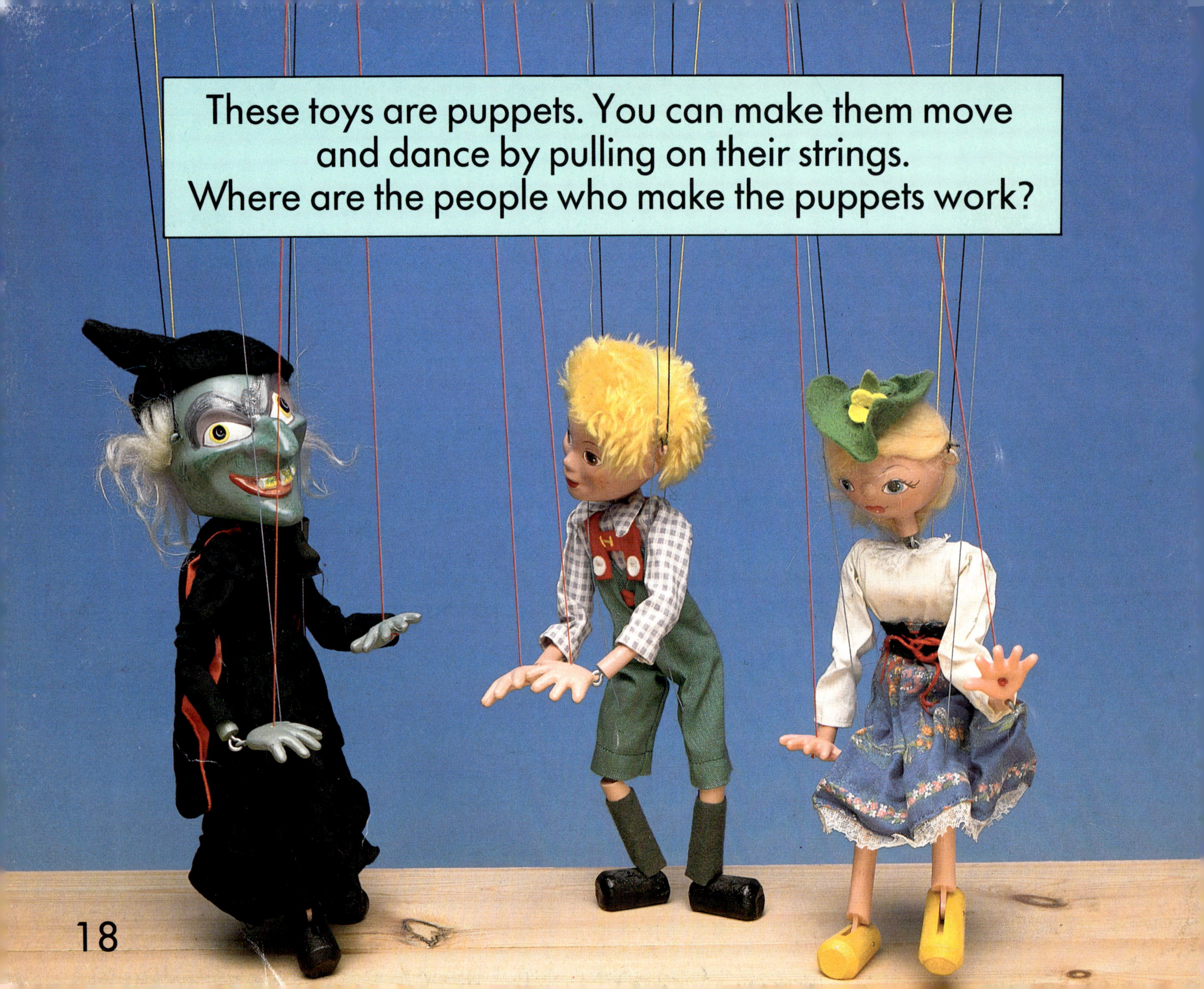

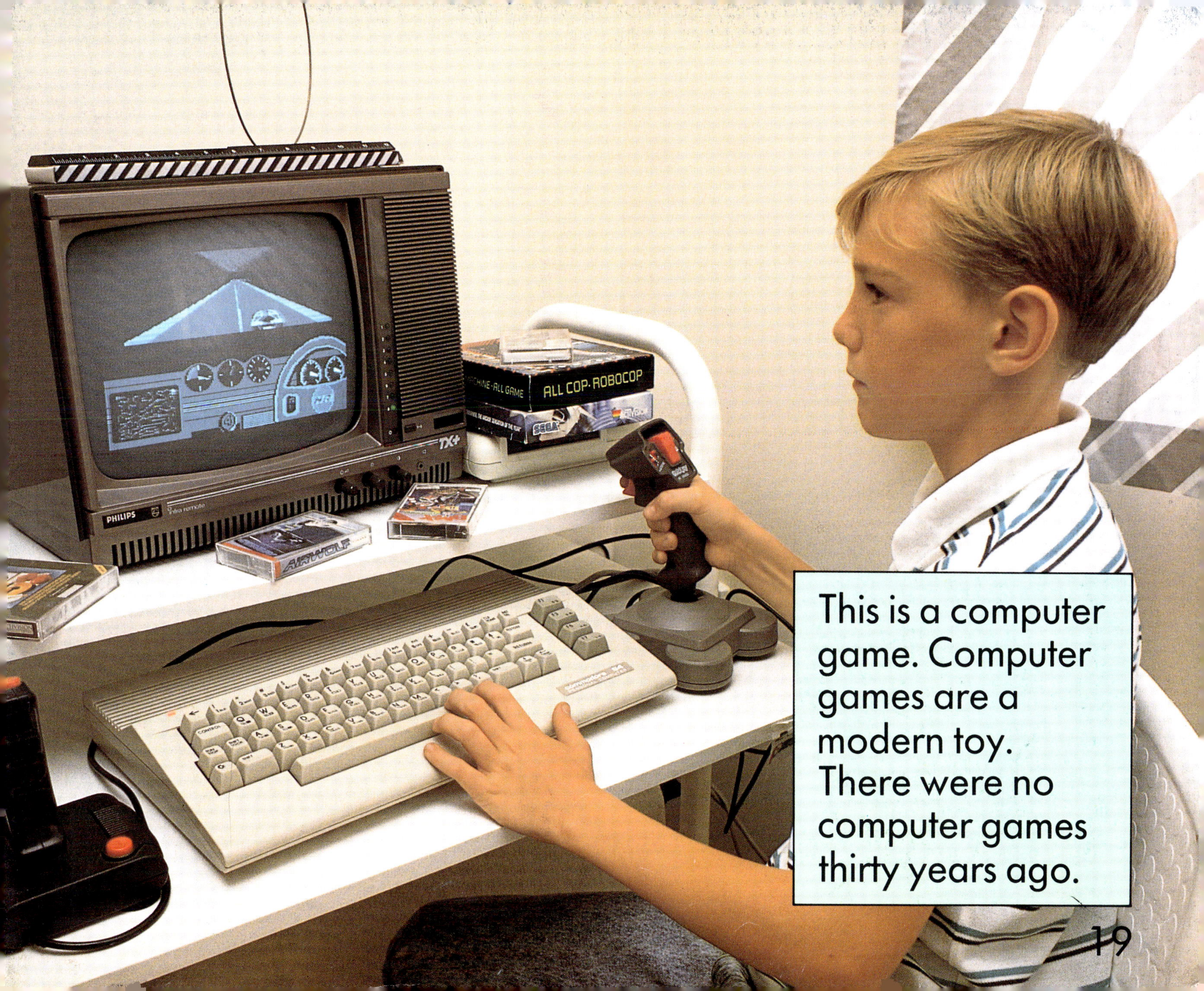
PHILIPS
TX+
ALL COP·ROBOCOP
SEGA
AIRWOLF

This is a computer game. Computer games are a modern toy. There were no computer games thirty years ago.

You could build a model like this. It has **levers** and **pulley wheels** to make it work.

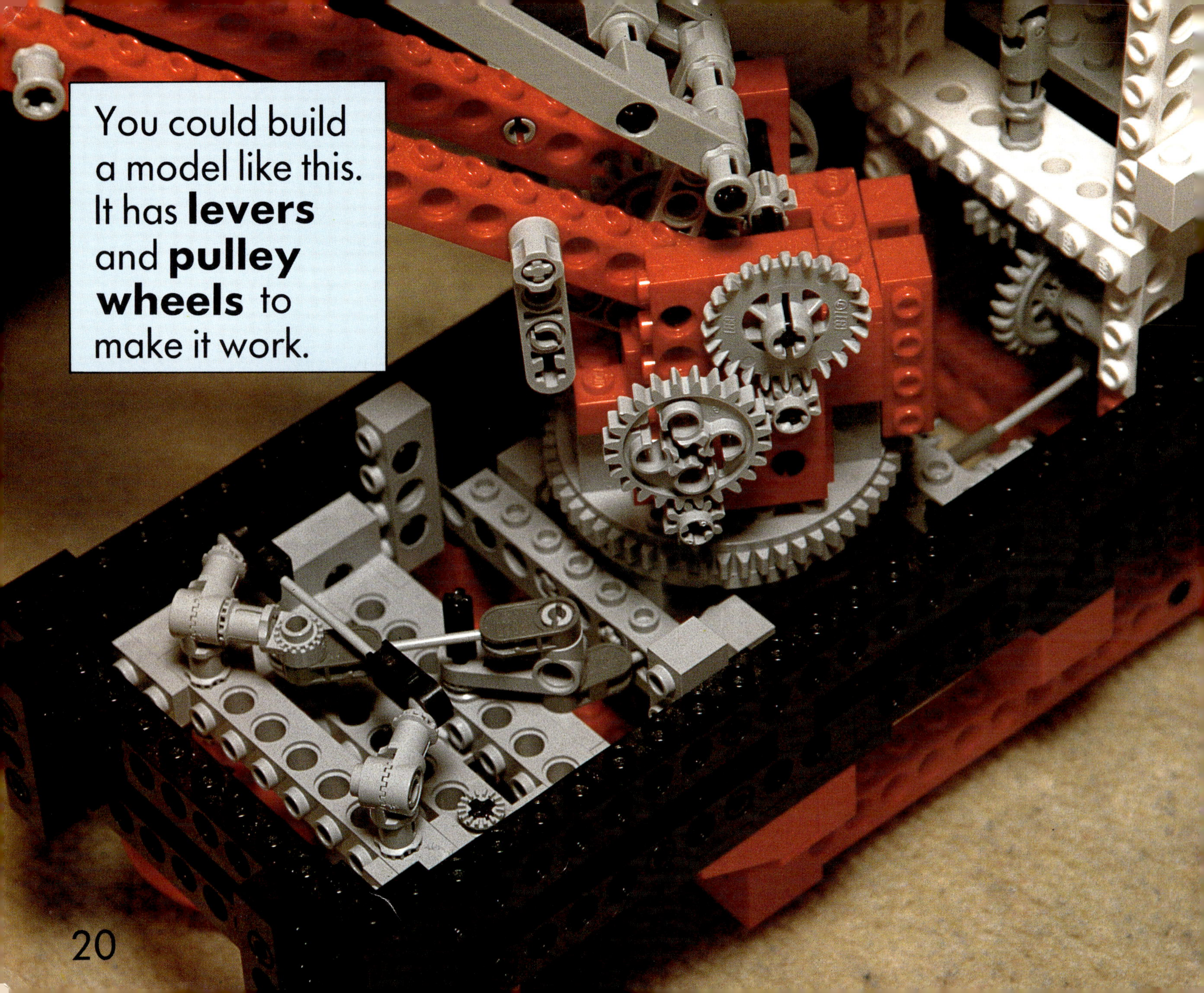

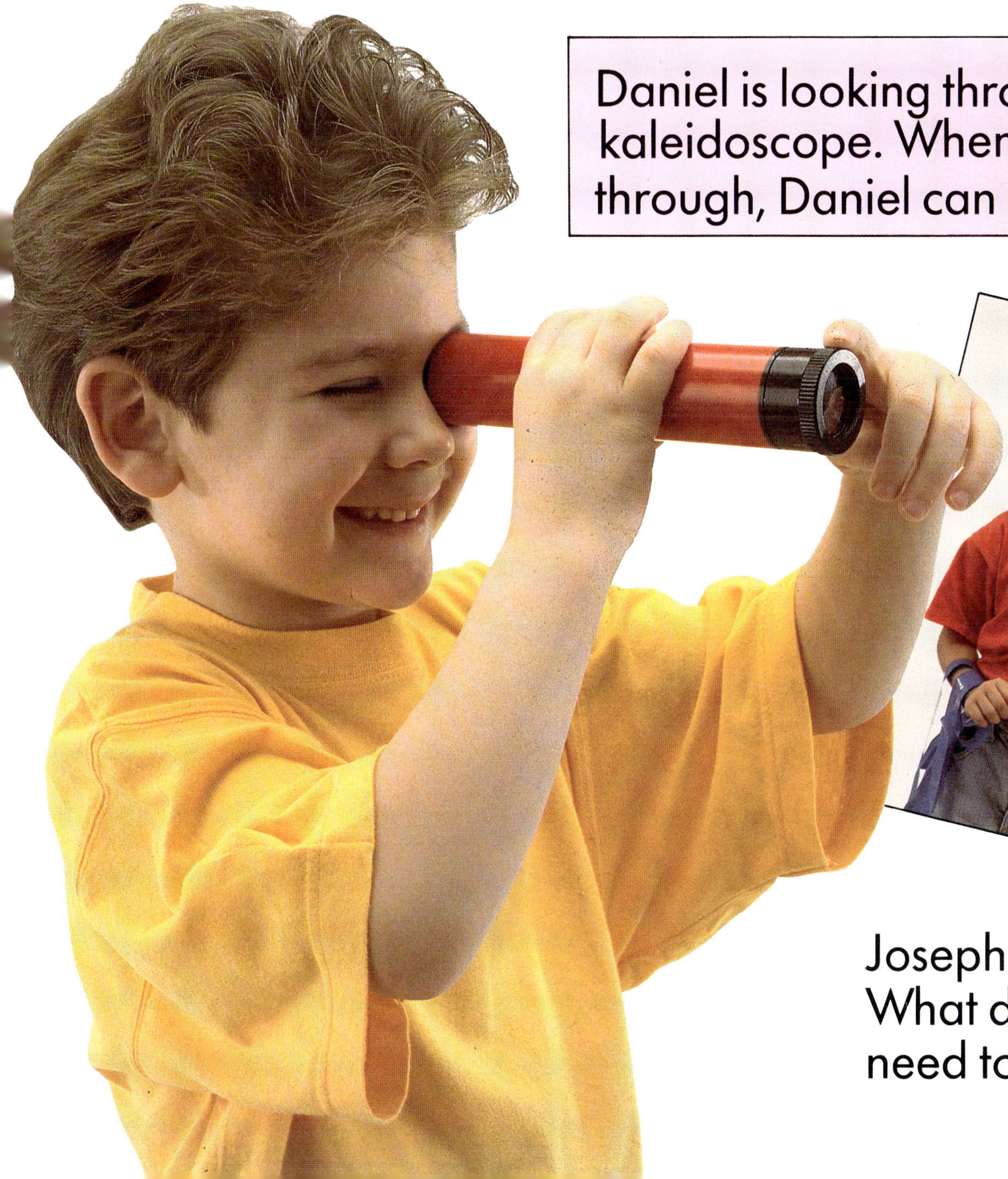

Daniel is looking through a kaleidoscope. When light shines through, Daniel can see pretty patterns.

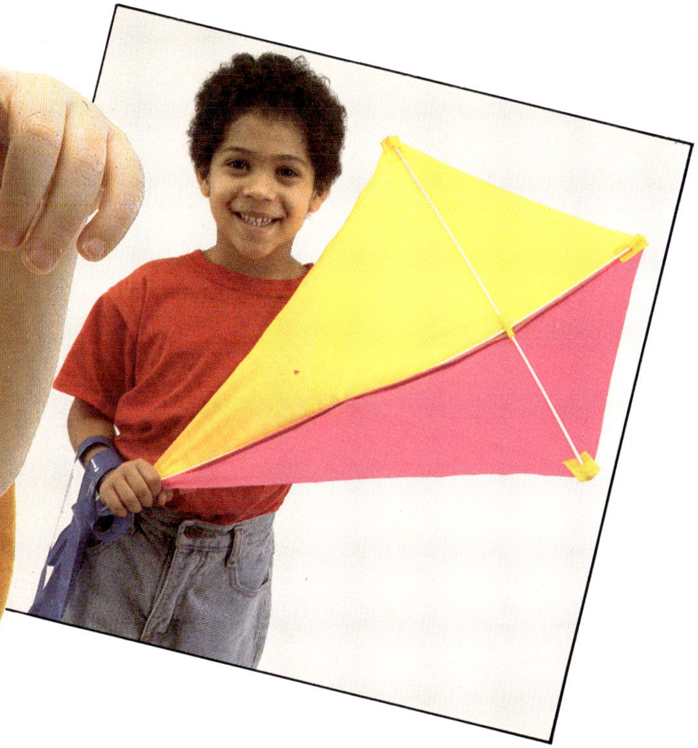

Joseph is holding a kite. What does the kite need to make it fly?

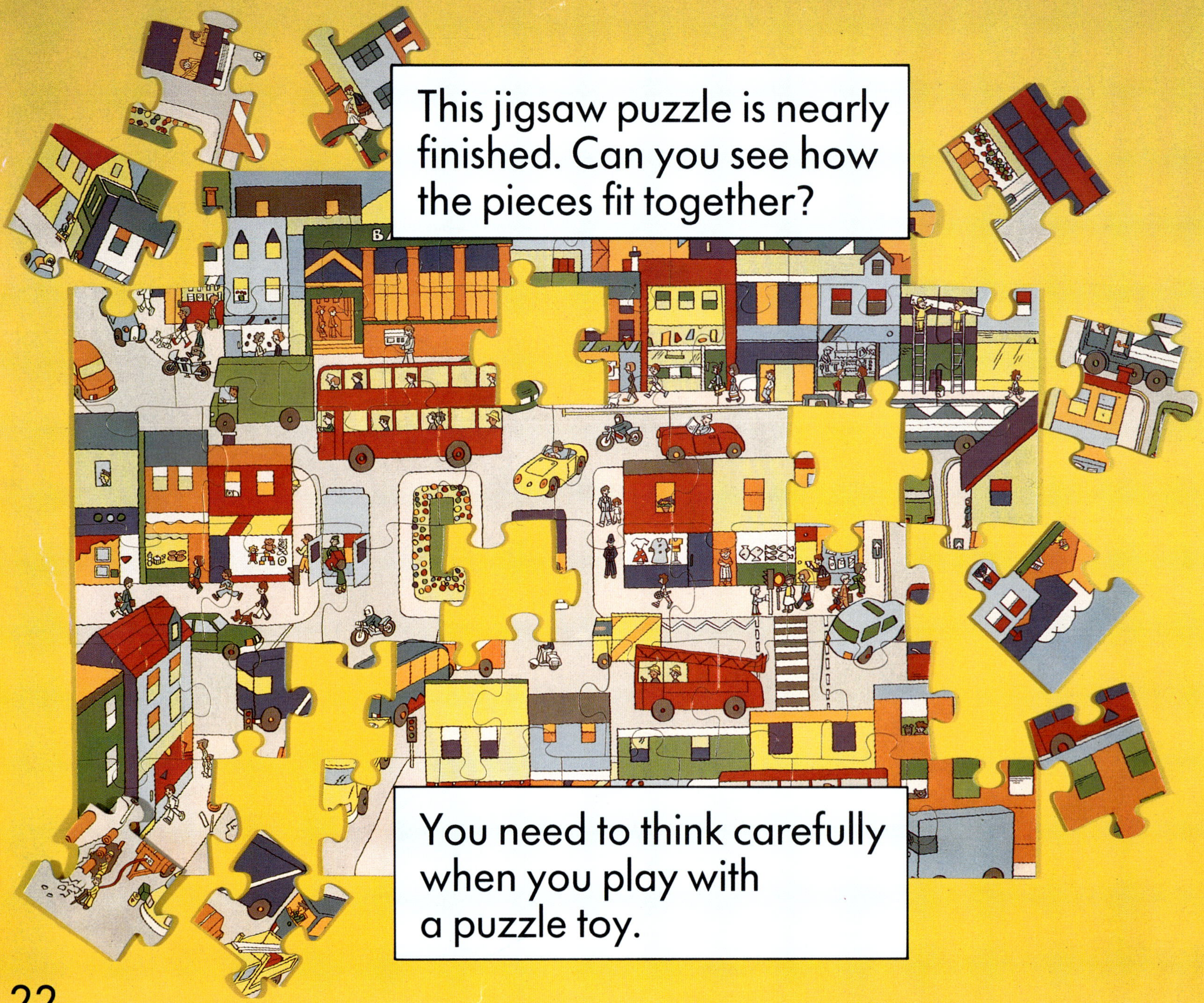

This jigsaw puzzle is nearly finished. Can you see how the pieces fit together?

You need to think carefully when you play with a puzzle toy.

These old toys are made from **materials** that are not used for making toys anymore.

**Tin** train

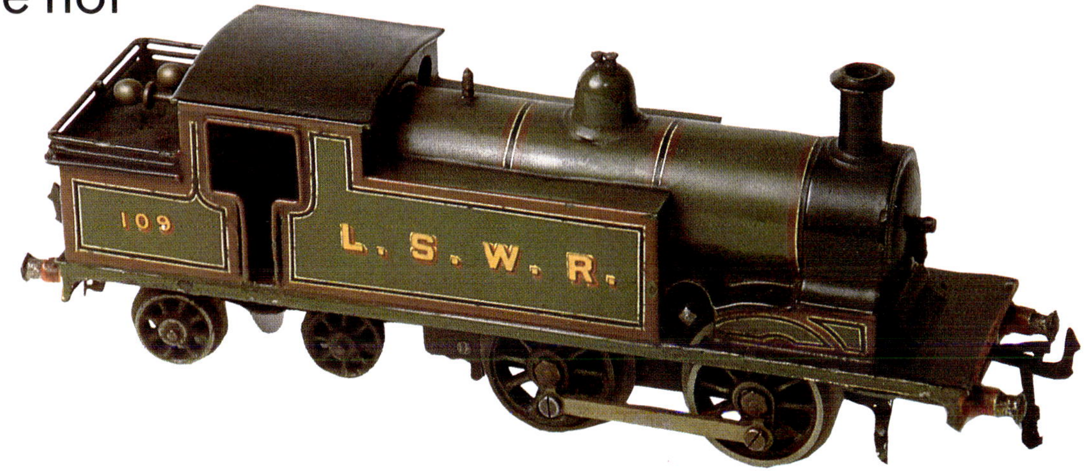
109
L. S. W. R.

**China** doll

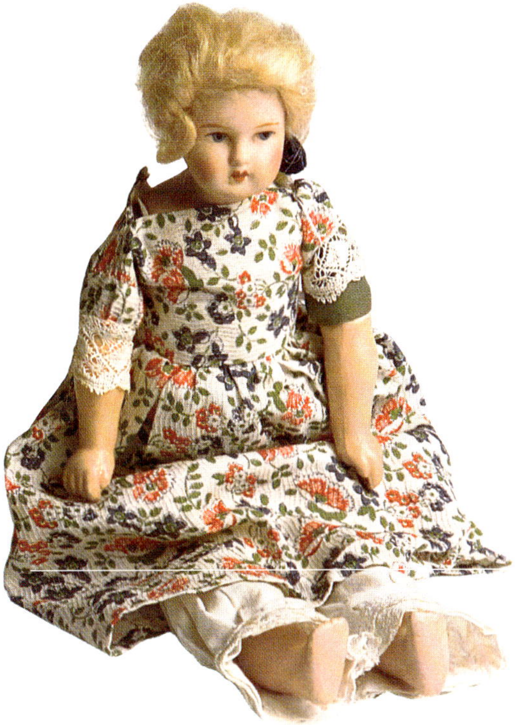

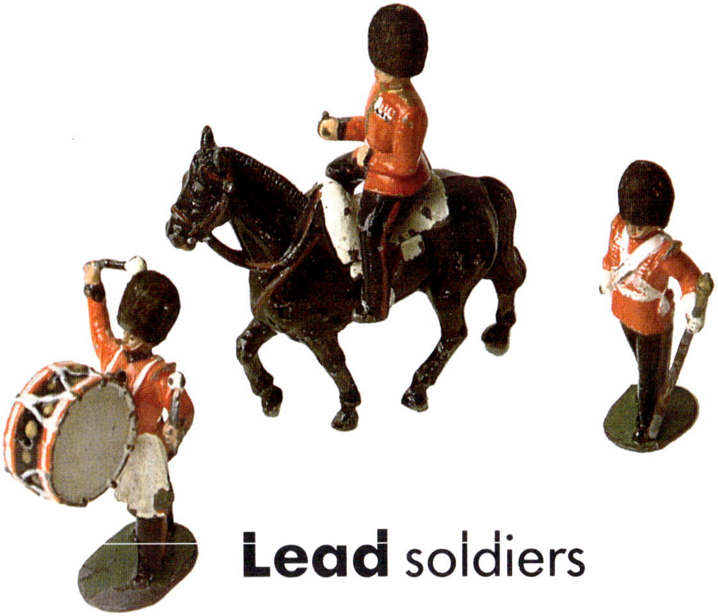

**Lead** soldiers

These three modern toys are made of **plastic**. Plastic can be made into any shape we like.

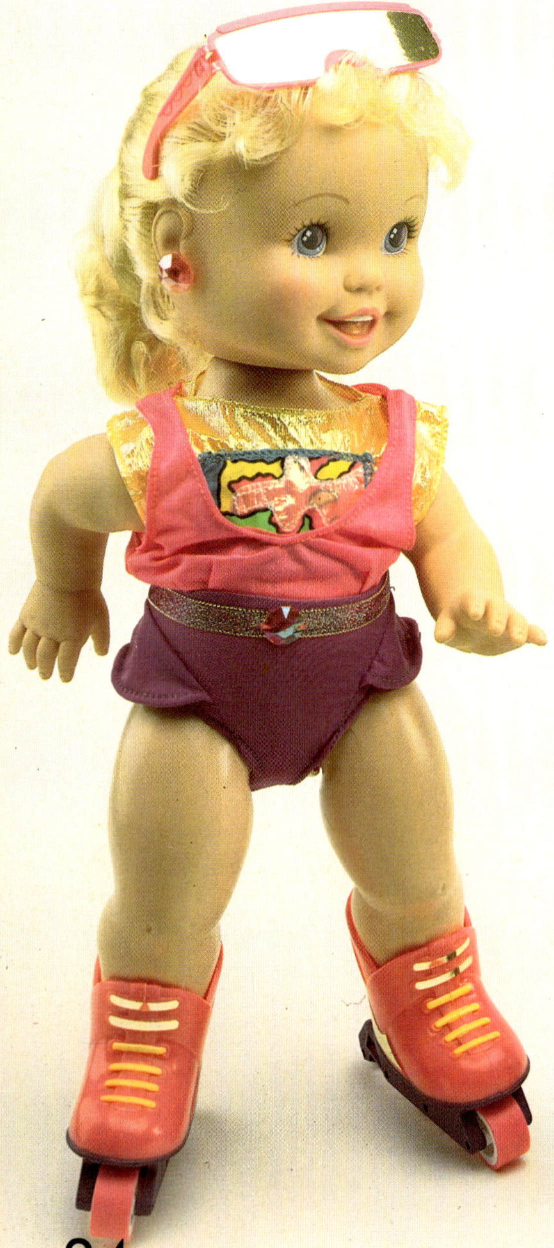

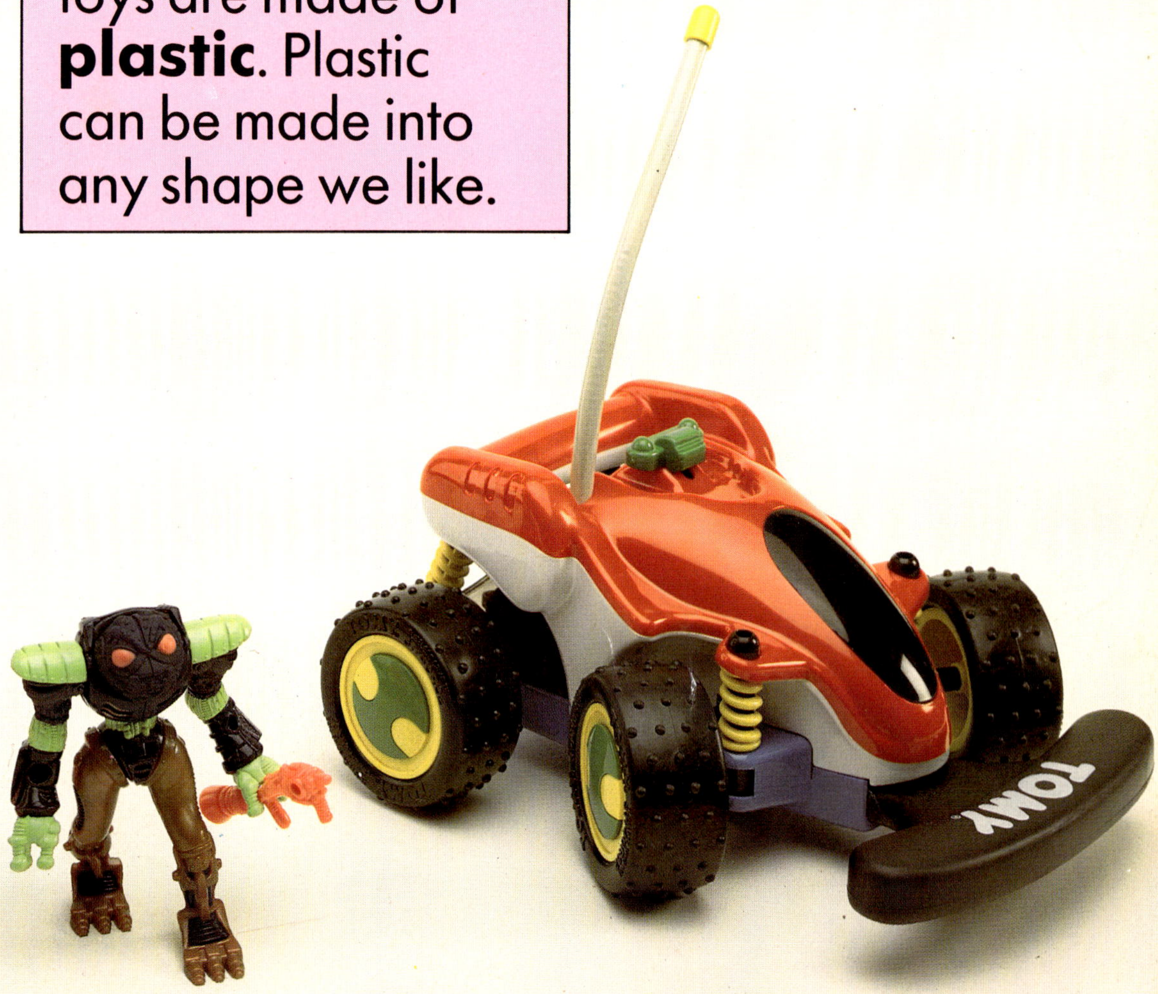
TOMY

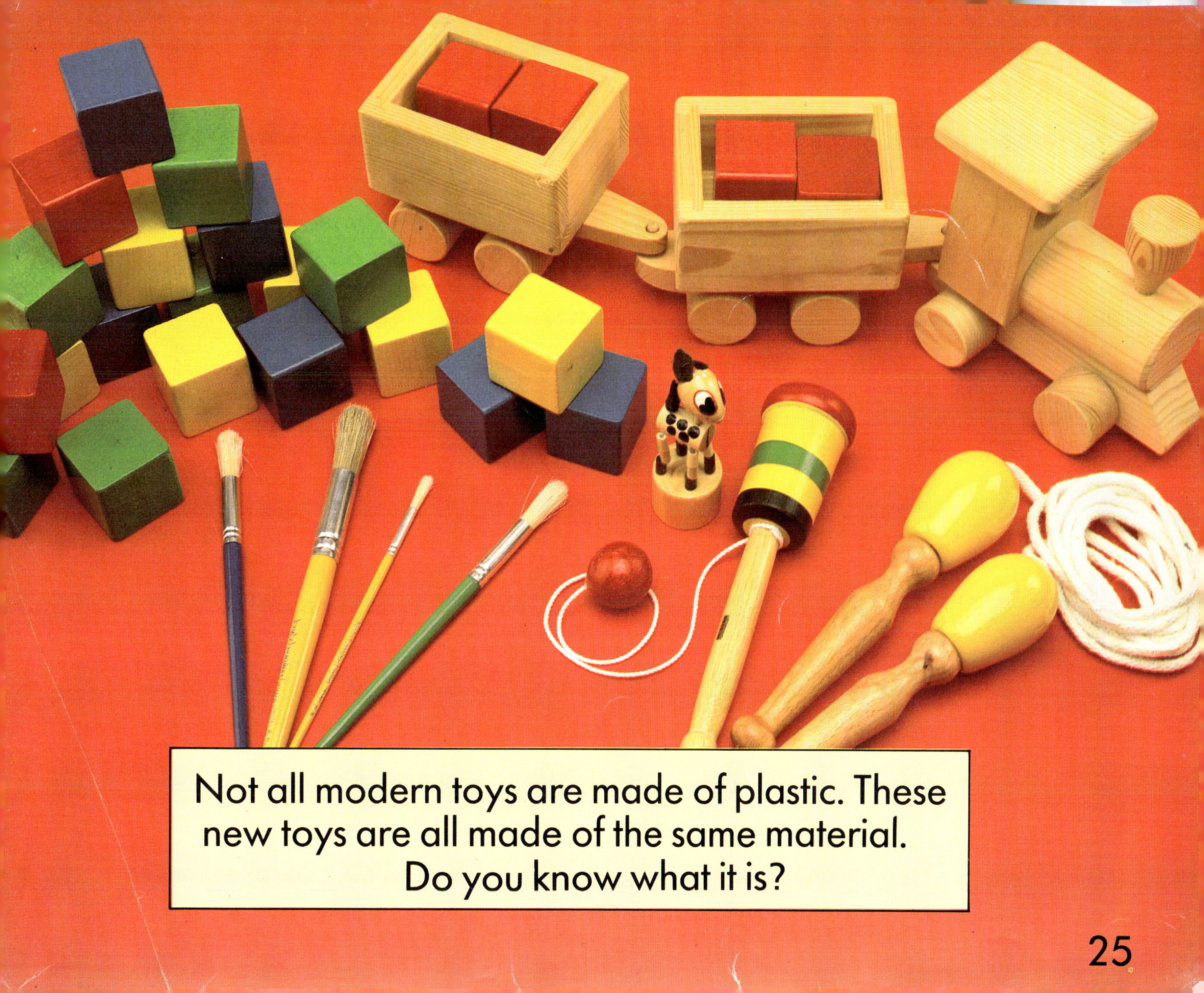

Not all modern toys are made of plastic. These new toys are all made of the same material. Do you know what it is?

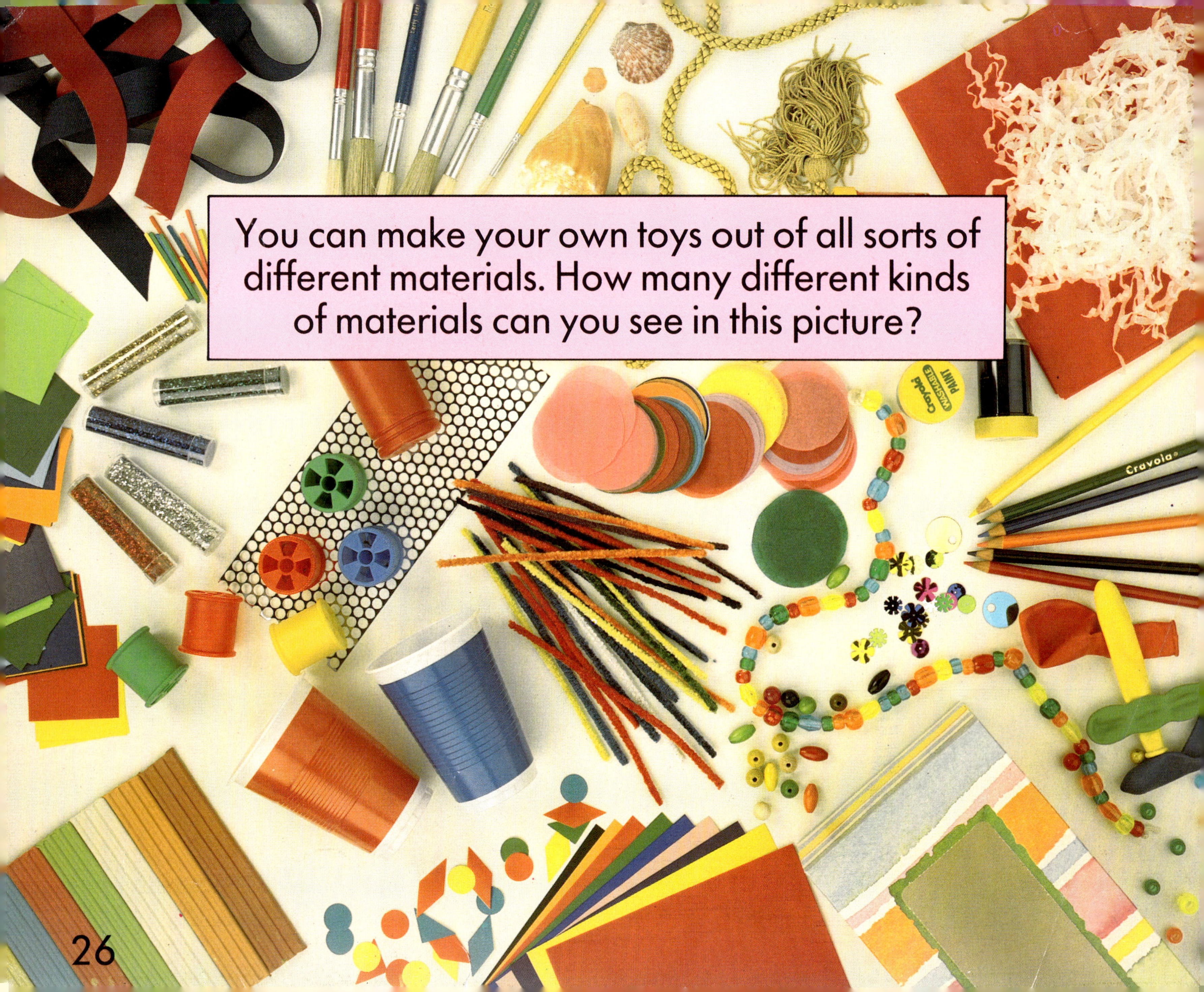
Crayola

You can make your own toys out of all sorts of different materials. How many different kinds of materials can you see in this picture?

Melissa is making a toy car. Can you see what she is using to make it?

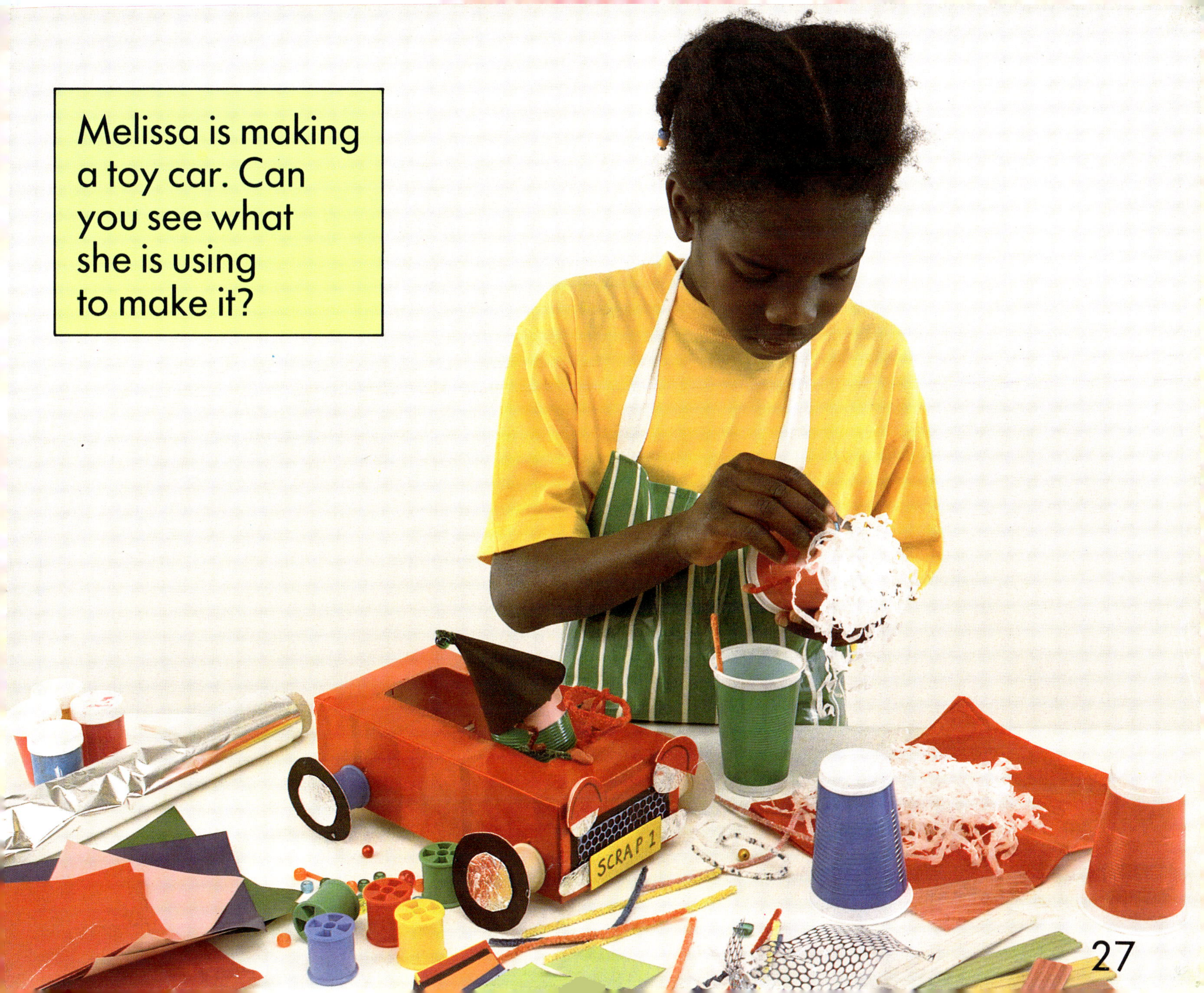
SCRAP 1

## Making a jumping machine

1. Cut the rubber band in one place.

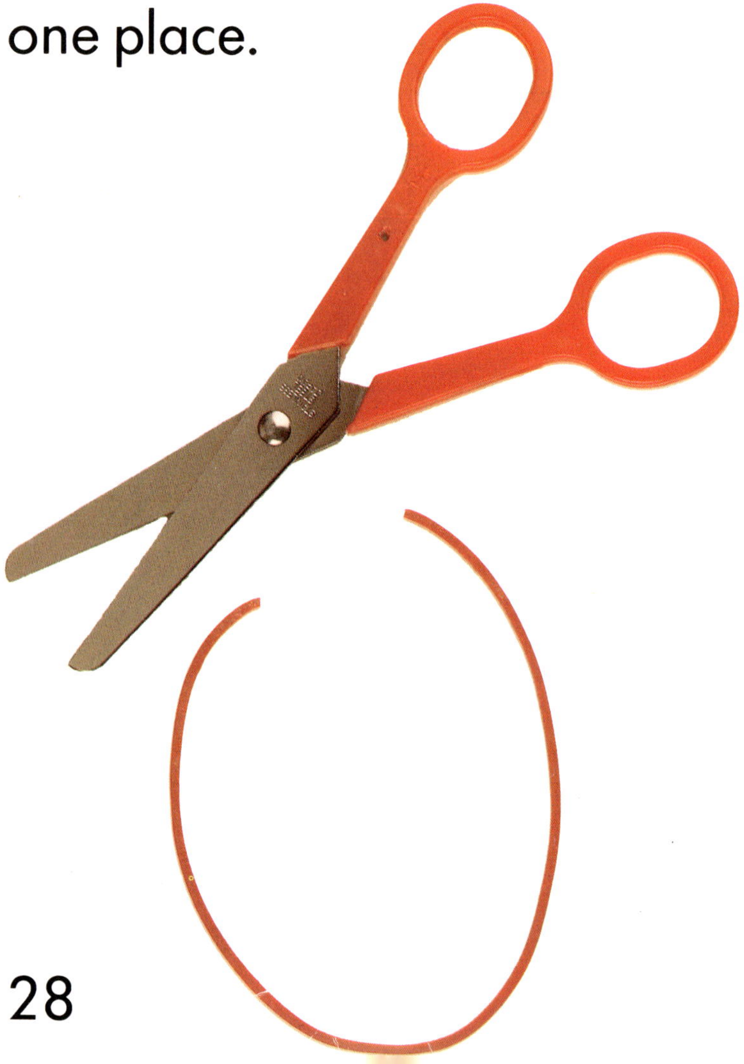

You will need a large rubber band, a cotton reel, a thin piece of wooden dowel (20 cm long) and some sticky tape.

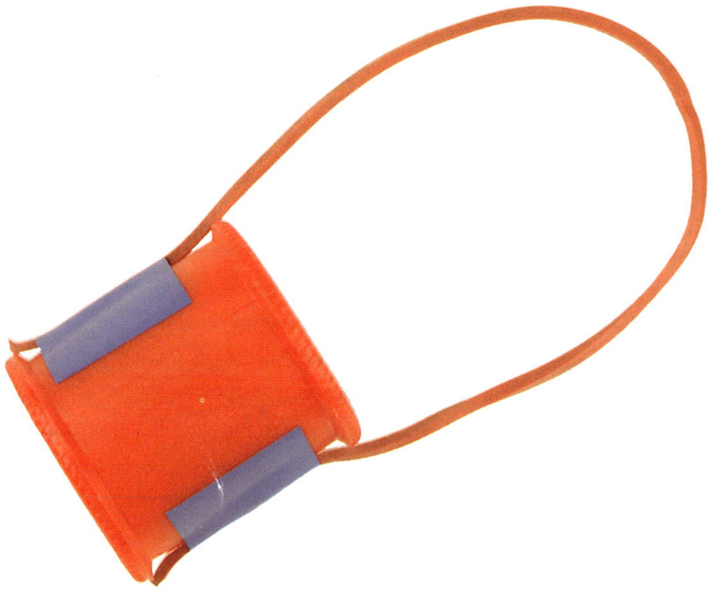

2. Stick the rubber band to each side of the cotton reel with sticky tape.

3. Slide the cotton reel over the wooden dowel, and fix the middle of the rubber band to the top of the dowel with more tape.

4. Put the end of the dowel on a table and pull the cotton reel down. Stand clear and let go!

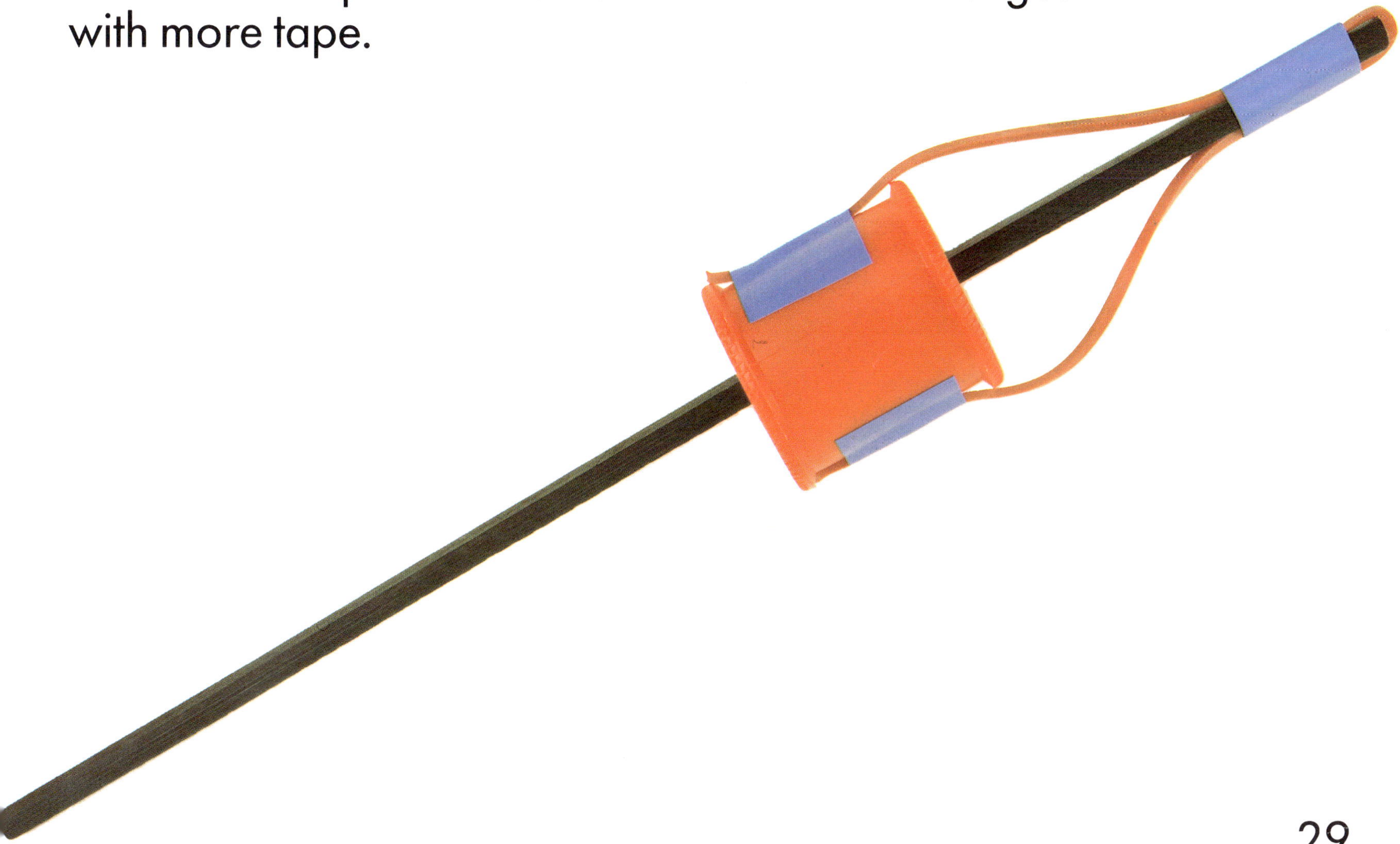

# NOTES FOR TEACHERS AND PARENTS

Play is a vital part of a child's development, and toys are an essential part of this process. They provide both a stimulus for the imagination, and a focus for the child's pretend world.

Toys can also introduce children to other aspects of the wider world. The materials from which toys are made, and their design and testing, are all parts of manufacturing processes.

How a toy works, whether by electricity, steam, sound or a rubber band, can introduce children to the concept of energy. Toys that need to be pushed or pulled can introduce children to the concept of forces.

Making their own toys will help children to develop greater manual dexterity and will allow them to test their own observational skills. They will also gain firsthand experience of simple scientific and technological processes.

**Making the Jumping Machine**

This simple machine obtains its energy from the stretched rubber band. It transforms the potential (or waiting energy) of the stretched rubber band into the kinetic (or moving energy) of the jumping toy. These two forms of energy combine to produce mechanical energy. Older children can use this toy as a push-pull force measurer. For this purpose a slightly longer piece of dowel should be used.

# GLOSSARY

**Batteries**   Special objects which make electricity.

**China**   A very fine sort of clay which breaks quite easily.

**Electricity**   A kind of energy that makes things work.

**Joints**   Special pieces used in toy-making. They allow the arms, legs and heads of the toys to move and bend.

**Lead**   A kind of metal. It can be poisonous.

**Levers**   Bars of metal, plastic or wood, which are used to help lift things.

**Material**   What something is made from. Metal, plastic, cloth, wood, china, tin, lead and paper are all kinds of materials.

**Plastic**   A special kind of material which can be made into any shape we like.

**Pulley wheel**   A wheel with a groove round it. A rope or chain fits in the groove. Pulley wheels are used to help lift things.

**Stuffing**   Special material used to fill soft toys.

**Tin**   A kind of metal.

# INDEX

batteries 15
board game 5

cars 12, 15, 27
clockwork 14

electricity 15, 16
electronic game 16

game 5

jigsaw 7, 22

kaleidoscope 21
kite 21

materials 23, 25, 26
   china 23
   lead 23

plastic 24, 25
tin 23
metal cutters 8
model 20

puppets 18

remote-control car 15

scooter 13
shapes 4, 24
stuffing 10

teddy bear 11
top 17
toy caterpillar 13
train 14

TEL 021-440 3431